ALSO BY BARBARA LEAMING

If This Was Happiness:
A Biography of Rita Hayworth

Orson Welles:
A Biography

Barbara Leaming

SIMON & SCHUSTER

New York   London   Toronto   Sydney   Tokyo   Singapore

Bette Davis

A BIOGRAPHY

SIMON & SCHUSTER
SIMON & SCHUSTER BUILDING
ROCKEFELLER CENTER
1230 AVENUE OF THE AMERICAS
NEW YORK, NEW YORK 10020

DESIGNED BY LEVAVI & LEVAVI
MANUFACTURED IN THE UNITED STATES OF AMERICA

1   3   5   7   9   10   8   6   4   2

LIBRARY OF CONGRESS CATALOGING IN PUBLICATION DATA
LEAMING, BARBARA
BETTE DAVIS—A BIOGRAPHY / BARBARA LEAMING.
P.   CM.
INCLUDES BIBLIOGRAPHICAL REFERENCES AND INDEX.
1. DAVIS, BETTE, 1908-   . 2. MOTION PICTURE ACTORS AND
ACTRESSES—UNITED STATES—BIOGRAPHY.   I. TITLE.
PN2287.D32L4   1992
791.43'028'092—DC20
[B]   92-4643   CIP

ISBN: 0-671-70955-0

PICTURE CREDITS

Bettmann, 1,2,5,18,21,27,37; Benny Baker, 4; Fred King, 6,7,8,9,10,11,12,13,14, 16,17,19,20,22,34; Marcel Hart, 15,23,24,25,26; Charles Pollack, 28,29,30,31, 32,33,36; Larry Cohen, 35.

CONTENTS

BETTE DAVIS   7

STAGE, FILM, AND TELEVISION CREDITS   361
ACKNOWLEDGMENTS   367
NOTES ON SOURCES   371
SELECTED BIBLIOGRAPHY   379
INDEX   383

hree days after Christmas, on the evening of December 28, 1961, a buzz of tense anticipation filled Broadway's Royale Theatre as the curtain went up on the ramshackle, moldering tropical veranda of the Costa Verde Hotel, where Tennessee Williams's *The Night of the Iguana* takes place. The time was the summer of 1940, the place Maxine Faulk's crumbly Mexican inn perched on a jungle-covered hilltop overlooking the sea at Puerto Barrio. Suddenly the theater erupted in whoops and whistles of delight as, with a flash of ketchup-colored hair, Bette Davis's slatternly widow Faulk swaggered onstage, fresh from a sexual encounter with one of the handsome young Mexican workers who double as her casual lovers. Everything about her—the cocky, flat-footed walk, the blue work shirt brazenly unbuttoned to the waist of her hip-hugging jeans, the patch of middle-aged flesh disclosed—quickly, silently established the unabashedly arrogant attitude of this female Stanley Kowalski, who apologized to no one for seizing her pleasures like a man.

To Bette Davis's fans, who filled the Royale on opening night—especially the cheapest balcony seats, where the loudest whistles, foot stamping, and shouts of approval and encouragement could be heard—the actress's entire career seemed to have led to this triumphant moment, as the queen of the Hollywood cinema stepped out before them to conquer Broadway. Before she had uttered her first word, the ribald, forthright figure of Maxine Faulk seemed like a composite of all the daring, exuberant, rapacious, demanding women Bette Davis had portrayed on screen since the thirties. In the widow Faulk's insolent air one caught a glimpse of Davis's castrating virago Mildred Rogers in *Of Human Bondage,* of the predatory bitch-goddess Julie Marsden in *Jezebel,* and of the jealous murderess Leslie Crosbie in *The Letter.* Here, too, were intimations of Davis's nobler, finer, but no less resolute creations, the Judith Trahernes and Charlotte Vales, who, in signature films like *Dark Victory* and *Now, Voyager,* bravely reached out and grabbed more than life had seemed willing to give on its own.

Although other first-nighters in the audience briefly joined in the applause, they soon sensed that there was something exceedingly odd about the delirious ovation Bette's admirers persisted in giving her, long past the point where convention dictated that they ought to have stopped. Unlike the regular theatergoers who had come to see the newest drama by America's greatest living playwright, the large Davis claque who had lined up on West Forty-fifth Street the week before to purchase tickets for her Broadway opening were here for one reason only, to pay tribute to the fifty-three-year-old film star and the enduring power of her legend.

"Bette!" someone called from the balcony, whereupon the actress seemed to lose concentration, slip out of character, and survey the crowd, whose cheers grew the more vociferous and disorderly, her attention having been caught. Director Frank Corsaro watched, transfixed and appalled, from his orchestra seat as Bette's eyes lit up, her chest swelled, and her lips curled into a tiny satisfied smile. To actor Patrick O'Neal, although only seconds had passed since the mad ovation had begun, it seemed like an eternity. He was waiting in the wings in fearful anticipation of his entrance as the defrocked Reverend T. Lawrence Shannon—if Bette ever got back on track and delivered his cue, which she ought already to have done. Far from returning to the text, however, Davis suddenly broke her position and strutted down to the footlights, where she clasped her hands above her head, waving her arms at the audience like a punch-drunk pugilist.

The prizefighter's victory gesture was strangely appropriate, suggesting as it did "Battling Bette," the quarrelsome, contentious, uncompromising female synonymous with the Davis image. This was the Bette Davis who, throughout the Depression and World War II, had inspired America with exhilarating on-screen depictions of a woman's capacity for far-reaching self-transformation and bold, independent, efficacious action. This was the Bette Davis who, in the thirties and forties, had waged war against the all-powerful Hollywood studio system; the short, scrawny, self-proclaimed Yankee dame who, legs spread wide, arms akimbo, and head held high, had publicly and repeatedly stood up to the studio bosses and their teams of lawyers, to directors, writers, and other actors —to anyone, in short, who had the audacity to fail to see things her way. And this was the Bette Davis whose matchless gift for expressive gesture and movement had allowed her to give several of the most lucid and compelling acting performances ever recorded on film. Her stardom had allowed her to realize the long-frustrated personal ambitions of her famously devoted mother, Ruthie Favor Davis, who had once sacrificed every hope of her own to Bette's career and happiness.

It had not yet been six months since her mother's death when Bette stepped forward to acknowledge the ecstatic applause of her fans at the Broadway premiere of *The Night of the Iguana*. Although Williams's awarding her the role of Maxine Faulk seemed like a fitting culmination of all her many struggles through the years, Bette had no qualms about derailing the play like this, momentarily leaving the text and the other actors far behind. Let Patrick O'Neal linger frantically offstage, waiting to hear his cue; let Tennessee Williams continue to pace back and forth, anxious for New York's response to his latest major effort; let Frank Corsaro, recently expelled from the production at her behest, go on staring daggers at her from his orchestra seat. As Bette Davis faced her legion of admirers, she felt that she had more than earned this glorious moment, earned the validating shouts of praise and approbation that had always meant more to her than anything else. O'Neal had nearly despaired of being summoned onstage, when suddenly, at long last, he saw Bette step back, reenter the world of the fiction, and cry out lustily, "Shannon!"—the signal that the drama was about to begin.

ONE

*I*n August 1897, the Free Will Baptists who congregated each summer in Ocean Park, Maine, held a talent show in the auditorium of the Free Baptist Temple. Among the scheduled performers was a broad-shouldered girl of eleven named Ruthie Favor, well-known to her audience as a bold and incorrigible tomboy. Ruthie regularly paraded about Ocean Park in her elder brother's clothes and commanded everyone, including her own family, to call her Fred. It was no secret that Ruthie Favor despised being a girl. But now, much to everyone's astonishment, little Ruthie seemed to have undergone a total transformation. The child emerged on stage cloaked in a flowing white gown and declaimed long passages from Lew Wallace's *Prince of India*. She gracefully illustrated her words with artistic poses and gestures in the then-popular Delsarte style.

Ruthie's metamorphosis was due to her having come under the influence that July of the local Delsartist, Miss Sadie Porter. Miss Porter's father, the Reverend Dr. Ethnan Porter, was cofounder and superintendent of the annual Free Baptist Chautauqua Assembly in Ocean Park and pastor of the Free Baptist parish in Lowell, Massachusetts, where Ruthie and her family lived during the year.

In its day, the church-sponsored chautauqua movement (named for the upstate New York town where it originated) offered secular educational and cultural programs in as many as three hundred local chautauquas throughout the United States. Founded in 1881, Dr. Porter's chautauqua in Ocean Park served anti-Calvinist Free Will Baptists from New England who timed their vacations to correspond with the evangelical camp meetings at Saco Bay.

Sadie Porter's much-attended classes in the Delsarte art of expression urged the Baptist daughters to liberate their bodies through gesture and dance, to express their souls. "Gesture corresponds to the soul," declared the French elocutionist and dramatic coach François Delsarte (1812–71). Delsarte's arcane theories of how the spiritual is communicated through the physical enjoyed an immense vogue in 1890s America that is difficult to conceive today, when his name is scarcely remembered. But as the nineteenth century drew to a close, impassioned disciples across the country heeded Delsarte's call. Self-anointed Delsartists echoed with varying degrees of accuracy the master's Law of Correspondences: "To each spiritual function responds a function of the body." And throughout America, their followers replied with the dramatic gestures and statuelike poses, the spiritually uplifting "aesthetic gymnastics," outlined in Delsarte manuals, including one published by the chautauqua movement in 1892, expressly for use in classes such as Miss Porter's.

Countless young women like the pastor's daughter had been attracted to the Delsarte system of relaxation exercises, calisthenics, and expressive movement for its curious intermingling of the spiritual and the sensual, which allowed them to cultivate an intense new awareness of their own bodies while remaining confident that it was really spiritual improvement they were so ardently seeking.

And for an eleven-year-old tomboy who had insisted on dressing and being addressed as a male, the Delsarte drills taught by Miss Porter would have given form to as yet vague longings for breaking loose from what Ruthie already knew were the constraints of her sex. Although François Delsarte had hardly intended his system for this purpose, to a great many American women of the day Delsarte-style poses and gestures had mysteriously come to symbolize something like a new awakening.

Ruthie Favor's *Prince of India* recitation was greeted in the temple by thunderous applause that became family legend. At season's end, William and Harriet Eugenia Favor, with their two sons and two daughters, left the beach cottage owned by William's mother to return to Lowell, where he worked in the mill town's Office of the Civil Engineer. Ruthie, the older girl, was determined not to allow the strange and romantic new sense of herself that Miss Porter had roused to slip away with the summer. Although for as long as Ruthie could remember she had seen Miss Porter every Sunday at the Free Baptist church, suddenly the pastor's daughter seemed to her to have acquired an almost mystical allure. No sooner had the school year begun than Ruthie secured her mother's permission to enroll as one of Sadie Porter's protégés in the expressive movement and elocution classes that she had conducted in Lowell since the mid-1890s.

For all Sadie Porter's influence on Ruthie's thoughts and dreams, there is no question that the dominant figure in her life (as in the lives of her sister, Mildred, and her brothers, Paul and Richard) remained her mother, known by her middle name, Eugenia. Eugenia's driving force, one son would fondly recall, was to dominate her children's lives for their own good. Her own mother having died when Eugenia was two, the child had been raised by her grandmother Harriet Keyes Thompson, on whose tombstone she would inscribe, in 1876: "Bearing the white flower of an unsullied life." Two years later, when Eugenia married William Aaron Favor, she made it known that her single most important reason for living was to bear children whose destinies she would direct. So now let Sadie Porter fill little Ruthie's head with romantic notions of self-expression and feminine awakening; Eugenia's task, as she saw it, was to equip her daughter with the spiritual refinement and vigorous Christian character needed for an unsullied life as a wife and as a mother who would someday do the same for her own children.

In later years, Ruthie's brother the Reverend Paul Favor liked to reminisce about the example of Christian zeal and evangelical devotion that Eugenia had set for her children, in whom she instilled the principle: "Where there is no vision, the people perish." By contrast with Eugenia's other children, however, Ruthie Favor, as she grew into her teens, seemed more and more to be developing the wrong vision. Under Sadie Porter's tutelage she had begun to harbor vague aspirations to a future on the stage, although precisely what she planned to do there remained unclear, even to Ruthie. By the time

Ruthie had entered high school, the Free Baptist community in Lowell had come to associate her with the artistic recitations and Delsarte pantomimes she performed regularly in church and school auditoriums. Even the pious older brother whose shirts and trousers Ruthie had once borrowed spoke openly of his sister's theatrical possibilities.

But possibilities they were to remain: ambitions thwarted, dreams unrealized. From the first, Eugenia had known (and even Sadie Porter would have agreed) that anything so alien to their tightly circumscribed existence as a theatrical career was inconceivable as long as Ruthie remained among them. Whatever the heights to which Sadie Porter encouraged her young protégés to soar, she beat her wings strictly within the confines of her father's church and with its blessing—and expected others to do the same. As Ruthie was soon to discover, in their world the only new awakening a girl really had any right to expect was beside a new husband, the morning after she'd been married.

🔺

Born in 1885 in the state capital at Augusta, Maine, Harlow Morrell Davis was the cosseted son of Edward and Eliza Davis, Free Baptists who lived in a big, comfortable Victorian house in Augusta and a vacation cottage at Old Orchard Beach on the southwestern tip of Maine, close to the camp meetings. Until he died, in 1903, Edward Davis operated a successful men's clothing store on Water Street in Augusta, where he served as a deacon of the Baptist church. The year of his father's death, eighteen-year-old Harlow entered Bates College in Lewiston, Maine, a small coeducational institution founded as a Free Baptist seminary a half century before. At Bates, Harlow distinguished himself in scholarship and debate, and at length as valedictorian of the class of 1907: the most brilliant student of his day, according to Harlow's friend of many summers, Ruthie Favor's brother Paul.

The sole blight on Harlow's college years was the persistent ill health of his mother, Eliza. In the aftermath of her husband's death, the fragile, dark-haired young widow, of an almost ghostly pallor, had clung all the more tightly to her son, who doted on her whenever he could break away from his studies. In May of 1906, a month past Eliza's fiftieth birthday, Harlow was finishing his junior year at Bates and preparing to spend the summer with her at the shore, when he received word from Old Orchard Beach that she had died of pernicious anemia.

Paul Favor, then a student at Andover Theological Seminary, knew Harlow Davis as someone who, like many a Yankee, with that breed's penchant for masquerade, disclosed his feelings to few people. Harlow's mask of indifference notwithstanding, the Free Baptists in Ocean Park were well aware of the depth of his feelings for his mother, and they did what they could to assuage his loneliness. At the Favor cottage especially, the cautious, solitary Davis was a frequent dinner guest that July and August. In the beginning, he seemed to come there principally as Paul's intellectual friend, but before long it was clearly Ruthie he kept coming back to see.

It had been fourteen years since Harlow caught his first glimpse of Ruthie. He was seven and she six when they met at one of the open-air gospel services the Free Baptists would hold on the windswept seven-mile-long beach they called the Grand Strand. Since both the Favor and the Davis families were members of the same close-knit religious community, united in their opposition to the dominant predestinarian Baptist theology of the period, Harlow was probably in the audience five years later when Ruthie recited and gestured to *Prince of India* at the Free Baptist Temple. In the course of many an idyllic summer at Old Orchard Beach, where once an apple orchard had stood, they had come to know and grow fond of each other, but only now in the season after his mother's death did romance flourish. By contrast to the solemn persona Harlow typically showed most people, the bouquet of love poems he composed for Ruthie in the months that followed suggested a hidden, more ardent side to his nature.

While Eugenia Favor had always expected to send both sons to college (before entering the seminary, Paul had attended Dartmouth, and his brother, Richard, would go to Harvard), she had never considered doing the same for Ruthie or Mildred. As far as Eugenia was concerned, Ruthie, having completed her studies at Lowell High School and Lowell Normal School, must pin her hopes on receiving a suitable marriage proposal.

And so it was that in 1907, on spring break from his senior year at Bates, Harlow Morrell Davis appeared at the maple-shaded Favor home at 22 Chester Street, in the Highlands section of Lowell, to ask Ruthie to marry him. Harlow Davis's proposal was all Eugenia could have wished for her daughter. Already in possession of a considerable inheritance—his father's business, two houses, and other properties—Harlow was scheduled to enter Harvard Law School in September.

Ruthie's always vague aspirations to a career on the stage seemed long since to have evaporated. For the time being, at least, she channeled into her relationship with Harlow the relentless driving force she was said to have inherited from her mother. Eight months after she became Mrs. Harlow Morrell Davis, in a small family ceremony in Lowell, she returned to prepare for the birth of her first child, who had been conceived by accident—family rumor had it—on Ruthie's wedding night. Her husband, in the midst of his first year at Harvard Law School, had temporarily stayed behind in the simple wooden row house they had rented at 11 Westminster Street in the Boston suburb of West Somerville. In his place came Mrs. Hall of Augusta, Maine, the jovial nurse who had cared for Eliza Davis during her pregnancy. "Let nature do her perfect work," she repeatedly counseled the high-strung Ruthie, who was grateful for what she recorded in her diary as Mrs. Hall's calming influence.

On Sunday, April 5, 1908, Harlow was in Lowell for the day, when Ruthie gave birth to their first daughter, Ruth Elizabeth.

"Too bad, too bad," Ruthie's sister, Mildred, was heard to cry out when she saw how small, sickly, and miserable the six-pound, nineteen-inch-long baby looked.

⚜

In later years, when Bette Davis—as Ruth Elizabeth would come to be known—was a venerable actress much called upon to reminisce about her youth, she consistently portrayed her scrawny, bespectacled, balding father as a cold and unloving figure, who sounded something like a cross between Scrooge in *A Christmas Carol* and Quilp in *The Old Curiosity Shop*. Again and again, in nearly identical words and phrases, she recounted Harlow's perpetual lack of feeling for her or her mother. According to Bette, the only creature he ever really seemed to care about was a vicious old dog. While her biographers have tended religiously to copy the details of this grim portrait, there exists—at least where Bette's earliest years are concerned—abundant and unambiguous evidence to the contrary: in the family photographs and copious notations in Bette's baby book, as well as in the richly cluttered Victorian-style scrapbook Ruthie kept in this period.

Eliza Davis's nurse, Mrs. Hall, had brought Ruthie the baby book, entitled "Baby's Record by Maud Humphrey," as a gift from Augusta, Maine; while the overflowing thick black scrapbook on whose first page was inscribed the heading "Ruthie's Book" dated back to Ruthie and Harlow's wedding day. Between them these vol-

umes document the halcyon days of the Davis marriage. The stereo-
typical poses and attitudes aside, Ruthie's photographs of Harlow and
his baby daughter unmistakably catch him without the mask of indifference most people seemed to see. For a man who reportedly
showed his feelings to few people, there is clearly an abundance of
emotion on display here.

Sunday night, immediately after Ruthie gave birth, Harlow en-
trained for Boston, where his end-term exams approached at Harvard
Law School, but by Wednesday the nervous, excited young father
was back in Lowell, awkwardly posing for the camera with four-day-
old Ruth Elizabeth, or Betty, as they had decided to call her, on his
lap. On the boyish twenty-three-year-old's face is a look of shy adoration shading into terror. In this their first photograph together, he
seems afraid he might break her, as if little Betty were made of glass;
not so in the flood of pictures that followed, taken by Ruthie during
the three months she and the baby remained in Lowell. With each
ensuing visit Harlow's confidence and ease with his daughter can
clearly be seen to grow. One such photograph, dated June 10, 1908,
shows baby Betty cradled in her father's arms. Under it Ruthie has
scribbled the notation that the child is having a comfy time. In another notation the equally contented mother gives us Harlow's pet
name for their newborn: Princess Bettina.

The presence of Mrs. Hall, who unbeknownst to Ruthie had
postponed her wedding to assist them, gave the young couple much-
needed time to be alone together. The kindly nurse took Princess
Bettina for her first glimpse of the outside world, a spin around the
block in her new wicker pram; while Harlow escorted Ruthie on her
own first trip outdoors since giving birth, a romantic ninety-minute
tour of the Highlands by horse-drawn carriage. Ruthie took special
pleasure in the fact that even now that she and Harlow were parents,
people often mistook them for honeymooners.

That July of 1908, Ruthie photographed Harlow and Betty as
they happily posed one last time at Grandmother Favor's house,
where the baby had recently learned to smile. Harlow had completed
his first year at law school with customary aplomb, already admired
by classmates for his extreme powers of concentration and prodigious
memory; and now he had finally come to collect his wife and daughter
for the train trip to West Somerville. In three months the baby
seemed barely to have grown, weighing a scant two pounds more
than when she was born. Upon their arrival at Westminster Street,

Ruthie noted with horror that the next-door neighbors had a new baby a day younger than puny Betty but already almost twice her weight.

Their daughter's perceived fragility seems to have endeared her to them all the more. Harlow especially was keen that she never be let out of sight. He doted on her as once he had doted on his sickly mother, Eliza. Ruthie recorded Betty's favorite place in the house as the sofa in Harlow's den. There the baby lay calmly for hours while Harlow pored over lawbooks. Of an August afternoon, when Harlow was not absorbed by his studies, he might sit with her on the front porch overlooking Westminster Street, where image-hungry Ruthie photographed Betty pressing her elfin face against his cheek, as the child loved to do.

And Harlow, in turn, loved above all else to play with the baby in bed in the morning while Ruthie dressed. For anyone who looks through Ruthie's old scrapbook, it is impossible to discover even the faintest tincture of the indifference usually ascribed to Harlow in what appears to be a candid shot Ruthie took that September; the photograph shows the young father tenderly reaching across the bed to his adoring five-month-old daughter.

By Thanksgiving, the Davis establishment was ready to host its first family holiday. Almost all the Favors—Eugenia and her ailing husband, William, Ruthie's younger brother, Dick, and her sister, Mildred, as well as two cousins and a family friend—gathered around Harlow Davis's bountiful table, where Betty was scheduled to eat in her high chair for the first time. As the baby banged the table with her rattle throughout the meal, it must have seemed to Eugenia Favor that she had succeeded brilliantly in directing the destiny of her elder daughter, Ruthie.

Already Ruthie's daughter seemed to display that indomitable will Eugenia fancied herself to possess. Although relatively slow to speak, Betty was quick to communicate her needs and wishes. The baby had learned from Harlow to shake her head to indicate displeasure (an oft-repeated gesture, most frequently accompanied by a robust little laugh) and in time loudly to cry out "No-no!" After a period of crawling on her stomach to get where she wanted to go, Betty learned to pull herself up by various articles of furniture. Then, when she could stand alone, she propelled herself by leaning on the go-cart her father had made for her. Able to walk at last, she regularly dashed across the front lawn to meet Harlow when he came home at night.

On Christmas Eve in the middle of Harlow's second year at Harvard Law School, the Davises visited the Favors in Lowell, where, as was to become his custom, Harlow dressed as Santa Claus to deliver Betty's first bagful of presents. Upon their return to West Somerville, Ruthie became pregnant again, this time by design. Whatever grave trepidation Harlow had initially felt about the prospect of parenthood his firstborn had almost instantly dispelled. Now, indulgent father that he had become, he and Ruthie theorized that a little sister or brother would do much to keep Betty from being spoiled.

As the birth of their second child approached, the Davises enjoyed a brief holiday in the cottage at Old Orchard Beach. Ruthie— now eight months pregnant—occupied herself photographing her husband and baby at play on the Grand Strand. Afterward, Betty was deposited in Lowell to spend a month with the Favors. At the time of her first pregnancy, when she and Harlow had been married less than a year, Ruthie had felt most comfortable giving birth in her mother's house on Chester Street. This time it seemed to Ruthie (as it did to Harlow) that her place was with her husband in West Somerville, where a maid called Margaret and a new nurse, Mrs. Worthington, would tend to her needs. Harlow was two months into his final year at law school when, on October 25, 1909, Barbara Harriet Davis was born.

At seven pounds, Bobby—as they would call her—weighed a full pound more than her sister had at birth. Still, when Mrs. Worthington placed Bobby in her mother's arms for the first time, Ruthie noted that the new baby looked much as Betty had.

"My big doll!" said Betty when she returned from her month in Lowell. Although Grandmother Eugenia had tried to explain that a new little sister awaited at home, from her first glimpse of her Betty seemed convinced that Bobby was her new toy. As long as everyone pretended that the baby was indeed a gift from her parents, she seemed content. But as her mother observed, Betty always had to be the center of everything and was clearly nettled at the prospect of losing any of the spotlight.

The situation came to a head when Betty saw Mrs. Worthington put Bobby in what had formerly been her crib. Until recently, Betty had slept every night a few feet from Harlow and Ruthie in the master bedroom. Exactly a year earlier, in October 1908, Ruthie had recorded in the baby book how Betty would wait quietly in her crib in the morning, darting glances in her parents' direction to see if they were awake yet. Sometimes Harlow and Ruthie would pretend to be asleep in order to watch Betty anxiously waiting for the moment when Harlow would take her into their bed to play. So it was now that, Mrs. Worthington having left the room where Bobby lay asleep, Betty slipped inside and performed what must have been (for a one-and-a-half-year-old) the Herculean task of lifting the baby out of her crib and placing her facedown on a small sofa across the room.

"There, there," Mrs. Worthington overheard Betty saying triumphantly. "I don't want Dolly here."

The arrival of a new baby was only one of the major changes that disrupted Betty's life. In June of 1910, Harlow graduated from Harvard Law School, and with his graduation Betty's familiar daily routines underwent profound alterations. As a student, Harlow had spent considerable time at home. Betty was very much her daddy's Princess Bettina, and she had grown used to Harlow's familiar daily presence. Nothing made the child happier than to be allowed at her father's side as he studied. Even though much of this was merely silent companionship, Betty had spent more time with her father in her earliest years than most children do. Now he would be going to an office each day, and all at once this life had become a thing of the past.

On graduation day, Betty accompanied her parents to Harvard. Ruthie left Bobby behind in West Somerville with Mrs. Worthington. In Cambridge, Ruthie and Betty watched from the crowd as former President Theodore Roosevelt, in town for the thirtieth reunion of his Harvard class, marched beneath the elms in the academic procession. Moments later, when Harlow marched past his wife and elder daughter, he was clearly excited, as a life he had long been planning unfurled before him. Harlow's reputation for what one law school classmate described as "a mental endowment and a will to work of the first order" had already attracted the offer of a position on the legal staff of a major Boston firm, the United Shoe Machinery Corporation on South Street. In keeping with Boston ideals of rootedness and stability, Harlow would work there for the next quarter century, rising steadily to be head of the Patent Department. And soon after graduation, a newfound sense of self-importance (but not self-indulgence; Boston frowned on that) would lead the promising young lawyer to move his family from their modest row house on Westminster Street to a considerably larger and nicer place (but no showplace; Boston frowned on that too), with a big open porch overlooking tree-lined College Avenue in Somerville.

Ruthie had eagerly anticipated the family's move to their new house, but her life in Somerville proved a disappointment. Once a constant presence in his wife's photographs, Harlow abruptly dropped out of sight, much as he did from the daily lives of his family. Single-mindedly preoccupied with his new job at United Shoe Machinery, Harlow had little time for Ruthie or the girls. During the early years of her marriage, Ruthie's energies had been absorbed by her relationship with a loving husband and by the births of two children in rapid succession. She had been preoccupied with Harlow's needs as he went through law school. There had been little time for her to think about her own repressed ambitions, her longing for something more than a conventional family and home. Now, with Harlow out of the house every day, working long hours at his new job, and her two pregnancies behind her, with no thought of more children on the horizon, a nagging sense of frustration seemed gradually to overcome her. Scarcely had the family moved to College Avenue when Ruthie began to experience periods of increasingly severe depression and lethargy. Harlow's reaction to his young wife's upset was to exacerbate her feelings of abandonment by pulling further away from her, seeming to cut himself off emotionally as well as physically from the wife who had once seemed a safe harbor and now seemed a burden.

Betty, who felt abandoned by the sudden absence of her adored father, reacted to the unspoken new dynamics between her parents, and to the feelings of discord and disorder they entailed, by developing an obsession with neatness and cleanliness. Family records trace the beginning of Betty's monomania to the summer after her second birthday. Dirt or disorder of any kind began to provoke violent tantrums. Betty would start shrieking, and as Ruthie soon discovered, the child seemed unable to control her outbursts. More often than not, her rages were wildly out of proportion to the things that appeared to trigger them. When Betty noticed a small grease spot and some wrinkles in a dress Ruthie had just put on her, she began to sob. Only when Ruthie replaced the soiled dress with a fresh one did the crying stop. There was no predicting when the obsessive thoughts associated with what Ruthie described as Betty's strange passion for order might overcome her. On a much-anticipated trip to the circus with Harlow, Betty suddenly noticed a crooked seam in the long green carpet that cut across the center ring. Immediately it was as if everything else had vanished for her except the terrible sign of disorder. The circus was forgotten. Not even the parade of circus animals marching the length of the carpet could distract her attention from the tiny imperfection that no one else seemed to see. Unable to put the senseless thought of it out of her mind, Betty spent the afternoon in a pout.

Lonely and depressed, and overwhelmed by Betty's violent outbursts, Ruthie tried to soothe her own agitated nerves by seeking a new outlet for her energies. If her husband was mostly absent from Ruthie's photographs in this period, something began to take his place: a newly discovered fascination with photography as a means of self-expression, which led her to experiment with light and pictorial composition as she had never thought to do before. Among the earliest of such images—perhaps the first of the many fantasy photographs Ruthie was to take of Betty in the years that followed—is one commemorating the child's third birthday, in April 1911. At a glance, the picture, which shows Betty posed on top of a table, seems like any other taken before it. Then one notices the way Ruthie has painstakingly bunched and arranged the curtains behind the child, pinning them every which way in an effort, however inept or unsuccessful, to manipulate light and shadow, to infuse her image with the lyrical atmosphere associated with the pictorialist photography of the day.

Ruthie had first encountered American art photography the previous summer in Maine, where she heard the Ohio-born pictorialist Clarence White lecture on photographic aesthetics. Along with such American camera artists as Alfred Stieglitz, Edward Steichen, Gertrude Käsebier, and Eva Watson-Schütze, White was a founder of the movement Stieglitz dubbed the Photo-Secession, dedicated to the critical and public acceptance of photography as a fine art. To Ruthie, White's lecture on the American pictorialists came as a revelation. The artistic poses and moods often discovered in their photographs connected them in spirit to the era's Delsarte-inspired interpretive dance, as practiced most notably by the likes of Isadora Duncan and Ruth St. Denis. This connection suggests why, with her long-repressed background in Delsarte and all it had once symbolized to her, Ruthie would have been so strongly drawn to art photography as a mode of expression.

Increasingly on edge and distraught, Ruthie sought a direct experience of the art that she hoped would sustain and fulfill her. Shortly after Betty's third birthday, Ruthie and a companion, Alice Canning, made a pilgrimage to New York City. Grandmother Eugenia took charge of Betty and Bobby at home. The previous summer in Maine, Clarence White had mentioned "291," the vanguard New York gallery where Alfred Stieglitz had mounted boldly original exhibitions of pictorialist photography. When Ruthie and Alice Canning arrived at "291," instead of finding a photography exhibition, they discovered Pablo Picasso's first one-man show in America. The New York critics had been mainly hostile to the exhibit. The *Globe*'s Arthur Hoeber, for instance, mocked the eighty-three drawings, watercolors, charcoals, and etchings on display as suggesting "the most violent wards of an asylum for maniacs, the craziest emanations of a disordered mind, the gibberings of a lunatic." But Ruthie seems to have been exhilarated, if pleasantly bewildered, by it all.

No sooner was Ruthie back in Somerville, however, than her crippling feelings of dejection and dissatisfaction resumed. On May 16, Betty had her tonsils removed. Ruthie's nervous debility kept her from escorting her daughter to Children's Hospital in Boston. Instead Harlow had to do the unthinkable: take the afternoon off from work. His attentions would have been a treat for the little girl, with whom he rarely spent much time anymore. When Betty awakened after the operation, at about five-thirty, Harlow lifted her into his arms, as he so often had when she was a baby, bundled her up, and took her home by cab. There Ruthie fretted over her during the five hours it took for the lingering effects of the ether to wear off and the restless night that followed. The next day, Ruthie judged the weather warm enough to allow Betty to play outdoors. When the child caught cold, Ruthie held herself culpable.

All the while, however, it was Ruthie's own health that seemed to have needed careful watching. Her wedding pictures of just four years before show a bright-faced, robust young woman whose years of Delsarte physical training have left her attractively poised and firm of flesh. Photographs from this later, troubled period reveal a depressed, stoop-shouldered figure with a haunted glint in her eye. On May 30, 1911, declaring herself miserable and in need of rest, Ruthie Davis checked into a sanitarium.

TWO

"Now she isn't going to be pretty!" cried Betty when Ruthie walked into the living room moments after the child had cut off all of Bobby's hair. "She isn't going to be pretty anymore!"

They were living in the Boston suburb of Winchester, in a charming old farmhouse on Cambridge Street surrounded by open fields and woods, where Eugenia would take the girls to gather wildflowers. There everyone seemed to hope that Ruthie might regain her health and start to enjoy life again as Mrs. Harlow Morrell Davis. As far as Eugenia was concerned, her elder daughter had much for which to be thankful. Following the recent death of Ruthie's father, William Favor, Harlow had assumed responsibility for his wife's two younger siblings: Dick, whose Harvard tuition he agreed to pay, and Mildred, whom he most advantageously married off to his cousin Myron Davis in Augusta, Maine. But instead of being grateful for what her mother lauded as Harlow's generosity, Ruthie seemed somehow to resent her husband's growing dominion over them all.

In the Winchester Private Kindergarten and later in the Winchester Public Schools, where she completed the fourth grade, Betty acquired a reputation as an aggressive, difficult child. Ruthie noted that Betty would play with other children only so long as she was the center of attention. Her teachers found her intolerant of criticism.

By contrast with Betty, who reacted to the troubles at home with bold self-assertion, poor beleaguered Bobby appeared only to recoil more and more deeply into herself. Finally, in the 1916–17 school year, seven-year-old Bobby, like her mother before her, seemed to experience a total mental collapse (as it happened, the first of many throughout her life), which forced Ruthie to withdraw her from the second grade.

Bobby's breakdown coincided exactly with a new source of turmoil in the Davis household: Ruthie's growing suspicions that Harlow had taken a mistress. "He had had a woman all that time, but I was the last to know," Ruthie would confide to a family friend, Ellen Batchelder, long afterward. The woman was Minnie Stewart, a thirty-one-year-old nurse who had been treating Harlow for asthma. The very existence of Harlow's mistress, let alone the fact that he eventually divorced Ruthie expressly to marry her, would long be the most deeply repressed aspect of Davis family history, especially as promulgated by Bette. Finding it far too painful to admit that her father had left them because he was in love with another woman, Bette always preferred to think of Harlow as someone incapable of love.

As was typical in the place and period, however, other family members would most likely have turned a blind eye to Harlow's extramarital liaison and encouraged Ruthie to ignore it as long as he was discreet and didn't ask for a divorce. Memoirs of the era suggest that even the most upright Yankee lady was capable of viewing an affair such as Harlow's "as unacceptable behavior, but behavior that had to be accepted." Almost certainly his cousin Myron Davis and Ruthie's sister, Mildred, would have known about Minnie. And given all Harlow had done and continued to do for the Favors, what position could Dick or even Eugenia have taken if, as was probable, they were among those who knew about Harlow's illicit sexual relationship long before Ruthie did?

For everyone concerned, divorce would have posed the far greater threat, on account of the scandal it would heap upon them all. A divorced woman had no proper place in their New England world, where she might be derided as a "grass widow" (as opposed to a true or "sod widow," whose husband had died). In a small New England town where everyone knew her story, a grass widow faced the almost certain prospect of finding herself subtly ostracized, even by old friends. Since mistresses frequently came from among the ranks of local divorcées, were the Davises to be divorced now, it would be Ruthie, not Harlow, whom other women were likely to shun as a threat to their own marriages.

The widely held attitude that women were somehow at fault when their husbands left them is reflected in a 1907 essay by Anna A. Rogers published in the Boston-based *Atlantic Monthly*, that most influential literary periodical of the New England Brahmins, of which Eugenia Favor is known to have been a longtime devoted reader. In "Why Marriages Fail," Rogers attributed "a marked increase in the evil of divorce in the United States" to recent changes in the status and aspirations of women—in particular: "1) Woman's failure to realize that marriage is her work in the world. 2) Her growing individualism. 3) Her lost art of giving, replaced by a highly developed receptive faculty." According to Rogers, any modern wife who failed to accept that it was her responsibility, not her husband's, to make the marriage work had "the germs of divorce in her veins." And to all women, such as Ruthie Davis, who longed for some other form of fulfillment than marriage alone provided, the *Atlantic Monthly* author offered "the plain fact" that besides being a good wife, "no other work really important to the world has ever been done by a woman."

▲▼▲

"I can only know how it affected me—it didn't," Bette Davis would insist years later when asked about her parents' marital problems. Her fourth-grade report card from the Winchester Public Schools for the 1917–18 school year, which she quietly preserved all her life, suggests otherwise.

That fall, when Ruthie finally confronted Harlow with her suspicions, things came to a violent head between them, as reflected in their nine-year-old daughter's mounting absence record: eight and a half days for the report period ending November 9; thirteen and a half days for the next, ending February 15. Whereas nothing in the small, neat, precise hand with which Harlow signed Betty's report card for both periods betrays him as a man whose wife has just given him an ultimatum, the scribbly parental signature for the two periods that follow indicates his response. The signature is Ruthie's. Her husband has left her.

In the third report period, between February 15 and April 18, Betty's teacher, Miss Elizabeth Hopkins, recorded her as having been absent for twenty-one days, more than four full weeks of school. During this time, Ruthie took the girls to St. Petersburg, Florida, to give Harlow an opportunity to move out of the house.

Only when they returned to Winchester, in time for Betty's tenth birthday that April, did Ruthie tell her daughters that Harlow wouldn't be living with them on Cambridge Street anymore. Bobby, who was repeating the second grade that year, was made miserable by the news, while Betty astonished her mother by blithely declaring, "Well, anyway, now we can go on picnics and have a baby sister!" In the fourth report period, ending June 29, Betty's absences would dramatically diminish to two and a half days. Betty had spent a good deal of the 1917–18 school year literally worrying herself sick, but now that Harlow was gone for good, the child made a great point of mimicking his Yankee mask of indifference. Betty had come to associate her father's indifference with strength, in contrast to Ruthie's long-established weakness.

The shabby bungalow court where Harlow had arranged for his family to stay in Florida in the winter of 1918 presaged the reduced circumstances in which the grass widow and her girls would thenceforth be expected to live on their unvarying $200 monthly stipend (while Harlow continued as before, with a new Mrs. Davis). At the end of the school term, assisted by Kathleen Campbell, the devoted young Irish nursemaid who had accompanied them to St. Petersburg, Ruthie moved their possessions to a smaller, more modest house, on Hancock Street in Winchester, where she had resigned herself to remaining, the scandal of her divorce and her mother's terror of that scandal notwithstanding.

Hardly did they settle in, however, when all three of them—Ruthie, Bobby, and Betty—were stricken with the then-rampant black flu, a virulent strain that claimed as many as five hundred thousand lives in the United States and almost twenty million worldwide. By the time they began to regain their health, many weeks later, Ruthie had acceded to Eugenia's persistent urgings that for their own good, the girls be sent away to boarding school.

Significantly, the school chosen, health-minded Crestalban, situated among white marble caves and prehistoric boulders in the Berkshire Hills village of Lanesboro, Massachusetts, was what Sadie Porter would have called a "breathing resort." Here students spent some eighteen hours a day out-of-doors, in accordance with Elizabeth Barrett Browning's dictum: "He lives most life whoever breathes most air." Ruthie had just emerged from her sickbed (and, on a deeper level, from the years of poor health associated with her marriage), and thus she was thrilled to learn that even in the bleakest New England winters all thirteen of Crestalban's hearty students regularly studied and slept on a healthful open-air porch. The students often enjoyed nude snowbaths in the morning and partook of that species of physical culture popularized by Dr. Lennox Browne as "lung gymnastics." In the winter of 1918, Ruthie made a preliminary visit to the rustic white farmhouse, large red barns, and brown-shingled schoolhouse that made up Crestalban. Afterward, she explicitly echoed the language of her old chautauqua Delsarte manual when she enthusiastically declared Crestalban "a school of expression, not repression." Her comment suggests the extent to which sending her daughters there resuscitated for Ruthie long-buried ideals of women's fitness and fulfillment.

Following her recovery from the flu, Ruthie boldly changed her own plans as well. Instead of remaining in Winchester, she would go to New York City, where her older brother, Paul, having recently completed his doctorate at the University of Dublin, was now assistant pastor at St. Bartholomew's Church on Park Avenue. Ruthie knew that, unlike her two well-educated brothers, she was miserably unprepared for the working world. At least she could stay with Paul until she managed to turn up a job, possibly as a domestic.

But first, as she outfitted the girls with the sleeping and sitting bags and warm under and outer garments they would need for their new open-air life, it seemed to Ruthie that in the excitement of the moment, neither Betty nor Bobby quite grasped the finality of their departure from Winchester. Nor, when Ruthie returned there alone after depositing her daughters at Crestalban, did she have a concrete idea of the life that faced her as she put most of their possessions in storage in anticipation of closing the house and driving to New York.

Putting on plays, usually truncated melodramas, was a favored activity at Crestalban. Ten-year-old Betty, keen as always for attention, enacted her first dramatic roles there—but not to great effect, according to the school's director, Miss Margery Whiting. Miss Whiting later remembered Bette as "considerably more self-conscious than most children at that age"; the child had "a high squeaky voice that was definitely unattractive on the stage."

As it happened, in Betty's three years at Crestalban, her most successful, even legendary, performance seems not to have taken place on stage at all. By Christmas 1920, after two years as a nursemaid in Manhattan, Ruthie had moved to Millbrook, New York, to assume the position of housemother at Miss Bennett's school for girls. Her previous job had given Ruthie little time off to be with her daughters and no proper place for them to visit her. Betty and Bobby had often spent holidays and even summers at Crestalban, endlessly exploring Lanesboro's marble caverns and underground passageways. This Christmas, however, Ruthie's new employer agreed to allow Betty and Bobby to pass the holiday in Millbrook, so long as Ruthie took responsibility for the handful of students at Miss Bennett's who would not be going home during the vacation. The night before the Davis girls were to meet Ruthie in Grand Central Terminal in New York, Margery Whiting held her annual Christmas party at Crestalban. At the party, much as Harlow had always loved to do, Betty appeared dressed as Santa Claus to distribute the gifts under the candlelit Christmas tree.

Disregarding instructions to wait until the teacher returned, Betty excitedly reached into the pile for her own present. Either her sleeve or her collar brushed against a candle, instantly bursting into flames that, when she tried to put them out, quickly engulfed her Santa Claus beard. By then, however, Miss Whiting had thrown Betty to the floor, where she vigorously rolled her in a rug until the fire was extinguished. As Betty emerged from the rug, something told her to keep her eyes closed, as if to prolong the oddly pleasing sensation of being watched and pitied by all. I'll make them think I'm blind! was her first thought (or so she later admitted to Ruthie), as teachers and classmates cried for fear that it was true.

By her own account, Betty took similar pleasure the next day at Grand Central when Ruthie cried out in despair at the sight of her badly blistered face, flecked as it now was with cinders from the train trip. Horrified to discover that only some cold cream had been massaged into the child's burns the night before, Ruthie promptly conducted her daughters to a nearby emergency ward. A Japanese intern used a pair of tweezers to pluck the cinders from Betty's blisters and to peel away much of the burned flesh for fear that it had become infected.

Reports of the extent of Betty's burns have varied widely through the years (with most chroniclers repeating the most dire version, which has the child's entire face affected), but photographs taken by Ruthie at the time show that the damage was mostly limited to the area beneath the chin, around the sides of the face, and the forehead. In Millbrook, Ruthie shared her bed with Betty, whose hands she tied at night to keep her from clawing at her wounds. She attached a small bell to her daughter's wrist in case she managed to break loose. Ruthie set her alarm clock to ring every two hours through the night so that she could dress her daughter's burns.

Betty's scrape with disfigurement so terrified Ruthie that initially she vowed not to send the child back to Crestalban after the vacation. But her employer, Miss Bennett, persuaded her that it would be better to downplay the accident lest Betty make too much of it. Although Ruthie finally decided to allow Betty to finish the spring term at Crestalban, the accident and its aftermath remained a major turning point for both of them. As she tenderly greased and bandaged the child's face twelve times a day for weeks on end, as if by an act of contagious magic Ruthie seemed to transfer some of her own long-thwarted dreams to her daughter. While the burns slowly healed, Ruthie encouraged Betty to believe that some special fate lay in store for her—that she was waiting for something. As with the always vague but no less ardent aspirations of Ruthie's own youth, precisely what the child was supposed to be waiting for remained unclear.

Late that summer of 1921, when Ruthie and the girls vacationed with Eugenia on heavily forested Mount Desert Island, off the coast of southern Maine, Betty's stomach swelled up hugely one day, as if she were pregnant.

Not long after they had arrived on the island, the lanky thirteen-year-old had developed her first big crush. The object of her affections was a handsome brown-eyed soda jerk named Francis Young. While walking her home one evening, Francis surprised Betty with a kiss on the lips. In the days that followed, Betty was torn by guilt that she had allowed herself to be kissed. She remembered that it felt not quite clean to her. As with those other maddening obsessions with dirt and disarray that she could never seem to put out of her thoughts once they had begun, all she could think about now was that the kiss would make a baby grow inside her. Soon, "quite like the false pregnancy of an animal," as she later described it, her worst fears seemed to have been realized.

But also like those other strange obsessions of hers, this one came at a moment of disorder in Betty's life. A difficult adjustment faced both Davis girls directly after the vacation. Instead of resuming the healthful outdoor existence they had known and loved for the past three years at Crestalban, they were to move with Ruthie to a furnished tenement apartment on West 144th Street in New York City. Ruthie had left her position at Miss Bennett's. With the money saved by not sending Betty and Bobby back to Crestalban, Ruthie enrolled for the fall term at the Clarence White School of Photography.

Founded in 1914 to promote the aesthetic potential of the medium, White's New York academy boasted among its alumni such distinguished American photographers as Margaret Bourke-White, Anton Bruehl, Laura Gilpin, Dorothea Lange, Paul Outerbridge, and Doris Ulmann. (The presence of so many women on the list was no accident; from the first, the American pictorialists had gladly received women photographers into their ranks.) To Ruthie, signing up with Clarence White was the end of a journey that had taken her a little over a decade to complete. It had been White who first inspired her to experiment with picture-taking as a means of self-expression.

Except for her role as Ruthie's principal photographic model in New York, almost everything about their new life there was repugnant to Betty. Her loathing of dirt and disorder made her a less than ideal candidate for tenement living in one of the poorer parts of the city. Nor did she relish her new school, badly overcrowded P.S. 186 (with classes of fifty pupils each and a student body of three thousand). Great numbers of boys and girls pressing in on all sides of her filled the child with dread.

But all that would instantly be expunged from her thoughts whenever she sat for her mother's daily picture-taking assignments. This soothing ritual—methodical, precise, repetitive—appeased what Ruthie had called Betty's passion for order. Disoriented by so much else in her life at the time, Betty throve on the long hours and repeated exposures it required for Ruthie to emulate all those idealized camera portraits of "enigmatic" women, dramatically posed, lit, and costumed, that were by now scarcely more than pictorialist cliché.

Long before she even dreamed of becoming a film actress, Betty, in these posing sessions with Ruthie, learned how to anticipate in her mind's eye how she might look from this angle or that; to visualize herself in terms of a larger pictorial composition. She struggled with showing ideas and emotions to the camera; with reinventing herself in front of it. One wonders whether, had Ruthie Davis succeeded as a camera artist in New York, had she joined the first rank of students at the Clarence White School, her daughter Betty would ever have become an actress at all. But unremarkable, even mediocre, photographer that these often hackneyed images proved her to be, Ruthie more than ever now would have to pin her hopes on Betty.

Or "Bette," as a neighbor on West 144th Street, Myrtis Genthner, had proposed that they call the girl from now on. The neighbor apparently thought the French spelling (borrowed from Balzac's *Cousin Bette*) more appropriate to the figure of vague female longing Bette regularly became in Ruthie's increasingly rapturous photographs of her. The pictures may have been of Bette, but their sense of yearning was surely Ruthie's: conveyed as much in the romanticizing pictorialist haze she routinely cast over them as in the wistful attitudes and off-camera glances that evoked the Delsarte poses of her youth.

In New York, while Ruthie focused almost all her attention on photographing Bette, twelve-year-old Bobby would disappear to Myrtis Genthner's apartment in the same building, to play the piano for hours on end. By now, as Bette's daughter B.D. Hyman explains, Bobby had fallen into being Bette's shadow. And according to Robin Brown, Bette's closest friend of more than six decades, Bobby was always the secondary daughter, who looked on quietly as Ruthie concentrated everything on Bette. For the younger and less caressed of the Davis sisters (both of whom had studied music at Crestalban), the discovery of Miss Genthner's piano offered what solace there was for such indignities as having to share a bed with her mother (the single spare cot went to Bette, of course) and finding herself suddenly two grades behind in school.

While scant attention seems to have been paid to Bobby's musical talents that year, everything changed the following summer. Ruthie had completed her studies and found employment as a photo retoucher in New York City, and she sent the girls for the summer to Camp Mudjekewis in Fryeburg, Maine, where an ancient Indian village had once stood. Up to this time, Bette had always been the family star, but now suddenly it was Bobby, whom the camp's co-director, Miss Perkins, anointed her musical protégé. After she had showered Bobby with unprecedented praise and attention throughout the summer, Miss Perkins told Ruthie that the young pianist had great things in store for her. Miss Perkins proposed taking Bobby as her private pupil at her studio in East Orange, New Jersey, beginning in September.

That fall of 1922, on the day before the school term was set to begin, Ruthie and the girls transported their possessions across the Hudson. They moved to the attic of a boardinghouse in East Orange, where Bette quickly grew sullen and withdrawn. Bette's jealousy of her sister did not have long to fester, however. Shortly after Bobby began lessons with Miss Perkins, Ruthie developed osteomyelitis of the jaw, a painful inflammation of the bone, which kept her from commuting to her job at Pierie MacDonald's portrait studio in Manhattan. To make matters worse, on her way home from surgery to relieve the condition, Ruthie passed out on the street, while the girls waited at the boardinghouse alone. Ruthie was sick and disheartened, terrified by what might have become of Bette and Bobby had anything more serious happened to her and fearful of what would become of them all if she was unable to return to work soon. She took the girls to stay with her sister, Mildred, in the Boston suburb of Newton, Massachusetts. Mildred and Eugenia (who lived with her daughter and son-in-law) could provide the comfort and support Ruthie so desperately needed now.

According to Davis's 1962 autobiography, The Lonely Life, Ruthie abandoned New Jersey not because she was sick and afraid—Bette neglects any mention of her mother's ill health—but because Bette had been miserable there: "Mother, realizing how desperate I was with my existence in East Orange, New Jersey, made plans to 'unstick' me." Inaccurate as the statement may be, it bears witness to what were still, many years later, Bette's strong feelings about a period in which, however briefly, she exchanged positions with Bobby and became in effect the secondary daughter.

Indeed, of the three Davis women, only Bette was beside herself with unalloyed happiness about returning to Massachusetts. Although in Newton Bobby would finally be able to proceed to the seventh grade, the thirteen-year-old was understandably distressed about quitting Miss Perkins and the only morsel of triumph she had ever known. Ruthie also experienced mixed emotions about taking up residence in the white clapboard house, at 37 Beaumont Avenue in

Newton, that Mildred and Myron Davis had purchased upon moving from Augusta, Maine. Myron's cousin Harlow and his new wife, Minnie, also lived in the Boston suburbs, which made it likely that at one point or another Ruthie would encounter them. And much as Ruthie longed to have her mother and sister near, she knew that by returning to their world she became a grass widow again: a difficult adjustment after New York, where no one in Ruthie's artistic set would have cared that she was divorced.

THREE

uthie's mysterious, softly focused camera por-
traits of Bette covered an entire wall of their
modest, sparsely furnished apartment on
Washington Street in Newton, Massachusetts.
The photographs were an object of immense
fascination to Bette's classmates at Newton High School. The Newton
girls marveled at the romantic poses and costumes, which gave Bette
an air of glamour and worldliness unlike anything they had encountered before. With her pale porcelain skin, enormous blue eyes, and
ash-blond hair shot through with golden highlights, Bette seemed
considerably more sophisticated and self-possessed than any of her
new friends. "I guess she had matured a little faster than the rest of
us," says one of the Newton girls, Ellen Batchelder, adding that Bette
was soon regarded as the prettiest girl in their group. A year of artistic
posing in New York had endowed Bette with a confidence and bearing unusual in a fourteen-year-old. "We couldn't compete with that!"
recalls Faith Wing. "We just weren't up to her."

Something else set Bette apart in Newton and made her seem

incredibly strange and exotic: what her classmates quietly described among themselves as Bette's "family situation." Bette was the only girl in her new group whose parents were divorced. She was the only girl who lived in an apartment; the only girl whose mother worked; and the only one who didn't have servants at home. Once a month, on Sunday, unlike the other Newton girls, who enjoyed Sunday dinner with their families, she and Bobby were expected to take a streetcar into Boston to see their father who had abandoned them.

Bobby was always anxious to spend time with Harlow and could scarcely wait to get dressed and leave for their all-too-brief monthly meeting. By contrast, Bette's friend Margaret "Miggie" Fitts recalls that Bette repeatedly searched for excuses to avoid seeing Harlow. "Do I have to go?" she would groan to Ruthie. "I don't want to!" The reason she usually gave for preferring to remain at home was that the complicated trip required her to change streetcars, which she claimed to detest doing. Bette's real motive for wanting to avoid her father remained unspoken but painfully obvious: the powerful resentment she had begun to feel about the impoverishment and humiliation to which his remarriage had condemned her.

To the Newton girls, most of whom had never even been to an apartment, a visit to the Davis flat, where Ruthie had set up her photographic studio, was a rare treat. As Virginia "Sister" Koops recalls, Bette's fiercely independent mother seemed so much more original and exciting than the rather sedate, conventional parents to whom they were accustomed. But there remained the scandal of Ruthie's divorce in a time and place when, as Sister Koops says, divorce was still "whispered behind the hand." Although Bette scrupulously avoided mentioning her unhappy family history to her new friends, Ruthie's shameful status as a grass widow was well known in Newton. The subtle ostracism that Ruthie might have encountered in almost any New England town of the period infected Bette as well. Ruthie's divorce caused at least one prominent Newton family to discourage its daughter from becoming too friendly with Bette. Sister Koops recalls that, much as her family liked Bette, they preferred that Sister keep her distance on account of the Davises' "family situation."

At Newton High, Bette Davis had swiftly established herself as one of the most popular and high-spirited girls in the freshman class; but Helen Elwell, who sat next to her in several classes, sensed Bette's gnawing embarrassment about her mother's circumstances.

Much as Bette struggled to conceal her feelings, she was privately in torment that even the least affluent of her new friends lived in big houses with all the luxuries that she and Bobby would have enjoyed had Ruthie and Harlow remained married. When Bette visited the other girls' homes, she often secretly made notes that emphasized what she imagined to be the great costliness of the furniture and decor: so different from the ramshackle castoff items with which Ruthie had furnished their studio. "Normally she would have been in our situation, but because her parents were divorced she was not," says Sister Koops of the charmed life Bette almost certainly would have led as the daughter of a prominent Boston patent attorney. "That might have been part of her drive: 'Well, I'll show them!' "

Resentment over her loss of worldly position caused Bette regularly to recoil from meeting with Harlow; but time and again, Ruthie insisted that the child go in to Boston to see him anyway. According to Bette's mother, maintaining regular contact with her father was "the only decent thing to do."

This was a very rare instance of Ruthie's insisting on anything with Bette, whom she indulged in most things. Ruthie's unabashedly vicarious preoccupation with Bette's social life at Newton High encouraged the daughter to view even the most trivial details as life-and-death matters. Ruthie stoically accepted and thus tacitly encouraged Bette's screaming fits when all did not go exactly according to plan. While most of Bette's schoolmates had family seamstresses at home, she had to rely on her mother to make her clothes in the spare minutes when Ruthie wasn't working as a portrait photographer. On one occasion, when Bette came home from school in anticipation of finding the dramatic marabou-fringed dress she was to wear to a party that evening, she was enraged to discover Ruthie still frantically sewing away. Before a word was exchanged between them, Bette burst into tears. "I want to wear it tonight!" she shrieked. "I have to have it tonight!" Ruthie clearly saw nothing odd in this irrational outburst. "I'll have it ready by tonight, don't worry," she said, with barely a pause to look up at Bette's tirade.

Bobby had enjoyed her fleeting moment of triumph in New Jersey, but in Newton she quickly reverted to a status that Sister Koops called "the little stepchild." Following the initial shock of discovering an entire wall covered with photographs of Bette, visitors to the Davis apartment invariably noted to themselves the astonishing absence of even a single picture of Bobby. Dismissed by most of

Bette's friends as "a plain Jane," Bobby scarcely did better the following summer when the Davis sisters returned to Camp Mudjekewis. The retiring thirteen-year-old had looked forward to recapturing past glory at the piano. This time, however, Bobby's tentmates ganged up on her, making merciless fun of the poor flustered child for striving to be teacher's pet. A recently diagnosed heart murmur, which precluded her participation in most group activities, compounded her agonies. Bobby was condemned to spend most of her time alone. Far too agitated to fall asleep at night and plagued with a nervous cough throughout much of the summer, she often lay awake in her cot for hours on end, using a flashlight to read under the covers.

By contrast with the ineffably miserable Bobby, Bette spent her summer in ceaseless activity. Nonetheless, she found the time to read at least one novel at camp, Booth Tarkington's calf-love chronicle, *Seventeen*. The novel's evocation of "the painful age" seemed to speak to Bette as no book had done before: ". . . these years know their own tragedies. It is the time of life when one finds it unendurable not to seem perfect in all outward matters; in worldly position, in the equipments of wealth, in family, and in the grace, elegance, and dignity of all appearances in public."

Like a great many other young Americans before her, Bette was touched by the plight of the novel's hopelessly lovesick protagonist, Billy Baxter, whose agonies of self-consciousness are all the more painful because they occur at an age when "such things are not embarrassing; they are catastrophical."

By the time she returned to Newton, Bette had quite consciously reinvented herself in the image of another of Tarkington's characters: the coy object of Billy Baxter's delirious affections, the incorrigible flirt Lola Pratt. In the past, Bette had incarnated a variety of characters in Ruthie's fantasy photographs; but that fall of 1923, playing the school heartbreaker was her first full-blown dramatic role. Although she showed no interest in joining the Newton drama club, Bette indulged her taste for theatrics in her excruciatingly passionate, if basically innocent, relationships with boys.

"Believe me, there was no one sleeping together in those days!" says Miggie Fitts, who became Bette's best friend when Ruthie rented a new apartment on the top floor of a two-family house on Lewis Terrace, near the Fitts residence on Pembroke Street. "If you had a kiss, it was something. Different world!" Arm in arm, Bette and

Miggie and perhaps one or two other girls would stroll the two miles home from school, almost always with a group of boys trailing behind. Ruthie declared her apartment boy-ridden, on account of all the lovesick young men who regularly swarmed there in pursuit of Bette. In Newton, where an individual was identified by who her family was, Harlow's mortifying absence had often caused Bette to agonize over her place in the world. That fall, her newfound role as class coquette seemed to accord her a satisfying status and identity she had previously lacked.

"All my memories are contained within," Bette would declare of the thick Victorian scrapbook she kept in this period. Up to this time, it had always fallen upon Ruthie to preserve and construct family history in scrapbooks, diaries, and photographs, but suddenly, as reflected in Bette's private memory book, the fifteen-year-old perceived herself as embarking on a life distinct and apart from that of her mother and sister. Still, the fancies recorded here might be those of almost any girl her age enchanted by what Van Wyck Brooks has called "the glamour of youth": a lock of Miggie's brown hair, a scrap of gray chiffon from one of the gowns Ruthie sewed for Bette that year, a prized invitation to the (hitherto off-limits) home of Sister Koops in West Newton, and a Harvest Carnival dance card overflowing, as always, with boys' names.

To judge by his ubiquitous presence in Bette's memory book, her principal young man in this period was George J. "Gige" Dunham, whom Ruthie had designated house favorite at Lewis Terrace. Son of the president and general manager of the Standard Steel Motor Car Company in Boston, the shy, well-mannered Gige Dunham charmed and delighted Bette with the adoring poems and love notes he regularly asked the other girls to pass on to her. "The boy poet" —as he fancied himself—had seen Bette for the first time the year before, at a lifesaving lecture at Newton High. Telling himself that "there never was such a girl," he could scarcely work up the courage to speak to Bette. Instead he promptly composed but dared not deliver a garland of whimsical verses for her, in which he proclaimed Bette his "special friend." Finally, that summer, he wrote to Bette at Camp Mudjekewis. It was Gige's good fortune that having just read Billy Baxter's love poetry in Seventeen, Bette was thrilled to have her own boy poet to suffer over her.

For all the gratifying attention she received from Gige and the other boys, Bette's memory book records the nagging fear that before the fall term was up, one absolutely crucial bit of affirmation would have eluded her: an invitation to join the select Sophomore Club, whose membership of fewer than thirty was limited to what she described as Newton's best families. According to Ellen Batchelder, the school administration struggled unsuccessfully to abolish the Sophomore Club on the grounds that everyone was not welcome to join. The club's exclusivity was precisely its attraction to Bette, who worried endlessly that her "family situation" would keep her from being accepted. Not even Bette's election as vice-president of her Newton class that term seems to have meant as much to her as the tiny pink envelope that she and fifteen of her friends (including Ellen, Sister, and Faith) finally received late in October, welcoming them to what was widely regarded as the Newton "smart set."

"This is the house where Bette lives," the boy poet declaimed that spring of 1924. "These are the cars that come to the house where Bette lives. These are the boys that come in the cars that come to the house where Bette lives." It was no secret that poor Gige Dunham was in despair over the older, faster boys—seniors headed for Harvard, Yale, and other New England colleges—with whom Bette had begun to keep company. Despite his father's position at the Standard Steel Motor Car Company, Gige was still without an automobile of his own. He could hardly compete with boys capable of driving off with Bette in the closed cars that were so radically altering the nature of the American date. That year, at least 43 percent of all cars manufactured in the United States were closed (by contrast with 10 percent in 1919): providing young couples with the sort of unsupervised mobile "room" that prompted one juvenile court judge of the era to proclaim the automobile a "house of prostitution on wheels."

"Bette dated more, certainly more than I was allowed to date," says Sister Koops. "But that is no reflection on Bette, because I wasn't allowed to go down to the corner."

Before long, Gige Dunham's distress about the bold new direction Bette's social life had begun to take came to be shared by Ruthie. Mrs. Davis confided to Miggie Fitts's mother her fears that things might be getting out of hand with her willful daughter. Much to Ruthie's chagrin, it was suddenly a question not of the sort of sweetly innocent flirtation described in Tarkington's *Seventeen* (and embodied by her daughter's blameless relations with Gige) but of that far

more serious phenomenon which F. Scott Fitzgerald had taught
America to call "petting." "None of the Victorian mothers—and most
of the mothers were Victorian—had any idea how casually their
daughters were accustomed to be kissed," Fitzgerald had written in
This Side of Paradise (1920). In that book, the Tarkington "flirt"
metamorphosed into a "baby vamp," capable of saying (as Lola Pratt
could never have done), "I've kissed dozens of men. I suppose I'll kiss
dozens more." As Ruthie was the first to admit, even if she prohibited
her increasingly unbridled daughter from getting into cars with young
men, since she was out working so much of the time she could hardly
monitor all that went on in the apartment in her absence.

It seemed to Ruthie that with the close of the spring term at
Newton High, her agonies over Bette's boy fever were about to come
to an end. The anxious mother wasted no time removing Bette from
Newton. Ruthie and the girls were to spend the summer in Provincetown, Massachusetts, at the tip of Cape Cod, where they would live
in the Winthrop Street parish house of H. M. Grant, a Methodist
student pastor. In Provincetown, Ruthie's hopes of removing Bette
from temptation were quickly dashed. When Bette wasn't modeling
for painters from the local arts colony, she carried on much as before,
filling the parsonage with a succession of houseguests from Newton.
Among these visitors were several of the older boys, whom Ruthie
hesitated to banish lest her daughter cling to them all the more
tightly. When to Ruthie's great relief the gentlemanly Gige Dunham
put in an appearance that July, Bette's attentions to a Harvard fresh
man named Jim Allen caused the boy poet to depart in a jealous pout.
Taking great pleasure in the histrionics of it all, Bette made a great
show of tearing up the heartsick letter Gige sent her from Newton.
Then, on second thought, she carefully gathered the pieces in an
envelope to preserve in her scrapbook.

Without friends—let alone boyfriends—of her own, Bette's sister, Bobby, spent much of the summer taking long solitary walks on
the dunes. Now and then a kindly Portuguese fisherman took her
fishing for the mackerel with whose red gills Provincetown ladies had
once been said to trim their hats. After a particularly violent storm,
Bobby was out "mooncussing," or beachcombing, when she plucked
a shattered toy sailboat from the debris that had washed ashore. In
the days that followed, the quiet, lonely child devoted herself to
repairing the little boat, adding a new mast and cretonne sail of her
own design. As usual, however, on launching day the honors fell to

Bette. While Bobby watched from the beach, Bette set the sailboat adrift. It headed out to sea and was lost. Bobby screamed and screamed for her sister to swim after it, but Ruthie declared the tide far too dangerous.

Bette's turn to scream came soon afterward, when, in hopes of isolating her from eager male admirers, Ruthie announced plans to send both girls to a religious boarding school some one hundred miles west of Boston. By contrast with the dramatically posed and costumed female figure shown in the pictorialist camera portraits that cluttered the walls of their various apartments, the photograph Ruthie attached to Bette's application for admission to the Northfield Seminary for Young Ladies envisioned her as the quintessence of Pre-Raphaelite feminine innocence: Bette Davis as Lewis Carroll might have photographed her.

Set among the woodland brooks of rural Northfield, Massachusetts, the seminary had been founded in 1879 by the evangelist Dwight Lyman Moody to educate the daughters of impoverished farmers, at a tuition roughly half that at other schools. Author of the popular book *Heaven: Where It Is, Its Inhabitants, and How to Get There,* the Reverend Moody had begun to take a special interest in the plight of poor girls everywhere when, on his way to a revival meeting, he paused before a mountain shanty to observe two young daughters of a paralyzed father braiding palmetto straw hats for their scant living.

Bette was mortified at the prospect of being shipped off to a school whose connotations of poverty and neediness were precisely those she had struggled to transcend in the eyes of her Newton friends. How was she to tell Sister Koops or Miggie Fitts that, instead of parties and dances, this year would be devoted to prayer meetings and Bible study; or that, like all the other poor girls at Northfield Seminary, she would be expected to help with housework to defray expenses? Back in Newton, where Ruthie had rented yet another new flat, on Gray Birch Terrace, Bette cruelly accused her mother of wanting to punish and humiliate her for having attracted the sort of masculine attention that Ruthie craved for herself. In fact, Ruthie had been worried, justifiably perhaps, that as a divorcée's daughter, Bette was likely to be far more closely observed and commented upon than other girls in Newton. The anxious mother sincerely believed that it was better to send Bette away than risk the public outcry that seemed almost inevitable had she been allowed to remain and take up with the Newton boys as before.

Predictably, Bette was miserable at Northfield. The seminary girls struck her as vastly inferior to her Newton "smart set." Her sole cohort was her equally disconsolate roommate, Duck Seager, with whom Bette dubbed their cheerless room "Cell 322, Sing Sing." From the first, Bette bristled at the Northfield rulebook and the schedules of required prayer meetings and household duties the administration had quickly thrust into her hands. She and Duck mocked the litanies of "We don't do it in Northfield!" with which her every inquiry seemed to be met. Before long, Ruthie wrote to say that she would be stopping off in Northfield the following Thursday after attending a photographers' convention in Swampscott, Massachusetts. A determined Bette preserved her mother's postcard in her memory book, along with a notation that perhaps there was some hope left. Indeed, by the time Ruthie's visit was finished, Bette had persuaded her that she and Bobby were far too unhappy in this prison of a school to remain beyond the fall term.

Mrs. Davis informed Northfield Seminary that she was removing Bette and Bobby for "financial reasons," and after the winter break the girls transferred to Cushing Academy, a coeducational preparatory school in Ashburnham, Massachusetts. At Cushing, her report card shows, Bette's grades promptly plummeted from the A's she had earned in Newton to C's. Bette had openly declared that after the rigors of Northfield, she intended to have some fun at Cushing. She lost no time creating a mystique for herself among the Cushing boys by announcing that she already had a steady beau at home.

Much as she dangled the name Gige Dunham before the Cushing boys, she remained flirtatiously noncommittal to Gige himself. At Christmas, when Gige had finally worked up the courage to ask Bette what his chances were with her, she had replied merely that he had as much chance as anyone. As usual, this caused Gige to pour out his heart on his father's company stationery: "If you don't watch out my little Miss / Upon those lips I'll plant a . . ." Gige could hardly bring himself to write the word "kiss," let alone put his threat into action: "You know I wouldn't dare / You'd slap me right across the face / And tell me to go to the hot place." As Bette was quick to discover, Gige's quaint inhibitions did not seem to be shared by the boys at Cushing. In Ashburnham, the regular Sunday coed hour allowed young men and women to pair off and stroll about the grounds. Each week, as Sunday approached, Bette fervently prayed for rain. She had learned how useful an umbrella could be on these rainy walks to shield a furtive embrace with a beau.

Although Bette strolled the campus with a number of boys that term and even spent a weekend in Cambridge, where her Province-town boyfriend Jim Allen escorted her to the Harvard Freshman Jubilee, by the evidence of her scrapbook notations there can be little question that her favorite male companion of the moment was Cushing senior J. Warren Blake, or "Blake," as she called him. Bette encouraged Blake to throw over his previous steady girlfriend, all the while, however, making a great fuss about her own refusal to give up Gige. In due course, like his predecessor the boy poet, Blake inquired where he stood with Bette. And she, with typical coyness, replied that it wouldn't be any fun if she told him.

One evening after chapel, Blake's agonies precluded studying for an English examination the next day. Instead he composed a sighing note to Bette, typical of the many lovesick missives from boys that crowd her scrapbook. Would she tell him that she cared for him just a little? Did she know that she could do what she wanted with him and that he cared for her more than he could tell?

And would she please, please give up Gige?

ette was in her element playing the coquette with Blake and the other Cushing boys. But Ruthie, as always restless and dissatisfied, had other roles in mind for her. Although routine work as a portrait photographer and photo re-toucher in Newton allowed Ruthie to help support herself and the girls, she never permitted herself to forget that she had failed as an artist in New York. As Ruthie would record, a familiar feeling of discontent continued to stir within her: a longing for something more than life in suburban Newton seemed to offer. Many years before this, Ruthie had sought that shadowy and elusive something in the Delsarte poses she so ardently practiced in youth; then she had sought it in the pictorialist photography to which she committed herself in later years. So perhaps it was inevitable that Ruthie would eventually find her way to the era's Delsarte-inspired interpretive dancing, whose powerful artistic influence she and the girls absorbed that summer of 1925 at the Mariarden arts colony, in the idyllic mountain hamlet of Peterborough, in southwest New Hampshire. By this time,

Ruthie's aspirations were consciously no longer for herself but for Bette, whose budding physical beauty convinced the mother that her daughter ought to be trained to dance in the bold, exuberant, hieratic manner of Isadora Duncan or Ruth St. Denis. St. Denis taught at Mariarden with her husband and dance partner, Ted Shawn.

Marie Currier, a retired actress whose wealthy husband, Guy, funded Mariarden, had once studied with "Miss Ruth," as St. Denis was known to her adoring pupils. Accordingly, the Curriers envisioned Mariarden as a temple of art dance, where barefoot children in flowing white robes might attain the highest phases of being when their bodies had been trained to respond to what Delsartists called "the movements of the soul." At Mariarden, entrée to the highest phases of being was expensive. When Mrs. Davis met with Marie Currier in hopes of enrolling Bette, Ruthie was distressed to discover that she could not afford the tuition. Ruthie anticipated earning only a minimal income that summer taking pictures at the nearby Mac-Dowell Colony for writers, musicians, and artists—not nearly enough to pay for Bette's lessons.

Bette was promptly enrolled instead at Peterborough's lesser, cut-rate school of interpretive dance, the Out-Door Players, whose director, Marie Ware Laughton, offered to waive tuition for Ruthie's daughter in exchange for free photographs of classes and performances. Clad in the Greek tunics that Isadora Duncan had made emblematic of female yearnings, Bette and Miss Laughton's other young nature dancers were out cavorting among the pines one afternoon when several of the girls froze suddenly at the sight of a tall, ethereal female figure in a rippling Oriental robe and jangling gold bracelets. At Mariarden that summer, Mlle. Roshanara, the exotic thirty-three-year-old Irish-English "priestess of Burmese dance and health culture" (whose real name was Jane Craddock), had attracted a passionate following for her classes in expressive movement, emphasizing the "natural" use of all parts of the body. As it happened, Ruthie was there taking pictures of Bette and the others when Roshanara introduced herself to Miss Laughton's students and explained that she had come to observe them in search of one or two young dancers with presence and magnetism enough to join her company.

The next morning, much as Ruthie had hoped might happen, a tiny girl whose copious robe and delicate, fluttering motions announced her as a disciple of Mlle. Roshanara arrived at the Silhouette Shop, Ruthie's Vine Street photography studio. The child brought a note from Roshanara:

My Dear Mrs. Davis,

Will you be kind enough to come and see me and bring your daughter
Bette, any time after four.

Very faithfully yours,
Roshanara

Twelve years after this, in 1937, Bette Davis was rehearsing her
on-screen entrance in *Jezebel*. Director William Wyler sent her home
with the leather riding crop and sweeping black riding habit she was
to wear in the scene, with instructions to devise a single large, comprehensive gesture that would instantly define the character of Julie
Marsden. In the beautiful cinematic moment that resulted, Bette
catches the train of her riding habit with the crop and sweeps it up
over her shoulder with a graceful ripple of voluminous black fabric,
reminiscent of her 1925 solo dance debut at Mariarden in Roshanara's
staging of one of Loie Fuller's famous "serpentine" numbers. "La
Loie," as the Illinois-born skirt dancer had been known to a worshipful French public around the turn of the century, had created dazzling abstract effects through the wavelike manipulation of the colorful
fabrics in which she draped herself for such signature numbers as the
Fire Dance, the Lily Dance, and the Butterfly Dance. With long
wands strapped to her arms, Fuller would lash her billowing costumes in the fluid curves and spirals said to express "the higher
emotions." So, too, for Bette Davis's debut in the Moth Dance at
Mariarden that August of 1925, Bette used long balsam sticks to
manipulate the layers of white Chinese silk that hung all about her, in
illustration of the classic Delsartean principle on which virtually all
interpretive dance was based and by which much of Davis's best
screen work would consistently be informed: "Every movement is the
manifestation of a thought, an emotion, or a passion."

As Ruthie and Bobby watched Bette dance on a pane of frosted
glass underlit to give the effect of flames, in which the Moth finally
perishes, they were beside themselves with excitement. Bobby had
made Bette's eight-week apprenticeship at Mariarden possible by
agreeing to play the piano for a dance class taught by one of Roshanara's disciples in the damp cellar of a church in Keene, New Hampshire, in exchange for free lessons for her sister. But any sacrifices
that had to be made were well worth it, or so it seemed to Ruthie,
especially when director Frank Conroy, in whose Mariarden production of *A Midsummer Night's Dream* Bette appeared as one of the

Dancing Fairies, declared that it would be a crime if Mrs. Davis didn't put her older daughter on the stage someday. "She has something that you can't buy," he told Ruthie, "something that makes your eyes follow her when she doesn't speak, and when she does, it is just added excitement."

Despite the higher emotions Bette's graceful stage movement expressed so eloquently, the seventeen-year-old's journal entries suggest that her thoughts continued to be preoccupied with more mundane matters: most particularly, the ongoing rivalry between Blake and Gige. Bette had coyly invited both of them to Peterborough to see her in Mlle. Roshanara's production of *The Magic Slipper*. She had not, however, mentioned to either boy that his fellow sufferer would be there. A heartsick letter from Warren Blake that she received after the calamitous weekend tells all. On the Friday night of Blake's arrival that August, Bette concluded her performance by tossing the magic slipper to him in the audience. Only naturally, Blake interpreted this as a sign of favor. Whatever joy he may have felt at that moment was quickly extinguished later that evening when Bette informed him that Gige was expected the following morning and Blake shouldn't be so dreary as to complain about it. In a burst of jealousy, Blake angrily decamped early the next day. As Bette later gleefully recorded in her memory book, at Saturday night's performance she tossed the magic slipper to Gige.

As the summer of 1925 drew to a close, there was little in Bette's scrapbook to indicate that she shared Ruthie's fierce ambition for her to become an artist. Although Bette had savored the praise and attention her dancing attracted at Mariarden, and while she dutifully preserved the autographed picture Mlle. Roshanara had given her along with some vague words about Bette's possibly becoming one of her disciples in the near future, with September's approach Bette seems to have been infinitely more excited about all the new social glories that awaited at Cushing Academy, where Blake was already set to escort her to her senior prom.

Back at Cushing, however, things were not quite as Bette had hoped or expected. Under pressure from the school administration, she reluctantly agreed to work as a waitress in the cafeteria to help pay her expenses. And while she eagerly accepted the praise of friends like Jim Allen, who wrote from Harvard to congratulate her for trying to assist Ruthie, Bette was in fact mortified at having to advertise her dire financial circumstances to fellow students. New humiliation fol-

lowed when she ran for president of the senior class. Bette received
only a single vote, her own: a blow rendered all the more painful by
the principal's having read the results aloud in the auditorium. But
the worst did not come until mid-October when, after escorting Bette
to the Cushing–Worcester Academy football game, Blake suddenly
threw her over for a girl named Marion, with whom he decided to
attend the senior prom instead of Bette. Blake's unexpected rejection
was a chastening experience, and Bette's arrogant self-confidence
seemed to evaporate overnight. The boys whose affections she loved
to toy with weren't supposed to reject her as Harlow had. It was
almost with a sigh of relief that at Thanksgiving break Bette con-
tracted measles, which would keep her out of school for the rest of the
term.

Things were scarcely any better for her in Newton. Bette's girlfriends there were all excitedly planning for college. Sister Koops
would soon be going off to Skidmore and Miggie Fitts to Mount
Holyoke. College, however, was a possibility that even the self-
sacrificing Ruthie could hardly consider for Bette on her erratic earnings as a photographer and the $200 monthly alimony she continued
to receive from Harlow. More than ever, as Bette made the rounds of
Christmas parties in Newton, including a dance at the Neighborhood
Club given by Sister Koops and her older sister Doris, she lamented
a fate that had robbed her of all she would have possessed had Ruthie
not been so foolish as to lose Harlow to another woman.

It was in this frame of mind that, on January 5, 1926 (six days
after Sister Koops's party), Bette accompanied Ruthie to the Blanche
Yurka production of Henrik Ibsen's *The Wild Duck* at the Repertory
Theatre of Boston: an experience she would later credit with having
inspired her to become an actress. In *The Lonely Life*, Davis recalls
the powerful identification she felt with the English actress Peg Entwistle in the role of Hedvig. "I was watching myself," Davis would
write. "There wasn't an emotion I didn't anticipate or share with
her." But beyond saying that she was "thrilled" by Entwistle's performance, Bette offers no clue to precisely what it was in *The Wild
Duck* that stirred her. More useful is the theater program she preserved from that momentous day. Even before the curtain went up,
if Bette read George Bernard Shaw's "Analysis of the Play," Shaw's
references to the Ekdal family—to the mother Gina's "photographic
work," the father Hjalmar's feelings of intellectual superiority to his
wife and his subsequent abandonment of her and their teenage daugh-

ter, Hedvig—can only have struck a strange and disturbing chord. Whether Bette read the Shaw text in her program we cannot know; but knowing what we do of her life to this point, it is possible to imagine the powerful sense of recognition she must have felt when the curtain went up on a set littered with Gina's photographic equipment and camera portraits. In eerie resemblance to Ruthie Davis, Ibsen's Gina Ekdal has studied photography and earns her scant living as a photo retoucher. Like Harlow Davis, Hjalmar Ekdal was once (as another character says) "accepted amongst his fellow students as the great light of the future." Hjalmar's disdain for what he perceives as Gina's dull-wittedness and vulgarity exactly parallels the dynamics between Harlow and Ruthie, whose "inability to share his intellectual life became a source of irritation"—as Bette recalls in her memoir, careful to add that she can "understand" her father's impatience with Ruthie's "lesser gifts." Also as in Bette's experience, while the father in Ibsen's 1884 play is presumed to be the superior partner, it is the mother whose labors in the photography studio provide the money on which she and her daughter must live.

More and more as she grew older, Bette would consciously prefer to identify with Harlow. She would openly share his "irritation," even "contempt," for Ruthie, especially in those periods when Bette most intensely blamed her mother for having abdicated the comforts and position life with Harlow would have offered. Feeling, as she did that winter of 1926, the vexing precariousness of her circumstances in contrast to Newton friends like Sister Koops (whose adoring father, a well-to-do widower, provided all that Bette might have had from Harlow), Bette can only have experienced a pang when in *The Wild Duck* Hjalmar promises his daughter: "Hedvig, I am determined to make your future safe. You shall live in comfort all your life." Almost certainly, however, the section of the play that would have spoken most directly to Bette was what Blanche Yurka (who portrayed Gina) described as "the big emotional scene where Hedvig weeps hysterically over her father's leaving her," as performed by the seventeen-year-old Peg Entwistle. "My heart almost stopped," Davis would write. "She looked just like me." If, by her own account, Bette anticipated and shared the character's every onstage emotion, it was because in Hedvig's screams as she clings to the departing Hjalmar— "Father! Father! No, no! Don't turn away from me. No, no—he will never come back anymore. Mother, you must get him home again! Why won't Father have anything to do with me anymore?"—Bette heard the cries of anguish she had felt, but for fear of seeming weak dared never express, over Harlow's repudiation.

Since the moment in 1918 when Ruthie declared that Harlow had left them for good, Bette had struggled to conceal her tempestuous feelings about her father behind the mask of indifference she had copied from him. Peg Entwistle's Hedvig suggested a new possibility, a new mask: speaking those very emotions at long last without the danger of having them attributed to oneself. And so it was that when the curtain fell on Act Five of *The Wild Duck,* Bette turned to Ruthie and solemnly announced, "Mother, if I can live to play Hedvig, I shall die happy!"

🍷

The doodles in Bette's class notes at Cushing Academy during the spring term of 1926 suggest that the prospect of pursuing a theatrical career after graduation was suddenly much in her thoughts. In the upper-right-hand corner of a piece of lined notebook paper Bette has sketched a theater marquee:

ZIEGFELD THEATRE
STARRING
BETTE DAVIS

In the lower-left-hand corner one discovers Bette's childish rendering of a chauffeur-driven limousine, with a stick-figure version of herself in the back seat, captioned:

A CERTAIN NEW BROADWAY STAR
AND HER NEW ROLLS

Other significant fancies surface here as well, such as the Skidmore banner that Bette idly sketches, with reference to the college Sister Koops will be attending. In contrast to the theater marquee, the college banner represents what might have been in Bette's life: the road she probably would have taken had her parents remained married. If, of all the Newton girls, it is Sister Koops (certainly never her closest friend there) about whom Bette has chosen to daydream, it may be because, like Bette, she came from a single-parent home— except that to Bette's way of thinking, Sister had the correct parent, the father. Harlow was scarcely aware of his daughter's day-to-day life, but Sister's father showered her with attention that included the careful monitoring of her every activity, especially where boys were concerned. Which may be why, although one might not notice it at first, when Bette prints Sister Koops's given name near the Skidmore banner, she does it this way: "VIRGIN/IA?"

That term Bette landed the starring role of Lola Pratt in a student production based on her favorite novel, Tarkington's *Seventeen*. If there was any part the aspiring actress was particularly well suited to play, this was it. In the course of work on the production, Bette surprised classmates by embarking on a romance with Harmon Oscar Nelson, Jr., or "Ham," as everyone called this shy, lank-limbed, Ichabod Crane sort of fellow. Ham had been cast as one of Lola's suitors. Unaccustomed to being pursued by girls, Ham was hardly the glamorous figure at Cushing that Blake had been, but therein lay his appeal to Bette, who continued to feel upset and embarrassed by Blake's defection. She feared being rejected all over again should she take up with one of the faster, more popular boys. Intent on having a steady boyfriend during her senior year, no matter who he might be, she invented the unlikely, unthreatening Ham Nelson in the role. Ham's childish notes to Bette from this period (notes that, she confided to her journal, she found disappointing) suggest that he was bewildered and perhaps even a bit frightened by Bette's persistent advances. For her part, declaring it "humiliatingly obvious" that he was more interested in music than in her, Bette promptly involved herself in all of the school's abundant musical activities where Ham, a talented singer, was certain to be encountered: the Cushing Glee Club, the Music and Minstrel Show, and the Fireside Sing. Her single-minded pursuit paid off. By the time they appeared onstage together in *Seventeen* later that spring, Bette could happily note in her memory book that she and Ham were now considered every bit as much a couple as Blake and Marion.

Although Bette had invited her father to attend her Cushing dramatic debut, he failed to appear. On opening night, Harlow sent his regrets and a bunch of sweet peas for good luck. When she wrote to thank him afterward, she made the mistake of mentioning her newly acquired theatrical ambitions. Bette's declaration plunged Harlow into a fit of agitation. Yearnings such as these had caused him to draw back from Ruthie when she experienced them, and now it was happening all over again with Bette. It seemed to Harlow that, like her mother before her, Bette failed to comprehend that her only happiness in life could be in marriage and motherhood. Unwilling to send her to college or to listen to any further talk of a stage career, Harlow instructed Bette to find work as a secretary until a suitable marriage proposal materialized.

By this time, Bette was preoccupied with the romance of her senior year at Cushing, and she seemed to give hardly a thought to the dilemma posed by Harlow's steadfast refusal to contribute to her boarding school tuition. While Bette talked and wrote of nothing besides the upcoming graduation festivities, at which she and Ham planned to outshine Blake and Marion as that year's golden couple, Ruthie faced the prospect of her daughter's being denied her diploma if Ruthie failed to pay her tuition in full. Harlow did not respond to his ex-wife's plea for funds, so Ruthie undertook to pay both daughters' Cushing bills by signing on as school photographer. Added to her already heavy work schedule, shooting and developing all the class portraits before June 11 was a formidable task for one person. But even if she had to stay up night after night developing the student pictures, it was worth it to Mrs. Davis to avoid disappointing and humiliating Bette. So long as Ruthie had the pictures ready in time to collect her fees from the students, she could pay the final installment of Bette's tuition before the graduation ceremony, from which the anxious mother feared her daughter might otherwise be barred.

As Friday, June 11, approached, Bette, oblivious of her mother's ordeal, was all feverish anticipation of the Glee Club recital, set to launch the week's commencement activities. Watching Ham Nelson step out to sing a solo of "Moonlight and Roses" would be his parents and his younger sister, Lois. With a teenager's all-consuming determination that everything be absolutely perfect, Bette could hardly keep herself from agonizing about what the Nelsons would think of her bohemian mother. When the big day arrived and, at the last possible moment, Mrs. Davis rolled into Ashburnham in her battered Ford to deliver the portraits, Bette was in agonies of embarrassment at her mother's appearance. Weeks of overwork and sleepless nights had shrunken Ruthie's frame to a mere ninety pounds. From a distance, she seemed haggard and oddly wraithlike as she frantically gathered the dollars for Bette's tuition. Only when Bette came closer could she make out the hideous rash that covered large areas of her mother's face, the effect of the harsh chemicals used to develop the school portraits. There could be no more tangible sign of the price

Ruthie willingly paid to fulfill her daughter's dreams, but all Bette could think of for the moment was the appalling impression her mother would make on the Nelsons.

When Bette hesitantly presented her mother to the Nelsons at the Glee Club recital, they were charmed by Mrs. Davis, whose single-minded devotion to Bette they much admired. Ham apparently had told them about the deluxe engraved calling cards Ruthie had had printed for Bette's final year at Cushing and the array of party dresses she had made by hand for various senior dances and social occasions. Ruthie announced to Mr. and Mrs. Nelson that after paying off both daughters' tuition, she had even had a bit of money to spare from the photographic fees she had collected that afternoon. Hearing this, Bette went to work on her mother for one last necessity for the senior dance on Monday: a white satin evening coat like the one she had borrowed from a classmate earlier that spring to attend a campus party with Ham. For the rest of the evening, nothing could divert Bette from the subject. When no promise was forthcoming from Ruthie, her daughter suddenly announced plans for them to drive to the town of Fitchburg the next day for lunch.

A glance at the Cushing schedule for Saturday indicated a full day of activity for Bette: chapel in the morning, a baseball game that afternoon, and later that evening the senior play, in which Bette was set to appear. Still, the next morning Ruthie did as her daughter insisted. They drove to Fitchburg, where Bette dragged her immediately into a clothing store. As Ruthie might have expected it would be, a white satin coat was on prominent display. Mrs. Davis protested that the tiny sum left over from the portrait fees was hardly enough to pay for such an extravagance. Her daughter, whose self-centeredness she had nurtured and encouraged through the years, angrily refused to leave the shop until Ruthie, worn out and embarrassed, relented.

Bette received her Cushing diploma Monday afternoon, and that evening at eight she was wearing the white satin coat when Ham picked her up for the senior dance. At the dance, precisely as Bette had envisioned, she and her beau were widely regarded as the class of 1926's premier couple—or so Bette noted afterward when she pasted a satin swatch from the coat into her memory book as emblem of the evening's triumph.

After graduation, in open defiance of Harlow's wishes, Ruthie and Bette repaired to a one-room fisherman's shack at Perkins Cove

in Ogunquit, Maine, to plan Bette's next moves in pursuit of a theatrical career. Back in Boston, the exasperated Harlow secretly drew
up a new will, which left his entire estate to his second wife, Minnie,
adding: "This I do to the absolute exclusion of my children, Ruth
Elizabeth Davis and Barbara Harriet Davis."

Even as she was being excluded from her father's will, presumably on Bette's account, Bobby had been shut out of the cedar shack
in Ogunquit. Ruthie declared it far too small for the three of them.
Determined that Bette must have a restful summer at the shore
before embarking on her stage career, Ruthie sent Bobby to work
cleaning and fetching in a friend's lakefront house, where as many as
fourteen guests were known to spend the weekend. The lonely child
cried for days at a time when her employers scolded her for clumsi-
ness. Finally, Bobby broke down under the strain and was shipped to
Ogunquit. Bobby can only have been startled to discover that her
mother had invited Bette's new best friend—whom Ruthie had taken
to calling "my Southern daughter"—to live with them.

Although eighteen-year-old Robin Brown (then known as Marie
Simpson) had turned down Ruthie's offer to move in, she was a frequent visitor to the fisherman's shack at Perkins Cove, where she and
Bette (to whom she bore a marked physical resemblance) shared their
dreams of a stage career. The absolute certainty with which Robin
spoke about becoming an actress transformed Bette's hitherto vague
fantasies into something almost palpable, almost real. Bette's painful
sense of alienation from the Newton girls and the directions their
lives had taken drew her all the closer to Robin, who shared her lack
of money. Raised in West Virginia by the widowed mother of six
children, Robin was a scholarship student at Hood College in Mary-
land. She and five other Hood girls had taken summer jobs as wait-
resses in the brown-shingled old Sparhawk Hotel overlooking the
ocean in Ogunquit, where Bette had already made quite a sensation
that summer as the only girl to take and pass the lifeguard's test.

At the end of August, when there was still no concrete plan for
launching Bette's career, Ruthie proposed that they move back to
Newton. If Bobby went to public school instead of returning to Cushing, perhaps they could save enough money to make the big move to
New York the following year. At Thanksgiving, when Robin came to
stay with them briefly on Cabot Street, Bette seemed lonely and
depressed. Her old Newton friends seemed to have dispersed. When
a friend of Ruthie's arranged for Bette to pose for a wealthy Boston

sculptress, Bette leapt at the opportunity. The artist promised to send a limousine for her, and Bette hoped that if their neighbors saw her being whisked away by a chauffeur, they would think that Bette Davis had gone on to better things.

At Ruthie's suggestion, Robin met them in Ogunquit the following summer of 1927. They all shared a rustic cottage, while Robin and Bette worked two or three hours every afternoon at what Robin described as "a cinch job," serving tea and cinnamon toast on the porch of Mrs. Johnson's Tea Room. Shortly before leaving Newton, Ruthie had appealed to Harlow to provide the additional funds necessary to send Bette to drama school that fall. As might have been expected, he angrily refused on the grounds that Ruthie would do their daughter a far greater service by encouraging her to marry as soon as a suitable husband could be found. This, of course, Ruthie could not accept. As a woman who strongly perceived her ambitions to have been defeated in marriage, she was hardly about to urge the same fate upon her nineteen-year-old daughter. Ruthie's motives were not entirely selfless, however. In Bette's artistic fulfillment Ruthie clearly sought recompense for her own bitterly unrealized dreams.

That summer in Ogunquit, even as Ruthie pored over advertisements and brochures for drama schools in hopes of finding one where Bette might obtain a scholarship, her elder daughter was quietly falling in love with a dashing Yale man—precisely the sort of fellow Harlow had in mind. Every afternoon, when Bette finished her chores at Mrs. Johnson's sedate establishment on the Marginal Way, Francis Lewis "Fritz" Hall, of Portland, Maine, would roar up on the motorcycle Bette called "the two-wheeled devil" to take her home. It seemed to Bette that in his rakish leather helmet, Fritz bore a remarkable resemblance to Charles Lindbergh. The aviator's solo flight between New York and Paris that May had made him something of an American Galahad, which accounts for the incongruous picture of "Lucky Lindy" that Bette pasted in her scrapbook amid the numerous photographs Ruthie took of Fritz in Ogunquit.

For much of the summer, it had hardly occurred to Mrs. Davis that Bette's romantic relationship with Fritz was considerably more serious than her prior attachments. Even when Bette and Fritz formed what they playfully called a "summer family" with a German shepherd puppy whom Bette named Eli (after Fritz and his fellow Yale boys, or "Elis"), Ruthie saw no cause for alarm. Then, one afternoon in August, Bette arrived home from Mrs. Johnson's with the news that Fritz had asked her to be his wife.

Ruthie appeared to be in shock as Bette reported Fritz's insistence that the time had come for her to choose between marriage and a stage career. In Fritz Hall's old-fashioned view, a woman could not possibly have both. By abandoning her theatrical ambitions, Bette would prove that she loved him all the more. In response to all this, Ruthie suddenly declared that Bette would have to think over Fritz's proposal at drama school. Mrs. Davis had located a scholarship at long last. She and Bette would be leaving immediately for New York. Bobby was hastily sent to live in Newton with Ruthie's sister.

hen Ruthie and Bette returned to New York that September, the Broadway theater was in the midst of one of its busiest years. By the time the year was up, there would have been 268 shows produced on Broadway. That month alone, the start of the extraordinarily fruitful 1927–28 season, the curtain went up on thirty new plays and two significant revivals. And in October, an astonishing thirty-four new shows and three revivals would open. That season, one could see Barbara Stanwyck in *Burlesque*, Helen Hayes in *Coquette*, Claudette Colbert in *The Mulberry Bush*, and Mae West in *The Wicked Age*. Eddie Cantor held forth in the *Ziegfeld Follies* and Fred and Adele Astaire in *Funny Face*; and from Germany came Max Reinhardt's company with its stunning interpretation of *A Midsummer Night's Dream*.

Downtown at the Civic Repertory Theatre, on West Fourteenth Street, Eva Le Gallienne was readying a production of Heijermans's *The Good Hope* to open in October. In the grim old auditorium, which seemed always to reek of disinfectant, audiences paid modest prices ranging from fifty cents to a dollar fifty to see often first-rate productions of Chekhov, Ibsen, Molière, and Shakespeare. Ruthie had heard that Miss Le Gallienne's drama students worked off their tuition by acting in her company. Soon after she and Bette arrived in New York, they appeared at the actress's Greenwich Village office in quest of an audition. Although in *The Lonely Life* Bette would claim that Le Gallienne herself conducted the disastrous interview that led to her rejection, Ruthie's notes clearly indicate that Bette never even got to see the actress. It was Le Gallienne's secretary who promptly dismissed Bette after a brief, unpleasant exchange. When the secretary routinely asked Bette what she had read and how she had prepared to become an actress, Bette shrugged her shoulder and snapped that that was precisely what she was here to do: prepare. Bette's sharp tongue and presumptuous manner seemed perfectly normal to Ruthie; even in later years, the doting mother never really understood why Le Gallienne's secretary so swiftly sent them back to suburban New Rochelle, New York, where they had moved in temporarily with Ruthie's brother, the Reverend Paul Favor, on Westminster Court.

Ruthie had one other name on the list she had prepared in Ogunquit: the John Murray Anderson Robert Milton School of Theatre and Dance, on East Fifty-eighth Street off Park Avenue. The school's dean was Arthur Hornblow, the distinguished editor and principal drama critic of *Theatre* magazine. The next day, Ruthie and Bette applied there, only to discover that in order to be eligible for a scholarship in the spring, Bette would have to enroll that fall at the standard five-hundred-dollar tuition. The sum was well beyond Ruthie's means. And as the Reverend Favor pointed out that night in New Rochelle, there was no guarantee that Bette would be awarded a scholarship for her second term.

Unwilling to return in defeat to Newton (where her sister, Mildred, had already been paid five dollars for Bobby's expenses that month), Ruthie secured temporary work as a photo retoucher in Norwalk, Connecticut, through a classified advertisement in the *New York Times*. Soon Bette was devoting hours each day to frenziedly scrubbing every inch of the tiny furnished room they had rented. The lonely, disappointed girl was repeatedly observed muttering aloud to herself on the streets of Norwalk as she carried on angry conversations with those whom she imagined to have thwarted her in New York.

Bette's sole consolation that September and early October was the proximity of her fiancé, Fritz Hall, in New Haven. Fritz visited as often as he could and struggled endlessly to persuade Bette to give up what he called her "crazy idea" of becoming an actress. According to Robin Brown, Fritz was not alone in his objections to Bette's career. His wealthy family was adamant that Fritz's bride must abandon all thoughts of the stage.

This time Ruthie did not make the same mistake she had made in Ogunquit, where she seriously misjudged the threat Fritz posed to her long-range plans for her daughter. In mid-October, when Bette gave every sign of preparing to accept Fritz's marriage proposal with all its conditions, Ruthie quietly slipped into New York to work out a deal with the John Murray Anderson–Robert Milton School. Classes had already been under way for three weeks. The contract Ruthie negotiated at the last minute shows that she persuaded the school to cut its tuition to $340, which she agreed to pay in three installments. On October 24, 1927, Bette excitedly moved into the school dormitory on East Fifty-eighth Street, while Ruthie repaired to Burlington, New Jersey, where she had secured low-paying but steady employment as a housemother at St. Mary's School. It hardly mattered to Ruthie that this was precisely the sort of unsatisfying work she had done years earlier, before training in photography at the Clarence White School. Bette's career was all that counted now.

▲▼▲

"Remember that voice a month ago? Well, listen to it now!" the school's director, stage designer and impresario John Murray Anderson, said of Bette late in November of 1927. He had singled her out for praise to the elocution class, which she had entered several weeks before, affecting a faint Southern accent copied from her best friend, Robin, to mask her own distinctly Boston-flavored speech. Bette had come to drama school with much the same "high squeaky voice" that had irritated Miss Whiting at Crestalban nine years before. In her elocution class in New York, Bette would discover the "lovely, low voice" that she is recorded to have possessed at the end of four months.

Bette made other major discoveries in her dance studies with part-time instructor Martha Graham. Graham, then in her mid-twenties, was already a charismatic figure, whose daunting manner and evangelical tone caused one awestruck teaching colleague to compare her to John the Baptist, while others whispered that, like a heretic, she fascinated merely "by her contrariness." The dancer had apprenticed with Ruth St. Denis and Ted Shawn before joining John Murray Anderson's Broadway revue *The Greenwich Village Follies*. At the Anderson-Milton School, Graham liked to tell her barefooted pupils that she had learned her own first lesson in the dance from her father, Dr. George Greenfield Graham, whose work in a mental institution near Pittsburgh had led him to pay less attention to what his patients said than to how they moved. In girlhood, when Martha lied to her father, all he had to do was watch her body as she spoke to know that she wasn't telling the truth. As Dr. Graham told his daughter, "Movement never lies." Whereas at length Dr. Graham's dictum sent Martha in quest of her own "truthful" dance language ("There is no American actress more sincere than Miss Graham," wrote the dance critic Edwin Denby in 1945), its long-term implications would be very different for her student Bette Davis, some of whose most affecting moments on-screen would play precisely on the dissonance between word and gesture. Like one of Dr. Graham's patients, Bette's most finely wrought characters might find themselves saying one thing with words while communicating quite another message with their bodies.

"Project beyond perimeter!" Graham directed her students. "Take in space! Reach out! Complete every gesture down to the fingertips!" She told them that an artist must be in competition with only one person, himself; that to the artist, freedom can mean only one thing, discipline; and that she would do anything for her art, "even marry."

For Bette Davis, it was beginning to look as if she would have to do quite the opposite to become an artist: not marry, at least not marry Fritz Hall, who continued to demand that she give up her dream of a stage career. As proof that Bette would not be the first woman to make this choice, Fritz sent her a newspaper article about the young actress Katherine Wilson, who had abandoned her career to marry actor Richard Barthelmess. Bette saved the article in her scrapbook but declined to follow its example. Although she finally agreed to wear Fritz Hall's engagement ring that fall of 1927, she suddenly tore it off and returned it to him within three days.

The spurned fiancé had some rather formidable competition in New York. Besides falling under Martha Graham's powerful spell, Bette experienced her first sustained—and formative—exposure to the Broadway stage. An abundance of exceptionally fine actresses dominated the American theater of the period. According to Robin Brown, who frequently attended the theater with Bette in New York (where more often than not the only tickets they could afford were in standing room), the stage actresses who came to matter to Bette in the mid-twenties included Lynn Fontanne, Ruth Gordon, Pauline Lord, Laurette Taylor, and, most especially, Katharine Cornell. That fall, the nineteen-year-old Bette Davis returned again and again to Cornell's controversial performances in W. Somerset Maugham's *The Letter*, at the Morosco Theatre. At length, Bette had well-nigh committed to memory the dark-eyed actress's every ardent gesture and darting glance. "He tried to rape me and I shot him," Cornell's brazen murderess Leslie Crosbie lied nightly—"perilously well," wrote one critic—betraying herself by turns with her eyes, her voice, her hands, and, most strikingly perhaps, with the incessant, obsessive lacework that seemed to absorb her so.

Maugham's "thriller" had opened in London the previous March, with Gladys Cooper as the married Englishwoman who kills her lover. From the time of its American premiere, on September 26, 1927, the play had had a good many detractors. Most vocal were those in New York theatrical circles who argued that, by regularly choosing to appear in such melodramatic "rubbish," Katharine Cornell was unforgivably dissipating her gifts. To which Cornell replied that for a serious actress, Leslie Crosbie and the other innately unsympathetic characters she played throughout the twenties ("the loose, dissolute women," as her detractors called them) afforded "extraordinary acting opportunities."

While in years to come this lesson would by no means be lost on Bette Davis, for the moment she had to content herself with lighter fare: the mainly comic one-acters—Bertram Bloch's *Gas, Air and Earl*, Essex Dane's *Happy Returns*, and Alice C. D. Riley's *Their Anniversary*—in which she was to appear at the end-term performances of the junior dramatic class. Bette regarded these two nights as a nightmare. They would be the moment of truth when the faculty decided whether to award her a scholarship for the following term.

Dean Hornblow did indeed mark "Full Scholarship" on Bette's second contract with the John Murray Anderson–Robert Milton School. But by the time the spring semester began, on February 6, 1928, at Ruthie's urging Bette had accepted an offer of professional employment from one of the faculty members, director James Light.

On the basis of his work with her on a student production of *The Famous Mrs. Fair*, Light invited Bette to make her professional acting debut in *The Earth Between* at the Provincetown Playhouse in Greenwich Village. Rehearsals for the new, O'Neill-influenced play by Virgil Geddes would preclude Bette's return to drama school. In large part, Bette had been cast as the seventeen-year-old innocent Floy Jennings because of what people had started to call her delicate "Burne-Jones looks."

That February, while they waited to hear from Light about the date when rehearsals for *The Earth Between* were to begin, by way of preparation Bette and Ruthie attended performances of Eugene O'Neill's *Strange Interlude*, which had opened the month before at the John Golden Theatre. Although Bette scarcely understood what was going on most of the time, she was enthralled by Lynn Fontanne's bravura performance as Nina Leeds (reputedly the longest role ever created for an actress). Bette watched Fontanne almost as if her performance were detached from the rest of the recondite nine-act drama that Fontanne's husband, Alfred Lunt, had dubbed a "six-day bisexual race." Not to be outdone, Alexander Woollcott called *Strange Interlude* "a play in nine scenes and an epicene."

Like Bette's teacher Martha Graham, O'Neill was fascinated by those situations in which what we say is not the same as what we think or feel: hence the soliloquies in *Strange Interlude*, which allow characters to speak aloud the thoughts they can't, or won't, express to others. In contrast to Graham, O'Neill intended these asides to replace the actors' expression of inwardness through gesture. But if O'Neill held most actors in scant regard, Fontanne showed barely more respect for his text, which struck her as verbose and inelegant. "His speeches are clumsy, stilted," she complained publicly. "It's literary dialogue, not theatre dialogue." Twenty-five years before this, the great mentor of her youth, Ellen Terry, had provided what Fontanne would always call "the key to acting." "Think of the meaning of what you are saying," Terry had counseled, "and let the words pour out of your mouth." This was precisely what Fontanne did in *Strange Interlude*, so that even a bewildered nineteen-year-old like Bette could somehow appreciate and enjoy the fervent passions behind her words.

By March, Bette was still waiting to start work at the Provincetown Playhouse, when she and Ruthie paid a triumphant visit to Newton. The ostensible reason for the trip was to see Bobby play the role of Phoebe in a student production of James Barrie's *Quality Street* at Newton High School. Now in her senior year, Bobby had received a scholarship to attend Denison University in Ohio, where she hoped to emulate Bette by studying interpretive dance. After a few days of lording it over friends and family with Bette's impending professional stage debut (talk of which eclipsed Bobby's appearance in the Barrie play), Bette and Ruthie returned to New York to discover that *The Earth Between* had been postponed, probably until the fall. While the crestfallen Bette ranted on about how she should have gone back to drama school that term, Ruthie more calmly considered their options. She instructed her daughter to contact Frank Conroy, who had predicted such great things for her at Mariarden. Conroy passed Bette on to director George Cukor, then in search of a young actress to fill out his cast for the one-week Rochester, New York, engagement of Philip Dunning and George Abbott's popular melodrama *Broadway*.

Much to Ruthie's chagrin, her duties at St. Mary's School would make it impossible for her to accompany her daughter to Rochester. Instead she wrote a curious long letter to Bette, whose every conceivable action on the trip north the mother anticipated in what can only be described as maddening detail. On page after closely packed handwritten page, Ruthie lovingly choreographs the simplest events in the days to follow: what items to pack (Ruthie evidently knows every article of clothing her daughter possesses and every bottle in her medicine cabinet) in which of two suitcases, and in what order; when to get to the train station (down to the minute) and what to do there; how to behave on board, how to undress at night, in what sequence to remove her garments, and where to put each of them. And there are copious directions for how Bette is to act in all imaginable situations she might encounter. Ruthie instructs her daughter to enact her simple, quiet self in Rochester and to affect a less reserved demeanor during rehearsals with Cukor. All this Bette was urged to read several times over before she went to bed on the eve of her departure. Ruthie apparently understood as no one else did the soothing effect repetition had on Bette, whose passion for order she almost certainly inherited from her equally obsessive mother.

For luck, twenty-year-old Bette preserved the pink ticket stub from the April 27, 1928, train trip to upstate New York, where, on opening night at Rochester's Lyceum Theatre three days later, she received a telegram from New Jersey: MAKE BELIEVE I'M THERE. MOTHER.

Had Ruthie been able to accompany Bette to Rochester, in the course of her daughter's extraordinary week there she would have seen Bette leap suddenly from the smallest female role in the production to one of the most important, when the actress playing Pearl (the gangster's girlfriend, upon whom it falls to avenge his murder) injured her leg and was forced to withdraw from the show. Until this point, the twenty-eight-year-old Cukor had paid little attention to Bette, and he was admittedly rather startled by her performance. He was especially struck by the climactic murder scene, to which Bette added many heightening touches, such as the odd dancelike rhythm that made it seem almost as if she were willing her victim to die.

Following a summertime engagement at the Cape Playhouse in Dennis, Massachusetts, where she was cast as Dinah, a young English girl, in Laura Hope Crews's production of A. A. Milne's *Mr. Pim Passes By*, Bette returned to New York in August. In anticipation of starting work soon at the Provincetown Playhouse, she took up residence with Robin Brown in a furnished room with bath on West Fifty-third Street, hard by a Sixth Avenue delicatessen whose kindly proprietor regularly gave the struggling young actresses extra food to take home. Robin had acted briefly with a stock company in Baltimore after graduation from Hood. To support herself while she looked for dramatic roles in New York, she took a job as a hostess in a Manhattan restaurant. Before long, she was cast as Mow Dan Fah in Charles Coburn's revival of the 1912 Benrimo-Hazelton classic *The Yellow Jacket*, quaintly billed as a "Chinese play in a Chinese manner."

At the end of September, Bette was gravely disappointed when James Light announced a further postponement of *The Earth Between*. Again Bette found herself turning to George Cukor. The director was in town hiring actors for the Temple Players, a new repertory company Cukor and his business partner, George B. Kondolf, Jr., had formed in Rochester. Their season was to open in October with the recent hit comedy *Excess Baggage*.

▲▼▲

A few days before Bette was scheduled to leave New York City with the other Temple Players, Ruthie went on ahead to Rochester. There she rented a depressing but cheap ground-floor apartment for the two of them and excitedly waited for Bette to arrive. When the Temple Players finally stepped off the train in Rochester, Ruthie watched from a discreet distance of several yards as Bette and the others posed for photographs for the local newspapers. One of the assembled troupe was the actor and assistant stage manager Benny Baker, who noted with fascination Bette's surprising savoir faire with the photographers, for whom she shrewdly insisted on changing clothes, "so she wouldn't appear with the same outfit in rival papers."

Despite this outward show of serene self-possession at the train station, the moment Bette was alone with Ruthie, her anxieties burst forth in a furious tirade, ostensibly over the garish striped wallpaper in the apartment for which her mother had already signed a three-month lease. "I can't stand it! I can't stand it!" Bette cried, tears streaming down her cheeks as her eyes darted over the walls. Ever anxious to appease her daughter, Ruthie agreed to see what she could do to persuade the landlady to cancel their lease without penalty. By morning, Ruthie had concocted an elaborate story about a Peeping Tom who had lurked outside their window the night before. The apologetic landlady promptly returned their rent, and Ruthie moved their things out that day.

As Bette was soon to discover, it was no Peeping Tom whom she had to fear just now but Cukor's partner, Kondolf, who (unlike the homosexual Cukor) had designs on her from the first. "Kondolf felt that every ingenue who came into the company had to go to bed with him," explains Benny Baker, then in his second year with Cukor-Kondolf. "It was part of his routine." According to Baker, Bette repeatedly spurned Kondolf's sexual advances, and the actress's rejection was not taken lightly. The blow to Kondolf's ego may have been exacerbated by Bette's innocent carousing with other cast members, including actor Samuel Blythe Colt. Bette affectionately called Colt "the mystery boy," on account of his desire to conceal his identity as the son of Ethel Barrymore, who had sent up the blue Chrysler in which he regularly paraded Bette and other pals about nocturnal Rochester.

Before long, Bette had picked up a new earnest young suitor, Rochester businessman Charles H. Ansley, whom she declared every bit as rich and handsome as Fritz Hall. Moreover, in contrast to Fritz, "Charlie," as she called him, seemed to love the idea of her being an actress. Night after night, Charlie came to see Bette at the Temple Theatre, where he would fill her dressing room with great bunches of pale-yellow roses, on whose wonders she rhapsodized in her memory book.

In Rochester, the small parts Cukor assigned her in the likes of

Excess Baggage (as a young vaudevillian) and *Laff That Off* (as the "slavey") seemed trivial and unrewarding by contrast with the serious acting à la Katharine Cornell and Lynn Fontanne that Bette longed to do. Still, her consistently good notices in the local papers (which declared her "an attractive competent ingenue" with "some genuine ability" and "quite a bit of demure charm") led Bette to say no when James Light wired to ask if she could return to New York immediately to start the long-delayed rehearsals for *The Earth Between*. Not long after she informed Light that she would be unavailable until the end of the Rochester season, Cukor-Kondolf made the surprise announcement that Bette was being dismissed from the Temple Players. "When Bette was forced to leave the company, people wondered why, since she had done a perfectly good job as an actress," says Benny Baker. "Then it came out that the reason she'd been fired was that she hadn't wanted to do any 'bed work.' "

When the portly actor-producer Charles Coburn decided to play Henry VIII in a whimsical new musical called *A Play with Music*, he cast Bette's friend Robin for the role of his pageboy whose "wow finish"—just before the curtain fell on Act One—had her hit the king in the seat of his pants with a jumbo slingshot. Terrified that one night onstage she might miss her target, Robin practiced with her slingshot in the dark basement of 17 West 8th Street in Greenwich Village, where she and Bette had taken up residence following Bette's return to New York with the startling news that she and Charlie Ansley were engaged.

Day and night, nine floor lamps provided the only light in the strange bunkerlike apartment, whose lack of even a single window compelled Bette and Robin to walk out into the beer garden of an adjoining brownstone to see what the weather was like in the morning. Euphemistically declaring the apartment to be on the artistic side, Ruthie had secured it for Bette and her roommate on the basis of its proximity to the Provincetown Playhouse, around the corner on MacDougal Street, where Bette was finally set to open in *The Earth Between* in March.

Virgil Geddes's laconic text clearly shows why James Light—who had first observed Bette while she was briefly under Martha Graham's tutelage—would have thought it particularly well suited to her abilities. In eight evanescent episodes, running from three to ten minutes each and distributed between two acts, Geddes chronicles farmer Nat Jennings's incestuous passion for his childlike seventeen-year-old daughter, Floy, whom he imagines to be the reincarnation of his dead wife. The characters' brute inability to express themselves verbally, coupled with the farmer's suppressed feelings and his daughter's innocent incomprehension, results in an elliptical and sparely written drama. The actors must register its buried emotions less through words (of which there are astonishingly few in the script) than through movement and gesture. In contrast to the kinds of dramatic material with which Bette had hitherto been forced to work, *The Earth Between*, for all its weaknesses of pacing and story structure, afforded her abundant opportunities to show off her talents as an actress schooled in expressing herself wordlessly. Especially rich in potential were Floy's scenes with Jake, a sullen lout of a farmboy scarcely able to articulate his feelings for her. While on one level Floy clearly returns these feelings, her sheltered life with an overbearing and possessive father has left her strangely ignorant of normal passion. As photographs from the production show, confusion and fear hampers her every move. Unable to admit to herself, let alone to her violently jealous parent, what she has begun to feel for Jake, the actress playing Floy must communicate with her body the full, complex truth of her emotions ("Movement never lies") so that the audience may understand everything the playwright has forbidden his character to say.

On March 5, 1929, exactly one month before Bette's twenty-first birthday, when, along with all the critics and other first-nighters, Robin, Ruthie, and the Reverend Paul Favor crowded into the tiny playhouse on MacDougal Street for Bette's long-awaited opening in *The Earth Between*, Bette had to wait a little longer still. Onstage, actress Mary Blair nagged, complained, accused, cajoled, and threatened her way through the one-act O'Neill monologue *Before Breakfast*. In hopes of filling out the evening, James Light had chosen the shrill and unpopular sketch as a curtain-raiser—or "Strange Prelude," as Village wags dubbed it. From backstage, Bette heard the ceaseless torrent of words, words, and more words with which Mrs. Rowland, the disgruntled wife of the O'Neill play, tongue-lashes her husband. He is presumably working off his hangover in an adjoining room, from which only his hand may be seen ever so briefly to issue in quest of a bowl of shaving water. For Robin, Ruthie, Uncle Paul, and the rest of the audience, a further torrent of shrieks and screams from the lady signaled that, offstage, the husband had cut his throat to escape her; but for Bette, this last and most gruesome of Mrs. Rowland's tirades meant that her own big moment was finally at hand.

After the violent spate of language that forms *Before Breakfast*, the drawn-out silences of *The Earth Between* inevitably came as something of a shock. This is undoubtedly why Light juxtaposed them: to make the audience perceive Geddes's "Oriental" austerity all the more strongly by contrast with O'Neill's clanging verbosity. The juxtaposition was not to everyone's liking, however. "One may state of these two pieces that Mr. O'Neill says too much and that Mr. Geddes says too little," wrote St. John Ervine in the *New York World*. "One wonders why either of them troubled to say anything at all." A good many critics damned Geddes's play for its sluggish pace and clumsy staging, but nearly all had a word or two of praise for the "exquisite" and "entrancing" Bette Davis. They compared her beauty to that of "a Burne-Jones figure" and noted her "soft, unassertive style" of acting, which they faulted only for being perhaps a touch too "ethereal."

Back in her dressing room after the opening-night performance, although the reviews would not be available until the next day, Bette appeared serenely confident that they would be good, according to Robin Brown. Still, Bette waited until Ruthie and Robin brought the newspapers the next morning before she wrote to her father in Boston to let him know about her first major triumph as an actress. Bette also thanked him for the congratulatory telegram and basket of flowers, whose arrival on opening night seems to have stunned everyone gathered in Bette's dressing room, to judge by the Reverend Favor's detailed account in a letter to his wife, Gail. In her scrapbook, Bette clearly and carefully enumerated the bouquets received from friends and family members; only beside the entry for Harlow do we discover the faintest of question marks, as if she cannot quite allow herself to believe that the lavish arrangement of roses and jonquils can really be from him. For many years thereafter, Bette would repeatedly make a great point of saying, as she does in her memoir, that Harlow's flowers had arrived with only an engraved card coldly attached. Yet there in her scrapbook one finds the opening-night telegram (AM CONFIDENT OF YOUR SUCCESS) for which she thanks him in her March 6 letter, whose mingled affection and reserve anticipates the sudden spate of troubled communication between father and daughter in the weeks and months to come.

Bette had first longed to become an actress to play Ibsen's Hed-

vig. Now she was thrilled when Blanche Yurka, whose Boston production of *The Wild Duck* she had attended in 1926, sent word to the
Provincetown Playhouse to ask her to read for the part. A member of
Yurka's company, Cecil Clovelly, had seen *The Earth Between* in the
penultimate week of its run. Clovelly remembered Bette as one of
Roshanara's Dancing Fairies in the Mariarden production of *A Mid-
summer Night's Dream*, in which he had performed the role of Flute.
As chance would have it, Yurka had been doing Ibsen on Broadway
and was about to go on tour, when Linda Watkins, the young actress
who played Hedvig, announced that she planned to leave the com-
pany at the close of its Broadway run. Clovelly proposed Bette to
Yurka, who summoned her to the Bijou Theatre on West Forty-fifth
Street for an eleven o'clock audition the following morning, Saturday,
March 23, 1929.

"Now you must tell me what is the matter," implored Bette, essaying
the role of Hedvig during her audition onstage at the Bijou. "Why
won't Father have anything to do with me anymore?"

"You mustn't ask that until you are a big girl and grown up,"
replied Clovelly, as Gregers Werle.

"You *are* Hedvig!" Blanche Yurka shouted from the orchestra
when Bette finished. She rushed onstage to offer Bette a contract to
appear in the Actors' Theatre Inc.'s Ibsen program at a weekly salary
of $75. Rehearsals were set to begin the following week in anticipa-
tion of Bette's taking over from Linda Watkins on April 3.

By the time Bette returned from the audition to her dressing
room downtown at the Provincetown Playhouse, where she was due
to go on that night in the role of Floy Jennings, she felt as if she were
about to be ill. Her queasiness was badly exacerbated when a stagehand delivered a note. The familiar handwriting would no doubt have
loudly and instantly spoken to her even before she read the words.
The note was from her father. Without warning, he had come to New
York to see her play. He asked, in an awkward, strained manner, if he
might see her after the show to congratulate her and take her to
supper.

What thoughts may have raced through Bette's mind as, already
feverish and covered with a pink rash, she stepped out onstage that
Saturday night we cannot know. The Provincetown Playhouse, a
former stable, was extremely small, which makes it likely that at some

point Bette would at least have caught a glimpse of Harlow in the audience, nervously wondering if his daughter would agree to dine with him. His hesitation, his fear of rejection, was obviously based on all the times when Bette recoiled from visits to a father whom she correctly perceived to have rejected her first.

Although Harlow and Bette were alone together in her dressing room afterward, we may glean something of the tense, painful, largely unspoken back-and-forth that went on there from the evidence of a letter Harlow wrote to his daughter two days after his return to Boston. Known as a man who disclosed his feelings to few people, Harlow struggles, in his March 25, 1929, letter to say to Bette at least some of what had remained unsaid in the awkward, unsatisfying minutes they spent together. Besides telling her father that she wasn't up to dining with him, she seems scarcely to have talked about anything besides the impending Ibsen tour, while Harlow apparently praised every actor in the company but his own daughter. Monday morning, back at his desk at United Shoe Machinery, Harlow laments having seen her so briefly; her evident rush to get home on account of an illness he seems barely to believe in; his failure to ask her even half the questions he meant to, since, as he points out, he was counting on a long talk over supper. Lest Bette think that her father had merely dropped in at the theater that night because he happened to be in town on business, Harlow assures her that he came to New York solely to see her act. The man who once declared that she should become a secretary and give up all thought of a stage career reverses himself here. Harlow tells her how proud he is of her theatrical debut, how accomplished she seems, and (notwithstanding his failure to contribute money for tuition when she needed it—obviously a major sore point with Bette) how expertly taught she evidently had been at the John Murray Anderson–Robert Milton School. Only for a moment, toward the end of the letter, does a harsher voice seem about to erupt, when, perhaps thinking of the nervous breakdown that once sent Ruthie to a sanitarium, Harlow suddenly warns Bette that if she fails to take care of herself now, she may crack up.

"Y ou can't come in. Bette has the measles," Ruthie told Robin, who had just returned from the Saturday night performance of *The Yellow Jacket* uptown at the Coburn Theatre.

Following Bette's abortive encounter with her father, she had dragged herself home from MacDougal Street and collapsed into bed. Ruthie called a doctor, who diagnosed Bette's flaming rash as a serious case of measles; but as even Bette would come to realize, the rash and accompanying fever were almost certainly psychosomatic.

Insistent that she didn't want Bette's roommate to catch the measles, Ruthie banished Robin from the apartment. Sunday morning, Bette withdrew from the Geddes play for the week that remained of its run. For the next ten days, Ruthie endlessly read aloud to her ailing daughter from the three Ibsen plays in the Actors' Theatre repertoire: *The Wild Duck*, *The Lady from the Sea*, and *Hedda Gabler*. This would be in lieu of the rehearsals with Blanche Yurka that Bette (whose eyes were suddenly far too weak for her to study the scripts herself) had committed herself to undertake in that period. At Ruthie's urging, Cecil Clovelly had helped persuade Yurka to accept the unorthodox arrangement. It placed total responsibility on Ruthie to prepare her daughter for the single rehearsal on the morning of April 3 that Yurka required if Bette was to go on that night at the Bijou Theatre (as Bolette in *The Lady from the Sea*) before embarking on tour.

The difficulty with her eyes that accompanied Bette's affliction would only have intensified her psychic identification with Ibsen's Hedvig, who suffers from serious eye trouble. (Had Bette's extreme sympathy with the character gone so far as to make her virtually unable to read in the first place?) For all the personal reverberations Bette discovered in *The Wild Duck*, there is no evidence in anything Ruthie said or wrote to suggest that she recognized any of her own similarities to Hedvig's mother, Gina Ekdal. By the time Bette and Ruthie were finished with their ten days of rehearsal, however, as far as Bette was concerned Ruthie certainly had taken on important aspects of Gina's nature. On the eve of the all-important rehearsal with Yurka, Ruthie set the alarm clock for 7:00 A.M. That would give them more than two hours before Bette was due uptown. Unfortunately, Mrs. Davis neglected to wind the clock. They worked on Bette's lines long past midnight, and neither mother nor daughter awakened in the perpetually dark apartment until nine-thirty the following morning. What ensued then was the sort of shrieking and vituperation witnesses would often observe between Bette and Ruthie in years to come. While Ruthie searched frantically for a cab at the corner of Sixth Avenue and Eighth Street, Bette seems suddenly to have bitten her mother's shoulder, actually ripping through Ruthie's woolen dress with her teeth.

When the pair finally arrived at the Bijou Theatre, Cecil Clovelly was decidedly cool to them. "Why not think up a new one?" Clovelly snapped at Ruthie as she struggled to excuse their lateness with the story of the unwound alarm clock. Still weak from her illness and ten days with scarcely anything to eat, Bette let loose a barrage of invective at her mother. She ended with a loud command to get out and leave her alone. Yurka was intrigued and fascinated by this unexpected display of violent emotion—a display rendered all the more notable by its incongruity with Bette's extreme fragility and sickly pallor. While Yurka can hardly have imagined the source of all this pent-up resentment against Ruthie, she was nonetheless immediately aware that it could be put to splendid use onstage. Later, Yurka would remember this strange outburst as she encouraged Bette merely "to let herself go" in the scene in *The Wild Duck* where Hedvig breaks down because her father has abandoned her: a scene for which Yurka declared Bette would obviously need no rehearsal.

Ejecting her mother from the theater had been a major turning point for Bette. She had always privately blamed Ruthie for the loss of Harlow, and now she blamed her anew for the near sabotage of her long-awaited chance to speak to him through the character of Hedvig.

Anyone who doubts the immense personal significance that Bette's role in *The Wild Duck* held for both her and her father need only consult their uncharacteristically emotional correspondence on the subject that April of 1929, shortly after Bette turned twenty-one. For her birthday on April 5, Harlow had sent her an expensive suit-case to take on the forthcoming theatrical tour. The gift had mingled associations for both of them, since it came from a parent who had cruelly and unnecessarily allowed his daughter to travel about in poverty for much of her life. Having finally signed her contract with Blanche Yurka the day before, Bette would write to Harlow on her birthday to thank him for the luggage and to crow over her opening in *The Wild Duck*, scheduled for three days thence at the Boulevard Theatre in nearby Jackson Heights. After that, the troupe would go on to Philadelphia and Washington and then Boston, where Bette expresses the wish that she will see her father again.

Although Bette certainly mentioned the Ibsen plays during Har-low's visit to her dressing room on March 23, until this point he has expressed no special interest or alarm with regard to *The Wild Duck*. Now suddenly, on April 8—the very day that Bette has informed him she will be opening in the play—from his office in Boston, Harlow writes a letter whose barely suppressed frenzy about whether or not she has been cast as Hedvig suggests that in the interim he has read and been profoundly disturbed by the play that first caused his daugh-ter to want to become an actress. All too obviously, he, like Bette, has instantly grasped the story's personal implications.

Twice in the course of five sentences, he begs her to tell him if she is indeed to play Hedvig. The repetition suggests Harlow's des-perate need to find out whether his worst fear can be true: a need he struggles to conceal by transparently pretending to be interested in her other roles as well. Having written that he is especially anxious to know if she is to play Hedvig, on second thought he scratches out "if," replaces it with "whether," then adds "or Gina" to the end of the sentence. Ineluctably drawn to Hedvig's name when he goes over the sentence yet again, Harlow marks an "X" above it. The mark directs Bette to a scribbled footnote to the effect that, while he assumes that she has been cast as Hedvig, the part seems too wonderful for a newcomer (almost as if he is hoping against hope that somehow this may not be her role). Harlow is so anxious to get Bette's answer right away that, as he informs her, he has attached a stamped self-addressed envelope—something he has certainly never done before. Bette needn't even find a separate piece of paper for her reply; Harlow has written his questions at the bottom of the page, with plenty of room left for her answers. Needless to say, his first query is about Bette's part in *The Wild Duck;* next he inquires about her roles in *The Lady from the Sea* and *Hedda Gabler*. That the first play is all that he really has in mind is suggested by his erratically, unconsciously altering his numbering system after referring to it. Thus, after a general heading asking her to identify her roles in the plays that follow, he writes "(a) Wild Duck," then suddenly "(2) Lady from the Sea (3) Hedda Gabler."

And that Bette knows perfectly well what is principal in Harlow's thoughts is suggested by her boldly underscoring the name "Hedvig" when she writes it beside her father's entry for *The Wild Duck*—something she does not do for her roles in the other plays. Next, in a note to her father at the bottom of the page, Bette does something that she almost never did with anyone about any part she played; she enters into a heartfelt discussion of the role of Hedvig, why it appeals to her and what satisfaction she gets from playing it. After praying that she will come to Boston so that Harlow may see her do Hedvig onstage, Bette focuses on the immense pleasure she derives from making everyone in the audience weep at her performance of the hysterical scene when Hjalmar walks out on her. Freely taunting Harlow with emotions that have long been pent up within her, Bette goes on to say that she doesn't blame people for weeping over poor, abandoned Hedvig, whose cruel mistreatment has caused her to suffer so.

"Even I was not prepared for the torrent of emotional intensity which racked that frail body as she lay face downward on the sofa, crying her heart out," Blanche Yurka would say of Bette's opening-night performance in *The Wild Duck*, on April 8, 1929.

In Bette's Modern Library edition of the play, one discovers that she has underscored the stage direction indicating the loudness of her screams when she pleads with Hjalmar not to leave. She has scratched out the line "I think this will kill me!" presumably intending to communicate wordlessly the all-important foreshadowing of Hedvig's final decision to kill herself in hopes of retrieving her father's love.

Once again Bette accepted as well-nigh inevitable the adoring reviews she received for *The Wild Duck*. As predicted, her hysterical outburst in Act Four was especially relished for the "wistful charm and natural emotional ability" that led one critic to dub her "Bette Davis of the soulful eyes."

"I've read sufficient interviews given by prominent personages of the stage to have a comprehensive idea of the information you desire," Bette told her first interviewer backstage in Jackson Heights. "Some of my ancestors were prominent in the theatrical world—a fact that might be some justification for my stage tendencies. In any event I've always been filled with the lure and glamour of the theatre and determined to break into its ranks at the earliest opportunity."

She also remained determined to marry Charlie Ansley, who drove her from Jackson Heights to Philadelphia, where the Yurka company was set to open at the Walnut Street Theatre. Charlie had escorted Ruthie to at least one performance of *The Earth Between* in New York (on opening night he had sent his usual flowers from Rochester). All seemed to go well during his brief visit in Philadelphia; but hardly had he returned to Rochester when he stunned and angered Bette by following his father's advice to break off their engagement on the grounds that they were too young.

Bette promptly contacted Fritz Hall at Yale to invite him to her Wednesday matinee.

After Washington, D.C., where Bette cannot have failed to be struck by the irony of one critic's comparing her to Eva Le Gallienne, the Yurka company landed at the Plymouth Theatre in Boston at long last. There on May 13, with Harlow, Ruthie, and several of the Newton girls watching from different parts of the theater, Bette faced what she described at the time as the most terrifying night of her life. This was why she had decided to become an actress: to speak to her father through Hedvig's voice.

The personal resonance of the evening may be gauged by the especially revealing collage of newspaper clippings and accompanying

notations in Bette's scrapbook. Here one finds the Boston press notice of *The Wild Duck* that apparently means more to her than all the
others because, as she records, it comes from Harlow's paper and
identifies her (as she has almost certainly never been identified before) as "Miss Bette Davis, daughter of Harlow M. Davis, 204 Washington Avenue." And here is Bette's record of those members of her
Newton set in attendance on opening night; although several of the
girls are said to have been present, she mentions only Sister Koops by
name, suggesting precisely who among her old friends Bette longs
most to impress. And here, after years of dreaming about the comfortable Boston life that should have been hers instead of the impoverished bohemian existence she led with Ruthie, Bette has preserved
an item from the society columns describing a fashionable dinner
party given "in honor of Miss Bette Davis of Boston, Mass." Beside
the clipping, Bette has registered her horror and embarrassment over
the tasteless costume her mother wore for the occasion: a notation
whose cruelty is felt all the more deeply when one recalls that, anxious to savor her daughter's triumphs, Ruthie regularly and repeatedly perused Bette's scrapbook.

In November 1929, Ruthie's mother, seventy-four-year-old Eugenia
Favor, traveled to New York to witness her granddaughter's Broadway debut. Following the Yurka tour, Bette had been cast in *Broken
Dishes*, a comedy by Martin Flavin. Although the tiny white-haired
grandmother is reported to have applauded Bette's performance as
eagerly as Ruthie did, the situation in which Eugenia now found
herself can only have seemed strange and perplexing to her.

This was hardly the life Eugenia had planned for her daughter
and granddaughter. Long ago, Eugenia had worked relentlessly to
curb Ruthie's youthful ambitions and suppress her expressions of
discontent with her lot as a woman. All of Eugenia's efforts had been
designed to prepare Ruthie to assume the role of wife and mother. It
had been Eugenia's firm expectation that Ruthie in turn would someday shape a similar future for her own children. What can Eugenia
possibly have made of the unanchored, itinerant life in the theater
that Ruthie had chosen instead? In New York, Bette's spirited performance in the Flavin play as the rebellious and outspoken child of
a domineering mother struck the Favor family matriarch as every bit
as strange and exotic as Ruthie's flamboyant Delsarte recitations had

seemed in 1897 in Ocean Park, Maine. Afterward, a deeply perplexed Eugenia returned to Massachusetts, where she was to die five months later, on April 20, 1930. While Eugenia had known from the first that Ruthie's theatrical aspirations were doomed to amount to nothing as long as she remained in their close-knit religious community, it now seemed evident that Ruthie's dreams for her daughter were already (perilously?) close to fruition.

Bette would have far preferred to do the sort of material she associated with Katharine Cornell's "loose, dissolute women," but her role in Flavin's well-received and successful comedy soon resulted in a first screen test. Samuel Goldwyn's assistant Arthur Hornblow, Jr. (son of her former dean at the John Murray Anderson–Robert Milton School), saw Bette at the Ritz Theatre and wondered whether she might be right for *Raffles,* the story of a gentleman thief, to star Ronald Colman. Despite Bette's fears about a screen test, at Ruthie's instigation she accepted Hornblow's summons to the Paramount Studio in Astoria. The test was a failure. For all her experience posing for Ruthie's pictorialist camera portraits, it seemed to Bette that her apprehension caused her to freeze in the face of her first motion picture camera. She managed to project only tension and discomfort.

There was also considerable tension in Bette's personal life in this period. Fritz Hall's visit to Philadelphia had aroused new hope that he might finally accept her on her own terms. Bette declared herself still very much in love with him. Then suddenly, that January of 1930, she was plunged into a fit of shrieking despair by the news that Fritz had married a girl named Alice. Bette clipped an article about the wedding and the new Mrs. Hall's picture from the society page. In her scrapbook, she somewhat oddly juxtaposed them with a dramatic drawing of herself as she then appeared onstage in *Broken Dishes*—as if to underscore the choice she had made between marriage and a career.

While Bette failed to discover the acceptance and understanding she desired, her roommate and closest friend, Robin, was a good deal more successful with the man she fell in love with: Arthur "Bunny" Byron, Jr., a handsome newspaper artist, who had been crippled by polio at the age of twelve. Bunny, the son of the eminent actor Arthur Byron, who had played opposite the likes of Maxine Elliott, Maude Adams, and Mrs. Fiske, had no objection to her continuing her acting career after marriage. When they eloped, in February 1930, the couple made their vows at the Municipal Chapel in time for Robin to head uptown for a rehearsal. After learning the news from Bette, an anxious Ruthie turned up suddenly in her "Southern daughter's" dressing room to fulfill a mother's role, telling Robin the facts of life.

At twenty-two, Bette was in a wistful mood when she agreed to return to the Cape Playhouse in Dennis, Massachusetts, to do *Broken Dishes* in summer stock. More than ever now, Bette felt strangely out of place in New York, where it seemed that she would need the cleverness and wit of a Ruth Gordon to shine in the theatrical circles to which Robin, by virtue of her marriage, now had entrée. Although Bette continued to tell herself that instead of trifles like *Broken Dishes* she longed to do the sort of dramatic roles that might establish her as a great actress, something mysteriously caused her to falter when, on the basis of her Hedvig, the distinguished producer Arthur Hopkins (known for serious and important work on Broadway with the Barrymores, Alla Nazimova, Pauline Lord, Laurette Taylor, and others) asked her to come see him before she left for the summer.

Instead Bette went directly to Cape Cod, where by chance she found her old Cushing beau Ham Nelson, who was playing the trumpet at the Old Mill Tavern to help pay his tuition at Massachusetts Agricultural College, in Amherst. Four years earlier, Bette had embarked on a romance with Ham after Warren Blake abandoned her for another girl. And now—as Bette spent most mornings swimming and sunbathing with Ham, or driving about the Cape with him in her mother's Ford—it seemed to the ever-watchful Ruthie that her daughter was merely repeating the pattern in the aftermath of Fritz's marriage.

Back in New York that fall, Bette made her second appearance on Broadway, again in a comedy. This time she played a Southern belle in Lawton Campbell's farce *Solid South* at the Lyceum Theatre. The play starred Mariarden faculty member Richard Bennett as Major Bruce Follonsby, a julep-swigging, pistol-packing son of the Confederacy. Although the production was a failure, Bette's appearance in *Solid South* resulted in the offer of a second screen test.

In mid-October, Universal Studios' New York talent scout David Werner invited Bette to test for the role of Isabelle Parry—a Southern belle—in a film version of Preston Sturges's hit comedy of the previous Broadway season, *Strictly Dishonorable*. After the test,

Werner offered Davis a three-month contract that included round-trip train tickets to Hollywood for her and her mother and a weekly salary of $300. Bette and Ruthie failed to realize that the contract contained no written guarantee that she would actually get to do *Strictly Dishonorable*.

"It's obvious you're not the kind of person who's usually in pictures; you don't look like any actress I've ever seen," Werner suddenly told Bette, the moment after she had signed her first Hollywood contract, in his Fifth Avenue office that November. Bette had always thought of herself, and been treated, as an enchanting beauty. Her Pre-Raphaelite looks had appealed as strongly to the New York drama critics as to her long list of lovesick suitors, starting with Gige Dunham. Thus she was more than a little disconcerted by the talent scout's remark. It was Bette's first indication that by Hollywood standards, her appearance was decidedly unorthodox. Still, the contract had already been signed, and the nettlesome remark glided quickly past, followed by chitchat (most of it apparently directed at Ruthie) about the prestige pictures and great sums of money Bette would no doubt make at Universal.

Although Bette had left Werner's office fearful that she had made a terrible mistake, her trepidation about going to Hollywood was even greater after she went to see Lynn Fontanne in Maxwell Anderson's new play, *Elizabeth the Queen*, at the Guild Theatre. Fontanne's performance instantly and forcefully reminded Bette of the kind of bravura acting she had dreamed of doing in New York.

Not long afterward, determined to go to Hollywood after all, Bette was with her mother at the train station, where Robin and her new husband had come to see them off. Ruthie was all anticipation about the glorious new life that awaited them in Los Angeles, certain that her years of putting everything into her daughter were about to pay off. That Bette was less certain about exactly what faced her when she reported for work at Universal is suggested by her shocked and indignant reaction to Arthur Byron's good-natured teasing about all the "cheesecake" she would be expected to do in Hollywood. Even as Bette vigorously protested that she was a serious actress and would never consider doing such a thing, she could scarcely conceal her anxiety that he might be right.

n Saturday, October 23, 1937, two days before director William Wyler was to start shooting *Jezebel* at Warner Bros., he rehearsed the sequence in Mme. Poulard's New Orleans fitting room. Accompanied by her aunt Belle, Julie Marsden has come to be fitted for the gown she will wear to the Olympus Ball that spring of 1854. After they had read aloud from four pages of the script for some two hours in Wyler's office, Bette and actress Fay Bainter accompanied the director to Stage 22, where for the next ninety minutes the thirty-five-year-old director reviewed what does not appear in the screenplay: the sequence's complex choreography, much of it expressly designed to make use of the gestural abilities that were among Bette's distinguishing characteristics as an actress.

Most especially Bette would have to familiarize herself with the hooplike metal dress form that confines and immobilizes her from the waist down throughout the fitting room sequence, while Aunt Belle and Mme. Poulard and her employees seem constantly to be darting every which way, their frenetic motions redoubled by mirrors in front and back.

Fixing Bette in place in the midst of all this activity would have the effect of concentrating her expression in her upper body, particularly the arms, hands, and fingers, whose movements and pauses were to give the sequence its rhythm.

Bette Davis had already been in Hollywood for seven years when Wyler directed her in *Jezebel*, the film that would finally establish her as a great actress. Although Wyler seems to have responded to Bette's capacity for expressive movement as no one in Hollywood had done before him, his selection of the fitting room sequence as the first they shot together may have been his way of telling her that if she was to become the kind of actress she wanted to be, she needed to exert some restraint—or have it done for her. To Wyler's way of thinking, for all its exuberance, her gestural style was fussy, mannered, with movements that all too often blurred into one another because she hadn't learned to pace herself, to let a performance build and gather momentum. So desperate was she to exercise her powers at every instant that she tended to wear out her effects—or so it seemed to Wyler, who used the metal dress form to slow her down: to say, "Take it easy!" (as he seemed never to tire of telling her through all three pictures they would work on together).

Born in 1902 of Swiss-German parents in Mulhouse, Alsace, Wyler had come to the United States in 1921 to work in the New York office of Universal Pictures, whose founder, Carl Laemmle, was his mother's cousin. Within a year Wyler was in Hollywood, where, grinding out two-reel silent westerns in the Mustang series and five-reelers in the Blue Streak series, he learned what he called "the fundamentals of making films, which lie in movement." He often found himself, awake at night, trying to invent, among other things, new and visually more interesting ways for his cowboys to get on their horses.

After more than a decade of directing silent and then sound films, Wyler in 1936 worked for the first time with the cameraman Gregg Toland on Lillian Hellman's *These Three* (an adaptation of her play *The Children's Hour*). Fresh possibilities for the treatment of physical movement emerged, as Toland helped him to stage scenes without a great deal of cutting, in order for spectators to view the action as a whole almost as they would at a stage play or, for that matter, a dance performance.

This was another reason why in 1937, as he and Bette prepared to shoot the fitting room sequence in *Jezebel*, Wyler discouraged her from flinging herself at every moment. Wyler's predilection for allowing the action to unfold continuously (with cuts mainly for emphasis) made him want Bette to show the gradual unfolding of a series of gestures and all the gradations of feeling it encompassed.

As chronicled in the studio production reports (with further details gleaned from Davis's and Wyler's annotated scripts), on October 25, after two hours of work on her makeup and hair, Bette spent an hour rehearsing the four-page sequence, in which she never once moves off the raised platform around which the contrasting action in the fitting room swirls. For much of the sequence (although it all happens so briskly that we may not be quite conscious of it), Bette's immobility from the waist down is made to feel all the more curious by the dress form's being entirely concealed, along with the stool she perches on, by the ornate white ball gown in which Julie is being fitted.

"I don't like the collar," she says ("fretfully," according to the script). "And does it have to be so tight here? It binds. And the skirt—"

Called upon by the screenplay to "twist" about as she speaks, here Bette makes Julie Marsden a great fidget, her arms full of kinetic tension as she tugs at her fingers: the abrupt, petulant hand gestures (Delsarte called the hands "the direct agents of the mind") suggesting that it isn't so much the gown that agitates Julie just now as her fiancé's refusal in the previous sequence to leave an important business meeting at the Dillard Bank to accompany her to Mme. Poulard's.

In the midst of all this restless fluttering of arms, hands, and fingers, Julie's train of thought is suddenly interrupted when she notices one of Mme. Poulard's midinettes flitting past, with a red satin dress on a hanger. The screenplay has Julie "eye the dress with interest"; to which Bette and Wyler have added a subtle three-step gesture sequence that allows us to gauge her growing fascination with the "bold and saucy" red dress and how she may use it to get back at her fiancé for displeasing her.

First Julie's arms pause in midair—bent at the elbows, fingers curled against palms—forming a sharp contrast to what until now has been their ceaseless, nervous movement. Then, as Aunt Belle chatters on, oblivious to what her niece is thinking, we see Julie's left hand open just a bit, fingers uncurling like the petals of a flower: a limpid, delicate movement that we would scarcely have noticed if Bette had failed to pause first ("Take it easy!") and hold the previous gesture for an all-important instant or two.

Having made her decision (in the time it took for her hand to open), Julie signals the midinette with a Graham-like thrust of the left arm ("Reach out! Take in space!"), whose abruptness is felt all the more powerfully by contrast with the fineness of the gesture that preceded it; and in relation to the nearly imperceptible camera movement as Wyler pulls back a little, adjusting the scale to accommodate her arm thrust. Only after she beckons with the fingers of her outstretched hand ("Complete every gesture down to the fingertips!") does the camera return to its original position, as if in answer to her summons.

"Saucy—isn't it?" Julie says of the red dress to Aunt Belle, who replies, "—and vulgar!"; at precisely which moment Wyler cuts to a fresh camera angle, by way of emphasizing that the fitting room sequence has passed from its initial setup to the conflict that follows, as Julie and Aunt Belle argue about the propriety of wearing red to the Olympus Ball ("You know you can't!" "Can't I?"): an issue that will become the springboard of the narrative action when Julie's decision causes Pres Dillard to break their engagement.

While Aunt Belle frantically darts in and out of frame, with her back to the camera, this second shot brings us in much closer to Julie, who, assisted by Mme. Poulard's girl, struggles to unfasten the tightly cinched ball gown with an urgency that suggests she thinks undoing all the garment's intricate constraints will liberate her spirit as well as her flesh.

Wyler cuts again: to mark off the sequence's resolution, in which Julie calls out ("gaily—but firmly," according to the script), "Will you kindly get me out of this!" As (with a great flurry of hands) the voluminous white gown sweeps up and over her head, Wyler gives us the astonishing sight of space suddenly opening up behind, and layers of ornate undergarments encaged within the hooplike metal dress form, whose massively restricting presence we may scarcely have been conscious of until now.

Instead of rushing immediately to try on the red dress, as we might have expected her to do (and as she probably would have done before working with Wyler), Bette strikes a strange statuelike pose— left arm extended toward the camera, palm turned out, fingers curled inward—reminiscent of the artistic gestures Bette's mother had been known to practice before the turn of the century.

Whether or not Wyler knew it, there was a certain historical appropriateness to selecting the fitting room sequence as the first he and Bette ever shot together. With its immediate sources in Delsarte and interpretive dance, the style of expressive movement that (for all his criticisms) Wyler prized in Bette could trace its lineage even further: to a mid-nineteenth-century American desire to free women from tightly laced and overly restrictive clothing and the broader constraints on their sex that such garments represented. The sight of Bette gesturing from within the immobilizing confines of Mme. Poulard's dress form may remind us of the liberating connotations such gestures still had for a great many women in the early decades of the twentieth century: connotations that (as much as the roles she played or the film stories she appeared in) begin to account for the powerful image of female boldness that, from *Jezebel* on, Bette Davis's acting would come to embody.

In 1930—the year Bette Davis came to Hollywood—Garbo talked. "Gimme a viskey," she growled in her first sound film, Metro-Goldwyn-Mayer's *Anna Christie*. "Ginger ale on the side. And don' be stingy, ba-bee." That spring, Marlene Dietrich arrived from Germany to make *Morocco* at Paramount with Gary Cooper and director Josef von Sternberg. And at the third annual Academy Awards ceremony in November, *All Quiet on the Western Front* took the prize for Best Picture. George Arliss was proclaimed Best Actor for the Warner Bros. *Disraeli* and Norma Shearer Best Actress for MGM's *The Divorcee*.

When Bette and Ruthie arrived in Los Angeles that December, the United States was in the throes of its Great Depression. By contrast with the rest of the nation, Hollywood entered a distinct boom period, which—with the notable exception of a crisis phase in 1933—extended through much of the thirties as ever greater numbers of Americans sought escape at the movies. To meet the audience demand for film fantasy, cinemas changed programs twice a week and offered double features: innovations that put immense pressure on the studios to churn out enough films to fill all the newly created slots and keep the mind of America off its troubles.

The exceptionally heavy demand for "product" helped the Hollywood studio system that had evolved in the teens and twenties to flourish in the thirties. In the interests of getting out films as quickly and efficiently as possible, it seemed to make good business sense to centralize control of all aspects of production in the hands of a few studio bosses, who, as F. Scott Fitzgerald described them in *The Last Tycoon*, were "able to keep the whole equation of pictures in their heads." The filmmaking world Bette Davis entered in 1930 was radically different from today's more variegated Hollywood, where the only institutions even remotely approaching the all-engulfing power once wielded by the major studios are the large agencies capable of packaging the actors, writers, and directors on their client roster to get a film produced. The great screen actresses of the thirties operated strictly under long-term contract to their studios, which by and large selected, developed, and assigned each of the stars' succeeding projects.

"I, more than any single person in Hollywood, have my finger on the pulse of America," boasted MGM's Irving Thalberg; but it might have been any of the studio bosses confidently announcing that he and he alone knew how films ought to be made and talent employed. Violent conflicts and collisions with the talent were a regular feature of the studio system. Cutting recalcitrant actors and directors down to size was one way for Thalberg and the other film chieftains to establish their authority and superior wisdom. "I consider the director is on the set to communicate what I expect of my actors," said Thalberg, who relished coming repeatedly to blows with the brilliant and eccentric Erich von Stroheim, whose notions of absolute directorial control harked back to an earlier era that the studio boss was determined symbolically to extinguish once and for all. In 1924, Thalberg's controversial decision to mutilate von Stroheim's monstrously long masterpiece *Greed* by recutting it to normal feature length achieved archetypal status as precedent and backcloth for all subsequent collisions between the studios and the talent they controlled.

Men exclusively ran the studios, but the talent with whom they collided included women. In the twenties, Lillian Gish and Greta Garbo openly and unabashedly went to war with MGM's Louis B. Mayer, who prided himself on his ability to "handle" difficult artists and viewed both conflicts as a public test of his authority. Mayer "handled" the strong-willed Gish by overriding her passionate objections to the studio's alteration of the dark ending of what was to be her final film at MGM, director Victor Seastrom's *The Wind*. With Garbo,

Mayer had considerably less success. When she scored an immense box office hit with her third film for MGM, *Flesh and the Devil,* Garbo violated her contract by flatly declining her next assignment, as a "stupid seductress" in *Women Love Diamonds.* Declaring that she had no intention of playing "any more bad womens," she also insisted that Mayer raise her $600 weekly salary to $5,000. "They think I am mad!" Garbo told a friend in Sweden of her astonishing decision to walk out when Mayer failed to see things her way. "This is something nobody does here. But I get so nervous over these idiotic things that I lose my head. People say that they are going to send me back home. I don't know what will happen. Haven't shown up at Metro for over a month. Oh, oh." One month stretched into seven, at the conclusion of which, as all Hollywood watched in wonder, a chastened Louis B. Mayer reluctantly agreed to give the errant actress exactly what she wanted, if only she would return to work at once.

Like other young actresses coming to Hollywood for the first time, Bette Davis likely heard the stories of Gish and Garbo, and she almost certainly was aware of the battles against studio power that actors Edward G. Robinson and James Cagney were conducting during her early months there. Both men followed a first box office hit with demands for more money and a say in the roles they were to play on-screen. That January of 1931, Robinson had not been under long-term contract to Warner Bros. when the smash success of the film *Little Caesar* allowed him to demand and win a very handsome six-picture deal, at a fee of $40,000 per performance. Money was one thing, script approval another. Warners made a great point of refusing to give the actor any right to select the parts he played, it being an inviolable tenet of the studio system that the bosses knew best in all matters of production. Warner Bros. had a harder time with James Cagney after the overwhelming reception to his film *Public Enemy* that spring. Unlike Robinson, Cagney was a contract player at the studio when his career suddenly took off, and Jack Warner bristled at the appalling precedent that would be set should he allow the newly established star to insist upon a more generous salary and other rewards. "You got a contract; I expect you to honor it," Warner is recorded to have barked at Cagney, who promptly decamped for New York, where he announced plans to sit it out until the studio saw things his way.

For an obscure young actress like Bette Davis, just arrived from

New York, these and other tales of extravagant demands and bold rebellion against the studios must have seemed very remote. Shortly after Bette made her first appearance at Universal City—the 230-acre "film factory" that Carl Laemmle had built among the mustard fields of the San Fernando Valley in 1915—she discovered that (despite all she and Ruthie had been led to believe in New York, or believed they had been led to believe) the role of Isabelle Parry in *Strictly Dishonorable* had been assigned to another young stage actress from the East, Sidney Fox. A "Janet Gaynor type," as the studio quickly identified her, Fox had appeared in the comedies *It Never Rains* and *Lost Sheep* during the period when Bette was working on Broadway. Both young women were among the countless players Hollywood had begun to import from Broadway in the three years since 1927, when Al Jolson—in Warners' *The Jazz Singer*—inaugurated the era of the "all-talking" picture by crying out, "C'mon, Ma—listen to this!"

Unlike Sidney Fox, however, Bette was greeted with disappointment and bewilderment when, clutching the wire-haired fox terrier named Boogum that Ruthie had encouraged her to bring along as a prop, she posed for a calamitous series of portraits on her first day at Universal. Studio personnel whispered among themselves, presumably about what David Werner could possibly have had in mind when he signed "Bette from Boston" to a three-month contract.

But the most damning comment seems to have been silent. Ever eager to acquaint himself with newly arrived starlets, studio boss "Junior" Laemmle (Carl's twenty-two-year-old son, who had received Universal City as a gift on his twenty-first birthday) was said to have opened his office door, peered out at Bette and Boogum for a moment or two, then quickly closed it.

That night, there was so much screaming and shrieking in Bette and Ruthie's room at the Hollywood Plaza Hotel that, fearful of being asked to leave, Mrs. Davis called the front desk to complain about the noise in hopes that the management would think someone else had caused the commotion.

After years of sitting for her mother's camera portraits, Bette knew only too well how badly the photography session had gone. Looking at some of these photographs today, one sees that, much as Bette had feared, she appears uncharacteristically stiff and frumpy in them. Although, at Ruthie's suggestion, Bette had arrived at Universal City draped in a pair of silver fox scarves, she was promptly ordered to remove them before stepping in front of the cameras, dressed in a dowdy black coat and pumps that made her legs and hips appear heavy: astoundingly so, when one considers that Bette weighed scarcely 106 pounds at the time.

And where are the immense, eloquent eyes that so easily dominate page after page of Ruthie's albums of camera portraits? Here only the lids are visible, as Bette mysteriously persists in glancing downward at Boogum, whom she cradles in her arms as if it were the little gray-and-white dog who had just been put under contract to a Hollywood studio.

Bette angrily accused her mother of having given her bad advice about how to dress and conduct herself at the all-important photography session. Confronted with this barrage of vitriolic abuse, Ruthie maintained her equanimity. She blamed Bette's violent outburst on what she characterized as her daughter's panic-stricken state of mind: precisely the "thoughts of fear" that—in Ruthie's view—must have played havoc with Bette's photography session that day, working from within to transform her into the bland and oddly lifeless figure whom the camera seemed unfortunately to have recorded.

Ruthie's antidote to all this was to bolster her daughter's spirits by carrying on as if Bette's first day at Universal City had been an unequivocal triumph, instead of the disaster Bette more realistically deemed it. To Bette's unutterable horror, Ruthie wasted no time signing a lease on a storybook cottage at 4435 Alta Loma Terrace in the Hollywood Hills. No sooner had Ruthie announced that she was a pictorialist photographer visiting from New York than the real estate agent—Mrs. Carr—escorted her to the rustic hideaway Hollywood cameraman Gordon Pollock had built as a kind of "photographer's paradise," all rough wooden beams and open fireplaces. A quaint rooftop weather vane featured two fighting, screeching cats.

Mrs. Davis declared that in the aftermath of Bette's dismal first day at the studio, Alta Loma Terrace would help to restore their dreams.

Still, Bette was plunged into yet another shrieking fit when Ruthie urged her to request an advance from Universal, in order that they might rent the Pollock house. Her mother was putting too much pressure on her: how could she possibly ask Universal for an advance when they so obviously "hated" her? That night, as Bette wept and shook herself to sleep, Ruthie lay awake beside her, trying to think of a way to get the money.

Shortly after daybreak, Bette was still in bed when her mother crept off to the Roosevelt Hotel, where the former governor of Maine, Carl Milliken, an old friend of Harlow's family in the state capital of Augusta, was known to play tennis regularly at 7:00 A.M.

"What in the world is the matter, Ruth?" he asked, more than a little disconcerted to find Harlow Morrell Davis's ex-wife waiting for him there.

Although he readily gave her the four hundred dollars she asked for, Governor Milliken counseled Ruthie to secure a somewhat more modest accommodation than a house in the Hollywood Hills, so that she might teach her daughter the virtues of Yankee frugality; to which Ruthie replied, "No—Bette must be prosperous in appearance from the beginning, because someday she'll be someone here!"

For her part, Bette was scarcely so optimistic: especially when she received official notification that Junior Laemmle had awarded the role of Isabelle Parry to Sidney Fox—who, according to Bette, was generally known to be sleeping with the studio boss.

To make matters worse, although she barely understood it at the time, even as Bette had arrived at Universal City, the studio had been undergoing major changes that would drastically diminish the quality and range of film roles available to her there. In New York, David Werner had dazzled Ruthie with talk of such costly "prestige" projects as Erich Maria Remarque's *All Quiet on the Western Front*, with which Junior Laemmle had been successfully upgrading feature production at Universal (hitherto known for the mass production of profitable but less substantial fare). The Great Depression put an end to Junior's dreams, however, compelling him to reduce costs by reviving the old "factory" mentality of his father's day.

In the days following Christmas of 1930, Bette was all anticipation when Universal assigned her to appear in a new film version of her beloved Booth Tarkington's 1913 novel, *The Flirt*. The deliciously wanton and impudent part of Cora Madison seemed to make up for everything—until Bette learned that in fact the principal role of "the flirt" had gone to her bête noire, Sidney Fox, while she would be playing Cora's meek and mousy sister Laura, of whom Tarkington wrote: "Laura was in nothing her sister's competitor. She was a neutral-tinted figure, taken-for-granted, obscured, and so near being nobody at all . . ." In short, Laura was rather like the unprecedentedly bland persona Bette had somehow established for herself at Universal. She believed this first unwanted assignment could only reinforce the abundant damage that had already been done to her there. That is precisely what occurred when director Hobart Henley's *Bad Sister* (as Bette's first film was now called) opened in March 1931. Cast in a colorless and unrewarding role, Bette made scant impact on screen, where—almost all agreed—she appeared unsatisfactorily "lugubrious" (*New York Times*) and "camera-conscious" (*Boston Post*) beside the more vivid Sidney Fox. Harshest of all, perhaps, was Bette's own verdict on her less-than-auspicious Hollywood debut. When she glimpsed herself on screen for the first time at a preview in San Bernardino, California, a tearful Bette, with her mother, quietly slipped out of the theater less than halfway through the film.

EIGHT

"If she doesn't stop immediately, no one can tell what will happen," the doctor told Ruthie. "If she rests and stops worrying, she may pull through all right."

In the midst of Bette's crisis at Universal, a clearly neurasthenic Bobby had turned up in Hollywood from the University of Wisconsin (where she had transferred from Denison). The physician advised Ruthie not to send her younger daughter back to school (where she appeared to be driving herself too hard) but to allow her to stay with them in Los Angeles, to rest and receive medical treatment for her nervous debility.

Bette had decided to return to New York at the conclusion of her contract, which Laemmle had somewhat hesitantly renewed on the counsel of cameraman Karl Freund, who was renowned for such classics of the German cinema as F. W. Murnau's *The Last Laugh* (1924) and Fritz Lang's *Metropolis* (1927). Freund's considerably less momentous work on *Bad Sister* at Universal had left him with the idea that, for all her apparent ineptitude on screen, Bette Davis possessed some curious potential that remained to be explored. But as even Bette almost certainly would have agreed, that potential had hardly manifested itself in either of the actress's two lifeless performances after *Bad Sister:* in John Stahl's *Seed* and James Whale's *Waterloo Bridge*. On a nearly daily basis, she excoriated her mother for having urged her to abandon a promising stage career to come to California. Bette felt certain that if only she had remained in New York, she would have been a leading lady by now.

Vastly more painful than her failure to hit her stride as an actress was the jolt of Universal's regarding her as odd-looking, sexless, and even somewhat ugly. Laemmle had been heard to lament that the newcomer possessed "as much sex appeal as Slim Summerville" (the exceedingly homely actor who had portrayed Tjaden in *All Quiet on the Western Front*): a source of great mortification to Bette. The ceaseless rejection she experienced at Universal was all the more perplexing to her because it was so entirely unlike anything she had encountered in New York.

Just as Bette was preparing to abandon Los Angeles (quite sensibly, she thought), Bobby's sudden spate of medical bills compelled her to remain. Rather than head east to pick up her stage career, Bette had little choice but to linger at Universal. Her stock there had fallen so low that, despairing of using her in anything himself, Laemmle regularly loaned her out to other studios for such trifles as *Way Back Home, The Menace,* and *Hell House*.

At home on Alta Loma Terrace, Ruthie complained that her hands were full. One daughter was endlessly listless and dejected, and the other seemed in a perpetual rage over the terrible films she was forced to make. When Bette came home from a day's work, Ruthie would urge her to take a drink to calm her agitated nerves: the start of Bette's lifelong problem with alcohol. Ellen Batchelder—who became Bette's closest friend and confidante during the early days in Hollywood when Ellen accepted a teaching position in nearby Pasadena—could see that no matter how angry or upset Bette was about her film career, she dared not show her turbulent emotions at the studio. Hardly would Bette get in the door at Alta Loma Terrace when she would feel the urgent need to "let off all that steam," hence the abusive screaming fits to which she regularly subjected her mother and sister.

Bette's spirits appeared to revive when she was ordered to report to the Universal wardrobe department to be outfitted for tests for the

female lead in director William Wyler's *A House Divided*. Modeled
on Eugene O'Neill's *Desire Under the Elms*, *A House Divided* chronicled the furious competition between a father and son for a single
woman: the father's new young wife, who has come to him courtesy
of a marriage broker. Set to star Walter Huston in the role of the
tyrannical father, Seth Law, the John Clymer–Dale Van Every script
was streamlined by Huston's son John, who cut the dialogue "to an
absolute minimum" in an effort to diminish the story's more melodramatic elements. The role of the oddly inarticulate young bride,
Ruth Evans, bore comparison to that of Floy Jennings in *The Earth
Between*, Bette's first theatrical success in New York: a good omen.

But Davis also perceived herself to be under enormous, almost
unbearable pressure as she arrived at the Universal wardrobe department in anticipation of meeting Wyler for the first time. Bette could
have no illusions about her Hollywood career thus far. By any conceivable standard she had failed miserably in films, and with her
contract about to come up for renewal, Universal was more than
likely to dismiss her. Aside from being the only decent role for which
she had been considered since the loss of *Strictly Dishonorable*, Ruth
Evans in *A House Divided* was probably Bette's last chance to make
her mark at Universal. She felt certain that failing to capture Wyler's
attention in the day's tests might mean the end of her screen career.

By this time, on the advice of a Universal secretary, who counseled her to make herself appear sexier, Bette had already lightened
her hair and altered her makeup to conform with what she interpreted as Hollywood standards of beauty. Intent on making Wyler
notice her, she madly searched the wardrobe racks for a provocative
costume. Ignoring the various dresses the wardrobe ladies urged
upon her, she finally discovered what she had been looking for: a dark
plaid cotton dress with a snug bodice and a low-cut square neckline
that bared an inch or so of cleavage. For Bette, choosing the "chest
dress," as she called it, was an act of utter desperation. For all her
years of merciless flirtation with young men, Bette was still a virgin
and unaccustomed to offering herself so blatantly; but as she kept
telling herself, she simply could not afford to lose the role in *A House
Divided*.

As the studio wardrobe ladies clicked their tongues at the absurdly ill-fitting "chest dress," Bette dashed out of the wardrobe
department and over to the soundstage where Willy Wyler was conducting tests. Acutely uncomfortable in the revealing outfit, with all

it seemed to signify, Bette was nonetheless confident that by displaying the ample breasts she believed to be her best feature, she was guaranteed to catch the director's eye.

Instead, when her name was announced on the soundstage, Wyler merely cast a disgusted, dismissive glance in Davis's direction and groaned loudly to an assistant, "What do you think of these girls who show their chests and think they can get jobs?" As Bette later described it to Ruthie, at that moment her mouth went dry and she felt all the color drain from her face. Wyler, seeming to look directly through her, ordered the test to begin. Paralyzed with embarrassment and confusion, humiliated to have offered herself like that, only to be rejected, Bette muttered something about an incompetent wardrobe lady's having forced her to wear the ludicrously snug plaid dress, but Wyler would hear none of it. When the camera went on, he showed little patience as the strangely tongue-tied Bette Davis stumbled ineptly through her test.

Not long afterward, to Bette's chagrin, the role of Ruth Evans went to actress Helen Chandler; and worse, much as she had feared, Bette was dismissed by Universal when Junior Laemmle declined to renew her contract.

In September 1931, Bette and Ruthie had started packing to go back east when a Warner Bros. representative called to offer her a role in the new George Arliss film. Bette initially thought that the offer must be some kind of joke. Murray Kinnell, who had acted with Bette in *The Menace* (an adaptation of Edgar Wallace's *The Feathered Serpent,* which she had made on loan-out to Columbia), was set to appear in Warners' *The Man Who Played God,* starring the immensely popular English actor George Arliss, to whom he recommended Bette for an ingenue role that had yet to be cast. As chance would have it, Arliss had seen and admired Bette's performance as Hedvig in Blanche Yurka's *The Wild Duck* and he asked Rufus LeMaire to summon her for an interview. That interview would launch Bette Davis on her tumultuous eighteen-year career at Warner Bros.

"Mr. Kinnell tells me that he believes you would be an excellent choice for leading lady in the picture." Bette fondly imitated the sixty-three-year-old Arliss's English accent and courtly manner, as she recounted the successful interview to Ruthie and Bobby that night at Alta Loma Terrace. Ruthie wasted no time unpacking their bags at the glorious news that Bette had been offered a $300-a-week, one-picture contract with Warners.

Arliss was an anomalous character at Warner Bros., where he had been summoned in 1929 to play Benjamin Disraeli, a role he had first done on Broadway in 1911. At Warners, he artfully intimidated studio personnel with the carefully constructed persona of an august English gentleman: "Mr. George Arliss," as he insisted on being billed ("Sir George," as he was often mistakenly addressed). For effect, Arliss's batman regularly followed him around the film set. As part of his act, Arliss made a great show of taking his tea at exactly 4:00 P.M., whether or not the director was ready for a break. At hardworking, no-nonsense Warner Bros., where speed and efficiency were expected to take precedence over all, this was curious behavior. But the box office appeal of Arliss's kitsch impersonations of Disraeli and Alexander Hamilton won him the right to certain on-set eccentricities.

"Countless thousands have waited for his MASTERPIECE!" blared the Warner Bros. publicity machine about *The Man Who Played God*, adapted from a Gouverneur Morris short story about a celebrated musician (Arliss) who loses his hearing. Notwithstanding the six films she had made under her Universal contract, Bette was billed as "a newcomer to the screen": "Bette Davis, the young woman with the sad face." She portrayed the musician's young fiancée, Grace, who falls in love with another man but fears running off with him lest she devastate the old maestro. Before the critics had had an opportunity to upbraid her for speaking just a bit too swiftly for comprehension, at Arliss's urging, Warner Bros. signed Bette to a twenty-six-week contract (renewable for up to five years). Her starting salary was $400 a week, $100 more than she had been paid for *The Man Who Played God*.

"Me—as I really was," Bette would say of a photograph from this period showing her with eyes downcast: a shy, reticent, oddly fearful creature, so entirely unlike the virago she was to become at the height of her fame that it is difficult to reconcile the two. To understand what Bette was like in these early days in Hollywood, it is essential to keep in mind that, by contrast with the screaming fits of temper in which she regularly indulged at home, her public demeanor was characterized by a surprising degree of timidity and trepidation. In this lonely period, her old friend from New England Ellen Batchelder was one of the few outsiders she and Ruthie permitted to enter their lives on a regular basis.

Two years before this, when Ellen had gone backstage after a performance of *Broken Dishes* in New York, Bette had shown great pleasure at seeing her but failed to invite her home to visit Ruthie, as Ellen had hoped to do. Nor had there been any concrete suggestion of meeting again soon. That Bette's attitude was very different in California suggests how sharply her circumstances—and needs—had altered in the interim. From the time she learned that Ellen was nearby teaching dance and physical education, Bette eagerly invited her to stay with them almost every weekend in Los Angeles. She and Ruthie would drive out to Pasadena to pick Ellen up and would take her home afterward. Ellen's comforting presence must have reminded Bette of a time when she had been (or appeared to be) perfect master of her situation, so different from her life in Hollywood, where everything seemed frightening and beyond her control.

Such were Bette's emotions in the days following December 24, 1931, when she signed her first multipicture contract with Warner Bros. For the moment, however, whatever anxiety Bette may have experienced about her future at Warners was as nothing compared to her uneasiness about her first big Hollywood party. She had been invited to a New Year's Eve gathering at the home of actress Lois Wilson, in Beverly Hills. The thirty-six-year-old Wilson, whose long lists of credits included James Cruze's silent classic *The Covered Wagon*, had played Bette's mother in John Stahl's *Seed*, the younger actress's second picture at Universal.

Ellen Batchelder recalls Bette's acute agitation about the prospect of the party. Bette was going without a date, and she feared that she wouldn't know any of the other guests at what she presumed would be a star-studded evening. She was determined to look glamorous, and Ruthie's proposal to sew her a dress was quickly rejected. Nor, as far as Bette was concerned, could there be any question of Ruthie's other strategy: dragging her to one of the Hollywood thrift shops Ruthie haunted, in search of the gaudily embroidered Oriental robes she was forever pressing on her daughter. This time Bette insisted on their all going to Magnin's to select the most sophisticated and extravagant gown she could afford, something that would catch the eye of every man in the room. All too quickly she seemed to have forgotten the humiliation she had suffered when William Wyler cruelly remarked on her "chest dress." Once again, as Bobby and Ellen watched in wonder, Bette chose a costume with a neckline to draw attention to her large breasts.

The night of December 31, as Bette dressed for Lois Wilson's party, Mrs. Davis came in to warn her, as she so often had in the past: "A stiff prick has no conscience." For all Bette's ceaseless trifling with her young beaux back east, Ruthie wanted her daughter to understand that she must be a good deal more careful with the worldly men she met in Hollywood, who could scarcely be treated so coyly. Ruthie and Ellen dropped her off in Beverly Hills, and Bette announced that she would probably not call to have them pick her up until sometime the following morning. Bette then braced herself to make her entrance at her first Hollywood party.

Much as she had dreaded, inside the crowded living room she discovered not a single familiar face. She ended up lingering painfully beside a window on the fringes of the party. She was too scared to speak to anyone until finally a man who introduced himself as Douglas Fairbanks, Jr., then the husband of Joan Crawford, came up to her as she stood alone and awkward. As she later described the incident to Ellen, before she quite realized what was happening, Fairbanks had deftly slipped his hand inside her dress, grabbed hold of one of her breasts, and said, "You should use ice on your breasts the way Joan Crawford does." Recoiling from his touch, Bette rushed to a telephone to summon her mother to come for her at once, all thought of a daring and exciting late-night departure quickly forgotten.

"I can't depend on anyone!" Bette cried, so angry that she barely seemed to know what she was saying or doing. "This house is a pigpen!"

Ellen Batchelder had come for a weekend at the house Ruthie had rented on Toluca Lake, to discover a clearly distraught Bette sweeping out a closet with a dustpan and broom.

"Look at me! I have to clean up these floors!" Bette shouted at Ellen, who quickly surmised that she and her mother had just had one of their "terrible brawls."

A good many of these brawls were ostensibly about Ruthie and Bobby's purported failure to keep the house as clean as Bette expected. As Bobby would later recall, the moment Bette came home from Warner Bros., she would put on a white glove and run her hand along the furniture to check that all was dusted properly.

The new house had been decorated in what Ruthie called true Yankee style by its Massachusetts-born owner, actor Charles Farrell, Janet Gaynor's co-star in a successful series of romantic films beginning with *Seventh Heaven* in 1927. To Mrs. Davis's great delight, a model of the *Mayflower* perched on the fireplace mantel, near a lamp whose shade had been stenciled with a map of Massachusetts. Outside, weeping willows drooped over a private lake, where mute swans regularly glided past.

But Ruthie and her girls knew scarcely any peace here, for by this time Bobby's state of mind had begun to deteriorate considerably. Where doctors had once attributed Bobby's nervous prostration to the effects of her having perhaps studied too hard at school, it became evident now that her condition was far more serious than anyone had suspected. According to Ellen Batchelder, at times Bobby grew violent. She would suddenly shout and hit at Ruthie or whoever else happened to be around. Then, just as abruptly, Bobby would revert to her normal, withdrawn self. It seemed to Batchelder that Bobby's torment was the result of having been "thwarted" all her life as she and Ruthie tried to live through Bette.

For her part, Bette had her own apparently overwhelming pressures to deal with just now, and Ruthie seemed determined to prevent Bobby's illness from infecting her sister's career.

Sipping tea with George Arliss had hardly prepared Bette for the assembly-line style of production that caused Warner Bros. to be dubbed "the Ford of the movies." Reporting for work at the 135-acre Burbank studio on January 22, 1932, Bette found herself assigned to two films simultaneously. On her first day she was put to work portraying a flapper in director Alfred E. Green's *The Rich Are Always with Us*, starring Ruth Chatterton and George Brent; and the day after that, January 23, she plunged into the role of a young artist in William Wellman's *So Big*, with Brent and Barbara Stanwyck.

For maximum efficiency, Warner Bros. scheduled Bette to shoot her scenes with Wellman by day and with Green by night—all for the same $400 weekly salary they would have had to pay her were she making only one film at a time.

"We're not running any museum," ran the refrain at Warner Bros., where the dictum was that even a rudely done film could yield a profit if made quickly and cheaply enough. At its best, Warner Bros. austerity was capable of producing films as brisk as the pace at which they had been made. But neither *The Rich Are Always with Us* nor *So Big* showed anything or anyone at his best—certainly not Bette

Davis, who (much as she had at Universal) persisted in her fear of venting her displeasure at the studio.

Ellen Batchelder recalls this as an especially trying period for Bette, who complained of being repeatedly stepped on at Warner Bros. because she was "a little New Englander." Bette's nightly screaming fits eventually drove Ruthie secretly to rent an apartment of her own, in anticipation of moving out with Bobby. On the eve of Ruthie's departure, Bette discovered her mother's plans. She grew more frantic than ever, tearfully demanding that Ruthie and Bobby give up the new apartment and remain with her as always.

⚶

"You be careful!" Bobby screamed, gesturing to the visitor as if he were in danger. "Don't go near her—she's got syphilis!"

At which Bobby pointed at her mother, who sank back in humiliation before the latest doctor she had summoned to Toluca Lake to see what could be done about her increasingly agitated and irrational younger daughter.

Bobby's outburst may have been occasioned by Ruthie's incipient romantic interest in Robert Woodbury Palmer, a skinny, bespectacled thirty-nine-year-old businessman from Belmont, Massachusetts.

Palmer spent part of the year on a ranch in Palm Springs, in southern California, where Ruthie had suddenly taken to visiting him. More often than not, she brought along Bobby, who violently objected to what she seemed to consider Ruthie's betrayal of Harlow.

For once, Bette's and Ruthie's positions were reversed. Bette watched in bewilderment while her forty-six-year-old mother "pursued" a man seven years her junior.

With the exception of Ellen's weekly visits, Bette's fundamental solitariness in Hollywood persisted. She had developed "a kind of schoolgirl crush" on George Brent when they worked on two films together and was thrilled to discover that the suave twenty-eight-year-old Irishman lived in a house across the lake.

Just how innocent Bette still was is clear from the fact that when Ellen Batchelder dropped by one day, Bette excitedly took her down to the lake. There the two young women hid behind some bushes and took turns trying to catch a glimpse of Brent through Bette's binoculars.

This voyeurism typified the stultifying passivity that seemed to have mysteriously overcome Bette since her arrival in Hollywood. By the time of her twenty-fourth birthday, on April 5, 1932, she had completed nine films, and not one of them provided so much as a glimmer of the virtuoso acting that had once been her single-minded goal. That goal had seemed almost within reach at the time of *The Earth Between* and *The Wild Duck*, but it often appeared quite hopelessly beyond her now.

This is probably why Ruthie reacted as she did to a letter Bette received from her erstwhile fiancé, Rochester businessman Charlie Ansley, who had broken off their engagement at the time of *The Wild Duck*. When Ansley wrote to Bette asking to see her again, Ruthie did everything she could to encourage the reunion. Charlie's reappearance would take Bette back to the period of her theatrical successes. Bedazzled by the appearance of his former girlfriend in the movies, Charlie would scarcely have comprehended the downward slide of her career since last he had encountered her: all the better, perhaps, for restoring her former boldness and self-regard.

With Ruthie orchestrating and photographing the event, Bette's reunion with the former suitor took place at Smoke Tree Ranch in Palm Springs. Bette, her mother, and her sister had gone there on holiday after the April 9 completion of her fourth lusterless performance for Warner Bros., in director Alfred E. Green's political satire *The Dark Horse*.

Like Junior Laemmle before him, production chief Jack Warner was already grumbling about what he perceived as the actress's "bland" appearance on-screen. Ruthie's photographs of Bette and Charlie Ansley in Palm Springs, and later in Yosemite National Park, in eastern California, are the more remarkable for the distinct metamorphosis they record. Here are Bette and Charlie riding horseback at Smoke Tree Ranch; and here, exploring Yosemite Falls in the Sierra Nevadas. After Bette's many months of debilitating rejection in Hollywood, the attention and adulation from Charlie Ansley seem to have revived her sense of herself—happily, in ample time to carry over electrically into her next film, Michael Curtiz's *Cabin in the Cotton*.

▲▼▲

"Turn your back and look at those snapshots for a minute while I get into something restful," says Bette coquettishly, with the Southern accent she modeled after her friend Robin's.

As Madge Norwood, the spoiled daughter of a wealthy Southern planter, she has just lured one of her father's sharecroppers, young Marvin Blake (played by Richard Barthelmess), to her bedroom, where she plans to seduce him. A glimpse of Madge undoing the sash of her dress is followed by a shot of Marvin nervously, distractedly looking through the photographs, as Madge suddenly starts to sing off-screen.

We cut again: this time to a tight close-up of Madge's face and naked shoulders, as her arms seem to reach behind her, apparently undressing herself beneath the frame, in off-screen space.

Unremarkable in itself, the shot is of special interest on account of the peculiar expressiveness Bette imparts to her shoulder movements. Her background in interpretive dance has taught her to communicate depth of feeling by animating the shoulders (Ted Shawn: "No intensity of emotion is possible without the movement of the shoulders"), as her dancer's physical training has allowed her to engage the eye with subtle articulations of muscle and collarbone, made visible beneath the skin.

The seduction sequence in *Cabin in the Cotton* caused something of a sensation at Warner Bros., where Bette Davis had been in serious danger of finding herself dismissed. Although her December 24, 1931, contract gave the studio the right to retain her services as an actress for a total of five years, nothing compelled them to do so. Whatever the reasons for their displeasure, after the twenty-six weeks guaranteed in her contract it would be perfectly legitimate for them to decline to pick up her option and be done with her. But now Bette's watershed performance in the Curtiz film made that most unlikely.

Although Paul Green's brusque and insubstantial screenplay about the conflict between sharecroppers and wealthy planters in "the new South" seemed to provide scant opportunity for the actress playing Madge Norwood, Bette uses every precious second of screen time to draw attention to herself with what she had learned from Martha Graham to call "full-body acting": twisting hips and shoulders, flexing elbows, clenching and unclenching fists—boldly thrusting herself at the camera and at us.

Her performance lacks variety, however. Almost everything is acted at the same level of intensity, with no apparent attempt to modulate her effects: a serious flaw in her craft that would persist for a good many years to come.

Still, of one longed-for effect the young actress could be absolutely certain: On June 16, 1932, a week after she had completed *Cabin in the Cotton,* Bette received word that Warner Bros. was indeed picking up her option, apparently on the orders of Jack Warner, who declared himself delighted with her "transformation" in the Curtiz film.

Photographs of Bobby taken at Zuma Beach, north of Malibu, where Mrs. Davis had rented a vacation cottage for them in the summer of 1932, show a frail, wild-eyed, emaciated figure, whom Ruthie had come to fear as a source of potential embarrassment to Bette, should one of Bobby's violent outbursts occur in public. Bobby's eruptions often began by her becoming almost catatonic, as she curled up in the fetal position. Then suddenly she would leap to her feet and rush about, screaming uncontrollably at the top of her lungs, until someone restrained her. Hesitant to commit her younger daughter to a mental institution in California, where the news might cause a scandal that could jeopardize Bette's film career, Ruthie decided to take Bobby to Massachusetts. There they could also count on the comfort and support of her family. But what to do about Bette in the meantime?

Aside from worrying about who would care for her older daughter in their absence, Ruthie made no secret of her anxieties that without a mother's supervision, twenty-four-year-old Bette might succumb to the abundant temptations in Hollywood and lose her virginity before marriage. Ruthie's anxieties had recently redoubled when Bette came back from a studio-sponsored trip to New York to publicize *The Dark Horse* and complained of the ceaseless pressure leading-man Warren William had exerted on her to sleep with him.

Thus the unprecedented effusiveness with which Ruthie greeted Bette's old admirer Ham Nelson when he turned up at their door in Zuma Beach, after his graduation from Massachusetts Agricultural College. In hopes of reviving his romance with Bette, and perhaps even of eventually asking her to marry him, Ham had signed on to play the trumpet at the Olympic Games in Los Angeles that summer.

Although he had enjoyed an amiable correspondence with Bette that led him to suspect she might be favorably inclined toward him, little had he anticipated the vigorous encouragement he would receive from her mother. But by this time Ruthie had concluded that under the less than ideal circumstances, Bette's quick marriage to the innocent, malleable, good-natured New Englander might be best for all concerned. Although, fresh out of college as he was and with no prospects to speak of, Ham would obviously be in way over his head in a marriage to Bette, Mrs. Davis theorized that his lack of a career made him a perfect mate for her daughter, whose needs would always come first.

Bette was a good deal less certain about what was best for her. Much as she admitted to a physical attraction to Ham, the idea of marriage terrified her. Always in her mind was the unhappy precedent of Ruthie and Harlow's failed union, and she repeatedly cited her parents' experience as her excuse whenever Ham—or Ruthie—pressed his case with her.

At length, however, Bobby's rapidly deteriorating condition brought matters to a head. Ruthie announced that on August 19, she and her younger daughter would return to Massachusetts, accompanied by Ruthie's sister, Mildred, who had come west to assist her.

Still, Bette held out until two days before Ruthie and Bobby's departure before she capitulated to all the pressure and somewhat reluctantly agreed to become Mrs. Harmon Oscar Nelson, Jr. A wedding party was hastily convened (including Mildred and the intermittently violent Bobby) for the drive to Yuma, Arizona, where no waiting period would be required for a marriage license.

On Thursday, August 18, 1932, after a Baptist minister, the Reverend J. L. Goodman, pronounced them man and wife, Bette and Ham spent their wedding night at the Farrell house on Toluca Lake. Bette's exultant mother occupied the next room. She left for New England early the next morning.

NINE

*F*AILING IN FILMS, N.Y. ACTRESS DIVES TO DEATH, read the headlines on the morning of September 20, 1932. TWENTY FOUR YEAR OLD ACTRESS GIVES UP IN HOLLYWOOD, LEAPS OFF FIFTY FOOT SIGN, SUICIDE NOTE IN PURSE. Almost seven years had passed since Bette had seen Peg Entwistle portray Hedvig in *The Wild Duck* in Boston. Entwistle's performance had been a transforming experience that had seemed to make everything in Bette's life suddenly fall into place when she realized that above all else she wanted to be an actress like Entwistle, a girl her own age but already an accomplished performer.

"I was watching myself." Thus Bette would recall the intense identification she felt with the young English actress. "There wasn't an emotion I didn't anticipate or share with her."

And so it was now, as Bette studied the reports of Peg Entwistle's fatal plunge from the giant "H" of the "HOLLYWOOD" sign in the Hollywood Hills, after a year of failure and disappointment in the movies. "I am afraid I am a coward," read the actress's suicide note.

"I am sorry for everything. If I could have done this long ago I could have saved a lot of pain. P.E."

Although Bette had experienced considerably more success in Hollywood than her early role model, the Entwistle suicide crystallized the immense dissatisfaction with her film career Davis continued to feel. Even after *Cabin in the Cotton*, Warners persisted in assigning Bette to routine roles in such "factory productions" as director Mervyn LeRoy's *Three on a Match* and Curtiz's *20,000 Years in Sing Sing*. Scarcely present on-screen in the LeRoy film, Bette found herself with little more to do in Curtiz's bleak prison drama. The principal dramatic action (and screen time) went to Spencer Tracy, as was the custom at unabashedly male-oriented Warner Bros.

Bette's second film under Curtiz's (in her case) perfunctory direction typifies the actress's problems at a studio as yet unwilling or unable to find projects suited to her abilities. The quintessential Warners film was cut to be "fast and snappy": perhaps too much so for Bette's gestural style of acting, whose nuances tended to get lost in the interstices between shots.

While it has often been said that in the aftermath of *Cabin in the Cotton* no one at Warner Bros. could determine quite how to use Bette Davis to her best advantage, one discovers scant evidence that—at this point, at least—anyone there really had the faintest interest or enthusiasm for doing so. Instead, as in *20,000 Years in Sing Sing*, Bette would repeatedly find herself slotted into largely standardized roles, in this case the gangster's "fast-talking, hard-bitten moll," Fay.

Not that there was some dark conspiracy against the actress, some devious plan to hold her back or thwart her career. Warner Bros. just had a bottom-line concern with using one of its employees in ways the studio deemed most profitable.

At this point, Bette and Ham had decided to stay on at the rented vacation cottage in Zuma Beach, from which every morning at five he drove her to Warner Bros. Typically, the young husband then spent most of the day in his bride's dressing room, waiting to take her home. Much as Ruthie had calculated, Ham took her and Bobby's place with Bette, who now daily vented her pent-up rage and frustration in private with her husband.

Ham's perpetual unemployment became an object of some derision at the studio when Bette had emergency surgery to remove her appendix at Wilshire Osteopathic Hospital in October. She was compelled to ask Warner Bros. for an advance against salary in order to pay the bill. She had little choice but to explain that she shouldered "the entire burden for her family's upkeep," which encompassed two households: hers and her husband's on the West Coast, Ruthie's and Bobby's in Dover, Massachusetts. For his part, Ham took no pleasure in being supported by his wife. Mortified by his status as a kept man, he looked for work and finally landed a series of engagements as a dance-band pianist. Eventually he also worked as a nightclub orchestra leader in such popular spots as the Blossom Room at the Hollywood Roosevelt Hotel and the Colony Club. As far as Bette was concerned, however, her husband's employment created even more of a problem. The conflict between his night hours and her own exhausting daytime schedule suddenly made it impossible for Ham always to be there for her when she needed him.

> She accused him of every mean fault; she said he was stingy, she said he was dull, she said he was vain, selfish; she cast virulent ridicule on everything upon which he was most sensitive. . . . She kept on, with hysterical violence, shouting at him an opprobrious, filthy epithet.

In December 1933, Bette and Ham were ensconced in a rented house once occupied by Greta Garbo, at 171 San Vicente Boulevard in Santa Monica, when she read W. Somerset Maugham's *Of Human Bondage*. Director John Cromwell was planning to film an adaptation of the 1915 novel at RKO.

The portrait of young Philip Carey's sadomasochistic relationship with the vile and abusive Mildred Rogers touched a chord in Bette. She probably recognized something of her own biliousness in Mildred's ceaseless spate of "hysterical violence." Whether Bette was conscious of it we cannot know, but like Ibsen's Hedvig, Mildred offered the actress an opportunity to unleash reserves of violent emotion long hidden from public view though sadly familiar in private.

On the basis of Bette's performance as the petulant and manipulative Madge Norwood in *Cabin in the Cotton*, John Cromwell, a forty-five-year-old former Broadway stage actor who had directed more than a dozen films since coming to Hollywood in 1928, had unofficially summoned her to his office at RKO to discuss the Maugham project. Other actresses had already expressed discomfort with the role of the cruelly selfish Mildred Rogers, not least because of the anemic pallor and overall physical grotesqueness that play so large a part in Philip's perverse attraction to the oddly androgynous Mildred (who was widely thought to have been modeled on a crude cockney boy with whom the young Somerset Maugham had been painfully obsessed).

Bette was convinced the role could turn everything around for her in Hollywood, and she launched a campaign to persuade Jack Warner to loan her out to RKO. Warner tended to resist loan-outs of his actors. He preferred to reserve his stable of acting talent for his own more than ample production schedule.

By early January of 1934, Bette had nearly worn away the studio boss's resistance to loaning her out, when she discovered that she was pregnant. The news plunged her into despair, for she felt certain that her pregnancy would cause her to lose what she saw as her great chance.

Before Warner Bros. would even consider talking to RKO about the loan-out, the studio expected her to have begun director William Dieterle's *Fog Over Frisco*, which was set to start shooting on January 22. There was no telling how long the negotiations might drag on; or whether Warners might require her to do yet another film or more, before she went off to RKO.

It was in this frame of mind that Bette decided to have an illegal abortion. Although she consulted Ruthie and Ham (and subsequently ascribed her decision to pressure from both her mother and her husband), she appeared to have made up her mind well in advance. On January 20, two days before she was due to start shooting *Fog Over Frisco*, Bette had her first abortion. Ham notified the studio that Mrs. Nelson would need several days off to recover from sunstroke and flu.

Bette was in her second and final week of work on *Fog Over Frisco* (in which she played a reckless society girl who becomes involved in a securities theft scheme) when Warners notified her that they had come to terms with RKO. She was due to report to their Gower Street studios after a week's break to begin *Of Human Bondage* on February 14. Leslie Howard would co-star as the obsessed Philip Carey. Although *Of Human Bondage* would be Bette's twenty-second film, she regarded Mildred as her first substantial dramatic opportunity since Hedvig in 1929. If she failed to create a vivid portrait here, she was unlikely to have such an opportunity again.

Fortunately, in John Cromwell Bette Davis discovered an able collaborator. He was the first film director to show any sustained interest in adjusting his pictorial effects to the actress's expressive stances and movements. Even in Curtiz's *Cabin in the Cotton* (the strongest of her film performances thus far), Bette all too often seems to be struggling for the camera's attention. By contrast, in *Of Human Bondage*, Cromwell frames his shots expressly to emphasize the bold physical details of her tense and volatile performance.

As Bette's twenty-sixth birthday approached, less than a week after she was scheduled to finish *Of Human Bondage* and return to Warners for her next assignment, the actress felt newly confident about her career. Particularly satisfying to her were Mildred's ranting scenes, in which she mercilessly tongue-lashes the adoring Philip: tirades in which Bette believed herself to have exercised her powers as she had never been encouraged to do on-screen before.

Bette believed herself—and her career—to have been transformed by the experience of playing Mildred, but back at Warners, it was as if nothing had changed. She found herself assigned to what she regarded as yet another trivial role, as the "siren" who tries to break up George Brent's marriage in director Alfred E. Green's *Housewife*.

"Before Maugham"—as Bette liked to say—she would have dutifully reported for work as ordered, no matter how detestable she found the script: reserving for Ruthie and Bobby, and later her husband, Ham, the brunt of the violent dissatisfaction she dared not display at the studio lest her option be dropped when next it was due. Now, early that April of 1934, as if inspired by her character Mildred's combativeness, Bette gave her first public demonstration of displeasure since arriving in Hollywood. She refused to report for "wardrobe fittings and other necessary preparation" for *Housewife*.

Warner Bros. fired off a telegram to remind Bette of her legal obligation. Her contract included no provision for script approval; she must perform any role the studio chose to assign. The wire was followed by several sterner warnings, which ultimately seemed to persuade her to report to work on April 18, more than ten days after she had been due.

Still, the precedent had been set. Thenceforth, if Bette Davis disapproved of a project, Warner Bros. was going to hear about it.

In the aftermath of playing Mildred, Bette's attitude toward Ham also seemed to change. Like Maugham's vulgar cockney waitress, Bette appeared to take perverse pleasure in cruelly upbraiding and humiliating a worshipful husband whose adoration suddenly struck her as the most loathsome form of weakness. In this she received ample encouragement from Ruthie, who made no pretense about having returned to Los Angeles in time to share her daughter's long-awaited glory. Where once Ham Nelson's presence had seemed expedient to Ruthie, that was no longer the case now that she intended to come back into Bette's life on a daily basis.

Bobby was left in professional care in Massachusetts (where the young woman had been receiving shock treatment and other therapy), while Ruthie appeared in California on Bette's twenty-sixth birthday. With her she brought a photograph album she had compiled of her daughter's life and career "before Maugham." When Ham perused the album—as Ruthie must have known he would—he discovered picture after picture of Bette's loving reunion with Charlie Ansley: a mother's malicious comment on her daughter's having probably married the wrong man.

Before long, Ruthie's ceaseless carping about Ham's lack of ambition caused him temporarily to flee, until his mother-in-law returned to New England in May. He came back in time to serve as Bette's buffer in her latest conflict with Warner Bros. She had finished filming *Housewife* on May 5, only to find herself swiftly assigned to another unwanted role, as Della Street in the first Perry Mason film, director Alan Crosland's *The Case of the Howling Dog*. This time, however, Bette would not accede to pressure from the studio.

On June 13, 1934, on his wife's instructions, Ham refused to accept Warners' telegram ordering her to report for wardrobe fittings the next day. All afternoon Bette dodged the studio's telephone calls. Finally, at six-thirty that evening, Jack Warner called Bette himself, only to be told by her husband that "Miss Davis is busy" and would call him back later—which she failed to do.

Instead, on June 14, while Bette remained in seclusion with Ham, she sent her agent, Mike Levee, to Burbank to inform Warner Bros. that she declined to appear in *The Case of the Howling Dog*, on the grounds that the low-budget thriller was far beneath the standard she had already attained in *Of Human Bondage*. For this infraction Bette anticipated suspension without pay, for a period to be tacked on at the end of her contract. In hopes of returning to the Warners payroll as quickly as possible without risk of actually having to do the Perry Mason film, she waited until Alan Crosland had replaced her with another actress—contract player Helen Trenholme—before writing to say that she agreed to come back to work on June 25.

Studio records show that her stratagem was quickly recognized for what it was. Warners extended her layoff until July 14, by which time a new assignment would presumably await her (although there was no guarantee of its being any more satisfactory to Bette).

Before then, however, the June 27 release of *Of Human Bondage* considerably altered Bette's status at Warner Bros. Critics extolled her Mildred Rogers as "easily her finest performance" (*New York Times*) and "probably the best performance ever recorded on the screen by a U.S. actress" (*Life*).

Following some initial embarrassment and perplexity in Burbank—why had Davis been allowed to give "her finest performance" at RKO?—Jack Warner cast her opposite the studio's premier actor, Paul Muni, in director Archie Mayo's *Bordertown*. The film was set to go into production on August 17, with Bette's role to commence on August 31.

Muni was reputed to wield more power than any other actor at Warners. He had complete story and script approval and a lordly fee of $50,000 per film, based on the vast box office appeal of his *Scarface* and *I Am a Fugitive from a Chain Gang*. But the thirty nine-year-old actor was not powerful enough to push through his choice of Carole Lombard for the role of the high-strung murderess Marie Roark in *Bordertown*. Jack Warner's selection of Bette Davis for the part betokened the studio boss's sudden realization that Bette might be a more valuable asset than anyone at Warners had thought.

In the aftermath of her first two skirmishes with the studio, there may also have been a subtle, perhaps unconscious element in casting Bette as what screenwriter and staff producer Robert Lord called a "psychopathic woman," whose pugnacity leads only to madness and self-destruction. Where Mildred Rogers had spurred Bette to assert herself publicly as she had never done in Hollywood before, Marie Roark taught a harsher lesson. Enacting Marie's descent into flailing, self-consuming frenzy, the actress played out what might happen to any woman who reaches too aggressively for what she wants.

Jack Warner seemed to have honestly believed that he was making amends to the actress by awarding her a plum role in *Bordertown*. That his ironic commentary on Bette's newfound recalcitrance was probably unconscious suggests how deeply ingrained was the popular association between female boldness and the "psychopathic."

"Believe me, I know something of psychopathic women," Robert Lord insisted to Hal Wallis, the associate executive in charge of production, who wanted one of Bette's scenes reshot "in a more emotional-hysterical way" than Mayo seemed to have directed it.

For her part, Bette feared Mayo and Lord were demanding that she seem too much the "raving lunatic" on screen. Aiming for a more finely nuanced depiction of mental illness, Davis based such affecting details as the abrupt, groping hand play and other nervous tics on sustained observation of her sister's breakdowns.

⚜

"To Miss Bette Davis for her work in *Dangerous*, I—" The audience at the March 5, 1936, Academy Awards ceremony, at the Biltmore Hotel in Los Angeles, drowned out the rest of D. W. Griffith's speech with torrents of applause and stamping feet as Bette made her way to the speaker's platform to accept the Best Actress award.

The day had started out unhappily. Her newly retained attorney, Martin Gang, of Gang and Kopp, had informed her that at a March 3 meeting, Jack Warner and his staff—including studio general counsel Roy Obringer—had refused Gang's March 2 proposal that Bette be lent out again to RKO, to portray Queen Elizabeth opposite Katharine Hepburn in John Ford's adaptation of the Maxwell Anderson play *Mary of Scotland*.

Bette had been desperate to accept the recently proffered role, not least for the opportunity to appear with Hepburn. Her fellow Yankee's New England background had caused Bette and Ruthie to monitor obsessively every step of the rival actress's far more successful Broadway and Hollywood career. They had been painfully aware of Hepburn's 1932 New York stage triumph in *The Warrior's Husband*, her widely praised film debut in *A Bill of Divorcement*, with John Barrymore, her Academy Award for *Morning Glory*, as well as this year's nomination for Best Actress (in competition with Bette) for RKO's Booth Tarkington adaptation, *Alice Adams*.

All this, while Warner Bros. persisted in using Bette Davis (fresh from her searing performance in *Of Human Bondage*) in such banalities as *The Girl from Tenth Avenue*, *Front Page Woman*, and *Special Agent*, whose sole raison d'être could only have been to return more than their negative and distribution costs.

A new seven-year contract—dated December 27, 1934, and providing for Bette's weekly salary to rise from $750 to $1,350—had seemed temporarily to appease her; as had two somewhat better (although still not quite satisfactory) roles—as a faded actress modeled on Jeanne Eagels, in Alfred E. Green's *Dangerous;* and as a sensitive waitress in Archie Mayo's adaptation of Robert Sherwood's fashionable drama *The Petrified Forest.*

But the fuss and fume started again on November 29, 1935, when, with only a day to go before Bette finished *The Petrified Forest,* Warners ordered her to report back on December 2, to begin work on Hollywood's latest attempt to film Dashiell Hammett's *The Maltese Falcon,* William Dieterle's *Satan Met a Lady.*

The following day, pleading illness and nervous exhaustion, Bette wired Jack Warner her vehement objections to doing another film so soon after *The Petrified Forest.* On December 2, when a studio physician, Dr. Carl Conn, appeared at 6:00 P.M. at Bette's home to report on her condition to the Warners' general counsel, Ham declined to let him in, saying only that Mrs. Nelson was expected to be out all evening. Eighteen minutes later, Bette sent another wire to Jack Warner, to whom she denied ever having claimed to be ill (the November 30 telegram notwithstanding): hence her refusal to allow the studio physician to examine her.

Bette went on to beseech Warner to grant her a much-needed hiatus nonetheless. Instead the studio boss suspended her, but when Bette quietly showed up for work on December 6, Warner just as quietly canceled the suspension.

In February 1936, not long after Bette had been astonished to learn of her nomination as Best Actress for her merely adequate performance in *Dangerous* when she had not been nominated the year before for *Of Human Bondage,* she dispatched attorney Martin Gang to press her claims with the studio for a fresh contract. She wanted additional money and a limit to the number of films Warners could compel her to make each year, plus a guaranteed yearly holiday of three consecutive months. In addition, she pressed for the right to do an outside picture during that three-month holiday period (e.g., *Mary of Scotland*). All of this received an icy reception in Burbank. To end the conversation, Roy Obringer needed merely to produce the valid seven-year contract Bette had signed with Warners barely fifteen months before.

As the Academy Awards approached, the only thing likely to revive Bette's spirits would be Jack Warner's approval of the loan-out to RKO. Certain that Hepburn was going to win the Best Actress award for *Alice Adams* (in Davis's view, justifiably so), Bette initially planned to be out of town at the time of the ceremony, on vacation with Ruthie in Honolulu. Besides, although they could never really prove it, Bette and her mother had privately blamed her failure even to be nominated for an Academy Award for *Of Human Bondage* on Jack Warner. They believed he had steadfastly blocked it because the film had been produced at a rival studio. Although Bette's name had not appeared among the nominees in 1935, there had been a much-talked-about write-in campaign on her behalf, which suggested the strong sentiment in Hollywood that Davis's Mildred Rogers had been richly deserving of Academy recognition. In 1936, her nomination for *Dangerous* was widely perceived as a consolation prize for the previous year's injustice.

Only under pressure from Jack Warner (who had communicated his displeasure about the Honolulu trip to the actress's agent on February 27) did Bette finally agree to put in an appearance at the Biltmore Hotel—probably in hopes that this sudden spurt of cooperativeness would induce Warner to approve the loan-out to RKO.

But when March 5 started with the call from her attorney informing her of Warner's refusal to allow her to appear with Hepburn in the John Ford film, Bette only naturally felt scant enthusiasm for attending the Academy Awards ceremony that night: as suggested by the dowdy navy-and-white print dress she chose as her silent statement on the occasion.

At a table near the dance floor, a forlorn and dispirited Bette Davis spent much of the evening seated beside her husband, more appropriately dressed in white tie and tails.

It seemed to Bette that the fine print of her seven-year contract left her powerless, ineffectual. As if she were in servitude to Warner Bros., she had even had to request Obringer's permission to join Ruthie in Hawaii two days later, on March 7. And what hope could she have of salvaging her career when, even as Jack Warner was refusing to loan her out for *Mary of Scotland*, she had been squandering her abilities on the latest trifle to which he had assigned her: as a cashier who impersonates a cosmetics heiress, in Alfred E. Green's *The Golden Arrow*.

But then out came the sixty-one-year-old Griffith to announce the Best Actress award. Dramatically rattling the phlegm in his throat, he read not Hepburn's name, but Bette's.

As the spotlight found her rising from her seat and excitedly making her way to the speaker's platform, Bette must have realized that at one fell swoop everything had changed. Warner Bros. hadn't had an Academy Award–winning actor since George Arliss's *Disraeli* in 1930. Never before had a Warners actress been named. As Bette clutched the gold figurine, a new sense of power surged through her: all she had to do was exert it.

The Academy Award symbolized everything Ruthie had worked for during the long years of hardship. But when Bette received the award, Ruthie was on vacation in Hawaii. Then word arrived from Bette that she was canceling her plans to join her mother; instead she would head east to celebrate with old friends and family. Feeling suddenly unloved and unappreciated, Ruthie composed a petulant three-word telegram to her daughter. ANYONE LOVE ME? she wired from Honolulu, lest Bette forget what she owed her mother for sacrificing everything to help her reach this moment of triumph.

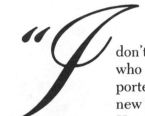

TEN

"*I* don't take the movies seriously, and anyone who does is in for a headache," Bette told reporters who had come to interview Warners' new Academy Award winner at the Algonquin Hotel in New York City in March 1936. "I really don't like the work, but it's amusing, even if it is hard. Honestly, every time I go to a preview of one of my pictures I wonder how soon they'll get wise and fire me. If they do, I'll probably go back to the theater, where I got my start."

Bette went on to explain that as soon as she checked in at the Algonquin, Jack Warner had wired her to return to Los Angeles immediately for additional work on *The Golden Arrow*. She gleefully reported that she had telegraphed back: YOUR WIRE NOT RECEIVED. "Studio executives hate to see a player take a vacation," Bette continued. "As soon as you get away, they start sending you wires about retakes. But I'm not going!"

There was, however, a definite subtext to all this: Bette's implicit threat not to return to Warner Bros. if they failed to give her the new contract attorney Martin Gang had demanded back in February.

On April 4, Bette was still in the East when her agent, Mike Levee, called Roy Obringer at Warners to convey the actress's willingness to do additional work on *The Golden Arrow* when she returned, in about ten days. Beyond that, Levee noted, Bette's appearance in any new film roles would depend on the studio's having agreed to a fresh contract.

In hopes of establishing evidence for a possible court case, Obringer asked to have Bette's ultimatum in writing—her current contract made any such refusal to work illegitimate in the eyes of the law—but Levee declined, insisting that all communications be oral. Martin Gang would be in touch in a day or so to hear Jack Warner's response.

In the meantime, Bette visited her friend Robin in New York. Then she enjoyed a triumphal side trip to Newton, Massachusetts, where she was the guest of honor at a luncheon at the Brae Burn Country Club, where she had attended bridge parties and dances some thirteen years before.

And there was a bittersweet reunion with Harlow. Bette's father had gone into semiretirement after a heart attack suffered in the months following Bette's appearance in *Of Human Bondage*. Harlow had invited Bette to his home in suburban Belmont, but that would mean an encounter with Minnie. Bette insisted he dine with her in Boston at the Copley Plaza Hotel, where eighteen years before, Harlow had taken Ruthie and their young daughters for a last meal together as a family.

Back in New York, Bette continued her public blasts against Warner Bros. On the West Coast, Martin Gang restated her demands to the studio, asking that Jack Warner and he come to an accord prior to the actress's imminent return.

In later years, Davis's reputation for doing battle with Warner Bros. would obscure the fact that in 1936, salary was the principal issue. Equating power with money, Bette wanted a salary commensurate with the status her Academy Award conferred. Where Bette earned $1,600 a week in 1936, four years before, Warners had paid stars Kay Francis and James Cagney $3,000 weekly, Ruth Chatterton $8,000. That same year, Edward G. Robinson earned $40,000 for each film he made; while Paul Muni's 1933 contract brought him $50,000 per project.

All the play she was suddenly getting in the national press for her flippant remarks about Hollywood seemed to have convinced Bette that forcing Warner Bros. to discard her seven-year contract was going to be a "pushover"—or so she told Mike Levee on April 7. She instructed him to inform Jack Warner that she had changed her mind. She declined even to do retakes for *The Golden Arrow* before her demands were met.

Warner, fearful of showing the slightest indication of weakness, on April 14 ordered a letter drafted to Gang. In it, he warned that the studio expected Gang's client to live up to the terms of her contract; there would be no new discussions or negotiations. Warner's legal staff advised him to withhold the letter until after Bette had somehow been wheedled into coming to Burbank to do the *Golden Arrow* retakes. When she reported for them on April 18, even as Davis was filming with George Brent, the studio was notifying her attorney of Warner's intransigence.

"I think it important that, just as soon as possible, we put a call in for her to report for work on a picture," Hal Wallis told Warner that same day, anxious to test Bette's threat to refuse all film roles until the contract dispute was settled. But neither of the scripts Wallis had in mind for her—*Mountain Justice* or *God's Country and the Woman*—was quite ready, so Warner ordered Bette placed on a six-week layoff without pay, effective April 20. Meanwhile Wallis would attempt to win Levee over to the studio's side and alienate him from Gang, whom Warner blamed for Bette's latest mutiny.

♈

By May 21, a week before Bette was due back for wardrobe fittings for her role as a female logger in director William Keighley's *God's Country and the Woman* (to be shot on location in Longview, Washington), Levee had persuaded the actress to dismiss her attorney. According to studio files, the agent informed Warners of Bette's willingness to come back to work and "try to secure a new contract in an amiable manner" by showing a new spirit of "cooperation with the company."

Within days of returning to the Warners' payroll (but not to work), Bette wired Jack Warner and requested a June 6 meeting. There she argued on her own behalf for all the same concessions Gang had demanded.

According to Obringer's notes (the always deeply suspicious Warner had arrived for the showdown with his general counsel at his side), Davis opened the meeting by announcing that "she had reached the point where she felt she was entitled to more money." As Warner watched her grimly and silently from behind his desk, the actress went on to specify that she would expect a set yearly salary for a predetermined number of pictures; whether the studio would pay her by the week or the film was for Warner to decide, so long as her yearly total was the same.

But before she could name specific sums, Warner cut in, reiterating his refusal to consider a new contract. He brushed aside Bette's desire to make a single "outside" picture each year, with the well-worn declaration "that he was continuously looking for good stories for her." He followed that by a throwing up of the hands and a last-ditch offer to raise her weekly salary from $1,600 to $2,000, in acknowledgment of the prestige her Academy Award had brought the studio, but only if Bette would agree to tack an additional two years onto her existing contract, whose other provisions were to remain as before.

All smiles and smug conviviality, Warner ushered her out of the office, with Bette promising to "think it over and advise him" of her decision as soon as possible.

When ten days passed without a word, on June 16 Obringer called Bette. She would say only that "she didn't know a lot about business and would rather have Mr. Warner talk to her attorney"— Martin Gang having been replaced by Hollywood lawyer Dudley Furse, who called in due course to set up a new meeting with Warner, on the afternoon of June 18.

That morning, as if to set the tone for the two-thirty conclave, Bette wired Warner, angrily denying all that her agent had said about her willingness to start *God's Country and the Woman*. One can only imagine the effect of such a telegram on the insecure Warner, who, above all else, dreaded being taken advantage of or made to appear foolish.

When Dudley Furse and Bette's business manager, Vernon Wood, appeared at Obringer's office at the appointed hour, they were met by the studio's general counsel and attorney, Ralph Lewis, of the firm Freston and Files, who regretted that Warner had been detained in Projection Room 5. Obringer wanted to start without him, but Wood pointed out that he and Furse were under strict orders from Bette to present her demands "personally" to Jack Warner. Thus the four men spent some twenty minutes making small talk until finally, at 2:50 P.M., Warner blustered in, complaining of the "excessive heat" and clearly expecting that the discussion was already well under way.

Instead Bette's business manager began by declaring that he and

Furse recognized the validity of her existing contract. They were here not to object to the December 27, 1934, document on legal grounds but to request Warner to consider negotiating new terms out of fairness to an actress who had, after all, just won the Academy Award.

Through all this Warner sat poker-faced; but when Wood accused him of "nonchalance" in dealing with Bette's demands, the studio boss launched into a harangue on the ungratefulness of stars whose "walkout tactics" punished the very studios that had created them. According to Warner, the studios put young unknowns (as Bette had been in 1931) under long-term contract in hopes of "grooming them into well-known screen personalities," at which time the studio's investment might finally pay off. But if performers like Bette Davis (and James Cagney before her, in his successful 1936 court case against Warners) continued to challenge their contracts whenever the studios declined their "outrageous demands" . . .

Dudley Furse interrupted Warner's litany of complaint by concurring that Bette's 1934 contract was "perfectly legal and binding" and "was too carefully drawn to afford Miss Davis any opportunity to attack its validity."

But when Furse asked Warner at least to consider Bette's demands, the studio boss snapped that he had already made his final offer: the $2,000 weekly salary (escalating to $3,500 after six years) he had proposed to the actress on June 6. Warner curtly refused even to listen to such other demands as a five-year contract and a four-picture yearly limit.

The next morning, June 19, Bette was scheduled to report for wardrobe fittings at ten, but on the basis of her lawyer's bootless meeting with Warner she failed to show up—knowing full well that the studio would almost certainly suspend her.

Before he ordered the suspension letter sent out, however, Warner invited her and Vernon Wood to his office. There, flanked by Hal Wallis and Obringer, Warner urged Bette to be "a regular trouper" and start work on the new picture. Not before the studio met her salary demands, she replied: $100,000 a year to start, escalating to $220,000 after four years. Plus she continued to stipulate that Warner Bros. allow her to do a single outside film every year; and declared her willingness to "take her chances and go out of pictures" if Warner failed to come up with the new contract.

"Miss Davis was very arbitrary and obstinate about the entire situation," Obringer noted afterward in his report.

When Warner budged only to offer a token additional $500 weekly in the seventh year of her new contract, Bette decided that enough was enough and strode out of the room. Her business manager stayed behind to assure Wallis that he would do all he could to persuade her to agree to Warner's latest offer.

It was now Friday evening. Wood promised Wallis that he would call him at home, on Sunday at the latest, with the good news. But when the business manager finally called on June 21, it was to report Bette's continued refusal to accept Warner's terms and come back to work.

By this time, Warner Bros. had formally notified Bette that as of June 19, 1936, they had suspended her without pay. Each day she remained away from the studio would be one more day owed at the end of her contract.

On the telephone with Obringer, Mike Levee announced that he was "through with her"—as a client she was "more grief than his commission was worth." According to Obringer's notes, the exasperated agent even offered to give the studio his file of correspondence with Bette (later he declined to do so, on the advice of his lawyer, who reminded Levee that his other clients might balk at his seeming to take the studio's side in the Davis affair). Levee believed that in appearing to accept his advice, then abruptly, inexplicably changing her mind, the mercurial actress was almost certainly "relying on the advice of others."

"Give me a blank check, because I don't know how much I'm going to spend today," Ruthie told Bette, in the presence of Ellen Batchelder, who explains that Ruthie expected to be paid back for all her years of struggle and sacrifice on Bette's behalf.

Ruthie and a newly sedate Bobby had moved back to Los Angeles. On their arrival they had promptly summoned reporters to declare Bobby's career plans: "I want to be an actress, just like my sister," Bobby announced on December 12, 1934.

Instead, eight months later, Ruthie married off her twenty-five-year-old daughter to a slender, rather languidly handsome young man, five years Bobby's junior: "Little" Bobby Pelgram, as Bette and Robin had called him in Ogunquit, where they had known his older brother Charlie. Although Ruthie was delighted by the match, Bette could hardly conceal her jealousy over Bobby's having landed the wealthy sportsman and aviation enthusiast. In his beautifully tailored white flannels and navy blazer, Bobby Pelgram reminded many of Bette's friends of a dashing, romantic figure in a Fitzgerald novel.

Because she wanted the same wedding anniversary as her older sister, Bobby eloped with her fiancé to Tijuana, Mexico, on August 18, 1935, accompanied by Bette and Ham—who was soon to suffer by comparison with his moneyed brother-in-law.

"When Bette started to become very successful, Ham decided that he didn't want people to regard him as 'Mr. Bette Davis,' " says Robin Brown of the period when Bette's husband insisted they abandon "the Garbo house" (as Bette called it) for considerably more modest quarters at 5346 Franklin Avenue in Hollywood (with a tiny rear cottage for Ruthie). And when Bette visited him in San Francisco, where he was earning one hundred dollars a week as a musician at the Villa Mateo in nearby Daly City, Ham was emphatic that she stay with him in cottage number 10 in the Mission Auto Court—a neat bit of publicity, perhaps; but a grave offense, as far as Bette's mother was concerned.

Where Ham quietly supported Bette's struggles with the studio, it was Ruthie first and foremost who prodded her to disregard the advice of her agent and keep fighting when Jack Warner offered so much less than she had demanded; and Ruthie who urged Bette to accept the strange proposal that reached them from London now. The mysterious and controversial forty-five-year-old Italian producer Ludovico Toeplitz—upon whom the King of Italy had conferred the title "de Grand Ry"—inquired whether Bette might be free to make a film for his Toeplitz Productions Ltd. in England. Toeplitz's previous productions included *The Dictator*, starring Clive Brook and Madeleine Carroll, and *The Beloved Vagabond*, with Maurice Chevalier.

Excited at the prospect of an opportunity to travel abroad, and even more by the fifty-thousand-dollar fee Toeplitz offered, Bette and Ruthie remained blissfully unaware of persistent rumors in the international film community that connected Toeplitz (a close associate of Gabriele D'Annunzio) with Fascist Italy. Having declared film "the most powerful weapon," Benito Mussolini was widely thought to have dispatched Toeplitz to London as a sort of "unofficial film ambassador" who would one day return to Rome to work in Cinecittà, the new complex of sixteen studios facing the Centro Sperimentale on the Via Tuscolana (known as "the artistic laboratory of Mussolini's time"). Giving rise to these rumors were Toeplitz's apparent economic ties to

the Banca Comerciale Italiana, despite Fascist prohibitions on export-
ing capital from Italy. Nor did Toeplitz seem to have been required,
as had other Italian nationals abroad, to transfer his principal funds to
Fascist Italy.

According to an August 27 letter from Toeplitz to Davis, Bette's
representatives responded to his preliminary inquiries with assurances that Warner Bros. had committed "numerous breaches" of their
contract with the actress, thereby freeing her to accept the starring
role in Toeplitz's production of *I'll Take the Low Road*.

Two days after Bette's suspension, on the evening of June 21, Jack
Warner called her at home to offer what he described as "fatherly
advice" to change her mind before popular opinion turned against her
when news of her "breach of contract" appeared in the press.

He cautioned that in hard economic times, Bette's rebellion over
a $1,600 weekly salary was unlikely to play well with the public. From
first to last, Warner controlled the conversation. Each time Bette
raised specific points about her contract or the suspension letter,
Warner admonished that that was not why he had called; he only
wanted to warn her to discontinue her belligerent and self-destructive
tactics "before it became too late."

That night, Bette dashed off a handwritten, undated seven-page
letter, in which she told the studio boss everything he had kept her
from saying on the telephone. (Neither the typed version prepared
by Warner's assistant nor the versions subsequently read aloud in
court and reprinted in the international press possess anything like
the raw passion of Bette's handwritten original.)

> In reference to our talk today—it seemed to me our main prob-
> lem is getting together on the money. You as Head of your firm,
> naturally know what your concern can afford and what they can't.
>
> I have no desire to be "off your list" and I feel sure—you do not
> wish it either. I agree lots of harm can be done through publicity.
> Believe me when I tell you I have thought and prepared for every
> angle of this for a long time now. I also know you have the right to keep
> me from working—a great unhappiness to me because I enjoy work-
> ing—especially after my long vacation. I am so rested it hurts! How-
> ever, there comes a time in everyone's career when certain things
> make working worth-while. I am now referring to the very few rights
> I have asked for. . . .

As to the "loan-out clause," I am the kind of person who thrives under change. I have never wanted this clause because I wanted to feel I was my own boss—have authority of my own—quite the contrary. I like a boss—someone to look up to whose opinion I respect as I do yours. Mentally—a change does me good—makes me do better work, I like working with new directors, new casts, etc. I am also ambitious to become known as a great actress—I might, who can tell. Every once in a while a part comes along particularly suited to me. I want to feel, should a role come my way, I am at liberty to take advantage of it. If no such part ever appears in five years, then I will not take advantage of my right. In that case I am very anxious to travel, thus the request for three consecutive months of vacation. Travel is also change—good publicity for you and me both and particularly important to me during the next five years as I have never been out of this country—it is broadening to one's intellect and will help me I'm sure in my work and thus help you. I am an essentially high-strung person—for that rea-son—change means rest and I must have rest.

To get back to our call and the purpose of this letter, I would be willing to take less money, if in consideration of this, you would give me my "rights." You have asked me to be level-headed in this matter. I feel I am extremely and I hope that you can agree that I am. I am more than anxious to work for you again, but not as things stand. . . .

As a happy person, I can work like Hell—as an unhappy one, I make myself and everyone around me unhappy. Also I know and you do too—in a business where you have a fickle public to depend on, the money should be made when you mean something, not when the public has had time to tell you to "go to hell." . . .

Unmentioned was the Toeplitz offer, which Bette's representa-tives had already virtually accepted on her behalf: thus her sudden willingness to take less money from Warner if only he would give her a "loan-out clause." But when—in a June 24 letter—he refused even this, Bette perceived herself to have little choice but to turn to the press, in an attempt to win public sympathy to her cause.

"I'm ready to quit for good," she told reporters at the beginning of July. "There are certain things I'm entitled to, and I'm darned well going to get them—or else!"

But what precisely was her cause?

She could hardly argue that she was fighting for better roles, when the film she was clamoring to appear in this time was the banal comedy *I'll Take the Low Road* (about an American girl who seeks a title), to be directed at Ealing Studios by the hack Monty Banks. Nor, as Warner had admonished, would she win much sympathy complaining about her weekly salary, when $1,600 would have seemed like a small fortune to most Depression-era Americans.

Hence the persistent vagueness of her public declarations: "It's a mess of little things that need adjustment—they've been wrong for a long time"; "I would hate to tell you how little the studio pays me—much less than many of the new players, especially men."

By contrast, Warner's pronouncements focused on one issue: the actress's repudiation of a contract whose validity even her own representatives seemed to recognize.

"We have been more than fair with Miss Davis," said Warner. "A year ago we rewrote her contract, which had considerable time to run, and gave her a new long-term one at considerable increase in salary. She expressed herself as satisfied with its terms and we proceeded to select outstanding stories for her and to launch a campaign to build her up. Now she is endeavoring to repudiate the contract and has refused to report for work unless demands for an exorbitant salary and other impossible stipulations are met. It is high time something were done to make people under contract to the studios realize that a contract is not a mere scrap of paper, to be thrown aside because they happen to make a good picture or two. We do not repudiate our contracts with our players and we don't intend to let them repudiate their contracts with us."

Fearful that should he learn of her negotiations with Toeplitz, Warner would seek an injunction to prevent her from leaving the country, Bette and Ham quietly boarded a midnight flight for Vancouver, Canada.

On August 3, when the Warners branch manager in Vancouver, Joseph Plottel, chanced to learn of Bette's arrival, he innocently rushed to her hotel to see if he could be of help in arranging publicity. Burbank, however, promptly wired him to keep his distance from the errant film star, who—much as Warner feared—was soon on her way to England, sailing on the Canadian Pacific liner *Duchess of Bedford*.

🔶

"At the moment I am one of the unemployed, for I am still under suspension by Warner Bros.," Bette told reporters on August 17, 1936, when her ship paused in Scotland on the way to Liverpool. "It is rather a long story to go into details. I am still bound to them by contract. I have five more years to go, and how or when the dispute will be settled I do not know. I should love to make a picture in

Britain but cannot do it. I am completely tied up with Warner Bros."

That same day in Burbank, appalled at *Variety*'s speculation that Bette was headed to England to make a picture for Gaumont-British, Roy Obringer directed Morris Ebenstein in Warners' New York office to notify major English producers—including Gaumont, Toeplitz, and Alexander Korda—that Bette Davis remained under contract to Warner Bros., which fully intended to prevent the actress from working elsewhere. Meanwhile Ebenstein brought to Obringer's attention a *New York Times* report that named Toeplitz as the true culprit; whereupon Warners' English attorneys, Denton, Hall and Burgin, promptly sought Toeplitz's assurance that he would respect the studio's exclusive right to Bette's services.

Instead the worried Italian producer submitted a copy of Bette's December 27, 1934, Warner Bros. contract to two English counsel, as well as to an American attorney practicing at the English bar. All three confirmed the document's validity. In their opinion, Warners would have no difficulty obtaining an injunction in the English courts to restrain the actress from working for Toeplitz Productions Ltd.

As even Bette now admitted, there existed no evidence to substantiate her earlier claims to Ludovico Toeplitz that Warners had blatantly and repeatedly breached her contract.

While James Cagney had successfully broken his Warners contract in court, it wasn't dissatisfaction with his screen roles that won the actor's freedom (although that had been the principal motive behind his suit) but a minor billing error: a marquee at Warners' Beverly Theater that read: PAT O'BRIEN IN CEILING ZERO, in clear violation of Cagney's contract, which guaranteed top billing.

As Jack Warner had understood well in advance, all Cagney had to do to prove breach of contract was produce a photograph of the offending marquee. Nonetheless, Warner had dragged out the legal proceedings to punish Cagney for his disloyalty and lack of gratitude and to warn all future insurrectionists of the lengths to which he would go to snuff them out.

If Warner had done all this against Cagney, whose case was open and shut, what would he do with Bette, who all too clearly had no legitimate case at all?

On August 27, Toeplitz Productions Ltd. notified Bette, at the Tudor Hotel in Rottingdean, that their lawyers' findings compelled them to recast her role in *I'll Take the Low Road* and to assure Warner Bros. that they were breaking off negotiations with her. This was a devastating blow for Davis, who pleaded with Toeplitz not to abandon her now that she had come this far at his behest.

Toeplitz calculated that even if Warner hauled Bette into court, a British judge would probably allow the studio to restrain her only until the end of the year, when her option next came due. After that she would be free to work for him as she wished: hence the option for future services he tacked on to the two-picture deal he made with her now, with the understanding that should all else fail, Bette would join him in Rome, where Jack Warner and the British courts had no influence.

Bette and Ham were in Paris for wardrobe fittings for *I'll Take the Low Road* when she learned of the September 9 temporary injunction Warners had won in the British courts, restraining her from doing any film work in England without the studio's permission.

"We consider the matter of the writ entirely one between Miss Davis and the Warners," Toeplitz announced in London, presumably to shield himself from legal action. "There is no question of enticement on our part. We intend to go right ahead with the film."

"Where are you?" Ruthie screamed into the telephone when Ham Nelson called from New York. "Let me speak to Bette!"

"She isn't here," Ham replied. "She's in England."

While Ruthie tried to suppress her anger over Ham's having left Bette to confront her court case alone, he explained that, having decided to abandon his career as an itinerant performer, he had returned to the United States to seek steady employment as a musicians' agent in New York, so that he could earn enough money to finance Bette's legal battle.

From this point on, Ruthie used Bette's ambivalent feelings about her husband's departure to turn her against him—as if he had forsaken her when she needed him most.

"Mother?" said Bette when Ruthie wasted no time calling London to commiserate about Ham's departure and propose coming to England in his place. Aside from her daughter's uncharacteristically tiny voice, the fact that Bette addressed her as "Mother" rather than the customary "Ruthie" spoke volumes about Bette's loneliness before the Wednesday, October 14, court hearing—*Warner Bros.* v. *Nelson*—before Mr. Justice Branson in King's Bench Division.

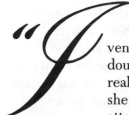

ELEVEN

"**I** venture to suggest that Your Lordship will doubtless come to the conclusion that this is really a rather naughty young lady and what she wants is more money," declared Warners' attorney Sir Patrick Hastings, as laughter wafted through King's Bench Court on the first day of the hearing to determine the validity of Bette's current contract.

Dressed in a red-and-blue tweed coat and matching beret and seated beside her expensive English lawyer, Sir William Jowitt (recommended, but not paid for, by Ludovico Toeplitz), Bette listened in horror as Sir Patrick alluded to the most seemingly infinitesimal details of her every action and utterance at Warner Bros. since December 24, 1931, when she signed her first one-picture contract, to make *The Man Who Played God* with George Arliss.

Although Bette had probably never noticed it before, at the bottom of every scrap of Warner Bros. interoffice correspondence was printed the dictum: "Verbal messages cause misunderstanding and delays (please put them in writing)." And now, from Warners' Borgesian "infinite library" of business records, Sir Patrick summoned up a dazzling profusion of detail, tracing Bette's dealings with the studio virtually minute by minute, from 1931 until that very day.

In the weeks since Bette fled to Canada, Roy Obringer had combed the Warners' files and transmitted all papers "relative to the Davis matter" to R. W. Perkins of Warners' legal department in New York, who in turn shipped it all off to Sir Patrick in London. Further, on September 9 and October 1, Obringer had furnished Sir Patrick with copiously detailed accounts of Bette's skirmishes with the studio, dating back to her April 1934 refusal to report for wardrobe fittings for the by now long-forgotten *Housewife*.

" 'In reference to our talk today—it seemed to me our main problem is getting together on the money,' " Sir Patrick read aloud in court from Bette's June 21, 1936, letter to Jack Warner—than which a more damning piece of evidence was scarcely imaginable.

Although Bette's camp seemed not to have realized it, Warners had quietly severed the matter of the actress's suspension clause from their case against her. Technically it was the studio's right to add the time she had been out on suspension to the end of her contract. The Warners' legal department preferred not to bring this up, lest Mr. Justice Branson rule the standard Hollywood suspension clause unenforceable (thereby opening a Pandora's box of dissension and complaint back in the States).

Sir Patrick asked only that Mr. Justice Branson recognize the straight amount of time Bette owed the studio under her current contract; and prevent the actress from working for Toeplitz or any other producer during that period.

"What this young lady is seeking to do is in effect to tear up her contract and say that whether she is right or wrong the court will not grant an injunction against her," said Sir Patrick of Bette's much-publicized charge that her Warners' contract was a form of "slavery."

" 'Slavery' has a silver lining because the 'slave' was, to say the least, well remunerated," he went on, rattling off Bette's salary history at Warners (and concluding with the weekly $3,000 she was to earn in the final year of her current contract). "If anyone wants to put me in perpetual servitude on that basis of remuneration, I shall be prepared to consider it!"

Even Bette—he argued—could hardly believe her own spurious claims, the real reason for all the brouhaha being the $50,000 offer to appear in *I'll Take the Low Road*: "There is a gentleman whose name

I cannot pronounce," said Sir Patrick. "A Mr. Toeplitz, I think. I suggest Miss Davis has been bribed and has been unwise enough to be flattered by the offer and say, 'I'll take it if I can get away from Warner Bros.' "

There followed testimony from Jack Warner, who, in typical fashion, wrung his hands over Bette's lack of gratitude to the studio that had built her up "from obscurity." Testifying on behalf of Warner Bros., Alexander Korda (Toeplitz's former associate and rival at London Film Productions, where the Italian had cut his teeth before founding Toeplitz Productions Ltd.) dismissed Bette's claims against her studio with the remark: "An actress does not always understand her will or what she wants to do."

The following day, Thursday, October 15, was devoted to Sir William Jowitt's argument that Bette's contract made her "chattel in the hands of the producer."

"The contract is so strict," said Sir William, glancing at Bette— whom Ruthie had advised to wear the same outfit as the day before, to discourage Mr. Justice Branson's thinking her a rich American movie star—"that Miss Davis could not become a waitress in a restaurant or an assistant in a hairdresser's shop in the wilds of Africa— whether for love or money."

Sir Patrick begged to interrupt, to remind Sir William that Warners had hardly sought an injunction to prevent Bette Davis from becoming a hairdresser in Africa; it was to prevent her appearing in a rival producer's film.

"I suggest," Sir William continued, "that the real essence of slavery is not that it is no less slavery because the bars are gilded, but because some superior authority says, 'You've got to continue work!' "

Bette's lawyer conceded to a paucity of evidence that Warners had breached her contract. He appeared to throw his client on the mercy of the court with the unexpected admission: "There are facts which might necessitate the court finding that Miss Davis has broken her contract." Still, he argued that it would be wrong for Mr. Justice Branson to conclude that Bette was "a mere money grabber."

"A breach of contract is always a serious matter," said Sir William. "But there comes a time when carrying out a contract becomes so difficult and irksome that a person is forced to say he cannot continue and must submit to the penalties which the law may impose."

Sir William ended without putting Bette on the stand, for fear of what she might say when Sir Patrick cross-examined her.

On Friday, October 16, Bette wore the identical red-and-blue tweed coat—but different shoes—to court, where Sir Patrick reiterated his plea that Mr. Justice Branson prevent her from acting elsewhere during the term of her Warner Bros. contract; while Sir William likened her contract to "a life sentence."

"This young lady is in the prime of life," said Sir William. "Supposing she cannot act in films until 1942, then she must stage a comeback, which would be an impossible position for her."

If the court must issue an injunction, he argued, let it be valid only until the end of the year, when her option next came due; or at worst, for that period plus the time that had elapsed since her June 19, 1936, suspension.

"I can see no reason for holding the contract unlawful," Mr. Justice Branson declared on Monday, October 19, as he granted an injunction that restrained Bette Davis from appearing in any but Warner Bros. films for the length of her current contract, or the next three years, whichever was shorter.

"In June of this year," he went on, "Miss Davis, for no discoverable reason except that she wanted more money, declined to be further bound by her contract, left the United States, and in September entered into an agreement in this country with a third person."

Mr. Justice Branson rejected Bette's contention that her contract was a form of "slavery"; contrary to Sir William's assertions, the injunction left her free to work as a waitress or a hairdresser's assistant, so long as she refrained from appearing on stage or screen.

"Miss Davis is said to be a person of intelligence and means," he continued, "and there is no evidence that she will not be able to employ herself usefully and remuneratively in other spheres of action, though perhaps not so remuneratively. She will not be driven to perform the contract, though she may be tempted to perform it. The fact that she may be so tempted is no objection to granting the injunction."

Finally, Mr. Justice Branson noted that his ruling extended solely to England; that having lost, Bette was responsible for Warners' court costs, as well as her own; and that she had fourteen days to appeal.

"This has been a real sock in the teeth," Bette said afterward, clearly shaken by the verdict. "I had not expected a one hundred percent defeat. Instead of getting increased freedom, I seem to have provided, at my own expense, an object lesson for other would-be 'naughty young ladies,' as Sir Patrick picturesquely described me."

"One thing is certain," Bette told reporters the next day. "I am not going to cut off my nose to spite my face. I am set on a film career, and if it means going back to Warners and being pleasant about it—why then I'm quite prepared to go."

But as Sir William explained to Jack Warner and his London attorneys, Denton, Hall and Burgin, on Wednesday morning, October 21, Bette would now give serious consideration to an appeal—unless Warner showed himself willing to make certain as yet unspecified modifications in her existing contract in exchange for the actress's immediate return to work. To which Warner replied that "obvious business reasons" precluded any concessions being made to Bette, who ought to "return to work unconditionally or proceed with the appeal." As his attorneys' November 3 notes make clear, Denton, Hall and Burgin believed Bette and her legal advisers to have been stunned by Mr. Justice Branson's ruling: "They were expecting at the worst an injunction limited to a period of one year. It is the three-year period of the injunction that has upset their calculations."

In the meantime, Bette conferred with Ludovico Toeplitz, who again raised the possibility of decamping for Italy, where he promised to make her his "Duse" in a series of "mythological films" to be shot at Mussolini's new studios near Rome. As she told Ruthie when she called her mother for advice, the unbelievable sum being named was one million dollars, tax free. Ruthie promptly insisted on joining Bette in London to accompany her to Rome should the impending appeal in the British courts come to nothing.

Bette received very different advice from her husband, who cabled her from his parents' home in Whitinsville, Massachusetts, on October 20: CLOCK IN STEEPLE STRIKES ONE. COME HOME. LOVE, HAM.

In further meetings with Bette and her representatives, Denton, Hall and Burgin assessed her as "anxious to return to work" but also "to find some concession that will save her from the humiliation of an unconditional return." In a report to Jack Warner, who had gone back to America in the interim, the attorneys noted that "gossip in the film world in London indicates that the defendant is receiving a consensus of advice to return."

"Either you work in California or you never work in this industry again," George Arliss told Bette (without letting on that he had come to see her at Warner's behest). "One road or the other—you've got to choose." And later, in an October 27 note to his former protégée, Arliss urged Bette to "review the thing dispassionately and choose the course that is likely to prove best for you in the long run."

"She promised me she'd come home!" a forlorn and angry Ham told Ruthie, whom he had come to see off in New York on the day she was to sail for England.

"What can you expect?" Ruthie replied. "It is a tempting offer."

To which Ham responded with grim silence.

They were standing on the dock—where Ruthie's car, its gasoline drained, was about to be hoisted aboard—when a crew member approached with a cable for Mrs. Davis.

Presuming it to be a Bon Voyage message from Bette, Ruthie was aghast to read instead: DON'T SAIL. COMING HOME. MEET ME IN NEW YORK. Speechless, she handed the cable to Ham. He joyously exclaimed, "I knew she couldn't do that! I knew it! I knew it!" as Ruthie went to see about having her car disengaged and the gas tank replenished.

That same day, Jack Warner's British lawyers wired him the news that Bette had accepted Arliss's advice to abandon her appeal and come back to work.

Appearing suddenly "very subdued and in a much more chastened spirit" (as the lawyers described her), Bette had arrived at the office of Denton, Hall and Burgin, where she was to be served with "an official sealed copy" of Mr. Justice Branson's injunction. Bette announced that although she had had "a good run for her money," she accepted that there was "no alternative for her but to return and perform her Agreement in accordance with its terms." She had booked passage on the *Aquitania* for November 4 and hoped to arrive in Hollywood by November 20, when she promised to report for work directly.

Still presumably "subdued and chastened," the actress did put forth several "mere suggestions"—as she now called them—intended for her and Warners' "mutual benefit." Upon her return, Bette persisted in hoping for better cameramen and scripts and a limit of four films a year.

The lawyers promised to convey Bette's suggestions to Jack Warner but not her renewed request for permission to do the occasional outside film (e.g., *I'll Take the Low Road*)—to which they responded with what they assured Warner had been their "strong objections" and warnings not to pursue the matter.

Nor could they be very encouraging when Bette asked if Warners might consider waiving their claim against her for court costs. And when Bette's lawyers mentioned "with some timidity" that it would be "very generous" if Warners would consider paying Bette's court costs as well, Denton, Hall and Burgin responded by calling it "a preposterous, even an impertinent suggestion," which they could scarcely consider mentioning to Jack Warner (although at length they reported it to him in detail, in a November 3, 1936, letter).

From the outset, the Warners camp recognized that the moneys she owed them—approximately two-thirds of their $14,683.71 legal bills—afforded the studio new leverage in its perpetual struggle to control her. The British lawyers informed Jack Warner of their suggestion to Bette that if all went well upon her return, the studio "might perhaps look favorably" upon her paying her debt in weekly installments deducted from her salary, rather than in a lump sum—the latter being beyond her means to accomplish, as she was known not yet to have finished paying her own legal bills.

In hopes of persuading the actress to come with him to Italy after all, Ludovico Toeplitz had offered to pay Sir William's fee; but—as Warners' British lawyers reported—Bette had declined the Italian's assistance, lest it put her under further obligation to him.

"I don't want to be misunderstood," Bette announced, shortly after arriving in New York, on November 11. "I don't want people to think I'm carrying the torch for downtrodden movie stars. That never entered my head. I'd hate to be a reformer."

She had come back to America, she told reporters who flocked to her suite at the Algonquin, "to serve five years in the Warner jail. . . . When I was a young thing and not very wise I signed the contract which ties me up until 1942. I'll be an old woman by 1942, but I'm going back and I'll be there in a week or so, and all I can say is the hell with it."

"The die is cast," Bette told reporters, upon arriving in Los Angeles with Ruthie aboard the Santa Fe Chief on November 18. "I'm just a working girl—not a crusader. 'Work, work, and more work,' is my motto from now on. No, there are no hard feelings. The law says

I have a contract which is inflexible until 1942. Whatever I am asked to do I shall willingly do. I am to have a conference at the studio within the next few days. No, there is no picture selected for me."

Puffing furiously on a cigarette, Bette drove off with her mother and Bobby, who had come to pick them up. The press corps was left behind to note that Warners' publicity people and the customary studio ballyhoo for a returning film star were conspicuously absent. They also were struck that Bette seemed exceptionally wan and emaciated. She had lost more than twenty pounds since last she had been seen in Los Angeles.

Despite the assurances Bette had received in London that upon her return to Burbank there would "be nothing in the nature of any recrimination or victimization" on the part of Jack Warner, who promised to let "bygones be bygones," she desperately feared the studio boss's quickly cutting her down to size with an endless succession of bad parts in bad films.

Bette's note announcing her readiness to return to work was hand-delivered to Jack Warner on November 20. He ordered her to report to Hal Wallis on Monday morning at eleven-thirty. At that time, after casting an appalled glance at her, the associate executive in charge of production promptly sent her home to put on at least ten pounds and await delivery of the new script he and Warner had been working on for her.

"Anything worth newspaper space is worth a picture," declared Warners' producer Lou Edelman, whose latest project, director Lloyd Bacon's *Marked Woman*, was said to reflect a much-publicized vice investigation in New York. It was long-standing Warners' policy to use newspaper headlines as a source of free film plots, which had the added advantage that audiences seemed to enjoy recognizing thinly disguised true stories on screen. In the spring of 1936, Special Prosecutor Thomas E. Dewey had convicted flamboyant racketeer Charles "Lucky" Luciano with the help of a group of prostitutes in the mobster's employ. This formed the basis for the terse, elliptical script Wallis sent over to Bette, whose own recent "headlines" (was she only imagining this?) it seemed somehow to reflect as well.

Like Bette, "clip joint hostess" Mary Dwight is outspoken and pugnacious, unafraid of talking back to her boss, dapper racketeer Johnny Vanning (based on Luciano—but also, perhaps, on Jack Warner, who could scarcely conceal the strong sense of identification he felt with the "tough guys" who populated his films). And like

Bette, Mary dreams of breaking free from a job from which there appears to be no escape. Finally, the only place left to do battle with Vanning is in court, where (as Bette had not) Mary takes the stand and wins against her cruel and exploitative boss.

Had another actress portrayed Mary Dwight, *Marked Woman* would have alluded solely to the Lucky Luciano case; but with Bette in the title role, the film inescapably suggested parallels to her own recent court case, about which all America had been reading for days, weeks, and months on end, and of which the on-screen events must have seemed a kind of distorted, dreamlike continuation.

As this was Bette's first film since returning from England, the image of the rebellious, "naughty young lady" depicted in countless newspaper articles fed into how people perceived the character of Mary Dwight. In turn, Mary Dwight infected the way Bette Davis would henceforth be regarded. Something of Mary's efficaciousness, and even her sense of moral outrage, rubbed off on Bette, who may have lost her court case in life but won it, gloriously, on-screen.

But even as Bette was establishing herself in the popular imagination as what one exultant Warners' executive dubbed "a female Cagney," the studio was quietly doing all it could to see to it that her tangle of debts emanating from the court case guaranteed that she behave herself. Jack Warner appeared to show sincere concern when, on January 6, 1937, Bette scrawled a nervous note imploring him to advance $14,000 against future salary, to cover the British legal bills, which she described as having caused her "tremendous worry for some time now." Six days later, Warner personally guaranteed a Bank of America loan in that amount, which the actress agreed to pay back in twenty $700 weekly installments (to be withheld from her salary). In private, however, Warner expressed glee at the indebtedness that would tie Bette to the studio all the more tightly when her share of Warners' legal bills came due.

"All this is entirely up to Miss Davis to pay," Warner told legal staffer R. W. Perkins. "We are going to exact from her the just costs of the case."

For all Warner's bluster with the boys, however, studio correspondence indicates that he feared asking Bette for the money, lest she revolt anew before completing the swift succession of four or more films he had already scheduled for her. Although Warner Bros. had wasted no time paying in full its British legal bills, Jack Warner asked Denton, Hall and Burgin to make a show of billing her directly, in order that—as Obringer explained to Perkins—"the onus of being harsh and cruel in the matter would be removed from us."

Much as the studio recognized that Bette was at this point "financially embarrassed," Obringer declared that as far as Warner Bros. was concerned, "this is her own problem."

"Bette Davis suffered a sunstroke which will keep her confined to a hospital in Carpinteria, California, for at least four weeks," Ham told reporters. He refused to say more about Bette's mysterious disappearance in August 1937, shortly after the studio reluctantly suspended her anew—on July 29—for failure to report to work on what was to have been her fifth film since her return from England in November.

Until now, Bette seemed to have mended her ways, appearing, as ordered, in four films in swift succession—*Marked Woman*, then Michael Curtiz's *Kid Galahad*, Edmund Goulding's *That Certain Woman*, and Archie Mayo's *It's Love I'm After*. As early as March, however, the actress had quietly resisted attending wardrobe fittings for the Goulding film. She had asked that they be postponed to give her time to recover after the punishing work schedule to which she had adhered since November, as well as from the lingering strain of her legal battle.

From La Quinta Hotel, in Indio, California, where she had fled for rest and seclusion, on March 18 Bette wired Hal Wallis her plea for a week off, lest overwork all too quickly transform her into "a jittery old woman." Anxious to show no weakness in the face of Bette's first small sign of recalcitrance since the court judgment, the studio agreed to give her only two days more. In response, on March 19 her attorney, Dudley Furse, notified Wallis that Bette's physician had ordered her to rest on account of low blood pressure and overall delicate health. Bette claimed to have damaged her health when, in an attempt to show a new attitude, she had pressed ahead to finish *Marked Woman* though stricken with the flu. According to Furse, the physician warned that if Bette refused (or was not allowed) to follow his advice and take to her bed immediately, he would "not be responsible for the consequences."

Although in due course Bette returned to work as ordered, by the time she had completed the Goulding and Mayo films that July she was down to 104 pounds. She was scarcely in condition to press on to yet another film, and in a desperate, rambling letter dated July 17, 1937, she begged Jack Warner to excuse her from the comedy *Hollywood Hotel*.

Ruthie had rented a beach house for them in Santa Barbara, where she intercepted all calls to her daughter, who, like Bobby before her, appeared to be suffering from a complete nervous collapse.

Besides overwork, crushing debt, and residual depression over her failed legal case, a number of other factors contributed to Bette's repining spirit: principal among them was dissatisfaction with a salary that, she never tired of reminding herself, would have been so much higher now had she accepted Jack Warner's June 1936 offer.

Interestingly, Warner appears to have recognized the beneficial effects that a well-deserved salary increase or cash bonus would have had on Bette at this juncture, but he feared changing so much as a comma in her current contract, let alone salary figures. "We are not permitted to make any changes, in any form, shape or manner in the contract," he had warned Obringer in the aftermath of the English ruling. "If we do, it means that we violated the judgment and all our work has been in vain."

Even more, studio records show Warner's immense trepidation about suspending Bette now that she had failed to report for work on *Hollywood Hotel*. This was scarcely out of concern for the actress's delicate mental state, however. As Bette seems never to have realized at the time, Warner Bros., for fear of raising the general issue of the Hollywood suspension clause, had technically waived its right to add time on to the end of her contract. And now, when a team of Warner Bros. lawyers studied the waiver Mr. Justice Branson had required, they could not determine whether the studio had waived its right to add time on to her contract solely for the June 19, 1936, suspension or for all subsequent suspensions as well, though most of the Warners' legal staff leaned toward the latter conclusion. Hence Jack Warner's anxiety that Bette or her attorneys would sniff the considerable advantage this legal ambiguity afforded her.

On July 29, when Bette's failure to report for work compelled Warner to demonstrate firmness by promptly suspending her, he quietly directed his legal staff to word the suspension notice as vaguely as possible, lest she or her advisers perceive the loophole that the British court case appeared to have opened.

Bette spent the rest of the summer in seclusion at Santa Barbara, where Ruthie (newly converted to Christian Science) read aloud to her for hours on end from Mary Baker Eddy's *Science and Health with Key to the Scriptures*. The readings, with their emphasis on spiritual healing, appeared to soothe the troubled movie star—but not enough, apparently, to prevent her from indulging in a bit of malice against her now happily married sister. Bobby had put her miserable past behind her and had recently embarked on a round-the-world cruise with her rich, handsome husband. Not long after Bette had agreed to report back to the studio to meet with director William Wyler in anticipation of working with him in *Jezebel*, the press discovered the isolated beach house where she and Ruthie had gone into hiding several weeks before. Bette now publicly disclosed the nervous collapse that Ruthie and Ham had initially been anxious to cover up, and—to her mother's horror—she disclosed something more: the hitherto carefully concealed history of mental illness that had plagued her sister. Bette claimed that the example of Bobby's past mental problems made her fear growing so ill herself that she might never work again.

"I'll give you just two weeks before you blow up and quit," Humphrey Bogart laughingly told Bette when he heard that she would be doing *Jezebel* with William Wyler. The director's obsessive attention to detail and fondness for multiple takes was notorious for having sent such leading ladies as Ruth Chatterton, Miriam Hopkins, and most famously, perhaps, Margaret Sullavan (whom Wyler later married and quickly divorced) into fits of rage against him.

With Bette, things did not turn out as Bogart predicted, however. For all her (equally notorious) quickness of temper, the twenty-nine-year-old actress seemed to find Wyler's compulsiveness soothing, reassuring: as if at long last she had found someone whose strange passion for order matched her own.

Aside from Bogart's warnings about Wyler, Bette had approached their first encounter in six years with considerable anxiety about whether Wyler would attempt to humiliate her again by bringing up the "chest dress." In Wyler's office at Warner Bros., when

several minutes passed with his seeming not to remember that they
had met before, something suddenly compelled Bette to bring up
precisely the subject that she had most wished to avoid; whereupon
Wyler's all-too-prompt apology for disparaging remarks he claimed
not to recall having made suggested that he, too, remembered the
incident but was anxious to put it behind them.

Wyler's own well-known tendency to brood over the most seemingly infinitesimal details may have allowed him to comprehend some
of Bette's demons as scarcely anyone besides Ruthie had done before.
Prone to work-related insomnia, stomachaches, and teeth grinding,
as well as to persistent fears that his errors as a director would be
preserved on celluloid, Wyler could empathize with Bette's lifelong
inability to expunge certain obsessive thoughts from her mind. Her
oft-repeated tale about her childhood experience of finding herself
unable to enjoy the circus after she had noticed a crooked seam down
the center of a carpet hardly seemed peculiar to a director whose
nickname, "Forty-Take" Wyler, hinted at the deeply ingrained, almost manic perfectionism that some observers mistook (frequently
with Wyler's encouragement) for simple insecurity.

"When he can't get a scene exactly as he wants it, he almost loses
his mind," Bette said approvingly to a reporter who had come to
interview her on the set of *Jezebel*. Not surprisingly, called upon to
characterize Wyler's directorial skills, Bette used a metaphor that
summoned up images of cleaning and ordering: "You have the feeling
that at the end he'll have everything strung out in just the order and
sequence they should be," said Bette, hanging imaginary clothes on
an air line as the reporter watched in apparent bafflement.

By contrast with the actors who found Wyler's methods maddening, Bette responded much as she had to the endless hours of
posing for Ruthie's pictorialist camera portraits in New York, sixteen
years before: the repetition temporarily allayed her fears about things
suddenly spinning out of control.

"In the pictures she did at Warners prior to *Jezebel*, Bette had
tremendous energy and a striking personality, but I don't think she
was a terribly good actress," says director Vincent Sherman. "It was
Willy Wyler who taught her something about films and film acting
that she hadn't realized before: that the most effective moments in a
film were the silent moments."

"At that point Bette did not yet consider herself a successful
actress," explains the director's widow, Talli Wyler. "She knew how

much she didn't know. Therefore she was much more malleable and open to guidance than she would have been later in her career."

And says Bette's friend, actress Dori Brenner: "Wyler demanded things of her as an actress, and that to Bette was very attractive."

So attractive that before long it was no secret at Warner Bros. that Bette had embarked on an extramarital affair with her (then single) director, whom co-workers observed on more than one occasion slipping out of her dressing room, his face smeared with lipstick from her kisses.

Interoffice memoranda show that as early as 1935, Hal Wallis had considered Owen Davis's Broadway play (which had featured Miriam Hopkins as the perversely obstinate Julie Marsden) as a potential vehicle for Bette Davis. But when Wallis's executive assistant, Walter MacEwen, read *Jezebel*, he declared that while Bette could undoubtedly "play the spots off the part of a little bitch of an aristocratic Southern girl," Julie's character was far too unsympathetic to appeal to audiences. "Maybe I'm a Pollyanna," MacEwen told Wallis, "but I suspect that box office history . . . would prove that audiences prefer to sympathize with their leading characters. . . . In other words, while Bette Davis receives acclaim for nasty supporting roles, I doubt if a picture built solely around her in an unsympathetic part would be so well liked."

The consensus at the studio seemed little different two years later when, in an unabashed effort to cash in on the ballyhoo surrounding David Selznick's search for an actress to play Scarlett O'Hara in the film version of *Gone With the Wind*, Warner Bros. finally purchased the rights to *Jezebel*, whose female protagonist once again struck most people Wallis showed the project to as hopelessly unsympathetic. In a detailed six-page memo to Wallis, director Edmund Goulding warned that while Bette Davis would be more likely than most other actresses to win public acceptance in so negative a role, audiences would nonetheless have immense difficulty identifying with her character.

Unlike Goulding and the others, Wyler seemed to have no such problems with Julie Marsden when Warner Bros. borrowed him from Samuel Goldwyn to direct *Jezebel* (although at length he did appoint his friend John Huston to "represent" him in the rewrites he deemed necessary in the last half of Abem Finkel and Clements Ripley's screenplay, where Julie's character experiences a "regeneration through suffering"). Wyler's troubles on the picture came later, as Wallis and company repeatedly balked at the seemingly languorous pace necessary to achieve what unit manager Bob Fellows described as Wyler's "screwy shots." Fellows's production reports to studio manager Tenny Wright formed a litany of complaint against Wyler's multiple takes and endless hours of rehearsal.

"Is this possible?" Hal Wallis would ask in bewilderment after an entire day produced only a single shot. Wallis was anxious to speed up the production to allow Bette's co-star Henry Fonda (as her fiancé, Pres Dillard) to finish in time to return to New York, where his wife, Frances, was due to give birth in late December. By prior agreement, Fonda would be available for a maximum of eight weeks, so from the first Wyler was working with a time lock. But Wyler's differences with his hosts at Warner Bros. cut deeper: At an economy-minded studio, which prided itself on making fast-paced films at a fast pace, "Forty-Take" Wyler could only have seemed an exotic and incomprehensible creature.

Two days during the second week of shooting, Thursday and Friday, November 4 and 5, serve to suggest the kind of meticulous work Wyler did with Bette and its cost: a single intricate sequence that, according to studio records, put the production an entire day behind schedule. The sequence occurs inside Julie's home in New Orleans, where she has just arrived late for a party in honor of her forthcoming marriage. (The preceding exterior shot, in which she catches the train of her riding habit with her crop and sweeps it up over the shoulder with a Fulleresque ripple of voluminous fabric, would be filmed much later). In the script, Julie's last-minute decision to shock everyone by wearing her riding habit to the party prefigures the decision that brings about her ruin: wearing a red gown to the Olympus Ball; but equally indicative of character is the camera movement through the party that Wyler and cameraman Ernest Haller devised to show how the willful and "imperious" Julie (as the script describes her) has always successfully pushed her way through life—until now.

Before she sweeps into the drawing room, however, Wyler lingers characteristically on the brief anticipatory scene in the script, where Julie is said to "toss" her riding crop to the butler, Uncle Cato, as she hurries through the entrance hall. As in the sequence in Mme. Poulard's fitting room, Wyler is concerned with giving greater clarity and exactness to Bette's motions so that they do not all simply blur into one another. Whereas Hal Wallis undoubtedly would have had his director shoot this small, seemingly inconsequential linking scene as briskly as Julie is supposed to pass through it, Wyler does something that Bette seemed not to have experienced at Warner Bros. before. He articulates her motions by situating them in relation to surrounding architectural details as she traverses a series of three interior frames, her pace measured by contrast with that of the butler struggling to catch up from behind. First there is the front doorway, then the entrance hall's curtained archway, and finally (as Haller's camera pulls back to reveal) the column beside which she pauses, half turns, and steps back slightly to hand the riding crop to the butler. All this Wyler shot nine times (a single error of timing could ruin the entire take), with what he perceived as the collateral benefit of slowing Bette down in order to make her performance more various.

Constantly stopping and starting her like this is part of what gives the whole whirlwind sequence a kind of dance rhythm. Hardly has she handed Uncle Cato the riding crop and plunged forward when she abruptly stops again, this time at the entrance to the drawing room, a fourth interior frame. The pause is accentuated by a cut to a closer camera position of her back as—arms extended, elbows flexed, fingers curled into palms—she boldly greets the crowd who stare in astonishment at her riding habit.

"Terribly sorry to be late," she says, twisting her torso from side to side, her fingers opening exuberantly as she adds, "I had trouble with the colt."

This opening of the fingers timed to coincide with her second sentence may seem a small bit of business, especially since it all takes place so quickly (and so much happens immediately afterward) that we may scarcely have registered it; but it is with precisely such subtle effects that Bette and her director create their vivid portrait of Julie Marsden.

"The most powerful of all gestures is that which affects the spectator without his knowing it," Delsarte is supposed to have said: a cherished notion for Isadora Duncan, Ruth St. Denis, and those other exponents of interpretive dance from whom Bette had absorbed much of her gestural vocabulary long before she came to Hollywood. During the making of *Jezebel*, Wyler would try to strip away all the unnecessary business that he called Bette's "mannerisms" (once he even threatened to put a chain around her neck to stop her head from bobbing with nervous energy), in order that each of her remaining gestures serve as a forceful expression of character.

Davis is particularly effective as she dashes from guest to guest in the drawing room, especially in the deft passage where Julie struggles to explain her costume to a pair of staring harpies, Mrs. Kendrick and Mrs. Petion. Their disapproval is clearly communicated in the grimness of their countenances. Although neither woman utters a word against her so long as she is with them, the strong subtext of censure visibly affects Julie's body as her hands suddenly slip below frame, so that even as she jabbers on politely to the ladies, her agitation throbs in off-screen space, in the frenzied, as yet mysterious activities of her hands: gestures felt all the more deeply for their remaining mostly unseen. Only when Julie's right hand nervously tugs the bunched train of her riding habit over her shoulder do we reconstruct her left hand's having just gathered up the fabric before placing it in her right; but by then Julie has greeted her friend Molly beyond the two ladies and swept out of frame suddenly to meet her, leaving only Mrs. Kendrick and Mrs. Petion to vent their outrage as the camera lingers on them just long enough to frustrate our curiosity about where Julie has gone.

Continuing the single, serpentine long take, whose complicated blocking and reframing required Wyler to shoot it twelve times, the camera catches up with Julie, whom Molly is wishing all the best in marriage, as the bride-to-be nervously fiddles with the elaborate lace collar of her friend's dress. We find ourselves scarcely paying attention to Molly's words, so enthralled are we by Julie's strangeness of gesture (and the barely submerged fears and emotions it suggests). Apparently drawing on Bette's own lifelong tendency to express inner feelings of restlessness through compulsive straightening, rearranging, and touching, she and Wyler give Julie Marsden an abundance of such psychologically revealing movements throughout the film.

▲

"I can't bear my face," Bette was heard to utter in horror after watching rushes for *Jezebel*. "I can't stand it!"

Although it is barely visible in the finished film, a rather large pimple that erupted on Bette's face in late November was the subject of immense agitation on the set of *Jezebel*, where work was impeded for approximately a week and a half on its account. On November 26, Bob Fellows reported that Dr. Franklyn Ball, a Hollywood dermatologist, had been summoned to examine the pimple, which the unit manager described to his superiors as "pretty swollen." In the days that followed, further memoranda indicated that Bette's pimple had left Wyler "unable to make any close-ups" of her; as well as the determination that makeup not be applied until her face had had a chance to "heal over properly."

All of which would seem hardly worth mentioning now were it not for the production's being thirteen and a half days beyond schedule, making it increasingly unlikely that Wyler would be finished with Henry Fonda in time for the actor's scheduled departure on December 18. There were already whisperings about Warner Bros. that Wallis was seriously thinking of replacing Wyler with a more efficient director.

Since Wallis and his staff openly and unanimously blamed Wyler for the production's tardiness, they were not amused when, with a scant two weeks left to finish up with Fonda, the director insisted on shooting a two-page scene involving only Bette and George Brent, as Buck Cantrell, Pres's erstwhile rival for Julie's affections. In this scene, Julie incites Buck against Pres, who has startled everyone by returning from New York with his new wife, Amy (whom he has secretly married in the year since the Olympus Ball). The unit manager fired off a report blasting Wyler for wasting time with material that could have been postponed until after Fonda's departure. But even with the loss of his male star looming days ahead, Wyler was clearly far more concerned with the nuances of Bette's performance, which he believed he could best serve by filming the scene now in order to sustain the emotional line built up in related scenes she had just completed with Fonda.

Wyler may also have sensed the disastrous effects that too much wildly discontinuous shooting (and the abrupt and violent emotional transitions that went with it) might have on Bette's already overwrought nerves. Besides her pimple, a variety of ailments, including involuntary contractions of the leg muscle that reportedly made it "very difficult for her to walk," all seemed to attest to Bette's intensely agitated state of mind during the making of *Jezebel*. Indeed, after Fonda left to join his wife in New York (Wyler's having finished with him a day ahead of schedule, as it turned out), Bette was recorded to have suffered a hysterical fit when repeatedly called upon to shoot substantially out of continuity.

To judge by Bette's correspondence in this period, a major source of upset was guilt over her extramarital affair. On several occasions she refused to allow Wyler to drive her home on his motorcycle, lest her husband suspect what was going on between them. Although their liaison was certainly no secret at Warner Bros., Bette managed to conceal it from Ham, whose blind devotion had nonetheless come to repel and sicken her to the point that she could scarcely bear to be alone with him anymore. Far from looking forward to time off for Christmas and New Year's Day, Bette dreaded the thought of separation from Wyler. His presence had become such a necessity for her that on the pretext of watching him work, she regularly came to the set to be with him even when the scene he was directing didn't include her.

But she was at home on Franklin Avenue with Ham on New Year's Day when word came from Ruthie's sister, Mildred, that Bette's fifty-two-year-old father, Harlow Morrell Davis, had suffered a fatal heart attack at the home he shared with his wife, Minnie Stewart Davis. For her part, Bette had never publicly acknowledged Minnie's existence, telling her best friend, Robin Brown, that Harlow's relationship with his former nurse and mistress had been merely "a marriage of convenience," as Bette privately insisted on calling it. Since her visit to Boston in the spring of 1936 after winning an Academy Award for *Dangerous*, Bette had been acutely aware of Harlow's precarious physical condition following his first heart attack, in 1935.

And then, at the end of the first week of shooting on *Jezebel*, news of a second massive heart attack had come through Ruthie, who was still regularly collecting her monthly $200 checks from Harlow. Thus Bette's father was almost certainly much in her thoughts throughout the making of *Jezebel*—and, concurrently, her affair with Wyler, in which her betrayal of sweet, unsuspecting Ham seemed to recapitulate Harlow's betrayal of Ruthie so many years before. Harlow continued under the care of Boston physician Dr. George Lynch until his death at 6:00 A.M. on New Year's Day.

For Bette, there could be no question of attending her father's funeral, as *Jezebel* was already desperately behind schedule.

On January 3, 1938, Bette's father was cremated at Mount Auburn Cemetery in Cambridge. Minnie shipped his ashes to Augusta, Maine, where the frozen ground prohibited burial in the Davis family plot until April.

"What the hell is the matter with him anyhow—is he absolutely daffy?" asked Hal Wallis, upon learning that on January 6, Wyler had done sixteen takes of the shot in which Julie learns that Pres is to return from New York, where he has spent the year since breaking their engagement.

By this point, the production was twenty-four days behind schedule. Following her father's death, Bette had returned to Warner Bros. to discover that Wyler was quite possibly about to be replaced by William Dieterle. That the rumor was rampant concerning Dieterle's imminent takeover is suggested by a January 4 memo from unit manager Fellows, eagerly requesting concrete information about "if and when" Dieterle was due to arrive on the *Jezebel* set.

Although Wyler had repeatedly promised Wallis to work more quickly, his sixteen takes of Julie descending a staircase to hear from Aunt Belle that Pres is finally coming home made Wallis question the director's sincerity.

"Doesn't this man know that we have close-ups to break up a scene of this kind?" asked Wallis. "And with all of the care he used in making the close-ups, certainly he must expect that we would use the greater portion of the scene in close-up."

This takes us to the heart of Wyler's conflict with Warner Bros. about filmmaking and, even more, about how properly to use Bette Davis on-screen: something he passionately believed her studio had not done until now.

Whereas Hal Wallis would have him "break up" the scene with close-ups, Wyler more generously uses the long take to allow us to watch Bette change physically as powerful emotions slowly, visibly surge through her body in reaction to the glorious news about Pres: a kind of fluid, wavelike movement passing from one body part to another, which Bette would have learned to call a "succession" when she studied at Mariarden in 1925.

"This is the greatest order of movement for the expression of emotion," said Ted Shawn of the succession, "and the introduction into dance of this discovery by Delsarte was one of the major forces toward forming the type of dance called American modern."

The shot that caused Wallis to speculate whether Wyler might be "absolutely daffy" takes place in the hallway at Julie's house in New Orleans. In the course of urging Aunt Belle to leave for the country with Julie to escape the threat of yellow fever in town, Dr. Livingstone (Donald Crisp) has informed her that Pres is returning to New Orleans to argue publicly for health measures to prevent an epidemic. As Aunt Belle shows the doctor out, she pauses at a table arrayed with flowers, while Livingstone proceeds to the front door, where—in an exceptionally fine touch—Uncle Cato suddenly sweeps into frame to get the doctor's hat and walking stick. While he does, we watch Aunt Belle look to the left, then to the right, as the camera seems to follow her gaze (and the rightward swing of the opening front door) to the staircase, where Julie will be coming down any moment, even as the doctor departs and the butler closes the door in what is now off-screen space.

All of this graceful and carefully choreographed movement has prepared us for Julie's entrance, as we wait to see quite how Aunt Belle will tell her about Pres and—more important—how Julie will react: the momentum of the long take serving to build up dramatic tension.

By contrast with the gliding movements that precede it in the shot, Julie's descent seems languid, lackadaisical; her body is uncharacteristically lifeless as she drags her hand along the banister, then fiddles with her sleeve a bit, before twining her fingers together as she passes Aunt Belle, who watches her from beside the table.

Only when Julie is partway down the hall (just after Uncle Cato passes behind her) does Aunt Belle finally tell her the news: at which Julie stops with a sudden small backward whipping motion of the right shoulder, in keeping with the classic Delsartean principle that the shoulder is the "thermometer of passion and sensibility," moving automatically and involuntarily whenever we are stirred or agitated. Then, after a tense pause, the wave of emotion seems to rouse her head and left shoulder, before pulsing visibly into her sternum and her arms.

Until this point we have been watching Julie grasp the news emotionally, hence corporeally; only now, when she speaks the words given in the script, "Pres is coming," does she seem to grasp it intellectually as well, as the fluid movement finally passes into her fingers, causing them to unknit and spring to animated life again.

Another beat, as Julie casts a backward glance at Aunt Belle, then shows her profile to the camera and says, "Of course." This use of the profile was a deft bit of stage business Bette probably acquired from watching Katharine Cornell, who was famous for it on Broadway.

▲▼▲

"Bette was as innocent and naive as a child," recalls her friend from Warner Bros. days, actress Geraldine Fitzgerald.

So innocent that, for a time, she seems to have convinced herself that her on-the-set romance with Willy Wyler during the making of *Jezebel* was something a good deal more serious than the pleasant "fling" he quite openly considered it to be. Attracted to strong-willed women as Wyler undeniably was, he made no secret about his antipathy toward ever marrying another movie star after his turbulent union with Margaret Sullavan.

In mid-January, as their work together on the film drew to a close (Wyler having withstood Wallis's threat of replacing him with William Dieterle), Bette, whatever hopes she may have been harboring, must have realized that her daily contact with Wyler was coming to an end as well. Although in recent weeks she and Wyler had talked endlessly about his directing her in the role of Cathy in a film version of Emily Brontë's *Wuthering Heights*, the chances of Jack Warner's acquiring the Ben Hecht–Charles MacArthur script for her, or of his allowing her to do it for Samuel Goldwyn (should Goldwyn want her), seemed increasingly remote. Indeed, Bette's worst fears were realized before long when she learned that Goldwyn, not Warner, had acquired the script, with Wyler scheduled to direct Merle Oberon as Cathy. This left Bette unhappily to fend for herself again at Warners, while Wyler went on to a project that would no doubt challenge and engross him even without Bette in the starring role.

The final day of shooting was set for Saturday, January 15, after which—as part of a deal to stay on as director—Wyler had agreed to work without salary. Whereas until this point Bette had done whatever she could to help Wyler get through the picture, now suddenly at the last minute she fell ill. She refused to do a simple shot with George Brent, on the grounds that she feared coming down with a bad cold, but it was being quietly said on the set that Bette just wanted to hold on to Wyler a little longer.

Unknown and unsuspected at the time was that on Monday, January 17, 1938, when Wyler finally finished shooting *Jezebel*, twenty-eight days over schedule, Bette was pregnant with Wyler's child.

THIRTEEN

"In each of her eyes sat a devil," wrote Charlotte Brontë after seeing the legendary French actress Rachel. "These evil forces bore her through the tragedy, kept up her feeble strength—for she is but a frail creature. Hate and murder and madness incarnate she stood. It was a marvelous sight, a mighty revelation."

Following *Jezebel*, Bette wrote to Jack Warner asking him to allow her to star in a film about the life of this most celebrated of Delsarte's pupils, whom critic James Agate called "by common consent the most awe-inspiring actress of all time."

Instead, on Monday, January 25, a week after she completed principal photography on *Jezebel*, Hal Wallis sent her the script for Busby Berkeley's *Comet over Broadway*, with instructions to report for work the following Monday. Bette took umbrage at an assignment which seemed to suggest that in spite of *Jezebel*, Warner Bros. intended to proceed as in the past: rushing her from one ill-suited project to the next.

On Bette's instructions, attorney Dudley Furse wrote Warner to complain of the Wyler film's having been "an unusually strenuous assignment." Beginning a new role immediately thereafter would be "much too strenuous a program for her to undertake," particularly when Bette could not be said "to have completely recovered from the possibilities of relapse or recurrence" of the nervous debility that had stricken her in August.

Bette's physician concurred that the actress was "in no condition to start in a picture in the near future." When he called the studio on January 29, Dr. Noys declared himself "absolutely amazed that she got through the last picture, as her condition does not warrant the nervous strain she undergoes in the making of pictures." Should Warners "rush" his patient into *Comet over Broadway*, he warned, "she would be in danger of collapse and naturally that would result in loss and expense" to the studio.

Although Wallis finally agreed to give Bette a six-week unpaid "rest period," for the moment he and Jack Warner stood firm on the Busby Berkeley assignment, even when she wrote to point out that Warners already had a script on Rachel—by Jean Negulesco—in-house.

The end of her relationship with Willy Wyler; the abortion she had had soon after they finished filming *Jezebel;* the pressure of concealing both the affair and the pregnancy from Ham; and now renewed conflict with the studio—all made this a difficult interlude for Bette, who fled again to La Quinta Hotel in Indio, in hopes of reviving her spirits.

"I believe we are getting the well-known run-around," production manager Tenny Wright told Hal Wallis on March 28, when, having returned from her "rest period," Bette failed to arrive for scheduled costume fittings for *Comet over Broadway*. It can hardly have been coincidental that on the same day, Bette had appeared on the cover of *Time* magazine: "Popeye the Magnificent," they dubbed her, a reference to her odd exophthalmic eyes.

Bette may have expected the *Time* cover to strengthen her bargaining position at the studio, but the next day, March 29, Wallis suspended her. For nearly a month the actress remained out of sight, celebrating her thirtieth birthday, on April 5, with Ruthie and Bobby —and four servants—at her capacious new Spanish-style house at 1700 Coldwater Canyon in Beverly Hills. Even as Jack and Ann Warner were wiring their "sincere wishes" on Bette's birthday, the studio was quietly preparing an appeal to the Screen Actors Guild to intervene on its behalf against the wayward actress, who had rejected yet another Busby Berkeley project—*Garden of the Moon*—that Wallis had sent her.

And so it went, back and forth and around, until finally, when the Screen Actors Guild refused to get in the middle, Warners held out the tantalizing possibility of new salary negotiations, if only she would agree to come back to work in director Anatole Litvak's *The Sisters*—which would serve as a stopgap while screenwriter Casey Robinson adapted the play *Dark Victory* (in which Tallulah Bankhead had starred on Broadway) as a vehicle for Bette.

By contrast with the fragile truce Bette forged with her studio, all-out war raged at home, where, according to Ham's December 6, 1938, divorce complaint, his every attempt at normal conjugal relations caused Bette to become "enraged" and to lash out at him with an "array of epithets and derision." Where once they had enjoyed a vigorous sex life, in recent months she had been "inattentive and distant" to him, to the point of "humiliation." When he attempted to make love to her, she would coolly declare that she was too tired or that she preferred to read. Nor, according to Ham, had she spared his feelings in front of others. On numerous occasions when he brought home business associates from the Rockwell-O'Keefe talent agency, where he worked as a musicians' representative, Ham experienced more "embarrassment and humiliation" as Bette appeared to do everything she could to make his guests "uncomfortable and unwelcome."

Anxious as she may have been to end this marriage to a boy whom she had so clearly outgrown, Bette remained unwilling to assume responsibility for all that was happening between them. Hence, it would seem, her repeated attempts to provoke him, to make him lash out at her or even to drive him away, to cause him to be the one who finally broke things off. Instead, when he refused to answer her taunts, when he waited half the night for her to appear for dinners long grown cold, and when he steadfastly declined to speak ill of her to his friends or hers, Bette abused and tormented him all the more, as if to punish him for failing to comprehend how bad she really was.

Perhaps it was a mercy that Ham seemed never to recognize one of the worst public humiliations to which Bette subjected him. On July 4, 1938, with a seeming warmth and affection that she had scarcely shown in months, Bette presented Ham with what was to be her final birthday present to him. He happily interpreted the gift as a signal of a welcome turnaround in their stormy relationship. Ham experienced a pang at how much Bette had spent on his extravagant birthday surprise—a motorcycle and leather helmet. Bette had lately, inexplicably, discouraged Ham from visiting or coming for her at Warners, so he was in ecstasies of delight when she insisted that he come to the studio as soon as possible to show off the dashing new bike to her co-workers. Oblivious of Bette's liaison with Wyler as he remained, Ham had no inkling of the gratuitous cruelty of the birthday gift, or of her heartlessness in encouraging the cuckolded husband to ride about the Warners lot on a bike that, to all who observed him, would instantly, inevitably call to mind Willy Wyler's motorcycle on which Bette had often ridden during their affair.

For all Ham's fond hopes, Bette had no intention of healing the rift between them. Even as she was photographing her husband posed ebulliently beside his new motorcycle the day he visited Burbank, Bette's thoughts were filled with another man, whom she hadn't even met yet. With Bobby and Ruthie, both of whom had been well aware of the liaison with Wyler, Bette could speak of nothing but the prospect of meeting daredevil aviator and tycoon Howard Hughes, whom she had invited as guest of honor to the dog welfare fund-raiser she was hosting at the Beverly Hills Hotel on August 11. Hughes had already set several air speed records when, on July 10, 1938, taking off from Floyd Bennett Field in a twin-engine Lockheed 14, he set a new round-the-world flight record of 91 hours, 14 minutes, 28 seconds. The hero returned to a ticker-tape parade in New York, a congressional medal in Washington—and Bette Davis's Tailwagger's Ball in Los Angeles.

Davis had been named president of the Tailwagger's Club, a southern California dog-lovers' organization, in the spring. Assisted by Bobby, who attended to most of the detail work, the actress had devoted months to organizing the August gala to benefit stray dogs and the training of Seeing Eye dogs. With a lack of sophistication that set them apart from much of Hollywood, Bette and Bobby planned an assortment of childish games, including musical chairs and a dance event in which the gentleman found his partner by rolling a large ball across the polished ballroom floor and waiting to see which of the ladies' feet it hit first.

In order to stand out from the crowd of other actresses in attendance, including Lili Damita, Mary Pickford, Norma Shearer, Jean

Parker, and Lupe Velez, Bette decided to come "in costume": an elaborate lacy ball gown reminiscent of one she had worn in *Jezebel*. Although she seemed not to realize it, Bette's position as front-runner for Best Actress at the Academy Awards for her portrayal of Julie Marsden made her a likely target for Howard Hughes, notorious for his penchant for brief, mostly frivolous affairs with the hottest actresses of the moment, whoever they might be. Hughes's quite serious, and much publicized, liaison with Katharine Hepburn was a notable exception to this pattern. Bette may have been thinking of the rival Yankee dame when, upon finally meeting Hughes at the Beverly Hills Hotel that August, she wildly overreacted to his standard overtures. She misinterpreted his routine seduction as an invitation to something considerably more serious and long-lasting than the well-known Hollywood Lothario seemed to have had in mind. Bette's nagging insecurity about her sexuality and physical appearance was such that she later confessed to having been "flattered" when, disregarding her status as a married woman, Hughes made no particular secret of asking to see her again after the Tailwagger's Ball.

Soon after meeting him, Bette dragged the slightly bewildered tycoon to meet her mother, who enthusiastically declared Hughes a far more appropriate match than Ham Nelson had been. It must have seemed a lifetime ago to Ruthie that she was the last and only adult in her family not to know that Harlow had taken a mistress. Instead of being compassionate to Ham because of her own experience, she appears to have taken perverse pleasure in her daughter's extramarital affairs and, especially, the betrayed husband's obliviousness.

Where Bette had prevented Ham from discovering the liaison with Wyler, now she conducted her affair with Howard Hughes practically in front of her still adoring husband. Yet something in Ham compelled him to ignore all that was happening, even when, as detailed in his December 6 divorce complaint, friends and business associates had begun to ask "embarrassing" questions about the "stability" of his marriage. Finally, however, when it was reported on the radio that Bette Davis was about to marry an as yet unspecified "millionaire," even Ham could no longer deny his wife's unfaithfulness.

▲▼▲

In an effort to patch things up with Bette, Ham had arranged to go on vacation with her to New York at the end of August. Perhaps it would help to remove her from the pressures of Hollywood and from Ruthie and Bobby. But when he told her his big plans, he recalled, Bette responded with the announcement that "she preferred to be with her sister or her mother." According to the divorce papers, soon afterward Bette "departed with her sister," without so much as a word to Ham about how long they might be gone or where he might reach them.

Before she and Bobby slipped off to Glenbrook, Nevada, while the disgruntled Ham went to New York alone, Bette had finally signed a new contract with Warners, on August 17, which added to the exhilaration she already felt on account of Hughes's attentions. Although Bette seemed scarcely to have realized it at the time, or to have cared, in the end the new contract offered little besides more money. Studio records show that as late as July 7, Bette's camp had been pressing for a three-picture yearly limit, story approval, and the right to do one outside project a year in the final two years of the new contract. By August, however, to the evident stupefaction of Roy Obringer and other Warner Bros. executives, Bette, anxious to get a fresh contract signed, was suddenly content to accept a weekly salary of $3,500 (effective as soon as she started *Dark Victory*) and a release from her remaining $5,000 debt for Warners' 1936 British court costs.

All that remained, apparently, for Bette to start a new chapter in her life was to banish Ham from Coldwater Canyon once and for all. As the divorce records indicate, when she and Bobby returned from Nevada, she asked Ham "to leave her alone with her work and her family"—and, she assumed, with Howard Hughes. Bette had persistently blocked Hughes's dissolute reputation from her thoughts. She told herself that however many actresses he had been with before, she was "special." This made it all the more painful when, having driven her husband to move in with a colleague from Rockwell-O'Keefe, Bette did not hear from Hughes that September. To her mortification, Hughes evidently had lost interest in her less than a month after they met.

Already frantic over Hughes's desertion, Bette grew further agitated when she heard that Willy Wyler was back in town. The director had spent the summer in Europe, where he had gone to persuade Laurence Olivier to accept the role of Heathcliff in *Wuthering Heights*, after which he had taken off for a month of waterskiing in the south of France. In Los Angeles that September, Wyler met and quickly fell in love with the young actress Margaret Tallichet, a dark-haired beauty from Dallas. After her humiliating affair with Hughes, this was the last news Davis needed to hear.

"I am sure that Miss Davis is much happier than she has been since she returned from England," Roy Obringer crowed to Warners' New York legal office, in anticipation of her starting work on *Dark Victory*, her first picture under the new contract. "While it is true in this business that you do not know at what moment these temperamental people will fly off the handle, I have every reason to believe that we will go along on rather peaceful terms with Miss Davis for some time."

"That's Bette sitting over there," director Edmund Goulding told Geraldine Fitzgerald, on Thursday, October 6, 1938, Bette's first day on the set of *Dark Victory*.

When the young Irish actress, who had appeared at the Dublin Gate Theatre and in Orson Welles's Mercury Theatre, looked up, Bette seemed so unnaturally still and silent, it was almost as if she had "turned to stone."

"She's very unhappy," Goulding continued. "Her husband has just served her with divorce papers. Why don't you go and tell her an Irish joke?"

"I couldn't," said Fitzgerald. "I don't know her. I've never met her."

"Please. She's so upset. We don't know if she's even going to be able to work. Please try."

To oblige Goulding, Fitzgerald hesitantly approached the actress, whose secretary and best friend she was set to play in *Dark Victory*.

"Who are you?" said Bette.

"My name is Geraldine Fitzgerald, and I'm going to play Ann."

"Oh."

"Eddie Goulding told me to come over and tell you an Irish joke."

"What?"

"Well, Eddie says that he thinks you're a bit unhappy today and that you'd like to hear an Irish joke. I'm not at all sure he's right."

"All right," Bette said, after a long, ominous silence. "Go ahead. If you have an Irish joke, tell it."

"Well," Fitzgerald began slowly, "this is a joke my grandmother told to warn me that men are unreliable. A farmer's wife was chatting away to her crony, and this is what she said: 'You can't rely on men at all! You can't, you can't. You can't depend on them at all! Just the other day when my husband came in from the field, I put his stew down in front of him—and he pushed it away! So I took the bowl and I brought it out to the half-door, and I took out the mouse that was in the stew and I threw it out into the backyard. And then I brought back the bowl to my husband and put it down on the table in front of him—and he pushed it away again! You see, that's men all over. He wouldn't have it with the mouse in it, and he wouldn't have it with the mouse out of it!' "

At which Bette emitted a great shriek of laughter: signal to Goulding that she was ready to begin.

On Broadway, in November of 1934, *Dark Victory* had been widely regarded as little more than a "made-to-order vehicle" for Tallulah Bankhead. Her appearance as the doomed "Long Island playgirl and horsewoman" Judith Traherne was what the *New York World-Telegram*'s Robert Garland called the sole "reason for its being"; while Percy Hammond, in the *New York Herald Tribune*, recommended it as "an admirable utensil for its star's shiny technique"—replete with a good deal of "eloquent shivering" when Tallulah's "spoiled darling of Bridgehampton" learns she is going to die.

Two months later, in January, calling *Dark Victory* "the best modern woman's vehicle, potentially, I've read since *A Bill of Divorcement*," David Selznick wrote to urge Greta Garbo to consider portraying Judith Traherne on-screen (with a script by Philip Barry and direction by George Cukor) before she undertook a planned film version of *Anna Karenina*. Nothing came of Selznick's proposal, and exactly a year later, at Warners, Hal Wallis's executive assistant, Walter MacEwen, endeavored to acquire the rights from Selznick—this time as a Kay Francis vehicle, to be scripted by Casey Robinson. Since then, however, in the aftermath of *Jezebel*, Bette had displaced Francis as—in Roy Obringer's words—"our top rank female artist."

On September 26, 1938, less than two weeks before she reported for work on *Dark Victory*, when Bette learned that Kay Francis would be leaving Warners directly, she instructed attorney Oscar Cummins to press for the rival actress's "dressing room"—actually, a two-story cottage—as unequivocal symbol of her ascension.

Goulding and others in the *Dark Victory* company quickly recognized that Bette was decidedly apprehensive as she began work on her next major film. She was thrilled with Casey Robinson's screenplay about the terminally ill Judith Traherne and the handsome Dr. Steele, whose love transforms her before she dies, but the more she studied it, the more she wondered whether she would be able to do justice to the role. Robinson shaped his screenplay by giving it an exceptionally strong transformational arc as Judith passes from being a shallow, spoiled society girl, terrified of what the future may bring, to a woman of admirable strength, fortitude, and emotional depth.

It struck Bette that in its simplicity of line, this was a very different sort of transformation from the one she had so brilliantly enacted in *Jezebel*. As the *Jezebel* screenplay clearly suggests, in the film's final moments there is a strong element of duplicity in Julie Marsden's purported regeneration as she convinces Amy to allow her to accompany the dying Pres to the leper island. When Amy asks Julie to confirm that it is his wife whom Pres loves, the screenplay indicates that in the guise of being noble, Julie responds with a convenient lie, uttering the words of reassurance Amy "wants to believe." In the film, Davis adds immeasurably to the moment by refusing to make it too clear that she is lying. When Julie concedes to Amy, "We both know—Pres loves his wife," Bette leaves us uncertain whether or not she is telling the truth as she sees it. The actress discovered no such intriguing duplicity or ambiguity in Judith Traherne's metamorphosis in *Dark Victory*. Casey Robinson's considerably less subtle screenplay required her to show the beats by which Judith is transformed into the fine, courageous figure whom Bette intermittently despaired of being able to portray convincingly onscreen because, quite simply, she feared the ennobled Judith was so entirely unlike herself.

An unusually candid letter that Bette wrote to Teddy Newton, an actor she and Robin had first known in New York, discloses the intense feelings of self-loathing and doubt that tormented her during the filming of *Dark Victory*. In the course of four handwritten pages, Bette details the paralyzing guilt she feels about her admittedly cruel treatment of Ham. For the first time in her life, a lack of self-respect is making it hard for her to look at herself in the mirror. Her agitation over all she has done to hurt poor, sweet Ham has left her so sick that she is finding it difficult to perform satisfactorily in *Dark Victory*, a project she insists she adores.

Although Bette had desperately wanted to exile her husband and had seemed to do everything she could to humiliate him and force him from their home, now that he was finally gone she was tortured with regret. Part of this, as always with Bette, was sheer selfishness. For all her contempt for Ham, she had grown accustomed to having him at home as an audience for her tirades, the passive object of her abuse. Although she had deliberately driven him away, there were moments when she seemed strangely to regard his departure and divorce suit as yet another rejection of her.

However naively, she had fully expected Howard Hughes to take her husband's place. The tycoon's sudden, unexpected defection ("a blow to my ego," as she later described it) left her alone to brood over her two short-lived extramarital affairs, both of which had ended in rejection and sexual humiliation for Bette. Despite the high spirits with which she had flung herself into the liaisons with Wyler and Hughes, such behavior went against the grain of everything her background and experience had taught her to believe. Her father's adultery so many years before had unquestionably been the determining factor in Bette's life; his subsequent marriage to his mistress was a painful fact she had always felt it necessary to repress.

Having long perceived herself as a victim of her father's adultery, now she had emulated his behavior in her own extramarital affairs, and she began to find it unbearable to think of herself in these terms. Thus the absurd, oft-repeated story she started to tell in this period about Ham's having blackmailed Howard Hughes with a secret recording he had made of one of the tycoon's trysts with Bette. As Davis's friends knew only too well, such behavior would have been entirely out of keeping with Ham Nelson's gentle, temperate nature. Besides, so openly had Hughes conducted his brief affair with Bette that it would hardly have been necessary for her husband to resort to anything like secret sleuthing to prove her unfaithfulness. For Bette, however, the spurious story had the distinct benefit of transforming her into the victim of her husband's cruel behavior, rather than the other way around. To judge by Bette's letter to Teddy Newton, in which one discovers no trace of the indignation against Ham she regularly voiced among friends and associates, transferring her own unbearable guilt to her husband was something she very badly needed to do at the moment. And in her mortification over Hughes's having swiftly lost interest in her, the blackmail story possessed the added advantage of seeming to explain why the tycoon had so abruptly disappeared from her life.

Her emotions already in disarray over the loss of Hughes and the end of her marriage to Ham, Bette found herself scarcely able to continue work on *Dark Victory* when, in the midst of filming, she learned of Willy Wyler's marriage to Margaret Tallichet, to whom the director had proposed ten days after they met. Knowing his friend's desire to keep his wedding plans secret, John Huston had offered the house of his father, Walter Huston, in Running Springs in the San Bernardino Mountains as a good place to get married far from the Hollywood madding crowd. Only closest friends and family members would be present: John Huston and his wife, Lesley, Paul and Lupita Kohner, Wyler's lawyer, Mark Cohen, and the director's parents, Melanie and Leopold Wyler, and his brother, Robert. For all the attempts at secrecy, word about the impending marriage began to spread soon after Wyler and his bride-to-be signed a year's lease on a house just below Jack and Ann Warner's in Beverly Hills. That Bette had probably heard about the wedding in advance is suggested by her behavior as recorded in studio production reports when the second week of shooting drew to a close. On Friday, October 21, even as Willy and Talli were headed for the San Bernardino Mountains, Bette had begun to complain of not feeling well. And the next morning, October 22—Willy's wedding day—Bette's chauffeur, Brown, appeared on the set with a note to Goulding, informing the director that she was too ill to come to work.

Before long, Bette had fabricated another spurious story to mitigate her pain and humiliation over Wyler's marriage. In the version that Bette would tell through the years, the director married Margaret Tallichet only after he had sent a letter to Davis, with whom he had had a lovers' quarrel. According to Bette, she had been so angry with Wyler at the time that she foolishly allowed a full week to pass before she opened his letter, on October 22. In a true "movie moment," even as she was reading the director's ultimatum that unless she agreed to marry him within the week he would marry Talli instead, Bette claimed to have heard a radio announcement of Wyler's wedding.

All of which was quite impossible, of course, as there had been no recent lovers' quarrel between them. Wyler had ended his affair with Bette after *Jezebel*. Nor had there been any opportunity to resume the romance that summer, while Wyler was in Europe, or in the fall, when the director's friends knew him to be deeply involved with Talli. Still, much as we know Bette to have made it all up, if her story retains a faint ring of truth, perhaps it is because we feel somehow that we have heard it before. We have seen Bette in circumstances strangely similar to these: in love with a man whom she longs to marry, losing him through an act of headstrong foolishness, repenting her error only to discover that it is too late—he has married another woman. In *Jezebel,* when Julie Marsden realizes that Pres has married Amy, she knows that he cannot truly love his bride. Amy must be his second choice, Pres having married her only because Julie—his first choice, the one he really loves—blundered and let him go.

Her mind spinning with the lies she had fabricated about Hughes and Wyler, and with the hurt and perplexity that had driven her to invent them, as well as with the guilt she continued to experience about having betrayed Ham with both men, Bette returned to work during the week of October 25, and Edmund Goulding found her more insecure than ever about her ability to give a convincing performance of Judith Traherne's transformation. Considering how she felt about herself at the moment, enacting Judith's newly discovered fineness and courage was about the last thing she believed herself capable of doing. By the end of the week, convinced that she would not be able to do the character justice, Davis asked to meet with Hal Wallis on the evening of Saturday, October 29, to beg him to release her from the film.

"Here is this gallant little figure all alone, who can't tell anybody what the problem is and won't dare let anyone feel sorry for her," said Goulding, directing Bette in the role of Judith Traherne by giving her what Geraldine Fitzgerald describes as "images of her character's inner self." After Hal Wallis declined Bette's desperate request to leave the film, Goulding devoted himself to helping the actress somehow bridge the gap between her badly tarnished self-image and the strong, noble character she was called upon to portray. "Goulding worked very hard at building up Bette's ego," Fitzgerald recalls. "That was one of his most valuable gifts as a director: his ability to give an actor confidence."

By the fourth week of filming, Goulding was not alone in his attempts to repair Davis's bruised ego. In the days that followed Wallis's refusal to release her from *Dark Victory*, Bette suddenly found herself the object of George Brent's persistent attentions. Before the week was up, she and her leading man had embarked on a scarcely concealed love affair. At times Bette seemed oddly anxious to flaunt her involvement with Brent, to let people know that they were sleeping together. The following Saturday, November 5 (exactly a week since she had met with Wallis), Davis and Brent were recorded to have repeatedly dissolved in uncontrollable laughter over some faintly suggestive lines in the script, so that a simple scene in which Dr. Steele visits Judith in her hospital bed had to be shot ten times.

Neither her director nor her leading man seemed entirely capable of soothing her, however, during the fifth, sixth, and seventh weeks of filming, as Bette reacted with hysterical illness to the divorce negotiations with Ham. Repeatedly, she failed to appear on the set, causing the entire production to grind to a halt as Goulding scrambled to rush actors from their homes to shoot scenes other than the ones he had rehearsed and arranged the night before.

As the originally scheduled closing date of November 12 approached, it became increasingly evident that Bette would not be finished with *Dark Victory* in time to begin her role as the Empress Carlota in director William Dieterle's *Juarez*, starring Paul Muni as the Mexican freedom fighter. The "prestige" production's $1.75 million budget made everyone on the Warners lot anxious that all go without a hitch. Hence the foreboding tone of studio memoranda devoted to what quickly came to be known as "the Bette Davis situation"—as shooting began on the Paul Muni superproduction, with Bette still struggling to finish with Goulding, despite recorded absences of three and a half days that very week.

Juarez was in its tenth day of shooting when, on Tuesday, November 29, unit manager Al Alleborn appeared on the *Dark Victory* set to see what could be done about at least getting Bette fitted for her Carlota costumes; but Bette refused on the grounds that finding herself dressed as her next character would diminish her concentration on the role of Judith. Three days later, she refused again when *Juarez* producer Henry Blanke showed up on Goulding's set to pressure her to accede to the unit manager's request. For this show of firmness, Bette appears to have paid an emotional price. After Blanke departed, the actress seemed to experience a breakdown in the middle of a close-up where Judith prepares to die.

"Miss Davis was taken hysterical in the scene," recorded unit manager Bob Ross, in apparent bewilderment, on December 3. "She cried very heavily and it was very difficult and very trying to get the scene."

Despite these and similar scenes in which Bette's emotional turmoil was all too apparent, by the time she had completed *Dark Victory*, on December 5, Goulding seemed confident that, against all odds, the actress had turned in one of her strongest performances. Much as one misses the nuances of gesture, the complex choreography, discovered in *Jezebel*, watching her meticulous beat-by-beat delineation of Judith's growth and change is an exhilarating experience. If *Dark Victory* was destined to become one of her most popular films, it was undoubtedly because of its clear, compelling, upbeat image of a woman's capacity for far-reaching transformation, for overcoming obstacles and facing reality with a courage and bravery she never knew she possessed. For decades thereafter, female filmgoers regularly identified Bette Davis with her inspiring portrait of Judith Traherne: a mixed blessing for the actress, who continued privately to despair of the frustrating disparity between this most beloved of her film characters and the desperate, frightened, unfulfilled woman she knew herself to be.

FOURTEEN

"In what respect was your wife cruel to you?" attorney James A. Flannagan asked Ham Nelson on December 6, 1938, the day he sued Bette for divorce on grounds of "cruel and inhuman treatment."

"I expect it was as a result of her career," Ham replied. "She thought her career more important than marriage."

"Did she tell you that?"

"Yes, she did."

Bette was not in court as Judge Thurmond Clarke took scarcely fifteen minutes to end her six-year marriage—the divorce proceedings having been expedited to allow Ham to leave directly for New York, where a new job awaited him at the Young and Rubicam Advertising Agency. As chance would have it, Ham's widely publicized court appearance took place on Bette's single day of rest between finishing *Dark Victory* and starting *Juarez*.

By this point Ruthie had almost completed the incongruously formal decor she had planned for the onetime Kay Francis dressing room on the Warners lot: a mélange of English and French antiques with a rather grand four-poster bed as centerpiece. But as Bette was soon to discover, this "stately setting"—as her mother exultantly described it—constituted the mere trappings of power, not the thing itself.

Bette's designation as Warners' "top rank female artist" notwithstanding, from the outset Paul Muni held the reins on the set of *Juarez*, although he was not even scheduled to put in an appearance until January 9, when he would film his scenes separately from those of Bette and Brian Aherne (as her husband, Emperor Maximilian, the French puppet in Mexico). Still the studio's most powerful artist, Muni, with his contractual right of story and script approval, could demand revisions in the painstakingly crafted script by John Huston, Aeneas MacKenzie, and Wolfgang Reinhardt.

To establish a contrast between Maximilian, the imposed foreign emperor of Mexico, and Juarez, the "father" of the Mexican Republic, the screenwriters had made Aherne's character an eloquent speaker, while Muni was given what Huston described as an "Indian taciturnity" that made his every word count.

But Muni did not see it that way at all. A glance at the script disclosed that he had fewer lines than Aherne. Muni had yet to appear on the set of *Juarez* when he threatened to walk out of the big-budget picture if the screenwriters failed to give him more dialogue than Aherne—or if Muni's brother-in-law was not commissioned to do it for them.

Bette knew nothing about all this as she began hurriedly shooting her scenes on December 12.

Anxious to wield some of the power she believed *Jezebel* and *Dark Victory* had given her, she allowed scarcely a day to pass before she refused to do a scene as ordered—insisting, Alleborn reported to production manager Tenny Wright, that she didn't know the scene well enough. The production came to a standstill while Bette repaired to her dressing room to work up some "business." Dieterle frantically ordered Brian Aherne to the still department to have portraits made, for want of anything else to do.

But this was the least of the beleaguered film's problems. Alleborn chronicled the growing anxiety that Bette would explode when she realized that, even as she and Aherne were busy filming their scenes, Muni was daily hacking away at the script to diminish their importance.

By December 28, precisely as feared, Bette grew intensely suspicious and upset when Dieterle informed her that there was no need to shoot one of her big scenes in the script, as it was out of the picture for now. When no one dared to explain why, she demanded to talk to Henry Blanke, who was shooting tests of Muni at the time.

Anxious to avert the inevitable fireworks as long as possible, Alleborn decided to try to keep Blanke off the set until late in the day, so that at least that afternoon's work might be peacefully concluded before Bette discovered what Muni was up to; and, worse, that there was nothing she could do about it.

The dispiriting experience of finding herself slowly, relentlessly edged out of *Juarez*, so that in the end her performance was a mere fragment of what it might have been, led Bette to demand both female leads—a dual role as Charlotte and Delia Lovell—in her next Warners' film: Goulding's *The Old Maid*, based on Zoë Akin's Pulitzer Prize–winning dramatization of the Edith Wharton novel. It seemed to Bette that portraying the two contrasting cousins, rivals in love, would be a stunning tour de force, worthy of an actress who, meanwhile, would pick up her second Academy Award, on February 23, 1939, for *Jezebel*.

At the Biltmore Hotel, where the eleventh annual Academy Awards banquet was held, Bette's competition for the Oscar for Best Actress included Wendy Hiller for *Pygmalion*, Norma Shearer for *Marie Antoinette*, and Willy Wyler's ex-wife, Margaret Sullavan, for *Three Comrades*. Four years earlier, Davis's 1935 Academy Award for *Dangerous* had been widely and correctly perceived as a consolation prize for her having been passed over in 1934 for *Of Human Bondage*. In 1939, by contrast, Bette's pleasure in being named Best Actress could be unalloyed, confirming as it did the towering status she had achieved in the course of nine years in Hollywood: a preeminence she was working hard to sustain with the prodigious series of box office hits she was in the process of making.

Warner Bros. studio records indicate that even as she was being humored in her belief that she would indeed play both roles in the upcoming *The Old Maid*, screenwriter Casey Robinson was at work on a script that would render such an arrangement impossible, and negotiations were under way to get Miriam Hopkins to portray Delia to Davis's Charlotte. "I am wondering whether or not when Bette Davis gets a script and finds out she is not to do the dual role we will have any trouble with her," Roy Obringer warned Hal Wallis, in light of Bette's repeated requests to glimpse Robinson's work in progress.

But there was no explosion from Bette when, in due course, Warners delivered the script to her and she learned that Hopkins was set to co-star. Instead, from the outset, Bette appears to have emulated her phantom nemesis in *Juarez*. Like Paul Muni, she would work behind the scenes to enhance her role at Hopkins's expense. In this case, however, it was less a question of Goulding's agreeing to build up Bette's role than of his discreetly giving her the greater advantage in ways that Hopkins would scarcely be allowed to comprehend until afterward.

From Wyler, Bette had learned the careful consideration that must be given to an actor's first appearance in a film: thus the time he and Bette had taken to discover precisely the right gesture—the sweep of a riding crop and billow of black fabric—with which to establish Julie's character in *Jezebel*.

For two days now—March 15 and 16—Goulding worked with Davis and Hopkins on the script's opening sequence, set in Mr. Painter's "fashionable lingerie shop," where, accompanied by their ancient grandmother, the Lovell cousins have come to buy a trousseau for Delia. They had barely finished filming the eight script pages, when Bette began secretly maneuvering (with all the power two Academy Awards gave her) to cut the lingerie shop sequence, leaving the film to open with the sequence—set in Delia's bedroom—that follows.

But Hopkins knew nothing of this when, on Friday, March 17, Goulding proceeded to shoot the bedroom sequence. As this "second" sequence opens with Delia and her maid making some "hurried last minute adjustments to her bridal dress," Hopkins's call was at nine o'clock, an hour earlier than Bette's; Charlotte enters only after one and a half pages of script have been covered. On the assumption that her character would already have been introduced in the lingerie shop, Hopkins played her brief scene with the maid at a considerably lower register than she almost certainly would have done had she suspected that this was to be the audience's first glimpse of her.

By contrast, Bette already knew there was a strong chance the earlier sequence would be excised. Thus the unusually high degree of emotional excitement with which she makes her entrance: palpably overwhelming the rival actress, who later complained of having had little choice but to remain somewhere near the level of intensity she had established before Davis's arrival.

Not until April 12, when Goulding announced his decision to discard the lingerie shop sequence, did Hopkins begin really to grasp what her co-star had done; but already, by the third day of filming, she was regularly, gleefully throwing every obstacle she could think of in Bette's path.

Even before this, Hopkins, who portrayed Julie Marsden on Broadway, had bitterly resented Bette for having snatched a triumph from her in Wyler's film. Although they had barely known each other at the time, Hopkins had been the leading lady of George Cukor's Rochester, New York, company when Bette was an ingenue there: another source of enmity now that Bette was unequivocally the more powerful figure in Hollywood—although by no means the more formidable personality. Hopkins was precisely the sort of vivid, quick-witted woman—à la Tallulah Bankhead or Ruth Gordon—by whom Bette had consistently been intimidated in New York. Where Bette tended to recoil from bright, clever, verbal people, Hopkins was famous for surrounding herself with them in her jewel-box town house on New York's Sutton Place. But the nimble star of Ernst Lubitsch's *Trouble in Paradise* and *Design for Living* had not had a success since Wyler's *These Three* in 1936. With her career in eclipse, the Goulding film—with its woefully ramshackle script and ill-conceived characters—meant far more to Hopkins than it did to Bette, who needled her rival by regularly proclaiming her keen desire to be finished with *The Old Maid* as soon as possible, in order to get on to her next film assignment: the glorious Lynn Fontanne role in *Elizabeth the Queen*.

"Make every effort to rush this along," Hal Wallis urged the ever harried director, from whom the studio made scant attempt to conceal its intention simply to keep Bette working in *The Old Maid* until *Elizabeth the Queen* was ready. No matter that even Casey Robinson realized there were major structural problems in *The Old Maid* script yet to be solved. By this point, Bette Davis was far too valuable to Warner Bros. to be left idle for even the briefest interlude.

Handed the still unfinished screenplay, Goulding decided to shoot in continuity, in an effort "to build characterization." But nothing could solve the problem of the midpoint fifteen-year ellipsis, after which the spirited Charlotte returns, inexplicably, as a "testy, bitter" old maid.

In the first part of the film, Charlotte has secretly had an illegitimate daughter, whose identity she conceals—even from the child

—by presenting her as a foundling. Only Charlotte and Delia know that Tina's father was the man whom both cousins once loved, making for perpetual hostility between them. In the scene just prior to the midpoint ellipsis, the wealthy Delia, anxious to claim Tina for her own, has invited Charlotte and the child to move into her house, but Tina's echoing Delia's other children by calling her "Mummy" makes it most unlikely that Charlotte will consider the proposal.

Hence the peculiar absence of dramatic logic in what follows, as fifteen years pass away, and—without explanation or motivation—we discover that Charlotte and Tina have been living in Delia's house all this time; with Tina having become virtually a daughter to Delia, while Charlotte has mysteriously metamorphosed into a withered old woman.

Goulding and Robinson are known to have been acutely aware of this fundamental script problem, which no one dared discuss with Bette for fear of her reaction.

On Monday, April 17, 1939, the production was already five days behind schedule when Goulding shot the scene just prior to the midpoint, even as Robinson was still frantically churning out pages for the ill-conceived "old maid" segment. There is no record of what Bette might have been thinking as she faced the prospect of somehow embodying this abrupt and totally unmotivated change in her character. There are, however, references in the Warner Bros. files to the actress's having suffered a "bad fainting spell" on the set, at 3:50 P.M. on April 17, as the time for her on-screen metamorphosis drew near: presumably the latest of the hysterical illnesses with which Bette routinely reacted to feelings of disquiet and apprehension.

When the studio doctor arrived on the scene, he declared that "her pulse was way up" and sent her home, where she remained in Ruthie's care for the next three days.

🔻

"I have been studying the lady and, in my opinion, she is in a rather serious condition of nerves," producer Robert Lord told Hal Wallis on May 5, the penultimate day of shooting on *The Old Maid*. "At best she is frail and is going into a very tough picture when she is a long way from her 'best.' " Hence Lord's urgent suggestion that, to protect itself, Warner Bros. take out "some kind of health insurance policy" on Bette for the duration of *Elizabeth the Queen*.

"If she folds up, we stop shooting," warned the anxious producer, foreseeing the economic consequences should the over-worked, exhausted actress break down for a prolonged period, as the studio knew her sister Bobby had done.

Even as Bette appeared to teeter at the edge of a nervous collapse, at Ruthie's instigation she launched a new offensive against Jack Warner when her lawyer, Oscar Cummins, reported that Warners intended to change the name of Maxwell Anderson's *Elizabeth the Queen* to *The Knight and the Lady*, as if to shift the drama's emphasis from Elizabeth to her beloved Lord Essex (ineptly portrayed by Errol Flynn).

Where Lynn Fontanne had easily dominated the Broadway production over the no less brilliant acting of her husband, Alfred Lunt, as Essex, Bette and Ruthie feared that, with its record of unabashed preference for male action, Warners intended to make this Flynn's picture, not hers. Despite Jack Warner's assurances, their fears were not entirely without foundation. Studio interoffice memoranda, which Bette and Ruthie are unlikely to have glimpsed, repeatedly refer to "getting Bette into the Flynn picture."

When Oscar Cummins's persistent telephone calls to Jack Warner were unavailing, Bette, then in the final throes of filming *The Old Maid*, took matters into her own hands. She sent a telegram to Warner on April 28 (and, more angrily, on May 1), refusing to portray Elizabeth unless she was guaranteed top billing and a more suitable title. Bette, who had suffered from apparently psychosomatic chest pains since *Juarez*, informed Warner that the prospect of the title *The Knight and the Lady* had caused her to become "so upset mentally and ill physically" that she feared long-term "serious impairment" to her health.

With Warner's promising her top billing over Flynn, Bette agreed that as soon as she finished *The Old Maid*, on May 6, she would appear for costume and makeup tests for *Elizabeth the Queen* (subsequently retitled *The Private Lives of Elizabeth and Essex*) on May 9 and 11. While Flynn and director Michael Curtiz started filming on May 11, Bette would not be due until May 24, which would afford her some much-needed rest.

All was apparently well, until Bette appeared for the May 9 tests, only to discover that Flynn's salary for the picture had been budgeted at $41,300 to her $35,000. And worse, Flynn twice rejected invitations from the actress—whom he described as "not physically my type"—to join her in her dressing room after work for a drink.

▲

"We don't want to make Davis up as a female Frankenstein," said Hal Wallis, appalled at the actress's concept of the role, in which she sought even to outdo Lynn Fontanne in creating a "miraculous reincarnation" of the homely queen. "This is the impression I get from the tests she has made so far and I want to stop that immediately. After all, we have a story that we are going to try and make into a great love story, and this is not going to be possible if we try to do it with Flynn, as handsome as he looks in his clothes, in love with an ugly woman."

Where Lynn Fontanne had been widely admired in theatrical circles for her daring physical characterization of Elizabeth, Warners feared that Bette's gargoyle face and partially shaved head (to give the effect of baldness beneath a garish red wig) would strike film audiences as ludicrous and absurd.

Wallis worried no less about how Bette might react to his reservations about the gnarled physiognomy she and makeup artist Perc Westmore had devised—hence Wallis's order to Westmore to alter the actress's makeup without a word to her about what he was doing.

Mingling as it did "the body of a weak and feeble woman" with "the heart and stomach of a king," the role of Elizabeth should have been a good fit; but sad to say, for all Bette's preoccupation with Elizabeth's outward appearance, she utterly failed to give her character a suitable gestural style. The bizarre outpouring of tics with which, at intervals, Davis undeniably occupies the eye is no substitute for the dramatic intensity and delicacy of feeling the actress playing "our dread Virago" must convey in her every creaking, agonized movement.

Bette had seen precisely such a performance of Elizabeth in November of 1930, shortly before she came to Hollywood; and we may know something of what she saw from the glittering fragment of the Lunt-Fontanne production that exists as prelude to their 1931 film of Ferenc Molnár's *The Guardsman*. The film opens as the Maxwell Anderson play is drawing to a close at the Burg Theatre in Vienna. Elizabeth has condemned her beloved Essex to die; and we see them in their final moments together. Here is the famous grotesque makeup—the putty nose and sagging flesh—with which Fontanne gave the illusion of decrepitude. But here, too, is the sudden strange limpidity and grace of movement—the eloquent half-gestures and aborted reachings—with which she embodied her character's hopeless craving (and inner conflict: can she put to death the man she loves, no matter how great a threat to England he poses?), gestures that seem all the more poignant by contrast with Elizabeth's withered, immobile carriage, stooped with age and despair.

Beside this, Bette's more frenzied treatment of the same scene seems mannered and ineffectual: all tics and big showy movements (precisely the sort of thing Wyler had warned against), with none of Fontanne's nuance and poetry. Moments before the execution of Lord Essex, where Fontanne repeatedly reaches out to Lunt, aborting the gesture before they actually touch, Bette Davis simply throws her arms around Errol Flynn and clings to him tightly: encapsulating the subtle intellectual pleasure of the one performance and the all-too-frequent banality of the other.

In August 1939, as Bette Davis and Jack Warner struggled anew over her contract—with Davis asking for a two-picture yearly limit and Warner insisting on a minimum of four—the actress angrily declared that only if she were lying in her coffin would Warner be likely to recognize the justness of her demands.

When it became evident that the studio boss was not about to budge, Davis and her representatives proposed that Warners hire a "board of medicos" to determine the number of films she could safely make each year. On August 29, the studio general counsel recorded his horror at the prospect of having to seek the doctors' permission "any time we want Davis to appear in a picture."

Unbeknownst to Warner Bros., by that date Bette had already reluctantly abandoned the idea, when at least one of her personal physicians showed "a distinct lack of enthusiasm" for testifying on her behalf. In the course of lowering her voice for the role of Queen Elizabeth, Bette claimed to have ruptured several blood vessels. But when her business manager, Vernon Wood, approached the physician who had treated her three times for laryngitis, Dr. Cully's "rather disappointing" response was that if Bette would only stop smoking, her condition would be "largely relieved."

Davis did have cause to complain of fatigue at this moment. Virtually without letup, she had worked to complete a remarkable series of box office successes: *Jezebel, The Sisters, Dark Victory, Juarez, The Old Maid,* and *The Private Lives of Elizabeth and Essex.*

The unique combination of Warners' relentless assembly-line approach to filmmaking and Bette's phenomenal drive and stamina allowed the seemingly omnipresent Davis to dominate the American dramatic cinema of this period. Of Bette's two major potential rivals, Greta Garbo made her last important motion picture, *Ninotchka*, in 1939 and would abandon film acting after the disastrous *Two-Faced Woman* in 1941, and Katharine Hepburn was then devoting most of her energies to romantic comedy—leaving Davis virtually without peer in the field of serious screen drama. Had Katharine Cornell overcome her gnawing terror of film acting and accepted Irving Thalberg's invitation to come to Hollywood, or had Lynn Fontanne pursued her film career instead of forsaking the cinema with the famous line "We can be bought, but we cannot be bored!" who can tell what competition either far more formidable actress might have provided? But Davis had no such competition as she and her studio worked at full blast to turn out the six films that, however much they varied in artistry and ambition, forcefully staked her claim as Hollywood's preeminent dramatic actress.

Months after her confession to Teddy Newton that for the first time in her life she needed to take stock, Bette went east for a six-week vacation as soon as *The Private Lives of Elizabeth and Essex* finished filming, on July 6.

First she visited Robin (newly divorced) and other friends from New York theater days; then, accompanied only by her black Scottish terrier, Tibby, she drove her yellow wood-paneled station wagon to New England, where she visited old haunts in Dennis, Newton, Ogunquit, and Peterborough.

At intervals, she fired off long, rambling letters to Jack Warner; more often than not, her rapid scrawl filled both sides of the lightweight, tissue-thin paper she favored—giving her correspondence the curious air of a palimpsest, in which one layer of writing scarcely conceals another beneath it.

Page after page, the message is the same: She has shrunken to a mere eighty pounds. She is fighting for her health, for her life. Having completed five films this year—finishing one role, only to start another soon afterward—for the first time in her career she doesn't care if she ever makes another picture. She will not, she cannot, return to Burbank unless the studio agrees to reduce her work load.

And whatever his answer, will Mr. Warner please refrain from contacting her directly—as hearing from him upsets her very much.

On August 29, when Bette did not report to work as ordered, there was considerable debate at Warners about whether the actress was really as "ill and tired" as she purported—with Roy Obringer speaking for most when he described Bette's claims of "incapacity" as "pretty far fetched."

Even as Bette was conjuring up images of decayed health and premature death, the photographs in her scrapbooks for this period suggest the elation and boundless energy with which she pursued the good life—as her mother described it—in the White Mountains of New Hampshire, where, at Ruthie's suggestion, she had taken up residence in a tiny cottage at Peckett's Inn in pastoral Franconia. Bette has a new look now: the twill trousers and tweeds associated with the Eastern "horsey" set. Here she is, in full riding regalia, galloping along some remote mountain trail; and here, presenting prizes at the Littleton Horse Show; and here, perching atop an open-air car, surrounded by a group of attractive, fun-loving new friends.

At a glance one might easily mistake these photographs for stills from the F. Scott Fitzgerald world of *Dark Victory;* in most of them, there is even a trim, tweedy young man with slicked-back hair, who bears a distinct resemblance to George Brent—or rather to Dr. Steele, with whom the doomed Judith Traherne falls in love and retreats to a little white farmhouse in the New England countryside.

And like Judith, Bette is regularly accompanied by a faithful best friend who—like the Geraldine Fitzgerald character in the movie—doubles as her secretary (Bette having drafted Robin in this capacity when the latter complained of not having the money to join her in Franconia).

And then one comes upon the pictures of Butternut, the tumbledown little white farmhouse Bette has suddenly, impulsively purchased on Sugar Hill, summoning Warners' head carpenter to New Hampshire to restore it for her between his assignments constructing film sets.

In short, after a year of work, work, and nothing but, shedding one mask only to put on another, and scarcely a satisfying private life to speak of, Bette's six-week quest has ended with her reaching back into Hollywood's "Sargasso of the imagination," as Nathanael West called it, to appropriate a film character's richer, more satisfactory life for her own—including, apparently, the images of imminent death and the perpetual noble struggle against it that haunt Judith's otherwise idyllic New England existence with the man she loves.

The tall, tweedy Dr. Steele look-alike in the photographs was Arthur Austin Farnsworth, or "Farney," as Bette and Robin called the thirty-one-year-old desk clerk and assistant manager at Peckett's Inn. Robin had no sense that there was any grand passion between Bette and Farney. It seemed to Robin that although there was something rather "colorless" about Farney, Bette was drawn to him for his charming, impeccable manners, which instantly put her at ease.

Within seventy-two hours of checking in at Peckett's, Bette was being squired about Franconia by the suave, gregarious assistant manager, who—like Dr. Steele in the movie—seemed suddenly to have been put on earth solely to attend to her needs. Very quickly he abandoned his desk duties to amuse her with an endless round of barn dances, hikes, and romantic country drives in his convertible.

A man of attractive surfaces and diverting patter, an expert horseman and amateur pilot with a carefully concealed drinking problem, Arthur Farnsworth possessed scant ambition for a career of his own. After a brief stint in the office of a Boston oil burner company, in 1933 Farney had repaired to the White Mountains, where hotel work allowed him to play at being a country gentleman, always holding out the hope of receiving a substantial inheritance from his mother's "well-to-do" sister, whom he called "Mother Main." In the interim there had been a brief marriage to Boston socialite and aviatrix Betty Jane Aydelotte, but the couple had separated; and when he met Bette Davis that August, much to his chagrin he was still waiting for the divorce to become final.

▲▼▲

"Boy?" scribbled Jack Warner on the page of doodles he preserved from the October 22, 1939, meeting in Mountainville, New York, where he and Bette finally compromised on a three-picture-a-year limit. Having written this near the name "Mr. Farnsworth" and the notation "With Bette Davis," Warner is clearly trying to determine whether Farney is her new boyfriend and what role he may be quietly playing in the negotiations.

Suspicions had arisen that a new player was involved when, in hopes of luring Bette back to Los Angeles, George Brent had called her in Franconia recently, asking to spend some time with her there. Instead Bette had arranged to meet him in Boston, where she passed a few hours with him at the Copley Plaza Hotel, then rushed back to the White Mountains, leaving Brent with the distinct impression that he had been rebuffed.

Brent's mission having failed, Obringer indicated to the actress's representatives that if she did not report to work immediately, Warner planned to replace her at the studio with Vivien Leigh, who had recently finished her role as Scarlett O'Hara in *Gone With the Wind*: a role Bette had coveted, though Jack Warner had refused even to consider loaning her out when David Selznick decided not to distribute the picture through Warner Bros.

Studio records show that Obringer's was no mere idle threat. Warner was indeed about to make a move for Leigh if Davis's recalcitrance persisted beyond October 22.

"The story we want to give out is brief," Warner told Hal Wallis, after his successful meeting with Bette and the mysterious Mr. Farnsworth. "You can give out something to the effect that we want to make fewer pictures with Bette Davis as we want to keep making the high quality of pictures we have achieved with her."

After the photographs in Bette's album showing her idyllic existence with Farney in New Hampshire, one is momentarily startled to discover an image of her peacefully feeding a newborn baby at home in Los Angeles that November. Named after Ruthie, the child is Ruth Favor Pelgram (Fay, as everyone called her), to whom Bobby had given birth at Hollywood Hospital on October 1.

Following Bette's meeting with Jack Warner, she, Farney, Robin, and several other friends were driving cross-country when Ruthie tracked them down with the news that the birth of Bobby's baby had plunged the young mother into a new fit of uncontrollable mania, the first to blight her marriage to Little Bobby Pelgram, who was then working as a publicist at Universal Studios. It seemed likely that Bobby would have to be hospitalized again, and Ruthie asked Bette to cut her trip short and come home immediately. When Bette returned with Farney and Robin, she found Bobby a changed person, no longer the stylish, more confident figure she had been since marrying the wealthy sportsman. Bette had seen this behavior before: the haunted glances and erratic gestures, the screaming fits and paranoid ravings that had caused Bobby to be repeatedly institutionalized in the past. Ruthie summoned an ambulance to the Pelgrams' Laurel Canyon home. The shrieking, cursing Bobby was carried out of the house as Bette made a great show of promising to watch over Bobby's husband and baby, who were to stay with her during Bobby's hospitalization.

Farney lingered in Los Angeles through Christmas, after which he returned to Franconia, where Bette promised to join him in March. By that time she would be finished with *All This and Heaven Too*, the interim film Warners had scheduled until her next major project was ready: an adaptation of Somerset Maugham's *The Letter*, to be directed by William Wyler. In Farney's absence, Bette embarked on a brief affair with her director on *All This and Heaven Too*, Anatole Litvak, a close friend of Wyler's. In March, when Bette called New Hampshire to say she wouldn't be coming to Butternut after all, Farney appeared in Los Angeles to look out for his interests, Davis's on-the-set romance with Litvak having been widely hinted at in the press. Once again, however, as with Wyler, Bette failed to understand that that was all it was: a director's liaison with his leading lady, to last only so long as they were working together.

When filming was completed, on April 22, Litvak agreed to meet Bette in Hawaii for a quiet holiday together before she started work on *The Letter*. Three days later, Ruthie and Bobby (newly released from the hospital) saw Bette and Robin off on the boat to Honolulu. Also on board was Bob Taplinger, of Warner's West Coast publicity department, whose amorous attentions were a welcome comfort to Bette's badly wounded pride when, without a word of explanation or regret, Litvak simply failed to appear.

ou would never have thought that this quiet, refined woman was capable of such a fiendish passion," wrote Somerset Maugham in his celebrated 1926 short story "The Letter": a key line for comprehending Katharine Cornell's special fascination in the role of Leslie Crosbie when she played it on Broadway in the fall of 1927.

Then a drama student in New York, nineteen-year-old Bette Davis had made repeated visits to the Morosco Theatre, where Cornell's controversial performance of this latest of her "loose, dissolute women" was to become emblematic of Bette's own aspirations as an actress: aspirations that, in Bette's view, Wyler had finally helped her to realize during the making of *Jezebel*.

When one considers the importance that seeing *The Letter* on Broadway had had for Bette, it is certainly not too much to suppose that she might have discussed the Cornell production with Wyler during the filming of *Jezebel*. In any event, that Wyler privately associated the role of Leslie Crosbie with Bette long before it had been arranged for them to do it together at Warner Bros. is indicated in the director's preliminary notes by his use of Bette's name in place of Leslie's (whereas all other characters are routinely referred to by the names Maugham gave them). And that he had scant interest in directing another actress in the part is made clear in the April 9, 1940, contract that Wyler's agent, Leland Hayward, negotiated with Warners' general counsel Roy J. Obringer, where it is stipulated that Wyler had the right to withdraw from the project should Bette Davis decline to do it. This stipulation may also suggest Wyler's lack of certainty about whether Bette would want to work with him again after he had directed Merle Oberon in *Wuthering Heights* and— more troubling, no doubt—married Margaret Tallichet.

Wyler had not been the first director to propose *The Letter* for Bette Davis at Warner Bros. Studio records show that Edmund Goulding had "plugged" it to Hal Wallis and others on numerous occasions. But in the spring of 1938, when Jack Warner submitted the text of Maugham's play to the Production Code Administration, head censor Joseph I. Breen replied that there could be no question of his approving "the story of a wife, who murders her lover, but who, by lying, deceit, perjury, and the purchase of an incriminating letter, defeats justice, and gets off 'scott free.' " Besides the murder, particularly distressing to Breen's office were what he characterized as "all the sordid details of the illicit sex relationship between the married woman and her lover," as well as "very numerous references to the second mistress of the murdered man, who is characterized as a China woman."

Like other stories in Maugham's 1926 collection *The Casuarina Tree*, "The Letter" is said to have been based on an actual occurrence in the English colony in Malaya, where it had been Maugham's custom to gather material for his fiction. The source in this case appears to have been Singapore press reports concerning the sensational trial of Mrs. Ethel Mabel Proudlock for the April 23, 1911, murder of William Crozier Steward, whom she accused of having attempted to rape her while her husband, headmaster of a school in Kuala Lumpur, had been dining out with a member of his staff. Whereas the English colony as a whole seemed to believe Mrs. Proudlock's contention that, surprised by Steward's unexpected visit and appalled by his sexual advances, she had shot him six times in self-defense, the prosecution maintained that the headmaster's wife was, in fact, one of Steward's two mistresses: the other being a local Chinese woman.

According to the prosecutor, there had been no attempted rape at all, just simple jealousy of Steward's involvement with the Chinese woman: hence the crime of passion, for which Mrs. Proudlock was convicted and sentenced to death by hanging. Although the murderess was subsequently pardoned, she is recorded to have died not long afterward in an English insane asylum.

To this source material Maugham added the melodramatic plot device of the incriminating letter, which the murderess sent her lover, urging him to visit while her husband is away; and which her lawyer must retrieve from the Chinese woman afterward, lest she turn it over to the prosecution. For his short story and the 1927 stage dramatization based on it, Maugham also significantly altered the outcome of the trial, allowing the murderess to go "scott free" (as Hollywood's Production Code Administration noted with particular horror): her sole punishment suggested in the pungent line with which Leslie Crosbie famously closes the play: "With all my heart I still love the man I killed."

In spite of Joseph Breen's 1938 pronouncement, Wyler's personal papers show that he was actively pursuing the project in the summer of 1939 when he and Robert Stevenson conducted extensive talks that resulted in Stevenson's August 26 "Suggested Methods of Treatment" for a second film version of *The Letter* (the first having been made at Paramount in 1929, with Jeanne Eagels as Leslie Crosbie: a picture that, Breen noted in his letter to Jack Warner, had aroused "nation wide protest" at the time of its release).

Although by September of 1939 it was being said at Warner Bros. that Wyler was on the verge of convincing Samuel Goldwyn to secure the motion picture rights to *The Letter*, this was probably just Wyler's devious way of reviving Jack Warner's interest in the Maugham project, much as the director had once manipulated Goldwyn into buying *Wuthering Heights* by indicating that Warner wanted it. On September 28, Hal Wallis's executive assistant, Walter MacEwen, informed his superior about Goldwyn's purported "interest" in *The Letter*, the rights to which were being offered to Warner Bros. for $25,000. Another factor besides Bette's presence at Warners (and Jack Warner's perpetual distaste for loaning her out to other studios) made Wyler want to direct *The Letter* there rather than for Goldwyn, to whom he remained under contract: what he perceived as Goldwyn's nettlesome tendency to take personal credit for Wyler's artistic achievements, as when Goldwyn reportedly declared, "I made *Withering* [sic] *Heights*, Wyler only directed it."

By this point in Wyler's career, the credit he received for a picture had come to be far more important to him than the money he was being paid: or so it seemed to Hal Wallis, who, after making the deal with Wyler to film *The Letter*, recorded the director's preoccupation above all else with being given "the proper billing and publicity." Thus in his April 9, 1940, contract, besides spelling out the credit he required on-screen, Wyler wanted it specified that his name would appear in "all paid advertising and publicity . . . in type 33⅓% the size used for the title." The size of Wyler's ego and the extent to which Goldwyn may have pierced it is suggested by the Warner Bros. general counsel's August 1, 1940, warning to director of advertising and publicity S. Charles Einfeld that the studio "religiously" give Wyler precisely the credit indicated in his contract, lest the director "raise a lot of hell," as he seemed most likely to do should they disappoint him.

In addition to the potential problems of censorship that both MacEwen and producer Robert Lord had warned would have to be dealt with if Warner Bros. was to bring *The Letter* to the screen, from the first Hal Wallis appears to have been concerned about the difficulties presented by "photographing a play" that struck him as "very wordy." Wallis feared that if Wyler did not find precisely the right tempo for the material, if the action was somehow allowed to be too slow, the finished film might turn out to be dull.

Some of this, naturally, seems to have been the residue of Wallis's earlier conflicts with Wyler, whose directorial style had seemed so entirely out of place at Warner Bros. when he filmed *Jezebel* there in 1937–38. Since then, however, the immense triumph of *Jezebel* on all conceivable levels should have extinguished any doubts that Wallis and others may have had about Wyler's professional competence. But even now, as evidenced by the usual blast of threats, insults, and diatribes, there remained abundant concern at Warner Bros. about what was still widely perceived there as the inefficiency of Wyler's working methods.

Wyler's marks and notations on Robert Stevenson's August 1939 treatment and on the various drafts of *The Letter* completed by screenwriter Howard Koch at Warner Bros. provide rare glimpses of the director working through his material prior to filming it. (Talli Wyler recalls that whenever he began a new project, her husband's all-embracing concentration was such that it was almost as if he had suddenly gone "under water," where inevitably he remained for the duration.) Already, on the first page of Stevenson's pre–Warner Bros. treatment, Wyler's pencil marks seem to sketch out what he and cameraman Tony Gaudio would do in the opening moments of *The*

Letter. Stevenson devotes some fifteen lines and three short paragraphs to describing what he envisions as the film's initial images,
"establishing the Crosbie bungalow and the native huts around it":
alongside which copious account, in the right-hand margin Wyler has
scratched two thick black lines, one beside the first paragraph, and
another beside the third; and then, to link them, he has traced a kind
of semicircle, apparently to represent how he would film all of what
Stevenson describes in paragraphs one to three—the slumbering
dogs, the native houseboys, the fluttering birds, as well as the murder
itself—with a long, elegant sweep of the camera.

Almost always it is the visual—or potentially visual—things that
Wyler seizes upon. Marking off Stevenson's notes on Leslie Crosbie's
incessant lacework, he anticipates the presence of this motif in the
film, as well as the importance the film will place on Leslie's hands to
convey inner turmoil, by contrast with her outward air of control. It
tells us a good deal about Wyler's priorities that in the finished film,
he eschews the very elaborate lacemaking process as Stevenson describes it for something far simpler: preferring to use gesture to reveal
character rather than for purely decorative effect.

With evident excitement, Wyler scratches numerous lines beside what Stevenson proposes as the theme of the play: the difficulty
of guessing what is going on inside someone else's head, even someone you might think you know well.

Wyler's preoccupation with this theme, and how the actress playing Leslie Crosbie must embody it, is carried over in his annotations
on Howard Koch's second draft script for *The Letter*, dated April 10,
1940. The director's handwritten notes emphasize what he at one
point calls the "great deliberateness" of Leslie's gestures. Where
early in the screenplay Koch characterizes Leslie as addressing someone "with perfect control," Wyler underscores the description for
emphasis. Several lines later, where the actress's instructions read:
"her control slipping a little," Wyler first underscores "a little," then
changes "a" to "very"; and then, evidently still dissatisfied with this
characterization, he crosses out the directions altogether, apparently
preferring Bette at least temporarily to maintain the appearance of
"perfect control" established moments before.

Wyler's marginalia suggest that for him, part of the "action" of
The Letter must be the subtle alterations in Leslie Crosbie's manner
as we come closer and closer to the truth of what happened in her
cottage on the night of the murder. Only when we are almost exactly
midway through the script (having reached the pivotal scene, in which

Leslie's lawyer suddenly confronts her with disturbing questions about the incriminating letter) do the director's marginal notes indicate that Wyler is finally willing to allow her "perfect control" to show some cracks: "This is first time she lies badly," Wyler remarks of Leslie's nervous speech when asked about the existence of the letter. "Up to this point she has played it as if truly innocent—with a straight, frank and convincingly honest countenance—no by-play, etc."

◈

Whatever anxieties Wyler may have had about whether Bette would want to work with him again were soon dispelled when she accepted the role of Leslie Crosbie with an enthusiasm that she rarely allowed herself to express at Warner Bros. Aside from the personal associations the Maugham play had long held for her, Bette possessed a fair idea of what Wyler had done for her career in the past and was most anxious to be directed by him again.

Still, much as Wyler seemed to have anticipated, Bette's personal feelings about him were distinctly mixed. For all that she had been through with various lovers in the interim, Bette continued to harbor a good deal of resentment toward Wyler for so abruptly terminating their affair at the end of *Jezebel*. Whereas he reportedly had regarded their relationship as little more than a "fling," Bette had clearly attached far more importance to it at the time than he—and even seemed briefly to have held out hopes for some sort of future with the director.

Now and for the rest of her life, she would wonder whether Wyler had been sincere when, in the third week of shooting *Jezebel*, he had tantalized her with the role of Cathy in *Wuthering Heights*. Not long after she expressed interest in the part to Jack Warner, Samuel Goldwyn had snatched up the Hecht-MacArthur script, and "Bette's" role had gone to the unlikely Merle Oberon. Had Wyler, in putting her up to seeing Warner about the Brontë project, merely been using her to generate interest in Goldwyn's camp?

To make matters worse—although it is doubtful that Wyler knew she had become pregnant in the course of their affair—there was the problem of Bette's lingering bad feelings about her second abortion, especially now that Wyler had only recently become a father. The summer before, Talli had given birth to their first child, whom they called Cathy (after the role in *Wuthering Heights* that Wyler had promised to Bette!).

By contrast with the domestic happiness Wyler had so successfully built for himself since *Jezebel,* Bette's personal life seemed a pitiful shambles, particularly after Litvak's standing her up in Honolulu: a painful humiliation Bette feared Wyler would have heard about from Litvak or another of the men in their garrulous set.

All this Bette was determined to conceal from Wyler when she and Robin Brown returned from Honolulu, more than three weeks before she was set to begin work on *The Letter,* on May 27, 1940. Much as Bette privately dreaded meeting Talli and hearing all about the Wylers' new baby, she braced herself to behave with perfect equanimity throughout, lest her former lover be allowed to perceive her agitation. Bette knew that the affair with Wyler during the making of *Jezebel* was no secret at Warners; but now she was anxious that others see their relationship as "businesslike."

Whether Wyler understood her struggle to hide her turbulent feelings about seeing him again is impossible to say; but there can be no question that the struggle fed into the intense performance he got from her in *The Letter.* During the first week of shooting, Bette seemed to get through it all fairly well. even Talli Wyler's visit to the set, when Willy presented her to Bette for the first time. But then, as the week drew to a close, Bette was appalled to discover that she might quite possibly be pregnant again, whether by Arthur Farnsworth, Anatole Litvak, or Bob Taplinger she had no idea.

Was it her imagination that during the second and third weeks of filming, cameraman Tony Gaudio kept casting "sideways" glances at her? As Bette would have learned by now, cameramen, having trained themselves to be acutely sensitive to anything that affected the physical appearance of the people they photographed, often intuitively monitored such ostensibly private matters as menstrual cycles and pregnancies. Although not a word on the subject passed between them, Bette was racked with anxiety that Gaudio sensed she was pregnant—and, far worse, that he might tell Willy Wyler about it.

Intent on masking her distress from co-workers, in private Bette cried endlessly at the prospect of a third abortion, which—she recalled years afterward—she feared would make it impossible for her to have a baby should she ever marry again. Still, after she saw a doctor on Wednesday, June 5, to confirm her pregnancy (having called in sick at the studio, Warner Bros. records show), Bette declared that she knew what she "had to do." And so it was that, on Saturday, June 15, a free day during the third week of filming, Bette underwent a third abortion.

Aside from the fact that she was free that Saturday, the timing must have seemed optimal, since according to Wyler's production schedule, Bette was not due to go in front of the cameras again until Thursday, June 20, for the sequence in which, dressed in a form-fitting white eyelet evening dress, Leslie steals off with her attorney to retrieve the incriminating letter. Bette had hoped to handle the abortion secretly, but the moment she appeared on the set in the white eyelet dress, she heard Tony Gaudio exclaim, "Jesus, Bette, it looks like you've lost five pounds over the weekend!"

During the making of *Jezebel*, Bette had taken immense comfort in what she found to be the soothing repetitiveness of Wyler's notorious multiple takes. Now she learned the pleasures (and, more important for her art, the theatrical effect) of another kind of repetition: the subtle but precise echoing and modulation of gestures and moves from one sequence to another. Although Bette's own annotations on the script for *Jezebel* show her beginning to pencil in connections between shots, all evidence indicates that she continued to conceive of her role largely in terms of individual sequences, leaving the over-all unity of the piece to her director.

All this changed by the time of *The Letter*, whose complex structure, based on three interlocking "confession" sequences (Leslie's intricately woven "web of lies," as Katharine Cornell had described it), required Bette to develop what Wyler taught her to call "unity of conception."

In his preliminary notes, Wyler repeatedly scrawled "THE END" beside Leslie's astonishing admission to her husband that she still loves the man she killed. His words indicate that for the director, this was the point toward which all the film's action is inescapably headed and in relation to which all must be played (notwithstanding the additional scenes that eventually were tacked on to satisfy the Production Code Administration's demand that Leslie be punished for her sins).

Thus, at the time of Leslie's first "confession," when she claims to have killed Hammond after he attempted to force himself upon her, although we cannot yet be certain that she is lying, the actress playing Leslie must at all times be conscious that her character has indeed fabricated the entire story, however successfully she puts it across to her listeners, who include her husband, her lawyer, and the callow young district officer whose unhappy task it is to arrest her.

At the time of the New York stage production in 1927, one

reviewer had written of Katharine Cornell in this scene that the actress managed to tell her tale "as though at every instant a crack might open in the lacquer of falsehood." Indeed, this scene was one of the principal reasons Cornell took the role.

After more than ample rehearsals of this first "confession" sequence with Wyler (per the director's custom), Bette was all nervous anticipation as they began the filming on Friday, May 31, 1940, at the end of the first week of shooting. Her nervousness was no doubt exacerbated by fears that she might be pregnant and by Tony Gaudio's falling ill barely an hour after they had begun to shoot, so that a replacement cameraman had to be summoned at the last minute.

The entire company had had the previous day off, during which Bette seems to have gone through her script with a pencil, expunging any ellipsis marks and repetitions of words, presumably to make her speech pour out more quickly.

As the lawyer Howard Joyce (actor James Stephenson) will later suggest, for all the effectiveness of her initial presentation, Leslie rather too precisely and meticulously repeats her version of what occurred on the night of the murder every time she relates it ("The story she told him the first time he saw her," Maugham writes in his short story, "she had never varied in the smallest detail"): an indication perhaps that it has all been very carefully thought out in advance lest any incriminating contradictions, any cracks in "the lacquer of falsehood," be discovered.

As anticipated in Bette's notations, she plays a good deal of the scene on top of her lines, rushing ahead with her "confession" at full blast, sometimes almost as if she can't stop herself. Her momentum here is assisted by Wyler's uncharacteristically emphatic cutting, making for a total of twenty-one shots, whose rhythms convey the artfulness with which Leslie Crosbie manages to glide through this first version of the killing: by marked contrast to the single languorous long take that dominates the painful second "confession" sequence, as we watch the murderess falter for the first time.

Bette's lying back on a sofa through a fairly large segment of the first "confession" concentrates much of her physical expression in her hands, whose incessant hysterical fidgeting with a handkerchief ("Movement never lies") hints at a truth entirely at odds with the "perfect control" of Leslie's deftly orchestrated speech. As in a Martha Graham dance where movement expresses passionate, irrational depths of the self, Leslie's gestures allude to what she cannot yet say with words ("With all my heart I still love the man I killed"). Following the recounting of the murder, Wyler cuts to a close-up of her right hand as it unconsciously, involuntarily assumes again the strange shape it took in the aftermath of the killing: fingers oddly splayed, as if misshapen by the horror of it all.

While in Maugham's stage play Leslie makes a big point of wanting "to sit upright" before she begins her initial account of the murder, the film's placement of her on a sofa, with the camera hovering (almost obscenely) close above, makes her appear terribly vulnerable: so much so that we may think, Surely she must be innocent, or the most brazen of liars. And there is the added advantage of giving Leslie's speech several beats as she punctuates her account with a series of small, precise movements (all of them to be almost exactly repeated later, at the time of the third "confession"): first sitting up; then rising; then turning her back to her listeners and to the camera, as if to conceal her face as she reenacts the murder—this last a touch borrowed from Katharine Cornell, who had done it on Broadway to great effect.

"This is the first time she lies badly," Wyler noted of Leslie's second "confession," filmed on Monday, June 10, during the third week of shooting. Only one other person is present: the lawyer who, in the course of visiting her in prison, confronts Leslie with the existence of the incriminating letter. Now we watch her breezy self-assurance about the outcome of her case metamorphose into agonies of apprehension. (Bette's impending abortion, scheduled for the end of the week, and her own desire to conceal her condition, must have made performing this scene in which Leslie vainly endeavors not to give herself away a vertiginous experience.) On account of the especially intricate blocking and reframing required throughout the sequence, which covered some six pages of script, Wyler had rehearsed Davis and Stephenson all day, Saturday, June 8, from nine in the morning until five-thirty at night; running through it all again for two hours and forty-five minutes on Monday morning before shooting a total of fifteen takes (which Lord justified to Wallis with the explanation that "Wyler made so many takes with the roving camera because he did not know exactly what speed and movement would cover the dialogue to go over them").

Whereas the cutting rhythms in the first "confession" register the deftness and fluency with which Leslie initially tells her tale, the long take that dominates this second sequence—spanning the time between Joyce's appearance and Leslie's frantic denial that the letter is hers—adds considerable tension and suspense by refusing to mask the agonizing passage of time as Leslie's panic builds to a crescendo. The relentlessly "roving camera" to which Lord refers in his June 10 memorandum heightens our sense of Leslie's frenzied struggle to escape the trap her lawyer has set for her.

After Leslie hastily concocts an absurd story about having invited Hammond to her cottage to seek his advice on a gift for her husband, the murderess realizes the ineptitude of this newest lie and falls into a faint. Wyler follows this with a piquant little scene in the prison's first aid room, where, by contrast with the bold full-body acting she has just been called upon to do, Davis must accomplish everything with scarcely more than her left arm (extended upward and poised against the wall) and the crown of her head, as this is all we are permitted to see of her as she lies in shadow on a cot with her lawyer hovering above. When the lawyer informs Leslie that her letter to Hammond is in the possession of his Chinese wife, her reaction takes the form of a dancelike "succession": a subtle fluid movement through Davis's upper body that starts in the fingers of her left hand as they curl slowly into her palm, followed by an agonized flexion of the wrist, then a small shudder at the back of her head as at length we hear a low mournful sound issue from her throat.

"Can't we go back to plantation for the end?—so Leslie can be at the same place where she loved and killed Hammond?" Wyler had scribbled on the second draft script in April 1940.

The idea did not find its way into the finished film, however. As it is, the third "confession" sequence takes place in Howard Joyce's house, where a party is to be given in honor of Leslie's acquittal. It is here that Leslie's husband, Robert Crosbie, discovers the contents of her letter to Hammond; and here that she tells the truth about the murder at long last, in a scene whose nuances of blocking and editing echo those of Leslie's first "confession" (providing the satisfying sense of balance that Wyler presumably had once hoped to achieve by returning to Leslie's cottage at the end).

At the time his stage play was first produced, Maugham had experienced considerable trepidation about whether audiences would sit for another long narrative from Leslie in the final moments of Act Three. After two or three rehearsals, he replaced her final account of the murder with what he called a "throwback" scene, in which (the stage having darkened for a moment) we cut back to the night of the murder, to observe the actual quarrel that led to Leslie's shooting her lover. Maugham believed that the realistic reenactment of Leslie's final meeting with Hammond avoided the "tediousness" inherent in her simply retelling the tale in the form of a dramatic monologue.

Robert Stevenson seems to have been attracted to this approach in the pre–Warner Bros. treatment he prepared for Wyler in August 1939; but where the treatment proposes the possibility of using "flashback construction," Wyler scrawled an emphatic "NO!" in the margin: anticipating similar objections to the flashback in Howard Koch's second draft screenplay (Wyler's April 1940 annotation: "NO FLASHBACKS"), according to which Leslie would recall the murder in a voice-over, while the actual events leading up to Hammond's death were shown on-screen in "pantomime."

Wyler does not appear to have shared Maugham's fear that another long narrative from Leslie might bore the audience. Possibly because from the first Wyler had envisioned doing *The Letter* with Davis (with whose capacity for expressive movement he was abundantly well acquainted), he repeatedly declined to insert a flashback in place of Leslie's third "confession," believing that its dramatic interest was far less the rather lurid events she recounted than her manner of recounting them.

How does a woman tell her husband that she has made a cuckold of him? Where Katharine Cornell is said to have played the scene all anguish for what she has done, Bette's Leslie is harsher, more sadistic: sister to her Mildred in *Of Human Bondage* (except that Leslie's "good breeding" makes the violent passions that erupt here so much more astonishing). To judge by his notes, Wyler seems from the first to have encouraged Bette in this interpretation: so much so that at one point, he demanded that she play it rather more "strongly" than she was prepared to do. Having conceived of everything in the film as leading ineluctably to the moment when Leslie tells her husband that she still loves the man she killed, Wyler instructed Bette to look Robert in the face as she hurls these appalling words at him: the first direction of Wyler's that Bette is recorded to have resisted, on the grounds that any woman would look away upon uttering a truth so harsh.

Although, in due course, Bette deferred to her director's judgment and delivered the line as instructed, the disagreement quietly marked a major turning point in their working relationship.

Bette and her mother,
Ruthie, on April 6, 1908,
the day after Bette's birth.

Bette; her sister, Bobby;
and their father, Harlow
Morrell Davis. Bette was
so traumatized by the loss
of her father after her
parents' divorce that, in
later years, she could no
longer bear to remember
the true story of her early
childhood.

3

Bette, age 15 (right) in the Fall of 1923, after her return to Massachusetts. At Newton High School, Bette was a class officer and wildly popular with boys, but she was privately in turmoil because of her sudden proximity to Harlow and his new wife.

5

Bette's first husband, Ham Nelson. They met in boarding school but married after Bette went to Hollywood.

4

Bette, age 20, in Rochester, New York, in 1928, as she began her stage career.

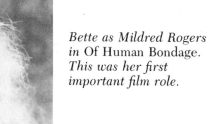

Bette as Mildred Rogers in Of Human Bondage. *This was her first important film role.*

Bette and Victor McLaglen in March 1936, the night she won her first Academy Award, for her performance in Dangerous.

Below, *Bette and Henry Fonda,
her co-star, on the set of
Jezebel.*

Top left, *Bette as Julie Marsden in* Jezebel, *her first fully realized dramatic
performance. In later years, Bette would weave a web of destructive fantasies around the story of this film.* Above, *Bette and William Wyler during
the filming of* Jezebel. *These were perhaps the happiest months of Bette's
life. She was not only madly in love with Wyler but also doing her best
screen work to date under his direction.*

Bette and Spencer Tracy in February 1939. She has just won her second Academy Award, for Jezebel.

Bette and Geraldine Fitzgerald in Dark Victory. Although this was a period of intense emotional turmoil for Bette, she managed to turn in one of her most powerful performances.

13

Bette and George Brent in Dark Victory. *The day this scene was shot, she and Brent had just begun a love affair and they kept breaking down in giggles over what they read as double-entendres in the script.*

Bette in The Private Lives of Elizabeth and Essex. *The role of Elizabeth had been performed on stage by Lynn Fontanne, one of the actresses Bette most admired.*

15

Bette and her mother,
Ruthie, out on the town
in Hollywood after Bette's
divorce from Ham
Nelson. Ruthie had
transferred all of her own
ambitions to her daughter
and she often seemed to
enjoy Bette's stardom
even more than Bette did.

Bette as Leslie Crosbie in
The Letter, *her second
film directed by William
Wyler and, arguably, her
greatest performance.*

16

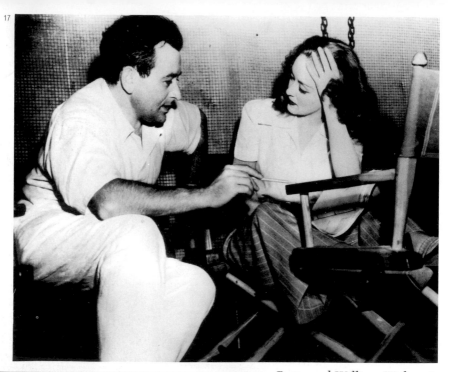

Bette and William Wyler at work on The Letter. *Their love affair was long over by now, and Wyler was married to another woman.*

Bette and her second husband, Arthur Farnsworth, at their wedding on December 31, 1940. Bobby and her husband, Robert Pelgram, are on the right. Three years later Farnsworth died under mysterious circumstances.

Bette as Regina Giddons in The Little Foxes. *Her collisions with Wyler during their third film together ended the collaboration that had produced her greatest performances.*

Bette and Paul Henreid in Now, Voyager.

21

22

23

Top, *Bette and third husband, William Grant Sherry, on their honeymoon.*
Above left, *Bette and Gary Merrill, her fourth husband, in* All About Eve.
*They met during this film and then imagined they could live their roles
during their marriage.* Above right, *Bette's daughter Margot Merrill, before doctors determined that the child had suffered brain damage.*

24

25

26

Top left, *Bette in Maine with her children Margot and Michael.* Top right, *Bette and her daughter B.D. in Maine. Bette adored the girl she called her "only natural daughter," but Davis's often violent relationship with Gary Merrill and her failure to shield B.D. from his wrath was particularly traumatic for B.D.* Above, *Gary Merrill with Margot, Michael, and B.D.*

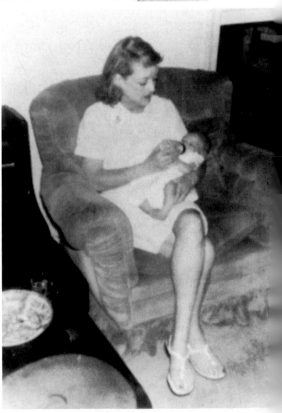

Bette and 16-year-old B.D.
on B.D.'s wedding day.
Bette was confident that her
daughter's marriage to a
much older man would be
short-lived.

Bette and her first grandson,
Ashley Hyman, in Connecticut.
Bette adored the role of
grandmother and doted on her
grandson.

29

B.D., Ashley, and Bette in Connecticut. Bette had moved to Connecticut to be near her daughter, but the tensions between them finally caused B.D. and her family to flee to Pennsylvania.

Bette and Mae West the night they met for the first time. Bette was so nervous at the prospect of their dinner that she was quite drunk by the time Mae arrived.

Bette "cleaning up" at the home of her friend Charles Pollock in Los Angeles.

B.D., Charles Pollock, Bette, and Ashley the night of the anniversary party Bette gave for her daughter and her husband in Los Angeles in 1983. Less than a year later, B.D. began to write her devastating memoir of life with Bette, My Mother's Keeper.

Rock Hudson and Bette's son-in-law, Jeremy Hyman.

Lillian Gish and Bette in
The Whales of August.
Bette's jealousy of Gish
would cause her to
destroy her own last
triumph as an actress.

Bette and director Larry
Cohen on the set of her
final film, Wicked
Stepmother. *Bette*
walked out on the
project after she saw
herself in the first
rushes.

Bette's friends Robin Brown and Dori Brenner in Los Angeles after Bette's funeral. Robin had known Bette since they were both teenagers and remained her best friend until Bette's death.

Bette Davis near the end of her life. Even after cancer and several strokes she was still "Battling Bette."

hile Bette worked on *The Letter*, Ruthie devoted herself to furnishing, and endlessly photographing, "Riverbottom," the English Tudor house she had selected for her daughter to buy among the riding trails and horse stables on Rancho Avenue in Glendale.

By contrast with the formal English and French antiques with which Ruthie had crammed Bette's Warners' dressing room, she filled Riverbottom with tattered, unpretentious odds and ends culled from local thrift shops, so that it looked as if she and her daughters had been hauling this furniture around with them for years. Every slightly shabby table and chair, every old Toby mug and hurricane lamp, hinted at a patina of memories and associations: the stable family background they had never really known. Ruthie may have thought: This is how my own furniture might look today had I remained in New England, had I not run off to New York.

Even the way Ruthie photographed Riverbottom was different: There is no pictorialist haze here, no sense of evanescence, of the inevitability of moving on soon. Ruthie has given a new sharpness to these carefully developed pictures of her daughter's first real home, whose air of permanence and stability is enhanced by Mrs. Davis's having printed them as eight-by-tens on heavy paper (so different from the fleeting, snapshot effect of her many pictures of previous—always rented—homes).

Until much too late, it seemed never to have occurred to Ruthie that the establishment she was lovingly, painstakingly creating for her daughter at Riverbottom would soon be home to Arthur Farnsworth as well.

Undaunted by the romances with Litvak and Taplinger, Farney stepped up his campaign as soon as Bette and Robin returned to Franconia at the end of July. (Bette was not due back at Warners until November, to film Goulding's *The Great Lie*.) Now that his divorce was about to be final, the hotel desk clerk with "a taste for good living" wasted no time proposing marriage. Bette Davis offered a quicker path to fortune than waiting for Mother Main to die. Where Ham Nelson had dreaded being "Mr. Bette Davis" for the rest of his life, Arthur Farnsworth clearly relished the prospect.

Robin Brown recalls being "surprised" when she learned that Bette and Farney were to be married on December 31, 1940, in Rimrock, Arizona; but hardly as surprised as Jack Warner must have been when, no doubt expecting one of the actress's usual diatribes, he opened his latest letter from Bette to discover a terse announcement that she had gotten married. Although Bette went on for several lines more to request time off from the studio, not once did she mention the name of her bridegroom, whom Louella Parsons identified in the papers the next day as a "wealthy Boston businessman," while other equally bewildered reporters described him as "a childhood friend" or, more simply, "Arthur Farnsworth of Boston." Bette's initially obscure second husband became a public presence soon enough, however, when that spring she utilized a month's vacation with him at Butternut to publicize the premiere of *The Great Lie*.

At the time of the wedding, Jack Warner had feared that Bette was about to use her new husband and home in New England as a means of escape from Hollywood. Did her marriage to a pipe-smoking "country squire" with leather patches on his elbows presage some fresh struggle with the studio?

That this was not the case became evident when, in mid-March, she called Warners' publicity director Charlie Einfeld to propose a charity benefit premiere of *The Great Lie* in Littleton, New Hampshire, on April 5, her thirty-third birthday: scarcely the behavior of someone who viewed New England as a refuge from Hollywood.

On the contrary, Bette seemed quite content, even anxious, to bring Hollywood with her to New England.

"The night of the big premiere, we arranged for all the lights in Littleton, New Hampshire, to go out at exactly the same time," recalls Bob William, Davis's publicist at Warners. Then moments later, the townspeople were dazzled by the sight of Bette and Farney leading a torchlight parade toward the theater. It was a spectacle calculated to be entirely unlike anything the little New England town had ever witnessed.

"Let's do something vital and strong even if you're not on the screen all the time," Willy Wyler had said to Bette during the filming of *The Letter*.

He meant Lillian Hellman's *The Little Foxes*, whose first draft screenplay the playwright had shown him by May of 1940. Wyler told Bette that he had immediately thought *The Little Foxes* ideal for her when he saw it on Broadway the year before, with Tallulah Bankhead in the role of Regina Giddens. But when Bette read Hellman's film script she was a good deal less enthusiastic than he, her principal objection being that Regina was off-screen far too often. Quite simply, it seemed to Bette that she had worked much too hard at becoming a star to accept a role in which she was not stage center almost all the time.

Nonetheless, at the time of *The Letter* Bette remained very much under Wyler's influence, so that when the director assured her that her craft was strong enough by now for her to carry a film like *The Little Foxes*, she agreed to approach Jack Warner with the proposal that he loan her out to Samuel Goldwyn, who owned the Hellman screenplay.

Bette was still shooting *The Letter* when she talked to Warner about *The Little Foxes*, following up with a letter dated July 10, 1940 (ten days before the end of filming), in which she made it clear that her sole interest in portraying Regina Giddens was yet another opportunity to work with Wyler. She stated that if some other director were assigned, she would not want to do it. So pleased was Bette with her work with Wyler on *The Letter* that in the event that she was allowed to make *The Little Foxes*, she offered to waive her three-picture-a-year deal with Warner Bros. to allow an additional film. This was scarcely the kind of concession Jack Warner was accustomed to receiving from her.

Initially, as in the past, Warner showed scant interest in loaning her out. Hadn't they gone to war over precisely this issue before; and hadn't Bette lost? Indeed, now more than ever, perhaps, Bette Davis represented an important form of capital to the studio. Yet so far was he from wanting to make her unhappy that (as alluded to in her July 10 letter) Warner even offered to try to purchase *The Little Foxes* from Goldwyn, in order for Bette to do the picture at Warner Bros.

In the end, although Bette seemed to have convinced herself that it had been she who finally persuaded Warner to loan her out for *The Little Foxes*, the decisive factor appears to have been Warners' desire to borrow Gary Cooper from Goldwyn for the upcoming *Sergeant York*.

Somewhat reluctantly agreeing to do what he had steadfastly refused even to consider in the past, Jack Warner made certain that the fine print of his December 23, 1940, preliminary letter of agreement with Goldwyn contained a clause prohibiting his rival from using Bette Davis's name in any general announcement of artists appearing in Goldwyn productions. Warner did not want Bette's prestige and publicity value to be used to any further advantage to Warners' competitor than was absolutely necessary.

And to assure that Bette would return to Warner Bros. as valuable an asset as she was when they loaned her out, Warner instructed general counsel Roy Obringer to stipulate that Goldwyn accord Bette full "star billing" in connection with *The Little Foxes:* adding that this was "for Davis' own protection as well as ours."

Something else repeatedly occupies the eye in the various legal papers and agreements prepared in connection with Bette's loan-out: the name Tallulah Bankhead. Again and again it is stipulated in one way or another that Bette Davis is being sent off to Goldwyn to appear in the Tallulah Bankhead role, so firmly and decisively had the stage actress managed to identify herself with the character of Regina Giddens after 408 performances at the National Theatre on Broadway and a very extensive road tour that would span some two years and 25,000 miles.

In Hollywood, there had been no great sense of Bette's having portrayed the Katharine Cornell role in *The Letter* or the Lynn Fontanne role in *Elizabeth the Queen;* even Bette, who had seen, admired, and borrowed liberally and, it would seem, unabashedly from both actresses' Broadway performances, appeared to suffer no particular anxiety of influence with regard to them. But, as presaged by the repeated impish appearance of her predecessor's name in the legal file on *The Little Foxes,* for Bette Davis, Tallulah Bankhead's already legendary portrayal of Regina Giddens would be another matter altogether: vexing, inhibiting, even somehow mocking her at nearly every turn.

In the beginning, Bette had not seen the stage production; certainly not when Wyler first persuaded her to talk to Warner about it; or even during the time when Warner and Goldwyn were hammering out their agreement. As late as March 11, 1941, when Goldwyn vice-president Reeves Espy agreed to Warner's final demand that Davis be "accorded sole star credit" and that her name appear above the film's title in the identical-size type (and that no other actor in the film be billed in type larger than 75 percent the size used for Bette), she seems still to have avoided seeing Bankhead in the role.

On April 14, 1941, Bette arrived at Goldwyn with an entourage including costume designer Orry-Kelly, makeup man Perc Westmore, and hairdresser Maggie Donovan, all of whom she had brought with her from Warner Bros. to execute the rather specific ideas she had worked up about how Regina Giddens must look.

As tests of makeup and wardrobe for *The Little Foxes* began, Wyler expressed grave reservations about the "dead white, mask-like" physiognomy (as he described it to Talli) with which Bette insisted on encumbering her character. It seemed to Wyler that by queerly covering her face with calamine, Bette had turned Regina Giddens into a "grotesque" rather than the complex, multifaceted character Tallulah Bankhead had discovered in Hellman's play. Before long, Jack Warner and Hal Wallis had been apprised that Wyler's abiding disapproval of the numerous makeup and wardrobe tests had greatly upset Bette, who seemed to grow increasingly "sick and hysterical" with each passing day.

At times it seemed to Wyler that Bette was out of spirits over finding herself at age thirty-three cast in the role of a forty-year-old woman, with a lovely daughter mature enough to conduct a serious romance of her own; and that Bette intended the grotesquerie of her makeup somehow to distance her from the part. Or perhaps, he speculated, the outlandish mask Bette had fashioned for herself was meant to lure attention away from the other players, to an actress who continued to fear the audience's somehow forgetting her on account of Hellman's having left Regina off-screen so much of the time.

That Bette's first major conflict with Wyler during the filming of *The Little Foxes* had to do with her makeup and other externals anticipated the larger discord that would erupt between them, as the actress persisted in building Regina Giddens from the outside, while her director repeatedly urged her to try to grasp her character from within.

From the time they first worked together on *Jezebel*, Wyler had been acutely aware of what he called Bette's "mannerisms": any gratuitous bits of physical business that did not serve to express character. Eventually Wyler's repeated threats to tie Bette's head back to stop it from twisting about madly had even become something of a joke between them (unusual for Bette, who by all accounts found it difficult to laugh at herself). But where she had allowed Wyler to curb her excesses during the filming of *Jezebel* and *The Letter*, the stardom that those films had helped her to attain made Bette substantially less malleable now.

"She had been another person when they made *Jezebel*," explains Talli Wyler. "By the time of *The Little Foxes*, everything was different. Because she had experienced such enormous success in the interim, Bette's ego had grown a lot bigger. She and my husband had always worked so well together in the past that I think, in a way, it really shocked both of them that they fought so hard now."

This time the actress bristled whenever Wyler urged her—as he recalled—"to be simple and dignified and not resort to a lot of gestures and accentuated speech and tricks that are just plain bad." While many of Bette's mannerisms were actually quite "good," he declared, especially when her role was that of a "high-strung or worried woman," Regina Giddens, as written by Hellman, "didn't call for that stuff."

But most of all, Wyler told her he wanted to be certain that she was planning to play Regina Giddens on-screen, and not simply "Bette Davis." In short, whatever the degree of stardom that Bette had undeniably attained by this point, her director was anxious that she continue to regard herself, and to function, as an actress. This, however, Bette struck him as being peculiarly afraid of doing, as if failing to repeat whatever had brought her success in the past might cause her to lose that success now.

"Bette was a woman very terrified of letting go of whatever she had," explains her friend Dori Brenner. "There came a point in her career where she began to imitate herself as an actress and to refuse to know that she was doing that."

And says veteran Warner Bros. script supervisor Meta Carpenter, "She had never learned to weigh the advice she was being given. It always had to be: 'I know what I'm doing! I'll do what I want to do! I'm controlling my life, and this is the way it's going to be!'"

△▼△

"For heaven's sake, why don't you get Tallulah Bankhead for the part?" Bette finally exploded at her director, whose ceaseless criticism is recorded in studio papers as having caused her to grow ill.

Even during the making of *The Little Foxes*, the influence that Bankhead's performance may or may not have had on Bette's was already something of a vexed question, which curiously persists to this day. Apparently at Wyler's urging, after Bette had finished the film, *The Bride Came C.O.D.*, she was en route to New Hampshire for a month's vacation with Farney when she stopped in Cleveland to see *The Little Foxes*, then in the final throes of its by now somewhat controversial national tour.

The road show was widely thought to have degenerated into almost a parody of its former self, as Lillian Hellman grew increasingly agitated by what struck her as Bankhead's cocaine-induced overacting, in contrast to the more expert and restrained performance the actress had turned in on Broadway. Even now, however, there lingered the magnificent gusto and voluptuousness that Tallulah had brought to the play, quite in keeping with the dramatist's intentions regarding Regina Giddens, of whom Hellman would say, "When I wrote it, I was amused by Regina—I never thought of her as a villainous character—all I meant was a big sexy woman": in short, someone quite like Tallulah. Long afterward, Hellman would savor her own special excitement when first she heard Tallulah's "deep thrilling offstage laugh" prior to the actress's entrance in Act One: "a laugh that had affected the audience like an electric current."

Set in the American South in 1900, *The Little Foxes* chronicles the internecine struggles within the Hubbard family as Regina (now Mrs. Horace Giddens) and her two no less rapacious brothers, Ben and Oscar, try to put together a business deal with Chicago business-man William Marshall. After Regina's ailing estranged husband re-fuses to give her the money she needs to be part of the deal, she allows him to die by refusing to get his medicine when he suffers what proves to be a fatal attack.

Ina Claire and Judith Anderson had both reportedly turned down the female lead in Hellman's stage play on the grounds that it was too "unsympathetic," when, on the advice of director Herman Shumlin, the role was offered to Bankhead (whose "scarlet" reputation is said to have worried the playwright from the first). Although her prior ap-pearances on Broadway had done much to advance her reputation as a formidable personality, Tallulah had yet to establish herself as a serious actress until February of 1939, when the critics extolled the "extraordinary variety" of her Regina Giddens, a character at once "seductive and dangerous," "charming and unscrupulous."

In later years, Bette liked to say that Willy had sent her to see Bankhead in *The Little Foxes* to ensure that she would give "a dif-ferent interpretation of the part." According to Davis, when she saw Tallulah in Cleveland, however, she realized at once that the stage actress "had played it the only way it could be played." Hence the discord that blighted her work with Wyler in *The Little Foxes*, in which, disregarding the director's objections, Bette insisted on por-traying Regina Giddens in the manner of Tallulah. "Miss Hellman's Regina was written with such definition that it could only be played one way," said Bette in her 1962 memoir: a version of the Wyler-Davis conflict that has turned up in almost all subsequent accounts.

But in a September 9, 1941, interview published in the *New York World-Telegram* shortly after the film was completed, the usu-ally laconic Wyler sounded off publicly on the Tallulah question; his comments indicate that, at the time, Davis was adamant about want-ing to avoid all comparison with Tallulah's interpretation. "Bette thought I was having her ape Tallulah Bankhead, who had done the part on the stage. Yet it's impossible to say the lines, wear the same period costumes and use a similar locale without having some simi-larity to the play. I couldn't say, 'Let's not do it at all because Tallulah did it'; that would have thrown out the whole play. Boy did it irritate me to read that I was making her copy Tallulah! That wasn't true. I was just making her play Regina Giddens and not Bette Davis when the camera started. She was inordinately frightened of the charge of mimicry."

Asked about all this many years afterward, Talli Wyler replies:

"As I remember, he wanted Bette to have more of the quality that Tallulah Bankhead had had on the stage: a quality of lustiness and sexuality. Tallulah had played it as if she was really enjoying herself! That's the kind of performance he wanted to get from Bette, but she had an entirely different idea and insisted on playing it her way, so that the whole experience became quite miserable for both of them."

Which takes us to the crux of Bette's dispute with her director— and why, in later years, she seemed to block out of her thoughts the painful objections he had had to an interpretation that struck him as shrill and sexless: lacking in precisely the intoxicating variety that (whatever its lapses) Tallulah's stage performance had so abundantly possessed.

While—in an apparent effort to differentiate her performance from Bankhead's—Bette seemed perversely determined to expunge all carnality from her character, Wyler agreed with Hellman on Regina's fundamental sexiness: like the playwright, Wyler wanted to be "amused" by Regina Giddens. Where once he had taught Bette to pace herself and to allow a gesture sequence to grow and gather momentum, now he urged her to do the same with the development of her character. Only if Bette first allowed the audience to be charmed and amused by Regina would the impact of her subsequent perfidy be felt as deeply as Hellman had meant it to be.

Southern California was experiencing the sultriest spring it had known in years. Temperatures exceeded one hundred degrees on the Goldwyn soundstage where Willy Wyler and Bette Davis were film ing *The Little Foxes*.

"Let me alone," the director growled at his wife when he came home after a day's shooting. Asked how things had gone with Bette, he growled again. "I don't want to talk about it. I had it all day. I don't want it here."

Even asleep, Wyler moaned and tossed about, fiercely grinding his teeth all through the night.

Beneath her voluminous flounced skirt and layers of petticoats, Bette wore a corset laced so firmly that it required two wardrobe ladies to pull the cords. Compelling her to breathe with her ribs rather than with the full diaphragm, the corset seemed only to exac-erbate what Bette's attorney, Dudley Furse, privately characterized as her "hysterical condition."

From the outset there had been unanticipated problems with the film script when Bette grew extremely agitated over the fresh point of attack Hellman had devised: adding new scenes at the beginning of the story in an attempt to open it up for the screen. Where the stage play had begun just as the Hubbards' dinner party is drawing to a close, allowing the actress portraying Regina instantly to make her mark with her "deep thrilling offstage laugh" (with which Tallulah had enthralled Hellman) and flirtatious banter with Mr. Marshall, the film script begins on the morning of the party as Regina's daughter, Zan (Teresa Wright), flirts with the handsome David (a character Hellman created for the screenplay), followed by a scene showing Zan having breakfast with her mother.

As Wyler was quick to recognize, Bette resented a younger actress's being established as the love interest in the opening sequence, as well as Regina's initial appearance in her capacity as Zan's mother. Minor and inconsequential as these new scenes may have appeared to Hellman and others, Bette regarded them as serious obstacles to establishing her character as vividly as she might have liked in the dinner scene that followed.

To make matters worse, the profusion of notes and marginalia regarding the character of Zan in Wyler's annotated script for *The Little Foxes* suggests that, where Bette's performance in *Jezebel* and *The Letter* had received the director's almost single-minded attention, this time he was no less concerned with the work of another actress in the film.

BETTE DAVIS POISONED BY MISTAKE and POISON ACCIDENT PERILS BETTE DAVIS, headlines announced during the second week of filming when Bette drank deadly household ammonia, which (after first aid was promptly administered) she said she had mistaken for the sedative her physician had prescribed for agitated nerves.

Not long afterward, word reached Jack Warner that, much to Wyler's chagrin, Bette's unusually overwrought state of mind had already ruined a good deal of the footage that had been shot. Artistic differences aside, there seemed to be a distinct personal subtext to the perpetual collisions with Wyler; from the outset, Bette had scarcely concealed an interest in rekindling her romance with the director, and when it became obvious that he had no intention of reciprocating, she grew moody and petulant.

Worst of all was the filming of the dinner party sequence, which—to judge by the copious revisions Wyler scribbled in his annotated script and by the extent to which it all had to be cut down in

the finished film—seems to have presented the most inherently trou-
blesome material. The Warner Bros. general counsel reported to
Warner and Wallis that Bette's nervous condition had kept her from
acting to any great effect in this sequence; whereupon an exasperated
Wyler tore into her performance to an extent that seemed only to
make her more "hysterical and ill" by the moment.

At length, exhausted from makeup and wardrobe changes, and
worn out by Wyler's persistent censure, Bette announced that she
had had enough. Let Wyler and Goldwyn replace her with whomever
they desired; Bette Davis was walking out of the picture. Before
leaving the lot, however, Bette appeared to collapse, which doctors
later attributed to the punishing heat coupled with the ill effects of a
tightly laced corset.

Warners' December 23, 1940, letter of agreement with Goldwyn
explicitly left them clear of any liability in the event that Bette failed,
refused, or neglected to complete her work on *The Little Foxes*. On
some level, her studio may have feared the trouble that now ensued
as Bette flatly declined to return to work, deeming herself ill with
exhaustion. Still, there was the matter of the $150,000 Goldwyn had
agreed to pay for Bette's services, of which her share was to have
been $66,667.72, with the rest going to Warner Bros.: hence Jack
Warner's abiding interest in monitoring events at the rival lot, where
Goldwyn had reportedly wasted no time sending word to Bette that
he was giving her some time off, May 12–21.

Before she was due to return, however, Bette's attorney, Dudley
Furse, told Roy Obringer that instead of improving during her days
off, her health and spirits seemed to have drastically deteriorated.
Her personal physician, Dr. Paul Moore, had declared her in need of
"additional rest" at the rented house in Laguna Beach, where she was
being cared for by Farney and Ruthie. Soothed by a series of whee-
dling telephone calls from Wyler and Goldwyn, Bette appeared to
have reneged on her vow to walk out of the picture. According to
Furse, both men had promised Bette "different treatment" when she
came back to the lot. As a further gesture of conciliation, Goldwyn
and Reeves Espy instructed Wyler to shoot around Bette from May
21 to June 5, on the assumption that by then Dr. Moore would have
pronounced her well enough to resume work.

There remained Goldwyn's insurance carriers to be dealt with.
Following a conversation with Bette's attorney, Lloyd's of London
dispatched their own examiner, Dr. Dorrel Dickinson, who promptly

seconded Dr. Moore's opinion that she needed to stay in bed for ten days. As Furse was to note, even if Bette was compelled to return to work before June 5, her "present condition" would make her of little use to Goldwyn.

▲▼▲

"Silence would scare them more," said Bette, suggesting that Wyler cut the line in which Regina answers her brother Ben's nervous inquiry about the dying Horace.

As Ben Hubbard knows only too well, with her husband dead, Regina may be able to gain a controlling interest in the business deal. So instead of saying "He's not conscious"—as indicated in Hellman's script and included by Wyler in the film—Bette thought it crueler and more effective to respond wordlessly.

Which, in large part, seems to have been her strategy with Wyler upon returning to the set of *The Little Foxes*. Although lurid rumors in the press went so far as to report Bette's having "jabbed Wyler unconscious" shortly after coming back to work, their ongoing battle was mostly subtextual. More often than not, she reacted to him with steely politeness, as if they barely knew each other. Rather than argue with him, when Willy said or did something she didn't like, she forced herself to walk silently off the set. But when Goldwyn—less patient now—threatened to take her to court, she returned and went through the motions of doing as Wyler told her.

Strangely enough, as actress and director they did some splendid work together in the tense and unpleasant days between June 5 and July 3.

Of particular interest is the sequence where Regina allows Horace to die by refusing to fetch his heart medicine. Cameraman Gregg Toland shows Regina seated impassively in the living room, while, behind her, a desperate Horace struggles to crawl upstairs for the medicine. Where Hellman's screenplay intercuts between Regina (in the living room) and Horace (on the staircase), Toland's deep-focus technique puts the two in a single intricately composed shot.

"I can have him sharp, or both of them sharp," the cameraman told Wyler, who preferred that only Regina be crisply defined in the foreground, in order that we might watch her face and body for signs of what she may be thinking and feeling as she leaves her husband to die.

Bette gets her effect by very gradually lengthening her spine, then extending the back of her neck, as, with great effort, Horace drags himself up the stairs behind her: making Regina's slow ascent in the foreground of the shot a grotesque reflection of Horace's in the rear.

And there are other fine details in Bette's performance: the sense of amplitude she projects with uplifted chest and outstretched arms; the degree of expression she places in her feet and legs, whose sudden "unladylike" extensions deftly embody her character's boldness.

Too often, however, Bette takes her details from past performances, burdening her character with what Wyler derided as meaningless and unnecessary gestures: appropriate for Julie Marsden or Leslie Crosbie, perhaps, but not for Regina Giddens, about whom they communicated nothing. Why, the director wanted to know, does Bette's Regina tug incessantly at handkerchiefs and other fabrics; why does she keep catching errant strands of hair and pulling them back from her face?

"What is acting, anyway?" Wyler would ask. "Are you thinking what the character is thinking or are you wondering, 'Shall I give them a bit of the old profile?' or 'Shall I wave my arm a little?' Well, you know the answer yourself. The camera catches all these things and tattles directly to the audience."

When these remarks appeared in the press after she and Wyler had finished their work on *The Little Foxes*, Bette went wild, angrily vowing never to work with the director again.

At which a gleeful Jack Warner leapt into the fray, to assure Bette of his "indignation" that Willy Wyler would dare to criticize her so. Unlike Wyler, the studio boss clearly had no objection to the star's playing "Bette Davis" on-screen, or to her repeating bits of physical business that had appealed to audiences before. In the past, Bette had repeatedly aligned herself with Wyler; now suddenly, that September of 1941, she found herself writing a note of unprecedented unctuousness to Jack Warner. She thanked him for taking her side against Wyler, whom she bitterly accused of having hurt her very deeply.

SEVENTEEN

ollowing *The Little Foxes*, Bette appeared in
director William Keighley's film version of
George S. Kaufman and Moss Hart's *The Man
Who Came to Dinner* and in John Huston's *In
This Our Life;* and in October of 1941 there
was a curious episode in which Davis was elected the first female
president of the American Academy of Motion Picture Arts and Sciences, only to resign two months later, publicly declaring herself too
busy to fulfill her duties as president while angrily protesting in private that the Academy had wanted her to serve as a mere figurehead.
That Davis was in no mood for opposition of any sort just now was
signaled by her choice of Irving Rapper, an amiable forty-four-year-
old Englishman who had worked as dialogue director on several of
her films, to direct *Now, Voyager*, her next major project at Warners.
She wanted a director whom she believed she could more easily
manipulate: hence the special enthusiasm with which she had urged
Warners to give the reins to the relatively inexperienced Rapper.

"She would take on Irving on the set in front of everybody," recalls script supervisor Meta Carpenter, to whom it seemed that the actress repeatedly "took advantage" of Rapper's gratitude for having helped him get the job. "She had to control everything and everybody." Where Wyler had often gone head-to-head with Davis on *The Little Foxes*, according to the script supervisor, Rapper "never took Bette on." His approach was gentler, more conciliatory. "Let's try it like this, and maybe you'll like it," he would urge the actress, in a manner that Carpenter recalls as "tentative." To which Bette would "grudgingly" reply, "All right, I'll try it. I'll look at the dailies tomorrow and see if I like it."

After the devastating collisions with Wyler during *The Little Foxes*, this is the film where, with her usual flair for off-screen theatrics, Bette begins to assert her dominion over directors. As if in reaction to Wyler's vexing remarks in the press (clipped from the *New York World-Telegram* and preserved in her album), henceforth she will stubbornly insist on elaborating her characters from the outside, rather than from within—at length, with unmistakably disastrous results as her art passes into a kind of decadence, a love of ornament and exaggeration for its own sake.

In *Now, Voyager*, however, the actress's emphasis on externals is dramatically effective because, in large part, those externals constitute the heart and soul of the film, which chronicles the remarkable metamorphosis of Boston Brahmin Charlotte Vale from a meek, neurotic, overweight, prematurely aged spinster to a strong, slender, attractive woman of impressive efficacy and independence. When Warners released the film in 1942, in the aftermath of America's December 1941 entry into World War II, Charlotte's transformation held a special meaning for American women, faced with the necessity of discovering their own inner strength and power. Compelled to assume the jobs and responsibilities left behind by the men who had gone off to fight, American women took immense comfort in Charlotte's message that even the meekest among them was capable of effective independent action. Significantly, Charlotte must finally learn to live without the man she loves; because Jerry Durrance is married to another, Charlotte has to find the strength to care for his daughter, Tina, on her own. Functioning bravely and forcefully in his absence, Charlotte proves her love for Jerry as she gives new meaning to her own life by accomplishing things she had never dreamed were possible. Coming as it did at that historical moment, *Now, Voyager* consolidated the Bette Davis image as a model of feminine power and independence: an image that, in 1942, resonated all the more strongly and importantly for American women hoping to find similar qualities in themselves while men were away at war.

✠

Now, Voyager was Hal Wallis's first independent production at Warners under a new arrangement with the studio, so that it was only natural for him to take a special interest in the film's day-to-day progress. Interoffice memoranda show an unusually high degree of creative input from Wallis (much of it devoted to quickening the story's pace), of a sort that Wyler would scarcely have brooked but that the more malleable and diplomatic Rapper apparently did his best to accommodate.

For her part, Bette was a good deal less flexible when Wallis called for several minutes to be reshot because he found the actress's line readings "stagey and artificial." Davis, apparently overwhelmed by fear, is recorded to have been stricken with laryngitis—almost certainly hysterical in origin—which held up the production for several days.

It was evident that Bette wanted to run the show, and the director was constantly put in the unenviable position of having tactfully to relay Wallis's "constructive criticisms" of her performance, or of other aspects of the production, without rousing her ire. The production head shrewdly steered clear of the set and "Queen Bette," as they called her.

Unit manager Al Alleborn's notes show that another drag on the production was caused by Gladys Cooper, cast in the role of Charlotte's domineering mother. The actress, who had played Leslie Crosbie in the London premiere of *The Letter*, repeatedly forgot her lines or botched her dialogue.

But mostly the problem was Bette—as Rapper declared in answer to two curt letters of complaint from Jack Warner when the production fell seven, then nine days behind schedule. Warner wrote to Rapper: "I want to impress upon you that unless there is a marked improvement, I must seriously consider the pictures you will do in the future." "Above all," wrote Rapper in response, "Miss Davis is a very slow and analytical lady whose behaviour had to be treated with directorial care and delicacy. Believe me, that in itself is a full day's work."

"Cut!" cried Rapper, at the close of a scene in which, costumed and made up as a homely old maid, Bette bursts into uncontrollable tears: a signal to the psychiatrist Dr. Jaquith (Claude Rains) that Charlotte is on the verge of a nervous breakdown. (Wallis, it should be noted, had ruled against the original monstrous makeup Davis and Perc Westmore had devised for the spinster Charlotte: a fantastically ugly face that struck the appalled production head as overwrought and self-conscious.) Bette had been sobbing, with tears streaming down her cheeks. Suddenly she turned it off, flashed a big smile at the crew, and shouted lustily, "How'd I do, boys?" Then, abruptly shifting gears again, a grim-faced Bette headed toward her dressing room as she snapped "Come on!" at Bobby. Day after day, Bobby haunted the set of *Now, Voyager*, silently watching her sister from the sidelines.

"Bette was one of the strongest and most determined women I've ever met, and the sister was one of the weakest," says Meta Carpenter. Painfully aware of Bobby's history of mental illness, studio workers did what they could to be kind to her, especially in light of Bette's brusque treatment: behavior that led Carpenter and others to speculate about the extent to which Bette might actually have been responsible for some of Bobby's breakdowns.

Davis and the script supervisor became better acquainted when the company moved to Lake Arrowhead for location shooting. After the day's work was done, the two women would take long walks together, during which Bette indulged in what Carpenter describes as "girl talk" about her marriage to Ham Nelson. But the more Bette talked, the more it struck her companion that, by this point, nothing was really meaningful or important to Davis except her work. "I don't think Bette was really capable of any great emotional depth or feeling," says Carpenter, with evident sadness. "Her whole life was her career."

"Bette Davis advises that she expects to be paid during the two weeks she devotes her time to the Bond Drive," wrote Roy Obringer to Colonel Jack Warner, on August 13, 1942. "There appears to be no chance of changing her mind on this, as she even went so far as to state that if there were any question, it had better be settled before any publicity broke relative to her going on the drive."

America was at war by now, which might have put into perspective Bette's perpetual, increasingly irrational skirmishes with directors and with her studio. But as Obringer's detailed report to Warner makes clear, when, like a great many other Hollywood personalities, Davis found herself recruited to participate in the War Bond Drive while she was between pictures, as if by reflex she promptly went to war with Warner, demanding that he pay her for her time.

Bette made up for everything, however, through her efforts as president of the Hollywood Canteen on Cahuenga Boulevard in Los Angeles, where American servicemen waiting to be shipped out to the Pacific mingled with their favorite Hollywood stars.

In her photograph albums one discovers numerous images of the actress posed with an endless succession of servicemen at the canteen. In a hurry to get through these bland, repetitious photographs, one might easily pass over several singularly odd shots hidden among them: eight-by-ten blowups of images taken at a considerable distance, presumably from across the former livery stable that Bette had leased to house the Hollywood Canteen, with funds raised by her agent, MCA president Jules Stein. Unlike her other mementos of the canteen, these photographs do not contain Bette, leading one to believe that she might have taken them—but why? of whom? Only on close inspection does one make out the scarcely recognizable face of William Wyler, repeatedly photographed unawares in his air force uniform, as he prepares to go overseas.

◆

"The Red Cross has nothing to do with Warner Bros.," scribbled Jack Warner, nervously drafting a March 15, 1943, telegram to Bette, who—on holiday at the Hotel Los Galmingos in Acapulco, Mexico, after completing the film *Old Acquaintance*—had angrily refused to appear at an upcoming reception to launch the Mexican Red Cross. She felt that the studio should pay her to attend.

The invitation to Davis had been part of a concerted government effort to strengthen inter-American relations by building up cultural ties. In hopes of countering the Axis countries' antidemocratic propaganda, the United States government regularly invited Hollywood personalities to serve as goodwill ambassadors in Latin America: hence the potential embarrassment to the Roosevelt administration when Bette Davis turned down the Mexican president's invitation to the charity function.

Drafting an answer to Bette's furious telegram accusing the studio of once again trying to dupe her into working for free, Jack Warner began with the sentence about the Red Cross having nothing to do with Warner Bros., then, as his draft notes show, crossed it out. He probably feared that too direct a response to her charges would only set her off again.

Next Warner tried a sentence about being "rather astonished" by her angry wire; but he crossed that out as well, replacing it with the less inflammatory "read your wire."

"We are all trying to do everything in our power to cement inter-American relations and assist our sister republic Mexico in launching its Red Cross with this event at which the president of Mexico will take time out twice to meet group," Warner continued, anxious to explain why it was important for Bette to attend.

He went on to remind her that "there is a war on and it's more important than Warner Bros., you, me, or any other individual"—but this, too, he scratched out, presumably because it might further provoke her: the last thing he wanted to do under the circumstances.

By this point, evidently, Jack Warner had taken to dealing with Bette as gingerly as her mother always had: anticipating the inevitable explosions, humoring her when they occurred, meanwhile doing everything possible to avoid setting her off anew. However, he seemed not to have comprehended the particular configuration of events that had sent her over the edge in Mexico.

After playing a secondary role in director Herman Shumlin's film version of Lillian Hellman's *Watch on the Rhine*, Bette undertook preparations for her next star vehicle, *Old Acquaintance*, to be directed by Edmund Goulding. She had been allowed to ride roughshod over Irving Rapper while filming *Now, Voyager*, and during preparations for *Old Acquaintance* Bette had expected to do the same with the infinitely less tolerant Edmund Goulding. Finally, Goulding issued Jack Warner an ultimatum—"Either I am working for Warner Bros. or Miss Davis and there is a difference." Before a choice was made, Goulding suffered a massive heart attack and was replaced by thirty-six-year-old Vincent Sherman.

"I was just a beginning director at that time," says Sherman. "Bette was a big star, who had won two Academy Awards. She was far above me, not just in standing at the studio but in terms of salary." Before long, the young director appeared to make a momentous decision about how to deal with his persistently out-of-control leading lady. "He went and slept with her," recalls Meta Carpenter. "After that, the next morning she was an angel. She came on the set a changed person." On several occasions, when shooting was finished for the day, Carpenter found herself asked to stay late while Bette and her director were alone together in her dressing room. Ordinarily, the couple would invite Carpenter in for a drink afterward. One night, however, while the script supervisor was reluctantly standing guard, Farney appeared at the gate, in search of his wife. When Carpenter informed Bette, the enraged actress sent word that her husband was not to be admitted to the studio grounds.

Following *Old Acquaintance*, Bette arranged to meet Sherman—who had a wife and small child—in Acapulco; but first there came the immense disappointment of the 1943 Academy Awards ceremony, at which Bette had expected to win for her Charlotte Vale in *Now, Voyager*. Instead the Best Actress award went to Greer Garson for Wyler's *Mrs. Miniver*. This was the film Willy had been about to make when he gave the damning interview about Bette, even going so far as to say how happy he was to be working with Garson, instead of Davis, who, for all her talent, seemed hell-bent on destroying her career.

Hence Bette's particularly foul humor when, shortly thereafter, Sherman failed to meet her as arranged in Acapulco.

That Jack Warner can hardly have understood the source of her upset is suggested by his having offered to send Farney to Acapulco, clearly in hopes of soothing her to the point where she might agree to attend the Mexican Red Cross reception.

"This is a wonderful opportunity for you to be the great lady all Mexico knows you are," wired Warner on March 15, confident at last that this was precisely the sort of thing Bette Davis wanted to hear.

"I was standing just inside the entrance of my store, and suddenly I heard a terrifying yell," said Dave Freedman, who owned a cigar shop at 6249 Hollywood Boulevard, near the office of Bette's attorney, Dudley Furse. "It made my blood curdle. The yell came from a man walking just inside my view, and as I heard him yell, I saw him suddenly fall straight backward and land on his head. He made no attempt at all to break the fall with his arms or hands, so that's why I think something happened to him before he hit the ground. Blood rushed from his ears and nostrils."

And according to advertising man Gilbert Wright, who was standing outside when Farney mysteriously collapsed shortly after leaving Furse's office at 2:30 P.M. on Monday, August 23, 1943: "I had seen him walk past the store entrance. When he was almost past, he let out a throaty cry, and the next moment he came down on the back of his head, just as if he were doing a blackflip and hadn't quite made it. I ran to him, and it was all I could do to hold him, because he was in convulsions. The blood was flowing from his nose and ears."

It had seemed to Dudley Furse that Farney was "in good spirits" as, a short while before, he signed tax papers pertaining to Bette's new independent production company, B.D. Inc., which—according to a June 1943 agreement—was set to produce some of her pictures at Warners after she had completed her next film there, *Mr. Skeffington*.

"Mrs. Farnsworth, we believe your husband has had an epileptic fit," said a caller from Hollywood Receiving Hospital, where an ambulance had delivered the unconscious Farney (who was recorded to have had no alcohol on his breath).

"There are a great many things my husband may have had," Bette replied, "but I assure you that an epileptic fit is not one of them!"

Within minutes, Bette summoned her personal physician, Dr. Paul Moore, to arrange for Farney's immediate transfer to Hollywood Presbyterian Hospital, where X-rays disclosed a fractured skull. By this time, Farney's condition had changed from "unconscious" to "semi-conscious."

"We have been unable to ascertain what caused the skull fracture," Dr. Moore told reporters at the hospital. "Mr. Farnsworth has not been able to talk coherently."

Meanwhile Bette and Ruthie had arrived at Hollywood Presbyterian, where Farney failed to recognize them; doctors urged the frantic wife to go home and rest. Contrary to what observers may have thought at the time, it seems unlikely that Bette's acute agitation arose out of any great love for her husband. Robin Brown points out that by the time of Farney's accident, the couple's romance was clearly over.

As late as October of 1941, Bette had rushed to her husband's bedside at Abbot Hospital in Minneapolis when he was stricken with a nearly fatal case of lumbar pneumonia; but after that, the couple's two-and-a-half-year marriage had deteriorated steadily, with episodes of drinking, infidelity, and domestic violence.

The press carried stories about the glorious Arabian horse Far-

ney had given Bette (without mentioning that it had been paid for
with her money); and there was much publicity about the airplane
Bette had purchased for her beloved Farney, who, while his wife was
busy working at the studio, happily filled the hours with a group of
amateur aviators called The Quiet Birdmen. Jack Warner's correspondence with Bette in this period suggests that he—like others in
Hollywood—mistakenly regarded the affable, impeccably mannered
Arthur Farnsworth as a stabilizing influence on Bette. After all, he
expertly squired her to a variety of studio social functions, where, as
Robin Brown recalls, Farney was particularly fond of all the attention
he received as Bette Davis's escort.

But by the time of *Now, Voyager*, husband and wife rarely slept
together anymore. Alcohol had rendered Farney impotent one time
too many. Temporarily Bette moved in with Bobby on Laurel Canyon
Boulevard (the address she quietly began to list on studio documents)
and talked of putting Butternut and Riverbottom up for sale.

Desperate not to lose any of the perks of being a movie star's
husband, Farney repeatedly pressed for reconciliation, suggesting
that, in the absence of passion, there might be benefits for both of
them in a sexless marriage. And so it was that after Vincent Sherman
failed to meet her in Acapulco, Bette agreed to go to Butternut for a
brief reunion with Farney, who had taken up war work as a "liaison
man" between airplane production plants in the South and the Hon-
eywell Precision Manufacturing Company. No sooner did they arrive
in New Hampshire, however, than the old hostilities resumed, with
heavy drinking on both sides. The fighting and drinking continued on
the train to Los Angeles, where Bette later admitted to having taunted
Farney by declaring herself in love with Vincent Sherman.

"The blood in the fracture was black and coagulated, not merely
purple and partially congealed as it would have been if the injury had
been received only last Monday," declared Dr. Homer Keyes, the
assistant county autopsy surgeon, who signed the autopsy report after
Farney died on Wednesday night, August 25, with Bette and Ruthie
at his bedside. "The fracture could have been inflicted as long as two
weeks ago, and, conceivably, Farnsworth had been walking around
ever since with the condition fructifying until it eventually caused his
death."

Within hours of the release of the autopsy report, Warner Bros.

distributed a statement from Bette that, at first, seemed to address the questions raised by Dr. Keyes's findings. "When I learned of the autopsy report," said the actress, "and was asked if I could remember any recent accident which might account for an earlier brain injury, I recalled a fall that Farney had at Butternut, our New Hampshire home, late in June. He was coming downstairs in his stockinged feet to answer the telephone when he slipped on the first landing and slid the full length of the stairs. He landed on his back and struck the back of his head and quite severely scraped his back. He suffered the usual lameness for several days but not being the complaining kind he said nothing more about it and so I thought no more about it. I realize now that little things that happened since, which I thought nothing of at the time, were a result of that fall, all of which have been confirmed by Dr. Moore. At least to find a reason for a seemingly ridiculous accident is a relief and a comfort to me."

Unfortunately, where Dr. Keyes had speculated about an injury that Farney would have suffered "as long as two weeks ago," it was now two months since the fall at Butternut that Bette described. An investigator from the district attorney's office visited her at Riverbottom that Friday, August 27, to review her statement in person.

In Los Angeles, rumor was already rampant that the fatal blow had been sustained the week before when a jealous husband mercilessly pummeled Farnsworth after discovering him in bed with his wife. It was a rumor Bette was particularly anxious to put to rest, lest it tarnish the myth of her perfect marriage to Farney, whose death soon had Bette seeming to believe in the myth herself.

"I didn't see the fall—I was upstairs—but I heard him and I came running down," Davis declared at the August 31 inquest. "He was kind of wiggly there for a few minutes and very limp. He was lame and stiff later—you know how a fall like that would affect one—but he never said anything about it, never complained."

Asked whether her husband had seemed ill recently, Bette replied: "During the past four weeks I have been away on vacation and he has been in the East on business and if anything has come up that troubled him physically during that time, I didn't know about it."

Without waiting for the coroner's jury to rule that Farney's death had been "accidental and the result of a fall" for which "no person was to blame," Bette, dressed all in black, swept out a side door of the courtroom, accompanied by Dudley Furse. Although a spokesman for the actress announced that she had to leave directly to accompany her husband's body on a flight to New England, Farney's August 31 death certificate indicates that the body had been shipped to Rutland, Vermont, three days before.

In 1939 in New Hampshire, Bette's romance with Farney had allowed her to play Judith Traherne to his Dr. Steele; so it was strangely fitting that Bette's testimony at the 1943 inquest inescapably called to mind Leslie Crosbie's courtroom appearance in *The Letter*. The story Bette told to account for Farney's death—his having fallen down a flight of stairs—even echoed the scene in *The Little Foxes* in which Regina Giddens's husband dies on a staircase after they have quarreled. Following the death of her second husband, Bette would coyly hint to friends that somehow she had been responsible. She would hint by turns that she might have pushed him at Butternut or on the train to Los Angeles; or that, like Regina Giddens, she had failed to help him when he fell. But this was merely her pattern of revising the prosaic details of her own life in terms of her movie roles. In 1939, Bette's relationship with Farney had begun as a melodramatic fantasy out of one of her own movies; and in a sense, that was how it ended as well.

EIGHTEEN

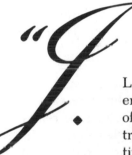

"J. L., I don't have to tell you, we're fighting every day," said Vincent Sherman, in the midst of filming *Mr. Skeffington*. "She gives me trouble on every damn thing and I'm not getting what I want from her. I think you ought to get somebody else to take over the picture."

"Oh, for Christ's sake, Vince," Warner replied, "you know her, she's emotionally unstable. And her goddamn husband just died. Be reasonable, go ahead and finish it. Putting somebody else on now would be a pain in the ass, you know what I mean?"

Although Davis had made a great point of requesting Sherman to direct *Mr. Skeffington*, almost from the moment she arrived on the set, on October 13, 1943, she began systematically to undermine his authority.

"It was the worst experience I've ever had," Sherman recalls. "She gave me hell. Whatever I did, she would say, 'I don't think that's right!' I wanted to kill her. My hair was falling out. I wasn't sleeping."

"Claude, tell me honestly," Sherman inquired of Davis's co-star, Claude Rains, "do you think the things I'm asking her to do are so wrong?"

"No, no," the actor comforted him. "I don't understand what's going on. I've never seen her like this."

Similarly bewildered were the writing-producing team of Julius and Philip Epstein. "Bette was in an unusual state of mind even for her," Julius Epstein explains. "She was taking over everything. We fought all the time with her on the picture. We figured she was a little more 'Bette Davis' than she usually was because of the death of the husband."

Unit manager Frank Mattison's notes suggest that the principal problem was Bette's insistence on ceaselessly rewriting the Epstein brothers' script, adding and subtracting dialogue according to whim: "It sure is tough on a unit manager to sit by with a show that goes like this where she is the whole band—the music and all the instruments, including the bazooka," Mattison recorded. "I suppose she wants to have her finger even in scenes in which she does not appear."

Repeatedly, the unit manager complained of Bette's unabashed efforts to usurp directorial authority: "There isn't a damn thing that can be done as long as Bette Davis is the director," Mattison told studio production manager Tenny Wright.

To make matters worse, it seemed to Mattison that Sherman was not doing all he could to control the headstrong actress.

Unlike Sherman—whom Warner had declined to release from the picture—the Epstein brothers had a clause in their (post-*Casablanca*) studio contract that gave them the option of going back east in October and November, as they often liked to do. Although, initially, they had waived this right in order to make *Mr. Skeffington*, before long Davis's ugly behavior on the set caused them to reconsider.

"I am sure that when the Epsteins see it they will be spinning on their heads like tops," Mattison warned Wright when Bette appeared with a long list of script revisions.

At length, when Bette declined to retake a scene as the Epsteins had written it, the writer-producers appealed to Jack Warner.

Julius Epstein says that by now the mere mention of the actress's name caused Warner to use "language that would make a sailor blush." Angrily declaring this the moment when he would confront her once and for all and reestablish the production's chain of command, Warner boldly strode off to the set—where the mere sight of her staring daggers at him caused the studio boss to smile weakly and blurt out, "Bette, darling!"

"We are in somewhat of a dilemma concerning the matter of our producers refusing to have anything to do with the picture," recorded Mattison, following the Epsteins' abrupt departure. "Miss Davis is not only the director, but she is now the producer, also."

At the end of a day's work, a weary, discouraged Vincent Sherman was sitting alone in the shadows on an empty soundstage. All he could think about was how to escape the actress who was making his life miserable.

Finally, he remembered an episode of sacroiliac trouble he had experienced several months earlier. "I know what I'll do." Sherman recalls his train of thought. "Tomorrow I'll help the boys pick up a table or something, and then I'll scream and fall to the floor and say my back is out. No doctor will be able to refute that—they'll have to get somebody else!"

Suddenly the click-click of Bette's heels pierced Sherman's reverie. He remained motionless. Perhaps she would go by without noticing him.

"Why are you still here?" she called, coming closer when he failed to answer. "Why are you sitting in the dark?"

"I was just thinking," said the director, hoping that she would turn around and leave him alone.

"You seem like you could use a drink," said Bette, beside him now. "Look, I've got a bottle of Scotch in my dressing room."

"That's one way to solve it," Sherman's wife, Hedda Comoro, told him the next morning. "But be careful."

Davis regarded the affair with Sherman as another token of her increased power; but even her having taken the director as her lover again did not cause her to heed his advice on how to portray the egocentric beauty Fanny Trellis Skeffington. Over the director's objections, Bette insisted on striving for effect with a "speech grotesque" achieved by raising her voice a full octave (purportedly because it made her character seem "more feminine").

That, by this point in her career, Bette may have been a good deal less interested in seriously exploring character than in playing to the gallery is suggested by an exchange she had with Sherman when he protested at another self-conscious bit of grotesquerie: the ludicrous wispy red wig she wore after a bout with diphtheria robs Fanny of her long-cherished beauty.

"Don't worry about it!" the actress insisted when she saw Sherman's look of horror. "My fans love for me to do something like this."

So there it was: the principal motive for Davis's tendency, thenceforth, to lay it on thick; to encrust her performances with bizarre costumes, wigs, and makeup, and (no less constricting) the curiously mannered technique of an artist in self-imposed decline.

"Audiences can make you rather vulgar as an actor," John Gielgud has said. "They are sometimes inclined to like very often the things that are not best about you and not to know the very best things that you do."

So, too, there was something in Bette that was recoiling from what was best about her as an actress. Where once she had been content to communicate wordlessly, to exercise her powers as an artist with a unique capacity for expressive gesture and movement, now she insisted on "bloating" the *Mr. Skeffington* script—as Julius Epstein says—with page after page of unnecessary dialogue, whose sole purpose was to declare her character a great lady, the actress a star.

On February 17, 1944, after 107 days of shooting, Sherman finished filming *Mr. Skeffington*, 59 days behind schedule. It was universally agreed that time and again Bette's erratic behavior had slowed the production's pace to the point of absurdity—but what to do about it? Jack Warner could scarcely box the ears of an actress who, from *Jezebel* on, had been nominated for Academy Awards five years in a row. Little as Warner cared to admit it, for the moment Bette's phenomenal box office appeal required him to come to terms with her at almost any cost. In consolation, Davis was almost certain to lose that leverage a few years down the line. Warner and his executives assumed that Bette needed only to turn forty for her immense popularity to begin to evaporate. Then they could deal with the termagant less gingerly than they needed to now.

"I am wondering if it would be possible to speed up the next Bette Davis picture by making it a Bette Davis Production, where she would understand that all these delays and slowly progressing through a script at one page or less a day would cost her a little bit of money," declared Frank Mattison during the filming of *Mr. Skeffington*.

This precisely reflected Jack Warner's thinking when, the previous June, he had signed a new five-year, fourteen-picture contract with the actress, whose usefulness to the studio, he calculated, would have been considerably diminished by the time five years had passed and Bette was forty-one. Set to go into effect after Davis finished *Mr. Skeffington,* the contract provided for her to shoot nine films directly for Warner Bros. and another five under the auspices of her own newly formed production company, B.D. Inc. Of the nine Warners' films, Bette would receive $115,000 for each of the first five and $150,000 for each of the four studio productions to follow.

But it was the five B.D. Inc. films that constituted Bette's triumph. Here at last was the creative freedom that she seemed desperately to have wanted for so long. Although, as in the past, the actress had no story approval on the nine films she was to make directly for Warners, the B.D. Inc. projects were essentially hers to choose. Warner reserved the right to veto anything he found particularly objectionable, although that seemed most unlikely to occur. In the B.D. Inc. films, Bette's role as producer would allow her to make the kinds of creative decisions and exert a degree of control that the studio had hitherto denied her. Besides all this, in addition to her salary Bette was to receive a portion of the profits earned by the five B.D. Inc. films. All in all, the new deal certainly appeared to be everything she had longed to achieve—and more.

But it was hardly anything like generosity that prompted Jack Warner to sign the new contract. His sole concern was to keep Bette working at full spate. As always at Warners, quantity, not quality, was all. The degree of stardom that Bette Davis had attained by this point made it necessary only for her name to appear on the marquee for audiences to pour into the theater. Thus the studio's interests would be best served by her making as many films as possible—good, bad, or indifferent—before she passed forty and, presumably, lost her allure. In short, Warner's scarcely concealed motive in signing Bette's new contract was to get the most out of his star before she was all used up.

Still, the new contract presented abundant opportunities to the actress. Aside from building experience as a producer, Bette Davis had the chance to take her film acting career in whatever unprecedented directions she might choose. The kinds of films she produced and appeared in under the auspices of B.D. Inc. would be limited only by her own imagination and artistic aspiration.

First, however, the new contract stipulated that Bette must make a film entirely of the studio's choosing. Her initial Warners' assignment was most promising: she was to play Miss Moffat, the idealistic schoolteacher in a Welsh mining village, in Emlyn Williams's *The Corn Is Green*, a role that Ethel Barrymore was considered to have made her "masterpiece" when she played it on Broadway in 1940. But to the studio's amply recorded perplexity, Davis approached the Barrymore role with what seemed like paralyzing trepidation. Perhaps the same anxiety of influence that had afflicted Bette during the filming of *The Little Foxes* was vexing her now. Hence perhaps the loss of voice that—to general amazement—caused her to fail to appear on the first day of shooting, June 21, 1944. Instead, as noted by unit manager Eric Stacey, Bette sent word through a secretary to director Irving Rapper that laryngitis was keeping her in Laguna Beach. Not until the sixth day of shooting, June 26, did Davis arrive on the set. Four days later, it became obvious that Bette's vexation of spirit threatened to bring down the entire production, as she insisted on obscuring her face and form with an absurdly awkward wig and thirty pounds of padding, as if with a security blanket. It seems incredible that an actress noted for articulacy of gesture would deliberately constrain her movements with a corset and great quantities of padding, but this is what Bette adamantly insisted on doing.

Refusing once again to comprehend her character from within, as Wyler had urged her to do, Davis repeated her by now familiar error of starting with, and rather overdoing, Miss Moffat's superstratum—with the lamentable result that her portraiture was as stiff and unyielding as was Davis in her relations with Rapper and producer Jack Chertok. Production reports show that, confronted with Bette's peculiar obstinacy about wearing the helmetlike wig she had selected, both men repeatedly sought gently to dissuade and "pacify" her; although, at one point, the usually more affable Irving Rapper was heard to groan with despair, "What she needs is a psychiatrist, not a director." But the studio files also show that, in the end, it was entirely for Bette to decide whether or not she wore her wig on-camera.

So much power did she wield that there was little anyone could do or say should Davis suddenly, blithely announce that she was leaving the set early because she had a date. "As you will notice, they did not shoot the last scene, which was ready at 5:30—they only rehearsed," recorded Eric Stacey on August 4. "This was due to the fact that Miss Davis did not want to remain and make the scene after having worked on it for an hour and a half as she had an appointment at the Canteen." Repeatedly, Bette disappeared from the Warners lot to rendezvous with her new "beau"—as she called wealthy New York real estate man Lewis A. Riley, then a corporal in the army Signal Corps. Although Bette's preoccupation with Riley threw new obstacles in the path of completing principal photography on *The Corn Is Green,* Jack Warner's notes to her from this period indicate that he warmly encouraged the romance—presumably on the theory that a new man in her life might calm her.

That Davis's perpetual war footing was viewed at Warners largely in sexual terms becomes clear on examination of studio memos and production reports, with their references to the actress's menstrual cycle and snide allusions to what was imagined to be her sexual frustration. Unfortunately, the arbitrariness and even irrationality that all too often characterized Bette's on-set outbursts made it easy to ascribe her biliousness to sexual causes and to assume that all that was really needed to relax her were the amorous attentions of Sherman, Riley, or some other man. Having easily won the battle over the wig, Bette seemed to lose interest in Rapper's film. Sadly, it was enough for her now to establish the character's facade. In the absence of any desire to perfect her craft, perhaps it was only natural that Bette's attentions would wander, causing her to find whatever excuses she could to steer clear of the film set to be with Riley. On Saturday, August 5, when a small flap attached to a lighting fixture came loose and grazed her head, Bette wildly overreacted. Although she is recorded to have attended a studio party that evening and to have gone out on the town the night after that, by Monday morning Bette was citing a head injury as her latest reason for failing to appear on the set. She intended to take a week off to be with her beau in anticipation of his departure for Fort Benning, Georgia, so Bette asked her physician to notify Warners that she had sustained "a slight concussion" and needed "a complete rest." That Davis was hardly as ill as she claimed became clear when the producer successfully persuaded her to return to work: The sooner they finished filming, the sooner she could be with her beau. The moment Riley left for Georgia Bette suddenly became most anxious to do whatever she could to expedite the film's progress. After three months spent chronicling Bette's numerous infractions, by September 6 unit manager Stacey found himself writing: "This company's progress, as for the last four days, has been excellent due no doubt to the fact that Miss Davis wants to get away."

On September 13, Bette completed her brittle and woefully unimaginative performance in *The Corn Is Green*. After that, according to the new contract, she was free to undertake her first independent B.D. Inc. production. But instead of remaining in Los Angeles to begin work on the first of the films whose artistic direction was entirely hers to determine, she followed Corporal Riley to Fort Benning and, with her sister, Bobby, rented a house in nearby Phenix City, Alabama.

On September 20, the actress gave a birthday party for her beau in Atlanta, to which she invited all the men in his company. Thenceforth there was no concealing Bette Davis's presence in Georgia, or her reason for being there. Many years before this, Bette had relished the status of most popular girl in Newton and Ogunquit—and now again, although she was there as Riley's girlfriend, she seemed thrilled by all the bedazzled attention his buddies lavished upon the movie star in their midst. So far was Bette from wanting to downplay her star status among them that in December she wired Jack Warner, asking to borrow a print of *Jezebel* to screen for the boys at Fort Benning.

Bette's sustained absence from Hollywood was a topic of considerable delight to Warner. He had expected her to waste no time exercising the creative freedom he had just given her and to launch into her first independent production with her usual monstrous zeal. That Bette was scarcely going to use her new freedom as her past audaciousness may have led people to anticipate had already been suggested by her curious choice for the first B.D. Inc. project: a remake of actress Elisabeth Bergner's 1939 *Stolen Life*. One certainly would have expected that during all these years of struggle, an actress of Bette Davis's caliber would have stored up numerous ideas for films she longed to appear in, characters she wanted to portray. That so many of the films Davis had made at Warners had been hopelessly trivial could hardly be blamed on her when, time and again, it was the studio that had assigned her to do them. Surely with Bette's theatrical background there were any number of serious dramas she planned to adapt for the screen now that she had finally won the power to do so. Warner had even been warily, reluctantly prepared for Davis to propose something from Ibsen or O'Neill. If that was the price he had to pay to keep her churning out more popular and profitable fare, so be it.

Instead, contrary to all expectation, Bette seized upon the Bergner remake. It was a story as thin and vapid as any she had ever been compelled to film. The years of working at Warners had caused her to absorb and assimilate its cut-rate aesthetic. Although they would hardly have cared to admit it, Bette and her presumed adversaries at the studio often thought as one.

According to the actress, friends who had seen Bergner's *Stolen Life* had recommended it to her as a likely vehicle. She had ordered a print from New York, screened it only the night before, and promptly written to Warner to announce her decision to film the story of twin sisters, one good and one bad, who fall in love with the same man. While the script was being written and the production prepared, Bette made the astonishing decision to abdicate responsibility as producer and remain in Georgia with Corporal Riley, who awaited combat orders. Having first squandered the opportunity to make a film different from any the studio would have dared to undertake on its own, now she was tossing away the right to exercise creative control over her first B.D. production.

"Your not being here makes it rather awkward in getting this film prepared," Jack Warner wired Davis on December 14, 1944. Not that Warner was encouraging Bette to return before the preliminary details of her February production were completed by other hands. "Hope you are having a wonderful time and that everything is really the life of Riley with you," Warner added, content for the figurehead producer to remain in Georgia until they were ready for her.

Bette showed little more interest in taking charge in any meaningful way when shooting started, on Wednesday, February 14, on location in Laguna Beach. Following the usual gratuitous clashes with director Curtis Bernhardt, who protested that what she really wanted was not a director but a "yes-man," Bette astonished everyone by going wild on her own first independent production. By February 22, Tenny Wright was reporting that despite her own money being at stake, Davis was proving every bit as uncooperative and recalcitrant as ever. When unavoidable technical snags caused two days to be lost at the outset, the actress-producer was indignant at the suggestion that she appear for work on Sunday. By March 2—according to ritual—Bette was out sick for a week, which, as recorded by unit manager Al Alleborn on March 10, caused the entire production to grind to a halt until she returned. When at long last, on July 28, 1945, *A Stolen Life* finished filming, thirty-three days behind schedule (almost all of the delay on account of Davis), no one at Warners could quite comprehend why she would have chosen to sabotage her own enterprise. Even Bette seemed not to understand why the long-awaited experience of producing had proved so entirely unsatisfying.

While it is impossible to know for certain, perhaps Bette's familiar tirades and overall bellicosity had become necessary self-soothing devices; or perhaps she had spent so many years at war with everyone that now that authority was finally hers, she discovered she had not the slightest idea of how to use it in a constructive, positive, disciplined manner. Bette appeared scarcely to comprehend that with control came responsibility. As producer she would have to accept responsibility for the success or failure of the product, and this she seemed disinclined to do. Years later, contrary to all extant evidence, Davis would blame the failure of her independent production company on the studio's unwillingness to "let" her do any real producing—but when had Bette Davis ever waited for Jack Warner, or anyone else, for that matter, to "let" her do what she wanted? Much closer to the truth is that, reluctant as Warner may have been to place the reins of power and control in her hands, the moment he did, whether she was conscious of it or not, Bette proved even more resistant to taking them.

How, exactly, did she use her freedom? The question is important for what it tells us of the scope of Davis's imagination and artistic aspiration. With five B.D. Inc. films to reaffirm her credentials as a dramatic actress before she turned forty-one, Davis need not have feared the loss of youth that loomed in Jack Warner's thoughts. Had Bette chosen a serious drama for her first independent production, she might have charted a whole new, no doubt more satisfying, direction for her acting career. But Davis made no bones about having been attracted to the mediocre *Stolen Life* for the gimcrack plot device of contrasting twin sisters, which allowed her to indulge her artistically self-annihilating preoccupation with the superficies of character. There was hardly any need to probe the psychological depths in Catherine Turney's screenplay, because to all intents and purposes, there were none. The bloodless writing required only that Bette invent contrasting visual styles for the identical twins, Kate and Patricia. After Pat—the bad, high-living sister—marries Bill Emerson, the man they both love, the dreamy, goodhearted Kate briefly takes up with a thuglike bohemian artist named Karnock. But when the bad sister dies in a boating accident, with only her twin as witness, Kate returns to shore pretending to be Pat, in order to take her place as Bill's wife. As in *Now, Voyager*, where the new Charlotte is plagued by the occasional attitude or mannerism belonging to her spinster past, in Davis's A Stolen Life, Kate reinvented as Pat is intermittently betrayed by the phantom gestures of a former self. In short, rather than use her prodigious gifts as an actress to explore and express the complexities of character, Davis chose, in this her first independent production, to waste herself on insubstantial, if mildly diverting, cinematic sleight of hand.

In the midst of shooting A Stolen Life, Bette poured out her feelings of boredom and restlessness in a May 1945 letter to Robin Brown. The focus of her dissatisfaction seemed to be the absence of Corporal Riley, who, she noted, had been in combat since March and had already been awarded a Bronze Star for gallantry in action. On May 7, V-E Day, the Germans had signed an unconditional surrender at Rheims. But even with the war in Europe over, Bette sighed, her beau was likely to be sent to Asia. To Bette's great despair, Riley had gone overseas without having actually proposed marriage. Although she had been expecting the wealthy real estate man to produce a diamond ring at the last minute, he asked only that she wait for him to return—whatever that might mean. Before long, although she had indeed indicated to Riley that she would be there for him when he came back, Bette was complaining that she was weary of living her life in a mailbox.

In this restive mood, Bette went off to Laguna Beach, where, to the consternation of her mother and sister, a month after V-J Day she took up with a muscle-bound sailor on weekend leave from San Diego. William Grant Sherry, seven years her junior, was an artist of sorts (with a fondness for painting clowns and other scenes of circus life), whose bohemian attitude and blunt manner seemed to remind Bette of Karnock, the quarrelsome ruffian-painter in A Stolen Life. Bette appeared to enjoy shocking people with the scarcely appropriate new beau, whom she impulsively decided to marry only a month after she picked him up at a party. The romance with the hot-tempered bodybuilder distracted her from the disappointment of A Stolen Life.

Although Bette's mother expressed violent opposition to Sherry, Ruthie was preoccupied: she was making plans to marry Robert Woodbury Palmer, the Belmont, Massachusetts, businessman whom she had been "chasing" for some years now. On November 21, 1945, three days before the sixty-year-old Mrs. Davis was scheduled to be married to Palmer in a ceremony at Smoke Tree Ranch in Palm Springs, Ruthie, in the course of filling out an Orange County mar-

riage license, heard herself utter the name of her mother, Harriet
Eugenia, whose sweetest hope had once been to see her dreamy,
artistic, ardent elder daughter contentedly married; and whose black-
est hour must have been Ruthie's irreversible metamorphosis into
that most wretched and reviled of old New England females: a grass
widow, or divorcée. Which makes it all the more striking when,
perusing the 1945 marriage license, one notes that although on the
document's left-hand side the prospective bridegroom lists his current marital status as "Divorced," Ruthie on the right declares herself
"Widowed": a tiny, harmless, forgivable falsehood certainly, but a
poignant one nonetheless, suggesting as it does a woman's unrelent-
ing secret sense of shame at having long ago been abandoned for
another. And what of Ruthie's years of violent effort: her menial jobs;
her study and work—and, ultimately, failure—as an art photographer; her successful nurturing—however often selfish, mean-spirited,
and cruel—of her elder daughter's talent and career? Beside "Occu-
pation: Trade, Profession, or Particular Kind of Work," Ruthie wrote
"Housewife."

Six days after Ruthie became Mrs. Palmer, her thirty-seven-
year-old movie star daughter startled America by marrying the recently discharged sailor whom she had known for barely five weeks,
in a much-publicized ceremony in the chapel of the Riverside Mission
Inn. Although Bette's uncle, the Reverend Paul Favor, had been set
to perform the ceremony at St. Mary's Episcopal Church in Laguna
Beach, at the last minute the Episcopal bishop ordered him not to do
so, Bette being a divorcée. Thereupon Dr. Francis C. Ellis, who had
officiated at Ruthie's wedding in Palm Springs the week before, was
recruited.

Like a fidgety character in one of her movies, marching down the
aisle on the arm of her new stepfather, Robert Woodbury Palmer,
Bette tried to soothe herself by repeatedly tugging at a lace handkerchief borrowed for good luck from her matron of honor, Bobby. She
continued to clutch and pull and tear at it all through the ceremony,
so that by the time Dr. Ellis had finished, the handkerchief was
nearly in shreds.

In turn, the hulking bridegroom—who posed as Hercules at the
Laguna Festival of Arts—never once looked at Bette during the ceremony, preferring to keep his gaze fixed rigidly on Dr. Ellis until it
was time to kiss the bride, which, according to newspaper reports, he
did with "considerable fervor."

"Who'll give me a cigarette and a glass of champagne?" Bette exclaimed afterward, adding: "That was the longest scene I ever played; the aisle seemed three blocks long!"

Bette alternated between deep drags on her cigarette and gulps of champagne all through the family picture-taking session that followed. Ruthie managed little more than a pained polite smile when her new son-in-law reached out with one mighty hand to show her where to focus her camera, meanwhile tightly clutching Bette's waist with the other.

After their wedding night at Smoke Tree Ranch, Bette and Sherry (as she called him) drove to Mexico City. Bette was scheduled to attend the Mexican premiere of *The Corn Is Green*. It was a calamitous journey, blighted by two flat tires, Bette's usual vitriolic tirades, and, apparently, her first glimpse of Sherry's "uncontrollable temper," as he responded to her cruel taunts by angrily throwing her out of the car and, later, hurling a trunk at her in their desert hotel room.

NINETEEN

"*I* have dinner ready for her when she gets home," Sherry would say, during his turbulent five-year marriage to Bette Davis. "I take off her shoes and bring her slippers and a drink. I press her dresses when her maid isn't here and draw her bath and give her massages. I feel it's a privilege to do things for her."

In letters that showed him to share his actress wife's flair for histrionics, Sherry wrote to her friend Robin (now newly married to New York advertising man Albert Brown) that because that was what he thought Bette needed, he had made her his entire life—perhaps even to the point of having smothered her.

And in her correspondence with Robin during this period, Bette rhapsodized about her third husband's good looks and dark curly hair, which she hoped their child would inherit someday.

While Bette was away at the studio, Sherry spent mornings at their home at 671 Sleepy Hollow Lane, painting in oils. His afternoons were occupied by working out and sunning himself with the other bodybuilders at Laguna Beach. In the beginning at least, his principal motive for unabashedly taking over the role of "housewife" (as Sherry described it) seems to have been to make Bette less dependent on Ruthie. Sherry correctly perceived Ruthie as an enemy to his agreeable new situation. Soon after he and Bette were married, Sherry discouraged mother and daughter from spending as much time together as had long been their custom. He even warned Ruthie never again to appear unannounced at Bette's door. The more docile Ham Nelson had permitted Ruthie to sabotage his marriage to Bette. Sherry quickly proved a shrewder adversary. Banishing Ruthie left him with only Bette to contend with.

Within eight months of marrying Sherry, Bette discovered that she was pregnant. When she was married to Ham Nelson, Bette had had an abortion because her pregnancy would get in the way of filming *Of Human Bondage*. This time, on the contrary, expecting Sherry's baby seems to have provided her with a way out of launching her second independent B.D. production: a prospect she had faced with considerable dread, as she had yet to comprehend why *A Stolen Life* had so badly misfired. Davis was in the midst of filming Irving Rapper's *Deception*—the second Warners production under her new contract—when she astonished Jack Warner with the news of her impending motherhood. Instead of announcing the B.D. production that was to have followed the Rapper film, Bette declared her intention to begin a maternity leave on December 15, 1946. Although she insisted she was merely postponing her next independent production, Bette quietly dissolved B.D. Inc. several months later, an indication that she had no intention of repeating the unhappy experience of producing her own films.

After the initial shock, Bette's decision to take a maternity leave was greeted with a general sigh of relief at Warner Bros. Sherry's presence in her life had hardly had the tranquilizing effect that Jack Warner and others had anticipated. If anything, production records suggest that her conduct during the filming of *Deception* had been even more arbitrary and destructive than usual. All too clearly there was no rational principle at issue, only an ugly display of power for its own sake, when she repeatedly insisted on altering the shooting schedule according to whim.

On the first day of shooting, April 25, Davis failed to appear on the set until one in the afternoon, giving the excuse that she had "attended a party the previous night and did not get home until 2:30

A.M." Thenceforth there was no telling at precisely what time the capricious actress would decide to show up for work. When the studio tried to accommodate her by agreeing to start filming an hour later each morning, she appeared for work at the earlier time—and protested angrily at being required to wait. Attempts to reason with her were met with bewildering fits of agitation: "Miss Davis got very excited and nervous, taking off her gloves and starting to cry," reported Al Alleborn of executive assistant Steve Trilling's ill-fated effort to come to some kind of terms with Bette. On several occasions she is recorded to have gathered the crew around her to denounce Warner Bros. for a variety of imagined offenses, but her vituperations served only to alienate the others, who, anxious simply to get on with their work, resented the star's waywardness.

"I am at a loss for words to express myself after having learned of the turmoil that existed last Saturday afternoon and today with respect to the production of your picture," Jack Warner wired Bette on June 24, 1946. "You must not lose sight of the fact that you are in a profession that calls for certain fulfillment of moral obligations to say nothing of legal ones." Hence the particular copiousness with which the studio recorded each fresh instance of Davis's unreasonable behavior on *Deception,* in anticipation of a possible lawsuit against her. When Bette declared her intention to take a few months off, Warner put up no fuss about advancing the $224,000 she and Sherry needed to cover their living expenses during the thirty-two weeks of her hiatus. Among themselves, studio executives expressed the hope that Davis would return from her maternity leave in a somewhat more rational and constructive mood.

▲▼▲

"Our host and hostess greeted us in slacks and matching plaid sports coats bearing the distinctive monogram which Sherry himself designed and which marks many of their personal effects," wrote a Sunday-supplement reporter who visited the pregnant thirty-eight-year-old actress in Franconia, New Hampshire, in 1946. "All hands promptly moved down to Butternut for a real New England breakfast of oatmeal mush, sausage, maple syrup and delicious pancakes made by Sherry's mother. You have only to meet Mrs. Sherry to know where her son gets his quiet dignity. And she commands the unstinted respect of her daughter-in-law. Mrs. Sherry, senior, together with Skippy, who is Sherry's younger brother, are spending the winter in the Butternut house with Bobby and her fair-haired little daughter Fay. So it will be a lively community sharing the fortunes of Sugar Hill this winter, of all sizes and sexes and ages."

Everyone, it seemed, except Ruthie, whose last glimpse of Bette had been at the San Bernardino railway station. The forlorn mother had photographed her elder daughter and son-in-law as they boarded an eastbound train. The couple was to spend Christmas at Butternut and remain there to await the birth of their child at the Mary Hitchcock Hospital in Hanover, New Hampshire.

Before Sherry entered their lives, Ruthie had supervised the dismantling of a century-old barn and its faithful reconstruction at Sugar Hill, where it would serve as Bette's permanent residence, with Ruthie installed in the charming old farmhouse. It was Ruthie who monitored the painstaking renovations and decorations; Ruthie who planted the fragrant beds of roses; and Ruthie who documented the step-by-step rebirth of Butternut in myriad photographs. But now, suddenly, Sherry's mother, a San Diego elevator operator, had usurped her place there—while Ruthie languished on the West Coast with her husband. The degree of Ruthie's agitation that winter may be measured by her January 1947 announcement that she and Palmer were separating after a mere fourteen months of marriage. In February, Bette and Bobby returned to California to comfort her.

Of all the photographs that Ruthie took of her elder daughter through the years, none can be more intriguing than those from April 30, 1947, the night before Bette planned to give birth by caesarean at Santa Ana Community Hospital. She had chosen the date expressly so that the baby's birthday would be May Day. Bette posed for the pictures on the waterfront terrace of the Sherrys' new house at 1991 Ocean Way in Laguna Beach. Their shoreline view—she had written Robin, that March, in a self-described state of enchantment—reminded her of their long-ago summers in Ogunquit. Ruthie's April 30 photographs show a voluptuous, luxuriantly pregnant woman in profile. This is hardly the image one associates with the vaguely masculine figure of Bette Davis—whose aura of sexual ambiguity was so deeply ingrained in the popular imagination that, the day after Bette brought her baby home from the hospital, rumor was rampant in Hollywood that the virago had never really been pregnant at all; that Bette Davis had secretly adopted seven-pound Barbara Davis Sherry.

According to her contract, *Deception* having been completed prior to the maternity leave, it was Bette's turn to produce and appear in a film of her own choosing when she returned to the studio on July 28, 1947. Instead, that September, she announced her decision to dissolve B.D. Inc. Jack Warner was only too happy to hear her say she would leave the producing to the studio, which promptly assigned her to a pair of lackluster films, *Winter Meeting* and *June Bride*, to be directed by Bretaigne Windust. (Bette's loud public protests that Warner Bros. would not allow her to portray Mary Todd Lincoln, or appear in a film based on Edith Wharton's *Ethan Frome*, seem extremely odd, coming as they did soon after she had chosen to give up the right to select and produce her own projects.) As it happened, *Winter Meeting* would be the first of Davis's films to lose money. This suggests that her decline in popularity was perhaps closer at hand than Warner or his executives had anticipated. There had already been disturbing indications that something was wrong. In the years 1938 through 1942, Davis had been nominated for Academy Awards five years in a row. She was nominated again in 1944 for *Mr. Skeffington*. But since then she had failed to be nominated for *The Corn Is Green*, *A Stolen Life*, or *Deception*.

And with the end of the war came a significant image problem for Bette, whose strong, combative, independent female characters had provided such excellent role models for American women. Now that the men had come home, a rebellious, threatening female figure like Bette Davis was the very last thing they wanted to see when they went to the movies with their wives and girlfriends. As far as a great many men were concerned, it was high time for the old male-dominated order to be restored; whatever freedom and power the women had exercised and enjoyed in their absence must be instantly relinquished. Now that women had seen what they were capable of accomplishing out in the world, it was going to be difficult for some of them to return to the old domestic routines as if the self-discovery of the war years had never taken place. On account of all she had come to represent to American women during the war, Bette Davis was a poignant, even painful reminder of the efficacy they had been required to give up with the coming of peace: hence the subliminal threat the actress seemed to pose to many returning GI's, who bristled at the image of female strength and independence she embodied.

Bette had shifted her tactics with Jack Warner, whose frantic, fearful private notes from the period indicate his distaste for the new sort of warfare he was being forced to fight: not with Davis herself, as in the past, but with Jules Stein's MCA agents. On January 5, 1949, hoping as always to check Bette's unbridled behavior with directors, Warner had called agent Lew Wasserman to propose the exceptionally tough Raoul Walsh to direct her next, in *Storm Center*. The furious studio boss recorded that when he uttered Walsh's name, "Wasserman started to chuckle and ridiculed my suggestion." The agent's glib mockery was enough to make the insecure Warner foam at the mouth.

How he longed for one of Bette's familiar fits of temper—so much easier to cope with than the agent's derisive laughter. Warner insisted on seeing Bette in person, to talk about *Storm Center* without her agent present.

When Wasserman caught Warner off guard with the suggestion that they tear up Davis's studio contract and start anew, Warner—by his own account—blundered by offering to sell it to her for $250,000. This was precisely what MCA seemed to have been waiting to hear. The agency stood to earn more money with Bette free to work for the highest bidder. Afterward, Warner logged his exasperation when MCA admitted to having informed Bette of his ill-considered offer to sell her contract but not his plea that she come in alone to talk to him about working with Walsh.

"It is not our desire to sell Miss Davis her contract at any time and never, irrespective of what money we could get, has it been my desire to do so," wrote Warner when word reached him that, bitterly perceiving the studio to have insulted and rejected her, Bette was about to accept his "offer" and walk out.

What neither Warner Bros. nor MCA seems to have counted on was Bette's deeply etched fear of change, which at length prompted her to signal her desire to return to the fold. On January 17, 1949, she and Jack Warner came to terms on a new one-picture-a-year, four-year contract (at a fee of $200,000 per picture, minus the $224,000 the studio had advanced during her maternity leave). Bette retained the right to do a single outside film each year, but she had no story or script approval over her projects at Warners. Much as the actress appears to have regarded the right to do the yearly outside picture as a great victory, it hardly seems the triumph Bette made it out to be when one recalls that in 1947, at her own instigation, she had dissolved her independent production company. Other than the potential of bringing in more money, the outside film scarcely accorded Davis the power she had already voluntarily relinquished.

Bette began filming director King Vidor's *Beyond the Forest* on May 24, 1949. It would be her first film under the new contract and, as it happened, the last she would make at Warners for a good many years. Through the decades, the story of Bette's abrupt departure from Warner Bros. has been much corroded by legend. But the studio's legal files provide important clues to the events that precipitated the final rift: Bette's having caused "a fuss" on the set when the estimable Vidor criticized the manner in which she had hurled a small bottle of medicine—evidently somewhat less strongly than the director thought appropriate. According to Roy Obringer's notes, this was followed by a frenzied telephone conversation between Davis and Warner, in the course of which the possibility of their "calling it quits" was hastily proposed and just as hastily agreed upon. Afterward, Warner was uncertain whether he or Bette had suggested it first. Although it has often been speculated that Jack Warner had simply wearied of Bette's ceaseless war fever, the real reason for his failure to try to make peace with her while she finished *Beyond the Forest* is given in a key notation in her legal file, which indicates that in the view of Warner Bros. executives, the actress had "lost her position as a sure money maker for the studio," as "over a period of recent years some of her pictures have made money and some have not."

Even now that the studio had unceremoniously ended its relationship with Bette Davis by tearing up her contract as soon as she finished filming *Beyond the Forest*, she and Jack Warner seemed wistfully, ineluctably drawn to take up the cudgels one last time. Bette could scarcely resist taunting him in the press with claims that she had deliberately "acted up" during the Vidor film to provoke the studio to break her contract. Warner, in turn, responded with the angry directive to his legal staff to find grounds for a suit against her—but all to what purpose?

On August 9, 1949, Bette Davis prepared to leave the Warners lot for the last time after eighteen years as a contract player. She was genuinely hurt and surprised that there was no one at the gate to wish her well. Bette appears not to have grasped the extent to which, weary of her by now entirely pointless and often ugly fits of temper, most of her co-workers were happy to see her go.

TWENTY

"Her whole world was starting to crumble," recalls baby B.D.'s governess, Marion Richards, of the turmoil at home as the forty-one-year-old actress's career anxieties fed into her increasingly troubled relations with Sherry. "When they were together, there was always a disagreement," says Richards, who lived with Bette and her husband during this period. It seemed to the governess (whom her former charge, B.D. Hyman, recalls as "a very serene kind of lady") that the only thing holding the couple together at this point was the strong physical attraction they continued to have for each other. At times Bette appeared to enjoy inciting her temperamental husband to violence. To the governess's astonishment, although Bette had often declared herself terrified that Sherry might kill her, time and again she would "fly off the handle" and lash out at him for no apparent reason, as if trying to provoke him. "He did get violent with Mother," says B.D. Hyman of her father, "but I think probably the apostle Paul would have become violent with my mother. I don't think you could avoid it if you had to be trapped with her."

By Sherry's own account, his "severe temper," provoked by Bette's constant needling, caused him to rush about the house, smashing furniture, during what he described as his intermittent "rages." "Many people have a temper but don't go so far with it as I do," Davis's third husband would say. "Sometimes I have to break a chair or a table to get release."

Although in some strange way husband and wife seemed to thrive on the enduring threat of violence, the ominous atmosphere quickly took its toll on their daughter. Like Bette, whose girlhood temper tantrums and obsessive behavior had begun at the age of two in reaction to tension between her parents, two-year-old B.D. seems to have responded to discord at home with misbehavior that—according to the governess—included repeatedly defecating behind the furniture. By October, Bette had begun to harbor serious fears for her own and her daughter's safety. More than once she threatened to end the marriage. To her threats, Sherry replied, "Just try to get rid of me."

"That girl and I were made for each other and I'm not going to let her go," Sherry told reporters after Bette disappeared with B.D. and Bobby on the evening of October 19, 1949, two months after the final break with Warners. "When I first heard about the divorce suit, I thought someone was trying to play a joke on me. When I learned it was true, I was just sick. I'm sure she'll come back when this whole thing blows over. It's just a matter of controlling my awful temper, but I know we can patch this up if we can just see each other again."

Asked about reports that he had smashed furniture in fits of anger, Sherry responded: "I fly into a temper at the slightest provocation, sometimes without provocation. Bette told me she was afraid of what I might do to her and the baby when I was in one of my rages. She said if she were a housewife it would be different. I don't blame Bette at all for what she did. It's tough for her to work hard in pictures and have this problem at home. I should be able to protect her and not frighten her."

Unable to communicate directly with his wife, he publicly appealed to her to return: "I think that Bette needs me. Aside from loving her, I felt, when we were married, that I could bring her stability, and I did for a long time before I lost sight of my path. I want to get back on that path. I never believed in that psychoanalysis stuff—I thought it was silly—but if a doctor can solve the cause of my temper and Bette will come back to me and cancel her divorce, I'll do anything."

Having left the house on the pretext of appearing on a radio program, Bette wasted no time filing for divorce to end her four-year marriage. She also requested that Judge Robert Gardner of the Santa Ana Superior Court issue a restraining order to protect her against Sherry. "The defendant has threatened the plaintiff with bodily harm," Bette's attorney declared. "And the plaintiff alleges she is fearful if defendant is not restrained from molesting the plaintiff, the plaintiff may suffer irreparable injury."

Meanwhile Sherry sent a letter to Bette through Dudley Furse, pleading with her "to call off the suit so I can go to a psychiatrist in the east whom I can talk to and who really knows about the mind." Bette reportedly wrote back: "Please remember there is no hate in my heart. I only want a solution to this thing."

By October 28, when Judge Gardner granted a temporary restraining order to prevent Davis's husband "from interfering with or molesting the plaintiff in any way," Sherry had voluntarily decamped for a house Bette owned on Toluca Lake, so that she and B.D. could return to Laguna Beach. "It's much better for her to stay there," Sherry announced. "It's a fortress, and all. It's protected by electric gates."

Even now that the court had ordered him to keep his distance, Sherry persisted in pressing for a reconciliation with Bette—who, three weeks to the day after abandoning him, surprised everyone by inviting her moody, mercurial husband to meet with her at Dudley Furse's office on the morning of Wednesday, November 9.

"Miss Davis and her husband have agreed to a trial reconciliation beginning immediately," Furse announced following the meeting. "Miss Davis has agreed to postpone any further action in her divorce in the hope of solving their marriage difficulties."

Even before the story appeared in the press, the Hollywood lunch crowd at Lucy's Restaurant was astonished to see the movie star and the muscleman—whose violent relationship had been abundantly documented in recent weeks—"laughing, talking, and holding hands," as they enjoyed a convivial lunch with Jack Skirball, producer of Bette's first post-Warners film, *Payment on Demand*, at RKO.

"I just need somebody to talk to me," Bette told twenty-two-year-old Marion Richards when she awakened her in the middle of the night. "Would you come downstairs? I'm in the mood to cook."

"I'm not very hungry," said the governess, only gradually comprehending that Davis's real motive for this curious behavior was a sudden surge of fear of her husband.

"Well, I'm going to cook anyway," Bette continued, with a manic rush of enthusiasm, "and I want to talk to you while I'm cooking, so get dressed and come downstairs!"

Whereupon, as Richards recalls, she dutifully got out of bed and accompanied her employer to the kitchen. Trying to lose herself in the rituals of cooking, Davis frantically prepared an enormous meal for the two of them at two-thirty in the morning.

Although Sherry (having briefly considered checking in at the Menninger Clinic) had begun psychiatric sessions with Dr. Frederick Hacker, his behavior with Bette continued to alternate between violence and subservience. Marion Richards watched in horror as Bette's husband "started to act like a servant." For all Sherry's efforts to run Bette's house, no sooner would she come home from the studio than she would fly into a rage. "You prince!" Bette would cry, jabbing him in the chest with her finger. "You're around this house all day doing nothing, while I'm out there being the breadwinner!" "There were times she was so cruel, it was unreal," says the governess.

As always, her sister Bobby provided another convenient target for Bette's nightly fury. She had divorced "Little" Bobby Pelgram in Las Vegas in 1945. Two years later, she had married David Roscoe Berry in Laguna Beach. When Bette learned that her new brother-in-law was a recovering alcoholic, she sent the couple a dozen cases of liquor for a wedding present. Bobby's second marriage was short-lived; and once again now, she had resumed her lonely role as Bette's shadow.

"Bobby was there for Bette when she was in her good moods, her bad moods, whatever mood she was in. And I must say, I've seen Bette treat her like dirt," says Marion Richards. But for all the abuse Bette regularly heaped on Bobby, it seemed to Richards that the waiflike younger sister continued to love and idolize the elder, whose needs and wishes she never questioned. In the Sherry household, Bobby often found herself thrust into the role of "peacemaker" between Bette and the more recalcitrant members of the domestic staff. Especially on those occasions when Bette hesitated to confront the staff for fear of being disobeyed, Bobby was sent in on her behalf. With one cook in particular, Bette despaired of ever getting her way when, enraged at the actress's meddling in her kitchen, the woman exploded at her, "Who and what do you think you are!?" Richards was astonished to see Bette dash out of the kitchen, "with her tail be-tween her legs," and run straight to Bobby. "Bobby!" she ordered imperiously. "I want you to go in there and tell the cook that Mrs. Sherry doesn't want it done this way!"

Accompanied by Bobby and the nursemaid, the Sherrys repaired to a rented house at Lake Arrowhead to celebrate New Year's Eve, 1949. Although Bobby timidly suggested holding the festivities in the early evening, Bette seemed appalled at the idea of a New Year's party taking place at any time other than the stroke of midnight. She also had very specific ideas about how they were to celebrate: with paper hats, party favors, and decorations, which Bobby was ordered to purchase and set up in the living room. Meanwhile Bette, all frantic nervous energy, went out with Sherry to the movies to see *Twelve O'Clock High*. In their absence, Bobby, who had spent a lifetime tirelessly laboring to please her difficult older sister, worked herself up into a frenzy of delight over the impending New Year's celebra-tion. She rushed about the living room, excitedly putting up the decorations, arranging and rearranging the noisemakers and party hats so that everything would be just right when Bette returned.

What neither Bobby nor the nursemaid could have known (until they heard Bette ranting about it later) was that Bette and Sherry had had a violent fight at the movie when she repeatedly goaded him with remarks about how attractive she found one of the film's actors, Gary Merrill. The couple continued to quarrel bitterly all the way home.

Minutes before midnight, as Bobby waited in the front hallway to witness the look of pleasure on Bette's face when she saw the elaborate party decorations, the elder sister threw open the front door, glanced contemptuously about the living room, and shrieked, "You didn't do it right!"

Bette swiftly tore apart all her sister's work: the place settings, the hats and noisemakers, the lovingly arranged cakes and sweets, everything. "We'll just have to wait another hour while I do it over myself!" the actress angrily declared. Knowing how much all this had meant to Bobby, the nursemaid cast a nervous glance in her direc-tion. Clearly unable to handle her sister's heartless cruelty, Bobby appeared to have gone "back into her shell like a little turtle."

"She hadn't told me she was going to a party," Sherry explained to reporters in April 1950, after his coming to blows with Bette's co-star in *Payment on Demand*, Barry Sullivan, caused Bette to move for divorce again. The occasion had been a combination wrap party and early forty-second birthday celebration for Bette, on April 3, at the RKO commissary, after which she and Sullivan had gone off to talk and drink in the dressing room.

"When she didn't come home to dinner, I called the studio," said Sherry. "Everyone else had left the party and there was no answer in her dressing room. I was worried. I drove out and found her. The studio gateman let me right in. She refused to go home. I was mad. I was jealous. She said I was a fool, that it was my imagination, that nothing happened. I blew my top. Any husband, any red-blooded man would have done the same."

"Where's your sense of humor?" asked the thirty-eight-year-old Sullivan, inviting Sherry to join them for a drink. "We're just relaxing."

"I don't want to hit you," Sherry replied. "You have to be photographed tomorrow."

"Don't let that bother you," said Sullivan, a moment or two before the jealous husband knocked him down.

Bette, meanwhile, had summoned a trio of studio policemen; but they kept their distance when the bodybuilder warned that he would hurt them if they came too close. When one of the guards tried to sneak up from behind, Sherry caught him and told him to get back with his friends.

Finally, Bette agreed to leave with her husband; but when she got into her chauffeur-driven automobile, Sherry warned the driver that he planned to tail him all the way back to Laguna Beach. If they tried to elude him, he would ram them from behind.

The next morning, Bette silently departed with B.D. and the nursemaid, leaving Sherry to tell reporters: "My wife is a troubled, mixed-up girl. She has never been really happy. She is not alone in this. All artistic people have great problems. I tried to help her as much as I could, but I can't go any further alone. I am too close to her and I lack the knowledge. If she would join me in consulting my psychiatrist, Dr. Frederick Hacker, I am positive that our marital problems could be worked out. But whether she continues with me or not she ought to have the treatment. If she does not, she will be a miserable woman all her life."

"Dear boy, have you gone mad?" Edmund Goulding warned Joseph Mankiewicz, who was set to direct Bette Davis as Margo Channing in

All About Eve. "This woman will destroy you, she will grind you down to a fine powder and blow you away. You are a writer, dear boy. She will come to the stage with a thick pad of long yellow paper. And pencils. She will write. And then she, not you, will direct. Mark my words."

The source material for Mankiewicz's loquacious backstage drama had been Mary Orr's short story "The Wisdom of Eve," which Twentieth Century–Fox story editor James Fisher had spotted in a back issue of *Cosmopolitan* magazine and passed on to Mankiewicz as "something unusual." Based on an incident in the life of stage and screen star Elisabeth Bergner, who had once foolishly taken a guileful young actress under her wing, Orr's story focused on understudy Eve Harrington, who employs her cunning to deprive an aging Broadway actress of her stage role—and her husband.

An aficionado of theatrical lore and personalities, Mankiewicz, on April 29, 1949, urged Fox production head Darryl Zanuck to purchase the Orr story as a potential vehicle for Susan Hayward.

Ten months later, in February of 1950, with the writer-director's enthusiastic approval, Zanuck signed Claudette Colbert to play the flamboyant leading lady—rechristened Margo Channing by Mankiewicz, whose screenplay had very substantially fleshed out the character and oiled her tongue.

Not long afterward, when Colbert suffered a herniated disk that compelled her to withdraw reluctantly from *All About Eve*, there was talk of hurriedly replacing her with Gertrude Lawrence or Ingrid Bergman. Speed was of the essence, as filming was set to begin in mid-April at San Francisco's Curran Theatre, whose management was able to make the premises available for a brief time only.

When both Lawrence and Bergman were ruled out, Bette Davis's name came up as a possible Margo Channing, but she was then in the midst of filming *Payment on Demand* at RKO and unlikely to be finished in time for the mid-April start date. In addition, Bette was known to harbor considerable ill feeling toward Zanuck. In 1941, when she had resigned as president of the Academy of Motion Picture Arts and Sciences, the furious Zanuck had warned Davis that she would never work in Hollywood again. This accounted for the actress's grim satisfaction when, nine years later, Zanuck offered her *All About Eve*.

Bette would co-star with Gary Merrill, the bushy-browed, faintly simian thirty-four-year-old actor over whom she had quarreled with Sherry on New Year's Eve.

RKO agreed to expedite the production schedule for *Payment on Demand*, and Zanuck signed Bette in early March, with shooting set to begin in San Francisco on April 15—less than two weeks after she left Sherry (had she deliberately provoked the fistfight on the RKO lot?) and announced her intention to seek a divorce.

In April 1950, accompanied by her daughter, B.D., governess Marion Richards, and a bodyguard to protect them all against Sherry, Bette arrived in San Francisco to shoot *All About Eve*. When the governess took B.D. to the Curran Theatre, where filming was under way, they would watch Bette "flirt like crazy" with Gary Merrill. The actor was married, but he seemed flattered to find himself the object of the star's ardor. Before long Davis and Merrill began spending nights together at the hotel, while Bette's daughter shared a room directly below with Richards. The governess recalls hearing the actress's bed "going up and down" all night.

When Sherry sent a conciliatory telegram from Laguna Beach, begging her to call off the divorce, Bette sarcastically read the telegram aloud, to the howls of an appreciative audience that included Gary and fellow cast members George Sanders and Anne Baxter. Despite her repeated claims that she was terrified of her estranged husband, Bette seemed oddly anxious to flaunt her sexual relationship with Gary, almost as if she longed for Sherry to hear about it and react. To avoid giving Sherry ammunition in the divorce case should his lawyers secure the testimony of Bette's bodyguard, Merrill usually made some perfunctory effort to leave Bette's room before the bodyguard arrived in the morning. On one occasion, seemingly desperate for someone to acknowledge that Gary had spent the night, Bette summoned B.D.'s governess to her room moments after the actor had gone; the smell of his sweat still hung in the air. When Richards arrived, she was embarrassed to discover a stark naked Bette Davis standing beside the rumpled bed whose creaky springs had kept governess and child awake for much of the night. As Bette smoked and talked about inconsequential matters, without making any effort to put on a robe, Richards decided to focus her eyes on Bette's face and to pretend that everything was quite as it should be.

"I'm forty and maybe a bit more—I have had a highly successful and gratifying public identity, which, since age four, has also functioned as my private identity, but which is not me—and when that public identity, that alias, ceases to exist, which will be any day now, I just don't know what the hell will be there in its place—and I love a man who, in turn, can love only the identity which I am about to lose because he has never known any other as me." Thus Joseph Mankiewicz characterized Margo Channing's crisis in *All About Eve,* as she ponders how to respond to the affections of her younger lover, director Bill Sampson (Merrill). The crisis seems obliquely to have reflected Bette's own, as (by her own account) she wondered with whom Gary Merrill was falling in love that April in San Francisco: Bette Davis or Margo Channing.

With her fondness for beginning a role by discovering the character's externals, Bette instantly seized on Mankiewicz's description of Margo as "a woman who treats a mink coat like a poncho" as key to the character's frisky, easygoing, unmistakably Tallulah-esque glamour.

Although Mankiewicz and Davis adamantly denied it, Margo looks, sounds, and acts so much like Bette's husky-voiced doppelgänger that it is difficult to believe the effect was entirely unintentional. Hitherto Bette had merely appropriated Bankhead's stage roles, claiming them for herself—and for postcrity—on-screen; now she seemed to snatch the rival actress's soul as well.

Mankiewicz introduces Margo Channing in a silent soliloquy that allows Davis to establish her character's pungent personality through the deftly choreographed movements of her eyes. Davis's opening shot derives its satisfying rhythm from the interaction between drama critic Addison DeWitt's acerbic voice-over narration and the play of Bette's eyes as she listens to an old actor's long-winded speech (mostly unheard by us) before Margo's nemesis, Eve Harrington, receives the Sarah Siddons Award. The camera has been scanning the dining hall of the Sarah Siddons Society as DeWitt introduces us to a number of the film's principal characters; we are still watching producer Max Fabian when we hear Margo's name uttered for the first time— dramatically anticipating the cut to Davis.

For a moment her heavily lidded eyes remain downcast, tantalizingly inaccessible—until the critic recalls Margo's first stage appearance. Thereupon Bette slowly, majestically looks up, a spare gesture of astonishing power and intimacy (and considerable irony: although Margo's gestures seem to respond to the critic's remarks, she cannot hear them—they are directed to us).

One can think of few other screen actresses since the silent era capable of making so exhilarating an entrance by means of the eyes alone.

Henceforth, although there is a good deal of other byplay (the lighting of a cigarette, the pouring of a drink), the beats of the shot are subtly punctuated by Davis's eyes, glancing modestly downward (when the critic alludes to her nudity onstage at the age of four); and up again, opening wide and holding in place for a long silent moment that italicizes DeWitt's final remarks on Margo's stardom.

Again, in a succeeding shot, moments before Eve accepts her award we cut back to Margo Channing: eyes downcast and head slightly bowed to conceal the tempest within.

Here as elsewhere in *All About Eve,* in her portrayal of a woman's struggle to master unruly feelings Davis proves herself capable of modulating her dramatic effects as she had scarcely done on-screen in years.

There are lapses: principally the familiar tendency to rant. But more often than not, Davis holds us with fine bits of physical business that crisply express the tension between emotion and restraint. Dressing to go down to her party, Margo learns from her faithful assistant, Birdie (who detests Eve), that Bill has been downstairs for twenty minutes without coming up to see her. There follows a wonderful mute dialogue between them: not a word more needs to be spoken; Margo knows he has been talking to Eve. An eloquent gulp of her drink tells all. Unwilling to disclose too much of her pain to Birdie (who is well aware of it anyway), Margo slowly makes her way to the door. Hardly does she close it behind her, however, when she breaks into a mad dash along the hallway and down a staircase, stopping abruptly before she comes into potential view of Bill and Eve. As Margo composes herself, Davis allows us to see the tumultuous emotions surging into her fingers, whose sudden strange, writhing movements make them resemble an octopus's arms.

Much as she had feared, there indeed are Bill and Eve, deep in conversation. Promptly dismissing the younger woman, Margo frantically propels herself about the room, ostensibly checking that all is ready for her guests: cigarettes; lighters; and a covered dish of candies, to which (in a brilliant piece of byplay invented by Mankiewicz) she returns three times as she and Bill argue about Eve. The first time she lifts a candy to her mouth, decides against it, puts it back. More pacing, and again she finds herself drawn to the candy dish— only to summon the will to resist once more. The third time, however, overcome by feelings of desperation that have been building throughout the sequence, she flings the candy in her mouth.

Long before Margo Channing tells her guests to fasten their seat belts, this small, significant gesture has given us ample warning that, indeed, it's going to be a bumpy night.

But what gave *All About Eve* its massive impact was less Bette's nimble and affecting portrait of Margo Channing than the film's watershed revision of the Bette Davis image. The most potent symbol of wartime female independence and self-sufficiency appeared suddenly to accept and even to recommend the retrograde sexual politics of the 1950s. Casting off the boldness and daring that Davis's powerful female characters had once adamantly insisted upon, Margo Channing loudly declared herself unable to live without her man: a declaration rendered all the more astonishing by Margo's vividly established sauciness and theatricality. At one fell swoop, in admitting that, yes, a woman must choose between happiness and a career, Margo seemed to undo all that Bette's gutsier characters had proved about a woman's capacity to function bravely and effectively on her own. Successful in the world as she may have been until now, Margo finally—wisely, the film insists—accepts that the time has come for this powerful, independent woman to stop fighting, step back, and let her husband take care of her. According to Mankiewicz's quintessential postwar male fantasy, for a woman to choose ambition and career over the man in her life is to condemn herself to the barren, pathetic, lonely fate of Eve Harrington. The hitherto headstrong, rebellious female like Margo who accepts domestic bliss with a powerful male protector is by far the wiser.

Had Claudette Colbert or some other actress portrayed Margo, *All About Eve* would scarcely have resonated as it did with "Battling Bette" in the role. Even before they had gone off to war, American men had been known to wince and recoil at the castrating viragos Davis portrayed on-screen; from the outset of her stardom, Bette's audience had been principally female. In the postwar years, the Davis image had seemed even more repugnant to these same American men—who rejoiced at Bette Davis's capitulation and disavowal of past follies in *All About Eve*, the first of her major films to exert a strong appeal on male moviegoers.

TWENTY-ONE

"Marion, quick, quick!" Bette cried, when she saw Sherry lurking outside her newly rented house in Los Angeles, where work continued on *All About Eve*. "He's here! Quick, get B.D. dressed and you get dressed! I don't want to be alone with him."

As usual during the day, two bodyguards were on duty at the front door. In early April, before leaving for San Francisco, Bette had accused Sherry of seeking to kidnap their daughter when, calling the house and happening to get the governess on the phone, he asked to see the child on one of their daily walks. A maid overheard the conversation, misinterpreted what was being said, and reported it to Bette, who angrily accused Richards of conspiring with her husband to take the child. On the evidence of Davis having asked Richards, shortly thereafter, to accompany them to San Francisco, where the governess was almost always alone with the child, it seems safe to assume that Bette could not have seriously believed that Richards had intended to help Sherry take his daughter.

"I want Bette! I want to see Bette!" Sherry could be heard now from the lower floor, as he pushed his way past the bodyguards into the front hallway.

Davis suddenly seemed "like a little girl" to the governess, who observed her to shake with fear in anticipation of facing her potentially violent husband downstairs.

"I want to see Bette!" Sherry continued, as the governess came downstairs with the baby, followed by Bette. "Bette, I just want to talk to you for a minute," said Sherry, in a calm, conciliatory tone.

Still trembling, Bette seemed unsure of how to respond.

"I don't want these bodyguards here when I'm talking to you," Sherry went on.

"No," said Bette. "They have to—"

"I want them out of the room!" he snapped, angry again.

Bette instructed the bodyguards to wait outside while she and her husband talked for the first time since her lawyers had asked the Santa Monica court, on May 10, to grant custody of B.D. to the actress, with Sherry retaining "reasonable rights of visitation."

Sherry had recently poured out his heart in a letter to Bette's friend Robin, in which—amid a sudden spate of references to God and prayer and how he and Bette belonged together—the beleaguered husband announced that he had decided not to fight the divorce. Still, he declared himself confident that the divorce from Bette was just God's way of helping them and that God would soon no doubt bring them back together as husband and wife.

When the bodyguards were gone, Sherry quietly explained that he was lonely and wanted to talk things over. Bette suggested that he take their daughter to the zoo for the afternoon. Perhaps they could have their talk afterward. But when he returned with the child several hours later, the security men blocked Sherry from entering as they briskly ushered his daughter indoors. One of the guards handed Sherry a note from Bette, declaring that she was afraid of him and did not want him to come around anymore. He could have two hours with B.D. every Tuesday and Thursday, but no more.

As always in their relationship, Bette seemed by turns genuinely frightened of her irascible husband and perversely anxious to stir him up. Sherry was living in their house on Ocean Way in Laguna Beach when Bette invited Gary Merrill to Laguna to meet Ruthie, who, on April 27, had stunned her daughter by eloping to Las Vegas with a sixty-three-year-old retired pottery packer named Otho W. Budd.

(Ruthie would divorce Budd eighteen months later on the grounds that he had proved "indifferent" to her.) Although it was natural for Bette to want to see the man her mother had married, bringing Merrill along was a curious decision. As if recklessly determined to provoke a confrontation with her husband, or perhaps just exhilarated by the danger of it all, Bette was observed about Laguna Beach with Gary, carousing in his yellow Oldsmobile convertible, and kissing and laughing late at night outside Ruthie's beach house.

Sherry apparently was still oblivious of his wife's liaison with Gary Merrill, but Gary's wife, actress Barbara Leeds, learned of the affair when, at a party soon after the *All About Eve* company returned from San Francisco, he drunkenly boasted of his hopes to marry Bette. On April 30, Mrs. Merrill left the couple's Malibu beach house in anticipation of filing for divorce in Los Angeles Superior Court on June 7.

With Gary's wife gone, Bette wanted to spend some time with him in Malibu as soon as they were finished filming *All About Eve.* Their week at the beach was marred by heavy drinking and raucous nightly quarrels, as B.D. and her nursemaid tried to sleep in an adjoining room.

Even during the day, when considerably less alcohol was consumed, things seemed to spin wildly out of control. One afternoon, Bette took a knife down to the beach to scrape mussels from the rocks. Trembling with excitement, she brought the shellfish back to the house, where she and Gary cooked them in an enormous pot, all the while talking about how hungry they were. There was a peculiar air of urgency about her as, barely able to wait until the mussels were ready, she began removing them from the pot, greedily stuffing them in her mouth and beckoning to Merrill to do the same. Bette devoured the mussels far too quickly, gulping them down almost as if she were starving. And Gary seemed equally insatiable, barely uttering a word as he pulled the shellfish from the steaming pot and crammed them in his mouth lest Bette get more than he. Gary was hovering over the stove, about to scoop up a fresh portion, when, at the table behind him, Bette suddenly doubled up and became violently ill, screaming with agony as she spewed undigested mussels on the kitchen floor. As the governess watched in horror, Bette shook and wept for a few minutes before Gary disgustedly picked her up in his arms and deposited her in the tiny bedroom, where she lay for hours, groaning that she was dying.

"You're not my type—I'm not interested in you," Marion Richards replied when, on the verge of being divorced from Bette, Sherry began to write love letters to the astonished young nursemaid—who dared not mention it to her employer.

Although Bette had planned to establish residence in Nevada in order to divorce her husband there, by this time she had become enthralled with the symbolism of getting a "quickie" divorce in Juárez, Mexico, on Independence Day, July 4.

"Marion, will you do me a favor?" Bette asked the governess before leaving for Mexico. "B.D.'s father wants her to go down to Laguna Beach while I'm away. Will you take her?"

"Oh, no, I don't want to!" said Richards, afraid to explain why.

"Marion, please. It's only going to be for about four or five days."

"No, no. Couldn't Barbara . . . couldn't she do it?"

"No, Marion. My sister has to take care of Fay. Please, I want you to do it. Don't worry, it won't be so bad."

"Well, okay."

"Good! I'll call Sherry and tell him. I'm sure he'll be delighted!"

With the nursemaid still beside her, Bette called Sherry, who, calculating that Bette would do exactly the opposite of whatever he appeared to want, pretended to object to the idea of Marion's being sent for the weekend with the child.

On July 4, when reporters knocked on his door in Laguna Beach for a reaction to Bette's having just divorced him, Sherry, instead of launching into one of his usual maudlin tirades, exhibited rare felicity: "I shall set off a great big firecracker in honor of my own independence."

Besides his daughter, waiting for him inside was Marion Richards, who, contrary to her expectations, suddenly found herself "a little bit flattered" to have Bette Davis's ex-husband take an interest in her. "I realized there was a kind of sweetness about him," says the governess, to whom Sherry opened his heart with stories of his brutal, derisive father; of being repeatedly bullied and beaten up in youth; and finally of his decision to become a bodybuilder in order to protect himself.

With Bette and Gary set to go to New England for an extended holiday, the governess had already given her employer notice that as soon as they left, she planned to seek another position, in her native

Pasadena. But now, when Sherry stunned and perplexed her by suddenly proposing marriage, Richards—who says that she had yet to enter into a physical relationship with him—found herself scarcely able to reply.

"No one is very happy, really, about a divorce," Bette told reporters at the Los Angeles airport upon her return from Mexico. "It's the end of one era in your life and sometimes the beginning of another. Who knows?"

"Now that you're divorced, do you plan to marry again?" called one reporter.

"One thing at a time," she replied. "I have no plans to marry anyone."

"How about Gary Merrill?" shouted another voice from the crowd.

"They always say an actress is going to marry someone right away." Davis laughed. "You can say I am not romantically interested in Gary. This is just part of the folklore of Hollywood."

Hardly had she left the airport, however, when her cab was observed to stop a quarter of a mile away, so that Bette could transfer to the yellow Oldsmobile convertible in which Gary Merrill had been waiting for her.

"Give me the phone," Sherry said to Marion when Bette called the next day to summon the nursemaid, who fumbled for words to respond. Sherry wasted no time happily informing his ex-wife that he and Marion were going to be married (although according to Richards, she had yet to accept his proposal).

"You son of a bitch!" Bette shrieked into the phone. She was still screaming and cursing wildly when Marion got back on the line—whereupon Sherry took the receiver out of Richards's hand and replaced it on the hook.

"After all the recent divorce unpleasantness was over," Sherry told reporters on July 6, "I suddenly realized that here is a girl who could make my life happy. She is beautiful and calm and spiritual and wants the really worthwhile things in life. She has no complexes."

Asked whether he and Marion had told Bette about their marriage plans, Sherry replied, "I'll leave her a note to let her know about it."

Suddenly it was being said about town that in the innocent-seeming young nursemaid with "the face of an angel," Bette Davis had discovered her real-life Eve Harrington. There was also speculation that Sherry's involvement with the twenty-two-year-old had been going on for some time and that Davis's affair with Gary Merrill was nothing more than a cover-up for her shame over having been abandoned for the much younger woman. To judge by Bette's frantic reaction in the days that followed, the abundant publicity that was being heaped upon her ex-husband's wedding plans must have made them seem like a debasing travesty of her own relationship with Gary.

Further evidence of Bette's state of mind at the time is provided by some of the women who had known her since youth. On several occasions, before stopping themselves to correct their "error," these women talked interchangeably about the marriage of Bette's husband and a nursemaid, Marion Richards, and her father's marriage to the nurse Minnie Stewart. Was memory playing a trick, confounding these two painful experiences, thirty-two years apart in Bette's life? More likely, their almost inevitable intermingling points up the similarities between the two events: similarities that, whether she was conscious of it or not, must have had a powerful impact on Bette.

Thus, perhaps, the distorted version of Sherry's second marriage that Bette would tell their daughter, B.D., in years to come. According to this account, Sherry had fallen in love with Marion while he was still happily married to Bette, who—like Ruthie with Harlow— seems to have been the last to find out what had long been going on, when her husband suddenly ran off with the nursemaid.

To this Bette added the spurious detail of Sherry and his mistress having tried to take B.D. with them when they fled, and of their having been "foiled in the attempt" by another member of the household staff: clearly a reference to the supposed "kidnap" attempt in April 1950, which even Bette appeared at length to have discounted, but also—it is tempting to conjecture—to what may have been an abandoned daughter's lifelong fantasy that when Harlow ran off with his nurse, he had really wanted to take Bette along but had somehow been prevented from doing so.

It is impossible to know what the fate of Bette's relationship with Gary Merrill might have been had Sherry not provoked her by announcing his impending union with Marion Richards. Gary was still legally married to Barbara Leeds, who—presumably to protect herself financially—was insisting on a California divorce decree. The Merrills' court date was set for July 26, 1950; even with both parties working to expedite matters, their divorce would not be final in California until a year after that.

Bette's frenzied state of mind rendered her scarcely able to wait so long. Her desperation to beat her ex-husband to the altar seems to have led Merrill to arrange to appear as scheduled in Los Angeles Superior Court—where all financial and property claims would be settled according to California law—then to rush off to Juárez for a "quickie" divorce.

Davis's vexation may be imagined when, the day before Gary was due in court, Sherry and Marion were said to have secured a marriage license in Orange County (coincidence or well-timed provocation?); and even more when, in court on July 26, in the presence of a gleeful Hollywood press corps, the current Mrs. Merrill strongly implied that twenty-seven-year-old Anne Baxter had been Gary's first choice for an affair during *All About Eve*. According to Mrs. Merrill, Gary had seized on Davis only after the younger actress proved to be—in Gary Merrill's words—"madly in love with her husband," actor John Hodiak.

The interlocutory divorce decree went through without a hitch, and two days later, on Friday, July 28, having secured a Mexican divorce in the morning, Gary Merrill became Bette Davis's fourth husband that afternoon (nine days before Sherry married Marion Richards, on August 6).

"An hour after I had married him, I knew I had made a terrible mistake," Bette told her assistant, Vik Greenfield, years afterward. A sudden panic seized her as she and Gary began the long drive from Juárez, Mexico, to Gloucester, Massachusetts, where Bobby and B.D. were waiting for them in a rented honeymoon cottage.

This probably accounted for Bette's tantrums along the way. "Each time we checked into a place," Merrill recalled, "something was wrong with it, and out we'd go. I'd be tired, saying, 'What the hell, it's a bed.' But no, it had to be better. Before the trip was over, my normally easygoing attitude was wearing thin, and I began to wonder."

"I'm horribly possessive," Bette told interviewer Gladys Hall in 1938. "I love the feel of things being mine. I could never adopt a child because I would have to feel that the child belonged to me, was my own flesh and blood or not at all."

But now, twelve years later, on their way to Gloucester in Bette's black Cadillac convertible, she lectured Gary on her desire to adopt a pair of companions for her "real" daughter (much as Ruthie liked to say that she and Harlow had conceived Bobby to keep their first child from being spoiled). "Mother didn't adopt two children," says B.D. Hyman. "She bought them for me to play with, the way you'd go out and get a puppy for your child."

Although Gary went along with Bette's plan to speak to a doctor in Maine about acquiring the healthy child of an unwed mother, he stipulated that they adopt a boy first, and—if Bette wanted—a girl second.

"Wrong fucking sex!" Merrill recalled having shouted into the phone when, on January 11, 1951, Bette called him in Key West, Florida, where he was filming on location, to announce that, contrary to plan, she had adopted a five-day-old girl—whom they agreed to call Margot, after Margo Channing (the character Bette desperately longed to emulate now with Gary by recognizing that there was more to a woman's life than her career).

Bette and B.D. were staying with Robin and Brownie, her husband, in Westport, Connecticut, when Bette arranged to pick up Margot, whom she described as "a real live doll" and "a present" for B.D.—as Bobby had seemed a gift from Harlow and Ruthie. "I had to go into the living room and sit down and close my eyes," B.D. recalls, "and there was this big 'present'!"

Soon after little Margot's arrival, Bette began to notice that the baby cried a good deal more than B.D. had—and differently somehow.

Knowing Bette's tendency to whip herself into a frenzy by turning things over and over in her thoughts beyond the point of reason, friends reassured her that all children are different.

Back in California, the Merrills settled into a Malibu beach house, which Bette had insisted on renting immediately when she learned that Richard Barthelmess had once lived there. Although her husband assumed that this was because Barthelmess had been Bette's co-star in her first important film, *Cabin in the Cotton*, it is tempting to speculate that she may have been thinking of the press clipping about Barthelmess that her beau Fritz Hall had sent her in 1927. Preserved in one of the Victorian scrapbooks that Bette continued to cart about nearly a quarter of a century afterward, the article told of how, at Barthelmess's insistence, his fiancée, Katherine Wilson, had abandoned her theatrical career to marry him: Fritz Hall's way of pleading with Bette to do the same.

Whether Bette was conscious of it or not, there was a certain irony in her selection of the Barthelmess house as the place where she would prove—or try to—that with Gary Merrill she could sustain both a film career and a family life.

At the Malibu beach house, Ruthie began to photograph the Merrills with their new baby. In the countless baby pictures Ruthie had once taken of Bette's "real" daughter, B.D., the child was almost always shown alone or with her mother, or—now and then—with Bette and Bobby: almost never with Sherry, whom Ruthie despised. By contrast, Ruthie's photographs of Margot for this period show her preponderantly with B.D., Bette, and Gary: the family Margot's adoption symbolized to Bette.

"She had hoped that she could have a regular family life, recalls Gary Merrill's brother, Jerry. "They adopted two children, and she hoped that this thing would work. And in the beginning, it worked pretty well. But it was very tough for her. . . . The only time Bette was ever happy, regrettably, was when she was working. It was sad to see it. . . . She tried as hard as she could to have a family life—I admire her for trying—but she couldn't handle it."

Bette's work in this period afforded her scant satisfaction. Because, by chance, *All About Eve* had been released before the inept *Payment on Demand,* Davis's departure from Warners had initially seemed to all the world a shrewd decision, providing Bette with the opportunity to select fine projects like the Mankiewicz film. *All About Eve* seemed to presage a vital new phase in Bette's film career, yet nothing of the sort followed. Having failed to revive her credentials as a serious actress when she had had the chance to do so with her independent production company, now again she chose unwisely, appearing with Merrill in such worthless fare as Irving Rapper's *Another Man's Poison* and Jean Negulesco's *Phone Call from a Stranger;* and on her own in Stuart Heisler's *The Star.* For all Bette's insistence on the freedom to pick her own projects, as in the past the actress displayed an inability to use that freedom judiciously in the service of her art.

"I was singing away," said Bette on Sunday, October 19, 1952, in Detroit, "then all of a sudden somebody was slapping my face hard and a voice was saying, 'Get up, Bette, get up.' I had blacked out completely."

The occasion was the out-of-town premiere—at Detroit's Shubert Theatre—of the ramshackle musical revue *Two's Company*, in which, at her husband's instigation, Davis was set to open on Broadway in two months. As Bette prepared to make her entrance by popping out of a magician's box, she felt a sudden sensation of whirling—but then she heard her cue, leapt from the box, and had barely begun her first song, "Good Little Girls Go to Heaven," when she collapsed to the stage with what one witness described as "a terrific bone-jarring bang."

As fellow cast members stood about, frozen, a stagehand rushed out to drag her into the wings. Having observed all this from the audience, Gary Merrill—now on his way backstage—assumed that his wife had suffered a fatal heart attack.

Within five minutes of regaining consciousness Bette was back onstage, straightening her hair and her dress as she put the audience at ease by remarking, "Well, you couldn't say I didn't fall for you."

"On the musical stage she is less an actress than a personality," Brooks Atkinson would say of Bette in *Two's Company* when she opened in New York on December 15, 1952. "Miss Davis's personal valor is not a substitute for experience in one of the theatre's most exciting genres; and this episode in her career is likely to be a wounding one."

Since her mysterious collapse in Detroit, Bette had never entirely regained her stamina. For the first few weeks of the New York run, she required revivifying injections from Dr. Max Jacobson, or "Dr. Feel Good," as he was known.

By March, however, Davis had more wisely turned to a prominent oral surgeon, Dr. Stanley Behrman, who, after removing an infected wisdom tooth, diagnosed her as suffering from osteomyelitis of the jaw: the painful bone disease that had caused Ruthie to collapse in East Orange, New Jersey, in the fall of 1922 (although in her autobiography, *The Lonely Life*, Bette oddly insists that before 1953, she had never heard of osteomyelitis). "Apparently, the infection has been spreading for months," the doctor told reporters, in anticipation of operating on the left side of Bette's lower jawbone. "It has been draining into her neck and shoulder, causing pain that was often severe."

Two days later, on March 10, *Two's Company* closed after eighty-nine performances.

Within the week, Bette underwent two and a half hours of surgery at New York Hospital, during which nearly half her jaw was removed, enough being left to allow all the bone to grow back. But that would take a year—during which Bette vowed to remain far from stage and screen, to allow her health to be restored.

TWENTY-TWO

A cab carrying Gary Merrill was making its way down the long private dirt road that led through an apple orchard and past a large trout pond to Witch Way, the sprawling, secluded oceanfront house he and Bette had bought at Zeb's Cove in Cape Elizabeth, Maine. On his way back from his regular two-day stint in a New York television studio, Merrill invited the cabdriver into the three-story colonial-style house for a late-night drink. Only naturally, the Bette Davis house was an object of considerable curiosity to the Maine locals, who, for all their fabled Yankee indifference, could scarcely repress their excitement about the legendary movie star's presence in their midst. But it was not Bette's celebrity alone that exerted such immense fascination in Cape Elizabeth. For some time there had been rumors of peculiar, even violent, goings-on in this house. The steady stream of servants who quit the Merrills' employ reported that Mr. Merrill, fond of the bottle, would walk about stark naked—especially, it seemed, when there was a maid around to shock and embarrass. Far more serious and disturb-

ing were reports of the physical abuse to which the actor repeatedly
subjected his famous wife, who had called the police on several occasions, only to refuse to press charges for fear of the dismal publicity
it would bring. And there was talk of the increasingly odd behavior of
their adopted daughter, Margot, who was said to be confined to an
isolated third-floor bedroom, where the shrieking child was regularly
tied to her bed all night in a straitjacket.

This night, however, as the driver followed Gary into the blissfully quiet fourteen-room house, where only the ocean's roar could be
heard, Witch Way seemed the picture of domestic tranquillity. Bette
appeared to be away, presumably having taken with her B.D., Margot, and young Michael Woodman Merrill, the son the Merrills had
adopted in 1952 when he was five days old. At first glance, there was
nothing to suggest that Witch Way, decorated with the same battered
Yankee furniture that Bette's mother had purchased years before for
Riverbottom, was a movie star's home. But as Gary poured a first
round, the cab driver's eye alighted on an incongruous thirteen-and-
a-half-inch-tall, gold-plated statuette, which he recognized at once as
one of Bette Davis's Academy Awards. Gary saw the driver excitedly
examining Bette's Oscar but said nothing about it, as the convivial,
increasingly boozy conversation turned to other subjects. After several hours and a good many drinks, when the driver thanked Merrill
for his hospitality and prepared to leave, Gary suddenly stopped him
at the door.

"Here, take this home with you," he said, thrusting his wife's
Academy Award into the bewildered man's hands. "We don't need
this around here anymore."

Although early the next morning the cabdriver sheepishly returned the Oscar to Witch Way before Bette came home and discovered it was missing, perhaps in some strange sense Gary had been
right; perhaps on some level Bette was anxious to be rid of the Oscar
and all it symbolized, for she had plunged into the role of wife and
mother with all the fervor and single-mindedness she had once applied to her greatest movie characterizations. But as so often with
Bette's acting, it was the "externals" of home life that preoccupied her
in Maine: the endless, obsessive cleaning and arranging, the overzeal-
ous preoccupation with minutely detailed household schedules, the
enthusiastic participation in the PTA and other local groups, and the
myriad domestic trappings with which Bette Davis struggled to create the guise of a happy, contented family.

But there was neither happiness nor contentment at Witch Way, at least not as most families would define those words. Family members like Jerry Merrill could see that an hour, perhaps an hour and a half, was the longest Bette could be with other people before the explosions started. On visits to Witch Way, as the hour mark approached, Gary's brother would pick himself up and head for another room to avoid the inevitable, often gratuitous brawling on which Bette and her fourth husband appeared to thrive. Although Bette and Gary clearly did not flinch from going head-to-head in front of others (and even seemed to enjoy having an audience), the worst fighting took place when only the children were there to see and hear.

According to B.D. Hyman, Gary saw nothing wrong in beating up his wife; to him such violence was "perfectly normal." Nor, according to her daughter, did Bette object to Gary's brutalities—far from it. "Mother had this peculiar relationship with Gary," says B.D. "She liked being brutalized. I think it was the only way she could understand a male-female relationship. And Gary was certainly very obliging on that score."

As she had done with Sherry, Bette often sought to provoke Gary to the physical violence she appeared to confuse with ardor. She goaded him with reminders that he failed to earn as much money as she at acting and with merciless mockery of his inability to satisfy her in bed. As her daughter watched in horror and perplexity, Bette would shove and push at Merrill until he showed some interest at last and knocked her to the floor with his fist. Whereupon Bette would let loose bloodcurdling shrieks of pain, accompanied by seemingly desperate pleas: "Don't hit me! I can't stand it!" At such moments, difficult as it was for the child to understand, Bette seemed honestly to have forgotten that she had brought the beating on herself.

The Merrills often drew the children into their quarrels, with Bette tending to target Michael as her husband's surrogate, while Gary (by his own account) did the same with B.D. To Jerry Merrill, it seemed that Bette regarded Michael as primarily Gary's son. Indeed, she often made a great point of distinguishing between her adopted children and her "real" daughter, B.D., about whom she spoke in what her friend Dori Brenner describes as a "totally different register."

Not surprisingly, perhaps in imitation of her parents' perpetual belligerency, B.D. was in the beginning frequently at odds with her younger brother. "I was a very overbearing older sister, apparently," she admits. "I used to play dreadful tricks on him and take terrible advantage." Still, as far as Bette was concerned, "If I wanted to abuse my brother, that was perfectly fine—after all, she'd bought him for me." According to B.D., the boy "was told that he had no right to irritate Mother in any way whatsoever and no right to complain about anything I did to him."

Much as Bette had once done to Bobby, B.D. taunted and tormented her essentially helpless younger sibling until the day when, appalled at this vision of history monstrously repeating itself, Bobby worked up the courage to intercede on Michael's behalf. She, after all, knew what it was to suffer a spoiled older sister's ceaseless abuse and to lack the protection of a parent who ought to have known better. Bobby had often observed B.D. gleefully exploiting Michael at Witch Way; but Bette had almost always been present, making it impossible for the eternally downtrodden Aunt Bobby to protest. On one occasion, however, Bette was nowhere in sight when B.D. hid one of Michael's toys, plunging the poor child into a fit of agitation. Accustomed as she was to Bette's undiscriminating approval, B.D. was stunned when her usually silent aunt angrily took her to task for this latest act of cruelty.

"Hey now, this is not a way to behave," Bobby reprimanded B.D., with a firmness and resolve she had never shown before. "Your little brother is in there crying, and you have no right to do that. You just did something that was downright mean. You taunted him and hid his favorite toy and won't tell him where it is. He's frustrated and hysterical, and you have no right to treat somebody like that. So you'd just better get hold of yourself, young lady, or you're in big trouble!"

Bobby's speech was like nothing B.D. had ever heard before. And for Bobby, too, her own words came as something of a shock, so different from the meek subservience to Bette that she had shown all her life. Bobby's elation was short-lived, however; Bette stormed into the room, furious that Bobby had dared to raise her voice to B.D. Within seconds, Bobby's newfound strength disappeared entirely. With Bette marching about, angrily demanding to know what had been going on, it seemed to B.D. that Bobby actually shrank physically. "Yes, Bette. Yes, Bette," Bobby muttered softly, retreating into a corner while the indignant Bette held forth.

Easy as it was for Bette to control her financially dependent younger sister, the actress appeared to take perverse pleasure in humiliating her before the children and, worse, before Bobby's own daughter, Fay. With B.D. for an audience, Bette loudly and angrily reminded Fay of all the money she had spent through the years to keep Bobby in a series of mental hospitals. Suddenly the actress launched into a heartless impersonation of Bobby in the midst of one of her breakdowns, bouncing off walls and weeping noisily and without restraint. "That's what your mother was," Bette screamed when she was done, "and she'd still be there today if it weren't for me!"

Although Bette regularly alluded to her sister's bouts of mental illness, for many months she refused to acknowledge that there might be something wrong with her adopted daughter, Margot, whose disturbing behavior included an attempt to choke a pet kitten, as well as nightly screaming fits that lasted until dawn. Initially, each instance of aberrant behavior was met with some new rationalization. When the child bolted in an apparent attempt (the first of many) to run away from Bette, Gary soothed his anxious wife with the remark "How fast Margot runs." And when, waiting in a parked car while Bette chatted with a neighbor, Margot suddenly started to strip off her clothes, the neighbor assured Bette that children often did such things. Even the attempted strangulation of the cat was explained away by someone's pointing out that, having yet to develop a moral sense, children are often cruel to animals.

However much she was capable by day of denying her adopted daughter's condition, at night, as Margot screamed and shook the bars of her crib in a third-floor bedroom, Bette could hardly put her out of her thoughts. She later said that Margot had seemed "driven," her inexplicable cruelty and restlessness "almost as if she was possessed by a demon." Bette recalled often praying to keep her temper—and her sanity. But her prayers were not answered; the actress was often observed shrieking uncontrollably at Margot, almost as if she thought she could "bully" the child into being normal. Margot's incessant repetition of words—"Hi, Hi, Hi, Hi, Hi, Hi, Hi"—drove Bette to distraction; as did Margot's random attacks on Michael, whose baby hair she yanked out in tufts. Once, Bette discovered two-year-old Margot and one-year-old Michael near the well-stocked bar, where she and Gary often collided. To her unutterable horror, Bette saw broken glass everywhere and Margot watching her brother weep at the sight of his bloody arms and hands.

Bette began endlessly to photograph Margot, in what appears to have been a last desperate attempt to assuage her anxieties. In hopes that the camera would somehow yield the truth about her adopted daughter, she relentlessly probed Margot's face for some sign of normality. Bette may have taken comfort, however fleeting, in many of

these images, for the photographs tend to show a sweet, lovely, an-
gelic child without the faintest sign of anything disturbing or abnor-
mal about her. But then one comes upon two very different pictures
(what motivated Bette to take them?) tucked away among the others.
The first shows Michael cringing facedown in a beach chair, as Margot
pummels him from above; the second focuses on the little boy as he
screams in pain from her blows.

After two-year-old Margot wreaked havoc in her room, smashing
everything she could get her hands on, Gary took her to Presbyterian
Hospital in New York. Doctors conducted a week-long battery of tests
before they pronounced the Merrills' adopted daughter "brain damaged." A number of possibilities raced through Bette's thoughts. Perhaps Margot's condition had been caused by drugs her unwed mother
had taken in an attempt to induce an abortion; perhaps it had been
the excessive pressure of the doctor's forceps during a difficult delivery; or perhaps the trouble dated back to a nursery accident soon after
her adoption. Whatever the cause of Margot's condition, one of the
doctors recommended that the Merrills send their daughter to the
Lochland School in Geneva, New York, where she could be educated
with other retarded children.

Margot's condition placed a new strain on Bette and Gary's already troubled marriage. Identifying Margot as his daughter (while
B.D. was Bette's), Gary bristled at her being labeled brain damaged
and retarded. When they visited the Lochland School, Gary recoiled
at the sight of two children with Down's syndrome, who were part of
the group Margot would join should she be sent there. By contrast
with these children, with their broad, flattened skulls and epicanthic
folds at the eyelids, Margot's outwardly normal physical appearance
was all Gary could think of.

Back at Witch Way, Bette huddled with Ruthie, who urged her
to return Margot to the hospital where she had been born almost
three years before and annul the adoption. If Bette refused to follow
her mother's advice, it was less out of compassion for Margot than for
fear of the bad publicity that would result were she simply to give the
child back. And so it was that, with Bette campaigning to send Margot
to Lochland, Gary suddenly announced that Bette could do as she
pleased with B.D., but his daughter was to remain at Witch Way,
where she belonged.

Although Gary believed that Margot would be best served by
their all acting as if nothing were wrong with her, he agreed to hire

a full-time nurse and to restrain her at night with a straitjacket to keep her from hurling herself out of bed. But even Gary would reluctantly come to admit that the arrangement was not feasible. Even in a normal, reasonably tranquil and supportive household, Margot would have had considerable difficulty. In the fractious, violent, alcohol-soaked atmosphere of Witch Way, a child with Margot's severe disabilities probably never stood a chance.

When at length the decision was reached to send Margot away to school, Bette seemed to withdraw emotionally from her adopted daughter, as if in preparation for putting the child out of her thoughts. Dori Brenner points out that for Bette, Margot was basically "eliminated" from the age of three. "What Bette didn't want to think about, she didn't think about," says Brenner. As the time for Margot's departure approached, Bette, declaring herself unable to face the eight-hour drive to Geneva, proposed that Gary take the three-year-old there himself. Bette would say goodbye to her in Maine. Nor did Bette change her mind when Gary rented a plane for the trip; she was, she reminded him, afraid to fly.

In Gary's absence, Bette told herself that life at Witch Way would be much better now that Margot was gone. Yet no sooner did Merrill return than it became obvious that sending the child away was only going to exacerbate the tensions between them. Bette hoped that Gary's agreeing to adopt B.D. would bring him closer to her "real" daughter and soothe his pain over Margot. Instead the adoption seemed to have the opposite effect. Gary resented B.D. all the more, as if Bette had pressed him to adopt her daughter in place of his own.

"It was a regular thing," says B.D. Hyman of the violence she suffered at Gary Merrill's hands. "He was drunk most of the time, and he'd just decide he was bored and was going to create some action. So he'd precipitate something. . . . Whenever he was around, there was no way of relaxing. It was like having a pent-up animal that at any minute was just going to suddenly zip around and attack." B.D. quickly learned that even so simple an action as crossing the kitchen could pose formidable difficulties if Gary was seated at the table, reading the newspaper. If she walked directly past Merrill's chair, he might suddenly jump up, drop the paper, and smack her with his fist—for no apparent reason other than that beating her and her mother seemed to give him pleasure. Violence was just as likely if she took the long way across the kitchen, quietly making her way around the other side of the table. Then, too, Gary might jump to his feet, angrily asking Bette's daughter why she was "creeping around," before he threw himself in her path and knocked her to the floor. At least the child would have braced herself for those beatings. Far worse were the attacks that occurred in the middle of the night when B.D. would be awakened by the sound of Gary kicking open her bedroom door. "He was bored, felt like hurting something, and I was there," says B.D., whose repeated complaints about Gary's brutalities her mother steadfastly denied.

For all her immense passion for B.D., Bette remained curiously unprepared to face up to Merrill's increasingly abusive treatment of her daughter. B.D. recalls: "It was a very strange mixture. I was her possession. I was the daughter, the child she finally had, the one thing that couldn't leave her. She owned me. I was hers, and she was obsessively doting." Still, when it came to B.D.'s complaints about Gary Merrill, Bette stubbornly refused to listen to her daughter. "She would not acknowledge that his brutality extended to me," says B.D. "She just couldn't accept that. She didn't want to part with him, and I was her precious darling. Mother had her own reality. She was very powerfully able to separate the truth from what she believed— this was no problem for her. So she denied in her own mind that he ever hurt me—that made it okay. She would just say, 'No, you're making this up. This isn't possible. I wouldn't let that happen to you. Forget it. You obviously fell down the stairs.' "

Merrill appears to have done his best to shield his adopted son from the family violence, reportedly going so far as to lock the boy in his room to keep him from observing the beatings to which Bette and her daughter were subjected. In time, as one Merrill relative observed, the boy seemed automatically to retreat to his room at the first sign of conflict between his parents. "Come with me—we'll go up here," Michael resignedly told a young cousin who was visiting Witch Way for the afternoon, when, as always, Bette and Gary began to quarrel. Michael calmly escorted the cousin to an upstairs bedroom, whose door he kept locked until the fighting seemed to subside. "Okay, now we can go out," said Michael, evidently accustomed to handling circumstances such as these.

Before long, in her frantic attempt to deny her husband's abuse, Bette found herself paying people to keep silent about events in the Merrill household. Sorely in need of funds on account of Gary's disinclination to work on a steady basis, Bette had resumed activity in Hollywood, where she appeared, to little effect, in the occasional bad film: Henry Koster's *The Virgin Queen*, in 1955; Daniel Taradash's *Storm Center* and Richard Brooks's *The Catered Affair*, both in 1956. The Merrills were living temporarily in Emerald Bay, California, when, confident that Gary would be absent for the weekend—he was out of state and not due to return until the following week—B.D. invited a girlfriend to sleep over. There could be no question of B.D.'s having friends to her home when Gary was about, to humiliate her with casual nudity and drunken violence. Saturday night, B.D. and her friend were quietly amusing themselves when B.D. heard Gary swagger in the front door and begin fighting noisily with Bette. Within moments, Merrill had found the girls and administered a particularly severe beating, which left B.D.'s friend badly bruised and emotionally shaken. Clearly, she could not remain in the house for the rest of the night, and it fell upon Bette to return the tearful child to her parents. Desperately pleading with them not to summon the authorities, Bette offered to pay a large sum for their discretion. Although the furious parents were anxious to report the incident to the police, and possibly even to file a lawsuit, they finally agreed to consider Bette's offer, but only after a physician had examined the child to determine whether Gary had abused her *sexually*. B.D. never again risked inviting friends.

▲▼▲

On October 9, 1957—four months after she had filed in Santa Monica Superior Court for "separate maintenance" from Gary Merrill, whom after seven years of marriage, she charged with "extreme cruelty"— Bette wrote a wistful letter to Robin Brown about her feckless recent attempts to start a new life for herself and the children. Not long after walking out on Gary, Bette had signed to appear on Broadway that fall in a dramatization of Thomas Wolfe's *Look Homeward, Angel,* rehearsals for which would take place in Los Angeles. Having rented a house in Brentwood, Bette opened what she presumed to be a closet door and plunged headlong down a ladder-type stairway to the basement.

A concussion and severe spinal injuries compelled her to withdraw from the play, send the children back to Maine (where they would live with Gary's brother Jerry), and move into Ruthie's house on Sleepy Hollow Lane in Laguna Beach. Bobby and her seventy-two-year-old mother would care for Bette there while she lay in bed waiting for her back to mend and wondering—as she told Robin— why she had not yet lost her mind.

By Christmas, she and the children were back together at Witch Way. And life with Gary resumed as in the past. "He came close to killing her a couple of times," says Bette's daughter, who had taken to hurling herself between them when Gary seemed to grow too dangerously violent with her mother. According to B.D., on several occasions a fearful Bette fled to Robin's house in Connecticut, where Gary, enraged at finding himself abandoned, quickly tracked her down. In the middle of the night he rushed about outside the house, drunkenly banging on windows and shouting, "I want to see Bette! I want to see Bette!" while Davis screamed uncontrollably, "I don't want to see him!"

One of Bette's favorite possessions was a jangling gold charm bracelet that Farney's mother had given her. At the onset of anxiety, Bette liked to fiddle with the gold charms on her right wrist, swiftly counting them one by one, as if to check that each was in its proper place. More often than not, hardly would Bette finish counting when she would start all over again: a comforting, anodyne process, whose speed and duration appeared to correspond to the degree of panic she happened to be experiencing. (This obsessive checking and counting with the fingers as a means of allaying anxiety suggests the tantalizing possibility that two of the actress's signature on-screen gestures—the expressive opening and closing of the palm and the rapid grazing of the fingertips with the thumb—may have had their origin in a form of compulsive finger-counting.) On May 6, 1958, moments before Bette, B.D., and Bobby set sail from New York for Europe, as they waved goodbye to Robin from the deck of the ocean liner *Independence*, Bette's charm bracelet slipped off her right arm and fell onto a wooden buffer between the ship and Pier 84, at West Forty-fourth Street. Although Robin feared that it had disappeared into the water, a longshoreman retrieved it. As the *Independence* was already on its way out to sea, the steamship company dispatched a tugboat to return the bracelet to the frantic movie star.

Which was just as well; as indicated in Bette's fretful, uneasy diary for this period, the journey that followed gave much cause for anxiety. While Michael stayed in Maine with his father, "the three B's" (as Bette called them) were off for two months in Europe. Davis had signed on to portray a decrepit bedridden countess in *The Scapegoat*, with Alec Guinness, in England; and to appear in a cameo role as Empress Catherine in *John Paul Jones*, to be shot in Spain. Bette had high hopes for neither film, but they were all she was being offered at the moment, and as she never tired of announcing, she needed the money to support herself and her children, as well as her mother and sister. Amid a good deal of apparently self-soothing talk about her makeup (always a sure sign that Davis was feeling especially anxious), the fifty-year-old actress quietly recorded her daily panic, even terror, at the thought of appearing on-camera.

When Gary Merrill married Bette Davis, shortly after the making of *All About Eve*, he perceived her as being at the peak of her career. He made no bones about looking forward to the prestige and publicity he would enjoy as her husband. "But at the point she divorced him," her daughter points out, "her career was kaput. That's basically the reason he didn't put up much of a fuss." For her part, Bette probably would have remained with Merrill for some time still; but as B.D. reached puberty and blossomed into what her friend Gay Bersteeg calls "a gorgeous Amazon," Gary's rough treatment of her—the senseless beatings and random attacks—took on a disturbing new aspect. Perceiving herself as a young woman who could no longer tolerate Gary's violent abuse, B.D. astonished her mother with an ultimatum that, friends say, the unusually self-reliant twelve-year-old would have been perfectly capable of carrying out. "Mother, I know it's not all the time, but I'm not going to live this way. Either he goes or I'm going to find somewhere else to live. I can't face this again."

The Merrills had meantime signed on to do a cross-country tour of *The World of Carl Sandburg*, in which they read selections from the author's poetry and prose. According to Jerry Merrill, although husband and wife lived apart during the tour and scarcely spoke to each other, onstage they made every effort to give no sign of the marital discord that had caused them to separate.

Gary Merrill failed to appear in Superior Court in Portland, Maine, on July 6, 1960, when, seeking a divorce, Bette told Judge Charles A. Pomeroy of her husband's "cruel and abusive treatment" of her for the past ten years. Declaring the children's welfare her primary concern, Bette argued the impossibility of their enjoying "a normal and wholesome life" so long as they were permitted to see their mother regularly "treated in this manner." The husband's brutalities were attested to by Bette's friend Robin Brown, who told

Judge Pomeroy that she had observed Gary abuse Bette in front of the children, who were palpably affected by it.

With Gary presumably gone from her life, Bette appeared to pin her hopes for emotional fulfillment on B. D., as Ruthie had once done with Bette. "Bette just worshiped B.D.," explains Ellen Batchelder, whom Davis asked to stay with her at Witch Way that summer after the divorce. To an old friend like Ellen, who had long ago observed the dynamics of Bette's turbulent, passionate relationship with Ruthie, history appeared to repeat itself in the all-too-familiar fights between Bette and her own spirited, willful, much-beloved daughter. It seemed to Ellen's daughter Gay Bersteeg that at times Bette's adoration could be so intense as to require B.D. to "defend herself" against it. "Bette would run your life if you let her, so B.D. had to somehow come up with what B.D. is," says Bersteeg. As for Margot, when she visited at Witch Way that summer, on vacation from the residence where she spent most of the year, Bette went off with B.D. and Gay, leaving the younger girl with Ellen and the maid. Margot ran upstairs in disappointment, and soon after Bette and the girls had gone, Ellen heard "a terrible commotion" on the second floor. Rushing upstairs to see what was wrong, she traced the loud, crashing noises to the music room, where, to her horror and amazement, she discovered Margot furiously hurling records in every direction to express her anger at having been left behind.

"Homemaker," said Bobby, on July 1, 1961, when asked her mother's most recent position of employment. Asked how long "Mrs. Davis" had held her current position (after her divorce from Otho Budd, Ruthie had reverted to Harlow's name), Bobby answered, "Life." Ruth Favor Davis, her death certificate tells us, was seventy-five years old when she died of coronary thrombosis after a serious illness of three months. Unable to maintain the house on Sleepy Hollow Lane in Laguna Beach in which Bette had installed her in the 1940s, Ruthie had recently moved to an apartment on Ramona Street near Bobby. (Bette was paying for both quarters, having long ago accepted that her mother and sister could not live under the same roof.)

Struck by the realization that Ruthie had died on the anniversary of her first wedding, Bobby wondered aloud whether it might be possible to bury their mother beside their father in Maine. Bette told her not to be so stupid: didn't Bobby know that the empty grave beside Harlow was reserved for another woman? And so it was that on Monday, July 3, 1961, Ruthie was buried at Fairhaven Memorial Park in Orange, California. Bette later told Robin that when the silver casket that had been Ruthie's deathbed request disappeared into the earth, she could scarcely believe that she would never see or speak to her mother again.

"Goddamn you!" Bette told Ellen Batchelder, to whom she complained of her loneliness in this period. "When you got married I gave you and Dean six months, and here you are still together—and I've been through four husbands already. Goddamn you!"

"You know very well that you deliberately chose the four dumbest men you could have," her old friend replied. "Why don't you find a nice man to support you for a change?"

Instead Bette remained as preoccupied as ever with Gary Merrill, with whom, now that they were divorced, she made a great point of maintaining what she called "amicable relations," despite (some might say because of) the tongue-lashings and beatings to which he continued periodically to subject her. Nor, court records show, did he spare B.D., at whom he drunkenly hurled obscenities during a Father's Day dinner in Los Angeles, to which Bette had invited him on June 18, 1961. Accusing Bette's daughter of having the mind of a seven-year-old, Merrill raved that B.D. would never be able to attract a man. When a call came for B.D. during his visit, Merrill grabbed the receiver from her and hung up, lest she be distracted from his boozy tirade. As Gary raised his hand to strike her, the fourteen-year-old rushed out of the room. He then turned his rage on her mother, who almost certainly would have continued their "amicable relations" had her ex-husband not publicly humiliated her—or so Bette seemed to perceive it—by embarking soon afterward on a much-publicized affair with Rita Hayworth.

Reports of the couple's drunken revels (which included Merrill's repeatedly battering Hayworth, much as he had beaten Davis and her daughter) drove Bette to file a motion in Maine's Cumberland County Superior Court to deprive her ex-husband of the right to visit B.D., Michael, and Margot. Although Bette claimed that this was to protect them from their father's "physical violence when in a state of intoxication," it was no secret that her real motive was to punish Merrill for his "notorious association" with the Love Goddess, which Davis cited in court papers as "a source of great embarrassment and humiliation to the children."

TWENTY-THREE

*I*n October 1961, puffing on her cigarette, making abrupt, jerky motions with her wrists and shoulders, and muttering angrily to herself, Bette Davis was stamping back and forth onstage at Broadway's Shubert Theatre. Rehearsals were under way for Tennessee Williams's *The Night of the Iguana*, in anticipation of the first scheduled public performance, in Rochester, New York, on November 3. Cast as the slatternly, sexually rapacious Maxine Faulk, who runs the ramshackle Costa Verde Hotel on a jungle-covered hilltop in Mexico, Bette was anxious to show everyone what she could do with the raucous, snorting, derisive "Ha!" with which Williams encapsulated her character's beguiling insolence. For the moment, however, director Frank Corsaro was preoccupied with a long, difficult, emotionally charged scene between Margaret Leighton and Patrick O'Neal. He had repeatedly asked Bette to sit with other cast members in the makeshift bleachers that had been constructed onstage for rehearsals. Fueled by an endless succession of cigarettes, the fifty-three-year-old Davis could not sit still. She marched, she groaned, she gesticulated. Although Leighton and O'Neal scrupulously resisted breaking out of character to glance behind them, they could sense Bette Davis's looming, malevolent presence, feel the ominous billows of smoke wafting in their direction. Hardly would Leighton or O'Neal utter a line or two when the spell of Williams's lyrical language would be swiftly shattered by Bette's pounding footsteps and agitated, erratic gestures, which the director feared were calculated to distract and disconcert them.

Things were scarcely any better when Bette's turn came to work with Corsaro. As the elegant and ethereal Margaret Leighton rejoined her fellow players in the bleachers, Bette strutted past the renowned English actress without a word or glance of acknowledgment. Taking her place beside the tall, gaunt, darkly handsome Patrick O'Neal, whose evasive, haunted eyes barely hinted at his raging fear and insecurity, Bette bristled with impatience when Corsaro, noted for his distinguished work with the Actors Studio, made a few preliminary comments to try to help them "feel their way" through the text. Before the director quite realized what was happening, Davis had hurled herself behind him, where, grabbing his shoulders and laughing raucously, she made a great show of rubbing her breasts against his back, in her latest attempt to undermine his authority before the other actors.

Bette's fierce antipathy toward Corsaro harked back to his early opposition to Tennessee Williams's having offered her the role of Maxine Faulk. What Bette had failed to understand, however, was that Corsaro had been opposed not to her per se but to her being cast principally because she was a major star whose name would ensure the acquisition of a good theater and attract the large theater parties so important to a play of this sort. Although the fifty-year-old Williams continued to be widely regarded as America's finest living playwright, the author of *The Glass Menagerie* and *A Streetcar Named Desire* had not had an unequivocal hit on Broadway since *Cat on a Hot Tin Roof*, in 1955. The plays of the intervening years—*Orpheus Descending, Garden District, Sweet Bird of Youth,* and *Period of Adjustment*— had caused some commentators to speak of an artist in decline: a perception Williams was especially keen to overturn in 1961 with what he suspected was his best play in years, perhaps the last great drama he had it in him to write.

By any standard, the other major female role in *The Night of the Iguana,* the itinerant artist Hannah Jelkes, who, accompanied by her ancient grandfather, Nonno, appears suddenly at Maxine's hotel, was clearly the more substantial (the "star part," as Patrick O'Neal calls it). But even when Katharine Hepburn declined to portray Hannah on Broadway, there was never any question of offering the richer, more rewarding role to Bette. Williams believed that, given the rigorous demands of the complex, lyrical passages he had written for Hannah, Davis would almost certainly have proved inadequate to the task of supporting the text. Even in her very best films, the playwright found nothing to suggest that Bette Davis could give Hannah's long, poetic speeches the subtle shades of color and expression they required. Not a word of this, of course, did Williams or his go-between, Violla Rubber, communicate to Bette, whose participation in the production was all the more essential without Hepburn. From the first, there were persistent whispers at the Actors Studio, where the *Iguana* production had been in development for two years, that in the earliest stages of Williams's discussions with Davis, the actress had not been shown a full-length text, only Maxine's lines, which, of course, would have made it impossible for Bette to gauge the weight of her role relative to others.

"When she discovers that the play is not really about Maxine Faulk, we're going to have a great storm on our heads!" Frank Corsaro groaned after his initial tense meeting with Bette, who, seeming to view *Iguana* as the big comeback her career desperately needed just now, mistakenly believed Maxine to be a role as important as Amanda Wingfield in *The Glass Menagerie* or Blanche Dubois in *A Streetcar Named Desire*. When, having studied *Iguana* in its entirety, Bette expressed her as yet vague disappointment to the playwright, Williams, in the interests of getting his play on, was not above allowing Davis to believe he might indeed do something to "develop" her character. Corsaro, by contrast, could give her no such assurances: hence Bette's violent resentment of the director, her need to contradict and humiliate him at every turn. Intimate with every nook and cranny of Williams's play after two years of working with it at the Actors Studio, Corsaro knew that Maxine Faulk was—and could only be—the "tertiary role," the drama's principal conflict being the war between Hannah Jelkes's spirituality and the carnality embodied by the defrocked minister, T. Lawrence Shannon. Through it all, the ribald widow Faulk is little more than a colorful onlooker to this furious battle of souls at the Costa Verde Hotel: hardly what Bette had had in mind or been led to believe.

In one of the Hollywood melodramas in which Bette Davis had

achieved stardom in the thirties and forties, *The Night of the Iguana* would have been a simple love triangle, with Maxine and Hannah fighting each other for the man they both love. Assuming that this was how, in rewrites, Tennessee Williams was going to "fix" the play in her favor, Bette sought to help things along by trying to launch a Hollywood-style feud with the actress playing Hannah. "We don't have to be friends to work together, do we?" Davis lashed out at Margaret Leighton when Corsaro introduced them, shortly after the thirty-nine-year-old English actress arrived in New York on October 3. Bette's acute self-consciousness about her own coarse, gouty phys-ical condition—the result of a decade of hard drinking and brawling with Gary Merrill—caused her to view the slender, graceful, fine-featured actress, fourteen years her junior, with scarcely concealed jealousy. Although she lacked Bette's far-reaching fame and box office appeal, Leighton was unquestionably the more seasoned and expert stage performer. At the Old Vic, she had appeared to great acclaim in *Arms and the Man*, *Richard III*, *King Lear*, *Cyrano de Bergerac*, *Henry IV*, and *Uncle Vanya*. From the first, much as Davis tried to bait the rival actress to create a passionate conflict between them that would somehow carry over into the play, Leighton serenely resisted being drawn into a catfight with Bette, whose indelicacies she wisely preferred to ignore.

This led Bette to set her sights on thirty-three-year-old Patrick O'Neal, who, by his own account, was then every bit as much at the end of his rope as the tormented ex-minister he had been portraying for the past two years in workshop productions of *Iguana*. Having come under the sway of the notorious Dr. Max Jacobson and his dangerous "speed" injections, the ambitious young actor was himself perilously close to a real breakdown when without the faintest en-couragement Bette Davis suddenly seized upon him to replace her recently divorced husband. Bette was coy and girlish at first when O'Neal, twenty years her junior, visited her rented East Seventy-eighth Street town house, where, to his amazement, he glimpsed Gary Merrill silently, mysteriously entering the front door and dis-appearing upstairs. Unable to attract O'Neal's interest, Bette soon turned ugly, publicly venting her rage at him and his dedication to the Actors Studio. Accustomed to arousing Gary Merrill's passion by taunting and provoking him to hit her, Bette seemed to have been trying to do the same with Patrick O'Neal, who in fact tended to recoil fearfully from her abuse.

Davis's attempts to send O'Neal over the edge had been escalating since the day at the Algonquin Hotel, in early October, when the *Iguana* company held its first, informal reading of the play. This appeared to be the moment when, whether or not she admitted it to herself, Bette felt oddly shut out, grasping that the most vital onstage action was the wistful, achingly beautiful dialogue Williams had written for Hannah and Shannon. Much as Bette struggled to conceal her anxieties, Leighton and O'Neal could hardly fail to be alarmed by the star's flailing, almost palpable desperation. Before long, during calamitous rehearsals at the Shubert Theatre that Frank Corsaro recalls as "nightmares," it became obvious that, madly marching back and forth behind them, Bette was going to do everything she could to undermine her co-stars. This left the director little choice but to meet secretly with Leighton and O'Neal at night in the darkened theater to work on Shannon's long key encounter with Hannah without Davis there to harass them.

Perhaps Bette had heard about the secret rehearsals, perhaps she was jealous of what she imagined to be O'Neal's burgeoning relationship with Margaret Leighton, or perhaps she was hysterical about the play, Williams's failure thus far to come up with the promised rewrites, or her own mortifying inability to get a handle on the small role she already had. Probably it was a combination of these factors that caused her to explode suddenly, without apparent provocation, while she was rehearsing with Corsaro, whom she accused of having colluded with Patrick O'Neal and the Actors Studio to destroy her. "She went crazy and paranoid, and accused Frank and me of hurting her, of sabotaging her performance," recalls O'Neal. As he watched Bette Davis rant and curse at him, O'Neal's thoughts began to spin with images of murder: thoughts that caused him to flee the rehearsal lest he grow violent with the shrieking actress. "It was just so outrageous that I went crazy," says O'Neal, "and ran right out of the theater, down Shubert Alley, and went straight to Max [Jacobson] and got a shot. As I used to say, 'In order not to kill her, I got the shot.' I was so outraged!"

"Ha!" barked Davis, before rushing angrily from the theater, to which she vowed never to return. In the days that followed, Bette, cozily ensconced in her friend Robin Brown's eighteenth-century house in Westport, Connecticut, declined to stir from the tiny upstairs guest bedroom, with its low sloping ceilings, piles of books, and cluster of familiar photographs, when, again and again, Tennessee Williams called to beg her to come back.

On October 30, the train carrying the *Iguana* company to Rochester was hurtling upstate when, to his perplexity and chagrin, Patrick O'Neal found himself summoned to Bette Davis's Pullman compartment. After putting Tennessee Williams through the torments of the damned by refusing to take his frantic calls or acknowledge the flowers with which he garlanded her Connecticut refuge, "La Davis"—as the playwright privately called Bette—had finally agreed to come back to work in time for the out-of-town tryouts. She had proved her point; the production's fate obviously depended on her, and she insisted that her own role be enlarged and Margaret Leighton's diminished accordingly. Having reminded everyone that the contract for Broadway's Royale Theatre, where *Iguana* was officially set to open on December 28, had been signed with her name as guarantee and that large theater parties had been amassed strictly on the basis of her participation, Bette made no bones about expecting to receive the rewrites from Williams as soon as possible.

To shore up her position further, Bette decided to enlist Patrick O'Neal as her ally, offering to help his career by taking him under her wing as protégé—and lover. Hence the message from Bette, inviting him to her private compartment. Scarcely having spoken to her since she had hysterically accused him of conspiring to destroy her, the actor proceeded through the train with considerable trepidation. But when he slowly opened the door, O'Neal was astonished to see, not the shrieking, foul-mouthed harpy he had expected, but Margo Channing, the warm, seductive, engagingly vulnerable, unabashedly adult woman Davis had portrayed with such flair in *All About Eve*. Averting his gaze to the moonlit landscape flitting past behind her, O'Neal heard Bette offer him a drink, then begin to talk in her most velvety tones about their upcoming stint at Rochester's Auditorium Theatre, where, she pointedly reminded him, their dressing rooms were to be on one side of the theater and Margaret Leighton's on the other.

"Don't forget which side of the theater you're dressing on," she reiterated, catching his eye to make certain he comprehended her meaning. Comprehending only too well, O'Neal awkwardly excused himself before Bette could go any further with her planned seduction. Running through the train, the actor searched out the stage manager, to demand, "Put me on the other side!"

By the time the *Iguana* company rolled into Rochester, they were, as Frank Corsaro describes them, "an embattled group." Enraged and humiliated after O'Neal rejected her advances, Bette became increasingly agitated when she heard that he had moved to a dressing room next to Leighton's. To make matters worse, it became painfully obvious at the cavernous Auditorium Theatre that Bette lacked the vocal technique to work subtly and effectively in so large a house.

"The opening was a raucous kind of success," says Corsaro. "The audience laughed as if they were at a farce. We didn't know what kind of play we had." One thing the company did know was that, having come out onstage to acknowledge a thunderous ovation from her fans, Bette could hardly conceal her upset and embarrassment at evening's end when it was Margaret Leighton who received the loudest cheers of praise and appreciation; the applause for Davis was little more than polite.

Before everyone left for the opening-night cast party, Bette stumbled and fell. Although afterward she attended the party "ostensibly in good physical shape" (as Tennessee Williams's agent, Audrey Wood, would recall), the next morning, with two sold-out performances to go, fellow cast members were shocked and disheartened by the sight of Bette being taken in a wheelchair to an ambulance. While some, like Wood, suspected that Davis's accident had been "subconsciously self-willed," Corsaro and others in the company questioned the seriousness of Bette's injury. "She just tripped over something, and it was an insignificant sprain which she turned into a major problem," says the director. "Rather than accept what it was, she got herself into a wheelchair. It was all her way of describing her rather embattled state. She was begging for attention, she was begging for relief. She was in panic, in total, absolute panic."

None of which seemed to have been a very great secret in Rochester, where, the day after an understudy replaced Bette in both the matinee and evening performances of *The Night of the Iguana*, one local newspaper reported that Davis was "suffering from a wrenched knee as well as a secondary part."

"I fully expected that we might actually close in Rochester," says Paula Laurence, the wife of *Iguana* producer Charles Bowden. "I didn't see how we could possibly go on with this."

Meanwhile, having failed to make Patrick O'Neal her ally, Bette suddenly turned her attentions to the director, to whom she placed a conciliatory telephone call from the hospital. "I was her only 'pal' by that time," says Corsaro. "She spoke to me in a manic way about the rest of the cast, who were all against her. She was violent about them, and yet she had a kind of manic joy about it all."

Davis's failure to appear at two out of three scheduled performances in Rochester, coupled with resentment over the star's "obstreperous behavior" in New York, drove exasperated company members to meet secretly to discuss the problem. "We realized that the play's future was at the mercy of a woman who was obviously manifesting personal illness," Corsaro explains. "A decision had to be arrived at whether or not she should be replaced, and of course everybody agonized." When the meeting concluded, with Corsaro's impassioned plea that they cast a new Maxine Faulk as soon as possible, word of it drifted to Bette, who, from her sickbed, angrily declared her intention to continue with the *Iguana* company on to Detroit, Chicago, and finally Broadway. From this point on, however, Davis notified the management, her being required to hobble about on crutches would preclude train travel with the others, hence the chauffeur-driven limousine she required.

One can only imagine Bette's astonishment when, leaving Rochester, she was ushered into the limousine, to discover that, in what Audrey Wood described as "a most kind and thoughtful gesture," Margaret Leighton had volunteered to ride with her to Detroit.

⚐

Frank Corsaro was meeting with Tennessee Williams in the rear of the deserted Shubert Theatre in Detroit to discuss the twenty to twenty-five minutes of cuts, many of them from Maxine's lines, that the director deemed necessary before they took *Iguana* to Broadway. Both men were rendered speechless by the sight of a seemingly delirious Bette Davis, who, clutching a basin of water and a rag, appeared suddenly onstage. Oblivious to their presence in the furthermost reaches of the auditorium, Bette wandered about the moldering tropical veranda of the Costa Verde Hotel for a moment or two before abruptly dropping to her knees to scrub the floor with a queer, obsessive fervor.

"I didn't believe what I was seeing!" Corsaro recalls. "We were absolutely transfixed and puzzled. It was really very pathetic—and even rather touching." Neither man suspected, as only Bette's closest friends and family members knew, that when her emotions were most disordered, she often sought to pacify herself through frenzied, apparently pointless cleaning rituals, such as the one Williams and Corsaro had happened upon. Listening to the actress cry softly as she washed the veranda, Corsaro felt a pang of embarrassment at having unintentionally violated her privacy. Instead of sneaking out of the theater, the director left Williams in the rear of the auditorium and hesitantly approached the stage to let Bette know they had been there all along.

Tears streaming down her cheeks, the actress continued to moan and sob as Corsaro climbed up onto the veranda to comfort her. "Nobody likes me," she bawled uncontrollably when the director asked why she was crying. "What am I doing that's wrong? I'm trying my damnedest!"

If Bette was this upset about Williams's having failed to build up her role, Corsaro shuddered to think how she would react to the news that at the director's urging, her part was soon to be made even smaller.

For fear that Davis would abandon *Iguana* before they even landed on Broadway, Williams hesitated to make the cuts he and the director had talked about that day in Detroit. Soon afterward, however, when they opened at the Blackstone Theatre in Chicago, the playwright knew he could procrastinate no longer. After reading a devastating review from his longtime fervent champion, drama critic Claudia Cassidy, Williams finally gave Corsaro the go-ahead to announce the cuts to the assembled company. As the director detailed the material to be excised, Leighton, O'Neal, and the other actors darted nervous glances at Bette, who responded with what seemed like unprecedented tranquillity.

Shortly after Bette left the theater, however, word came from her representatives that, from this moment on, if Tennessee Williams was going to make any changes in the text, it had better be to augment the role of Maxine Faulk. And there followed a spate of communications from Bette to various newspaper columnists, to whom she bitterly complained of her fellow actors' ineptitude, with Patrick O'Neal the target of her most virulent derision.

By this point, Bette's worst fears had been realized: she discovered that O'Neal had spurned her advances on the train to Rochester only to make an alliance with Margaret Leighton shortly thereafter. Driven wild by her sense of isolation, the jealous actress began calling O'Neal at all hours of the night to be certain that he was not with Leighton. In desperate hopes of escaping Davis, of whom he admits to having been "scared to death," O'Neal fled to an obscure hotel where she would be unable to track him down. "The poor man was falling apart!" Corsaro recalls. "He had allowed her to get to him, and he was a bundle of nerves."

Frustrated by her inability to discover the young actor's whereabouts, Bette repeatedly demanded that she and O'Neal go over their scenes together; in these turbulent sessions, Corsaro found himself functioning more as a referee than as a director. Day after day, Corsaro watched as O'Neal silently took Bette's invective and abuse, until finally, one afternoon, something seemed to snap in the actor. Waving his fists, he angrily informed Davis exactly what he and everyone else in the company thought of her. As O'Neal raged on, Davis's eyes brightened; she was triumphant at having aroused this show of passion at long last. "He let her have it in no uncertain terms, and she stood there smiling, loving every single minute of it," Corsaro recalls. "She really was the queen of the S and M club!"

Bette's happiness was short-lived. At Warner Bros. in the thirties and forties, Davis's box office appeal had given her license to grind writers and directors beneath her chariot wheels; why—she seemed to think—should Tennessee Williams be any different? Bette failed to understand that in Williams's world, the text, not the star, came first. Desperately as he may have needed Davis's name on the marquee, and willing as he may have been to hint that, yes, he might at length be inclined to embellish her role, unlike most of the people she had encountered in Hollywood, Williams regarded his principal responsibility as being to the play's artistic integrity. Patrick O'Neal points out that in a film, Bette might very well have gotten the changes she wanted. "She could have walked off the set," says the actor. "She could have threatened to leave the studio. She could have gone to bed with the director. All the things that she did do. But she couldn't do that here. The setup was different. Don't forget, Tennessee Williams was a great playwright." According to O'Neal, no matter what Williams may have indicated to Bette when they were drinking and "hanging out," he was simply not going to alter the play to suit her.

Whether Williams was prepared to admit it to her face was another matter. Sensing the importance of Bette's accepting once and for all that her role was now basically as she would be expected to perform it in New York, Corsaro decided to create a confrontation between Williams and Davis, where the playwright would be impelled openly to declare his intentions to her. At the Blackstone Theatre, Corsaro was working with Davis, with Williams observing intently from the stalls, when the director broke in to declare that she had better come to terms with the role as currently written; there was to be no new material for her character. "Tennessee, do you feel otherwise?" Corsaro turned to the playwright, who, put on the spot, had little choice but to agree, whereupon Bette coolly, silently drifted off the stage.

To remind Williams and the others that the show's continued existence depended on her, Bette began deliberately to miss performances. As if to strain everyone's nerves to the limit, at the last possible moment the actress would gleefully declare her unwillingness to go on. In the theater, the announcement that Miss Davis's understudy was to appear in the role of Maxine Faulk at that performance would lead crowds of ticket-holders to line up for refunds at the box office, where one of Bette's employees recorded their numbers with a clicker.

When it became evident that Williams was not about to budge on the rewrites, with less than two weeks to go before New York, Bette launched an all-out campaign to fire the director who had so vehemently opposed augmenting her role. Unlike her other enemies, Margaret Leighton and Patrick O'Neal, Corsaro was now expendable. He had done his work directing the play; the show could go on without him. But not without Bette, who flew into a violent rage when she learned that although Corsaro had been instructed not to deal with her directly, he was still in the theater, quietly monitoring rehearsals from the rear and sneaking notes backstage to the other cast members. Bette demanded that, thenceforth, Corsaro be barred from the theater; and in terror of her walking off again, Williams reluctantly agreed. While the *Iguana* company lingered for its final week in Chicago, Corsaro returned alone to New York, it having been agreed that in consideration of his many months on the production, he would of course retain billing as director. Whereupon Bette called members of the New York press to make it known that the director had been expelled.

With only a week to go before Broadway, Davis apparently continued to believe that getting rid of the director would allow her to take charge at long last. "I think if she had taken a truth serum," says Patrick O'Neal, "she would have said, 'Yes, I confess, it's going to be a play about Maxine.' "

"No, no, no, baby—stand over there," Tennessee Williams called up to the stage of the Blackstone Theatre. He was struggling to take over some of the directorial chores, even as his dependence on alcohol, pills, and the ministrations of Dr. Max Jacobson—the same "Dr. Feel Good" who had been treating Patrick O'Neal—hastened what O'Neal sadly calls the playwright's ineluctable "progression into darkness." It had hardly helped Williams's already precarious state of mind that in the course of the tour, his yellow-eyed black Belgian shepherd, Satan, had bitten him clean to the bone on both ankles, causing painful swelling and infection; or, worse, that the playwright seemed increasingly at odds with his devoted companion, Frank Merlo.

Williams's letters to the *Iguana* company are shot through with a sense of sadness over what he perceived as an impenetrable wall that had materialized between playwright and cast; a barrier that, perhaps, could only be overcome by Williams's committing to paper his thoughts on the work that remained to be done if his vision of the play was to be realized. Most problematic of all, it would seem, was the peculiar turn Bette's characterization had taken in recent weeks as she had endeavored to foreground Maxine Faulk by making her more striking in manner and appearance. Hence the brassy makeup, the too carefully coiffed and lacquered wig, the heavily boned push-up brassiere (designed to be worn beneath a blue work shirt unbuttoned to the waist), and the array of fussy mannerisms with which Bette was widely thought to have encumbered her performance, in unabashed disregard of the playwright's specifications.

To read the ineffably delicate letter in which Williams attempts to correct Davis's misconception of the character is to be reminded of William Wyler's strictures during the filming of *The Little Foxes*, urging the headstrong actress to try to grasp her character from the inside, instead of all too quickly assembling her from without. Now Davis was bestowing a tense, angular, self-conscious physicality on Maxine Faulk, the very antithesis of the easygoing natural grace, the freedom and openness of spirit, that Williams had envisioned. But where, in 1941, Wyler had suspected that the dead-white masklike physiognomy Bette constructed for Regina was a thirty-three-year-old's way of distancing herself from her forty-year-old character (and also, perhaps, of luring the audience's attention away from the other actors), in 1961, Davis's ketchup-colored wig, her stiff brassiere and

overpainted face, betokened the fifty-three-year-old actress's unease
about portraying a character Williams describes as being in her middle forties. Painfully insecure about her looks as she was, Bette
seemed to Patrick O'Neal to be trying to transform herself into the
woman who "gets the guy" and "wins" Shannon at the end of the play.

From first to last, despite the playwright's repeated attempts to
correct her, Bette persisted in misinterpreting the play and her character. As written by Williams, Maxine knows all along that she does
not need to fight Hannah for Shannon, who spends much of the play
struggling desperately to avoid taking a drink. Confident of Shannon's
fundamental dissoluteness, Maxine need only wait for the moment
when, inevitably, he starts drinking again. He will be hers to claim
after that. As Patrick O'Neal explains, when Shannon goes down to
the beach with Maxine at the end, it isn't because Maxine "won"; it's
because Shannon has given up and is being "sentenced to hell."

🦋

On the evening of December 28, 1961, as Bette Davis prepared to
make her entrance in the Broadway premiere of *The Night of the
Iguana,* she knew that her legion of admirers had filled the Royale
Theatre, especially the least expensive seats in the balcony. She knew
that when she swaggered out onto the veranda of the Costa Verde
Hotel, her fans would erupt in the wild cheers and applause that had
regularly greeted her in Rochester, Detroit, and Chicago. But she
also knew that, as had happened every night of the out-of-town run
since that fateful first performance in Rochester, when she fell and
injured her knee, by evening's end it would be Margaret Leighton
who received the loudest and most enthusiastic ovation by far, while
Bette Davis was invariably condemned to the brutal indignity of polite, even slightly embarrassed, applause. And so it was that, opening
night in New York, seconds after she made her entrance, Bette allowed herself the luxury of stopping the play before it had really
begun, in order to bask in the rapturous reception of her admirers.
Better to claim victory while she still could.

Strange to say, by the time *Iguana* had reached New York, the
violent offstage conflict between Davis and her co-stars had infused
their performances with a furious, primitive energy that, however
much the production had strayed from what Williams had had in
mind, contributed to a powerful and disturbing theatrical experience.
"We didn't act it: we lived it," says Patrick O'Neal to explain the

production's curious success on Broadway. "Dumb as the choice was for our personal health and well-being, it made the play work at a level it's never worked at again. It had Bette actually living Maxine; it had Maggie becoming Hannah; and me self-destructing all over the universe to be Shannon."

After the premiere, physically and mentally exhausted by the strain of these many months of preparation ("the longest and most appalling tour I've ever had with a play," Williams would recall), the author fled to the Silver Seas Hotel in Ocho Rios, Jamaica. There he wrote to Bette Davis, pleading with her not to withdraw from the play, as she had been seriously threatening to do as early as December 29, when the New York critics almost uniformly extolled *The Night of the Iguana*, with some recording their surprise that a star of Davis's magnitude would have accepted so "peripheral" and even "minor" a role, and one reviewer asking bluntly, "But didn't she read the script?"

As in past letters to Bette, Williams played the consummate diplomat: telling her how much he loved and admired her and how thrilled he was by her opening-night ovation, the likes of which he could not recall ever having witnessed before. Then, with a distinct edge to his words, Williams warned of the grave consequences of quitting *Iguana*. Despite the good reviews, Bette's departure would almost certainly close the show: a professional setback that the playwright and the actress could ill afford at this point in their troubled careers. We know from an April 15, 1962, letter to his friend Maria St. Just, written after Bette had been replaced by Shelley Winters, that he did not admire Davis's performance as Maxine Faulk, much as he appreciated the many tickets that her name on the marquee was capable of selling; hence, perhaps, the scarcely repressed desperation with which, in the earlier letter, the playwright struggled to charm and cajole La Davis into staying on.

Williams pressed all the buttons he could think of. Besides gently alluding to Corsaro's banishment (without mentioning that it had been done at Bette's behest), he broached the thorny subject of Bette's conflict with Patrick O'Neal, whose slight variations from one performance to another she perceived as attempts to sabotage and embarrass her before her fans. Arguing that O'Neal's variations were really the actor's efforts to improve his performance, comparable to the playwright's script revisions, Williams implored Bette to try as hard as she could to understand O'Neal's personal turmoil and thus to transcend the corrosive anger that was making it impossible for her to work with him.

Instead, pleading serious dental problems, Bette demanded to be released from her run-of-the-play contract. At intervals she seemed to suffer fainting spells that precluded her appearing in the play as scheduled. In one especially alarming instance, she passed out in the bathroom, and company members were unable to open the door because she had fallen against it. That April, although Davis finally managed to win her release on the grounds that she was phys-ically unable to continue, not everyone in the company believed that she was really ill. "It was all bullshit!" says Patrick O'Neal. "She was simply trying to get out of the play."

That Bette was hardly as weak as she claimed became evident on her final day as a member of the *Iguana* cast in April. "I'm soooo happy that you're all such a congenial group!" she bellowed at her grimly silent fellow actors. "I'm soooo happy that everyone thinks Maggie is so charming and Patrick is so brilliant! I'm sorry I had to irritate you for so long with my professionalism. You obviously like doing it your way much better. Well! Now you can, my dears!"

With that, Bette Davis stormed out of the Royale Theatre, and Tennessee Williams's *The Night of the Iguana*, never to return.

Several months later, Frank Corsaro, summering on Fire Island, wandered into a little beachfront bar. He had chosen a stool and made himself comfortable when he saw Gary Merrill drunkenly staring and pointing at him. Merrill stumbled to his feet and lurched toward Corsaro, who was ready to pick up one of the barstools to protect himself against Bette's famously violent ex-husband.

"You're Frank Corsaro, aren't you?" said Merrill, slurring his words as he hovered ominously over the director.

"Yes, I am, Mr. Merrill," Corsaro replied.

"Why didn't you just belt her?"

"What?!"

"That's what I did! I just gave her the biggest belt she ever got and knocked her on the floor and walked out on her. That's what you should have done!"

TWENTY-FOUR

"This role was truly the most difficult I've ever done," Bette told an interviewer in 1962. She was referring not to *The Night of the Iguana*, which she wrote off as one of the great mistakes of her career, but to director Robert Aldrich's *What Ever Happened to Baby Jane?*, which had begun filming that July, three months after she abandoned the Tennessee Williams play.

Bette had already given her notice to the *Iguana* management when Joan Crawford visited her dressing room at the Royale Theatre to deliver the film script about two reclusive sisters and their violent, abusive relationship.

"My husband, who knew Joan Crawford, brought her back," recalls Paula Laurence, "and Bette was so rude we were both terribly embarrassed. When Joan left, Bette screamed the place down: 'She's got the best property in California! I tried to buy it and she beat me to it. If she thinks I'm going to play that stupid bitch in the wheelchair, she's got another think coming!'"

285

At length, however, Crawford took the role of the disabled former movie queen Blanche Hudson, while Bette portrayed her insidious tormentor, onetime child vaudeville star Baby Jane Hudson, who, when she is not planning her own big theatrical comeback, tortures her invalid sister by serving her a rat for dinner and confining her, bound and gagged, to her bed. But the air of acrimony between Davis and Crawford persisted throughout the making of *Baby Jane* and afterward, with both women apparently well aware of the publicity value of their supposed feud. Indeed, the attention garnered by the actresses' snipes at each other suggests the extent to which *Baby Jane*'s popularity may be ascribed to the public's morbid fascination with the spectacle of two old movie queens colliding on and off screen.

With this gargoyle of a film Davis's Hollywood career would pass from kitsch to camp: that is, from the earnest banalities on which by and large she had stubbornly wasted her talents to ostentatious self-parody and burlesque. This is all the more disturbing when one recalls the precious handful of films—*Of Human Bondage, Jezebel, Dark Victory, The Letter, All About Eve*—in which Bette Davis had established herself as among our best screen actresses. Whether Bette knew that in *What Ever Happened to Baby Jane?* Robert Aldrich was asking her to enact a grotesque debasing caricature of herself is impossible to say. But she plunged into this self-consciously meretricious project with gusto, when only a few months before she had thrown away the opportunity to act in an important new drama by America's best playwright and thereby to signal her availability for other serious roles. This recalled the obstinacy she had demonstrated during and after *The Little Foxes*, when, as Meta Carpenter recounts, Bette's inability to weigh the advice of others caused her to behave in frequently self-destructive ways that declared: I know what I'm doing! I'll do what I want to do! I'm controlling my life, and this is the way it's going to be!

Having wantonly sabotaged *The Night of the Iguana*, Davis returned to Hollywood, insisting that "the only reason anyone goes to Broadway is because they can't get work in the movies." In one of many gratuitous public diatribes against Patrick O'Neal and Margaret Leighton, Davis told Hedda Hopper, "They are not to be believed. It's not like a movie, where you know you'll have only a few weeks with them—in a play it goes on for months. I don't understand that kind of person—I couldn't cope with it. I'd have been really ill if I'd continued in it."

In Hollywood, however, there was soon new cause for agitation when Bette discovered that, although Warner Bros. was set to distribute *Baby Jane*, Jack Warner had declined to allow Aldrich to shoot on the Warners lot. Ostensibly studio space was all booked up, but Davis interpreted Jack Warner's refusal as a lack of interest or faith in the project and perhaps even a deliberate snub to the onetime queen of the Warners lot. It seemed to Bette that Jack Warner's forcing her to work at the humbler Producers Studio on Melrose Avenue was supposed to be her comeuppance for past sins.

Nor, to Bette's chagrin, had financing for her comeback film been particularly easy to acquire. Aldrich had already unsuccessfully shopped the Davis-Crawford package around town when Elliott Hyman's independent production company, Seven Arts, agreed to bankroll *Baby Jane* as a low-budget quickie to be completed in no more than thirty days for under a million dollars.

That Davis had little idea of the immense box office success that awaited *Baby Jane* upon its release that fall is suggested by her having astonished and even irritated a good many people in Hollywood when, shortly after completing the Aldrich film on September 12, she advertised in trade publications in search of new film roles:

> MOTHER OF THREE— 10, 11 & 15—
> DIVORCEE. AMERICAN. THIRTY
> YEARS EXPERIENCE AS AN
> ACTRESS IN MOTION PICTURES. MOBILE
> STILL AND MORE AFFABLE THAN RUMOR
> WOULD HAVE IT. WANTS STEADY EM-
> PLOYMENT IN HOLLYWOOD. (HAS HAD
> BROADWAY.)

Although Bette apparently believed that the industry would be amused by the idea of a major star's advertising for work like this, the gesture backfired badly. Not only did the advertisement fail to attract any substantial offers but Bette's attention-seeking device had the unintended effect of further tarnishing her image as a serious actress.

That hardly mattered to Bette when, the following month, audience reaction to *Baby Jane*'s October 20 preview suggested that the film was going to be far more successful than anyone had even remotely imagined. It is a curious irony of Bette Davis's career that for all her many famous collisions with Jack Warner, she shared his view that the best films were the ones that attracted the largest audiences and made the most money. However much Bette Davis thought of herself—and was widely thought of—as a Hollywood rebel, during her years at Warner Bros. she had fundamentally, no doubt unconsciously, internalized its values. By now the only thing separating Bette and her old nemesis Jack Warner was that he was still in a position of power within the studio, while she was outside, longing to be allowed back in.

Hence the utter earnestness, the strange sincerity of feeling, with which Bette would solemnly declare Baby Jane Hudson "a great role" as she toured the United States to publicize the Aldrich film, whose brisk ticket sales convinced her that it was indeed among the best films she had ever made.

"The fact that the picture was a success is a miracle in my life," Bette told reporters, sounding a bit like Baby Jane herself talking of her comeback. "It's not to be believed. Perhaps it was the great law of compensation after ten hellish years. All I want now is a chance to prove my talent is still there for the big-million-dollar pictures." At other moments, Bette publicly crowed over what she imagined to be Gary Merrill's upset about her triumphant return to Hollywood: "The thing that's bugging Merrill is that I have a successful picture," she told Hedda Hopper. "He spent eleven years hoping I'd never work again."

After many years of distancing herself from the Hollywood milieu (even when she was in residence there) by emphasizing her status as a Yankee dame with austere New England tastes, now Bette decided to signal her return to film stardom by installing herself in grand style at Honeysuckle Hill, a charming white colonial house on Stone Canyon in Bel Air, whose purchase was facilitated by a $75,000 loan from Jack Warner. On January 25, 1963, *Baby Jane* was in its third lucrative month in local theaters across the nation when Bette signed a contract with Warner to appear in a dual role as twin sisters in *The Dead Pigeon* (later retitled *Dead Ringer*), set to start shooting that summer. Correspondence between studio representatives and Davis's lawyer Tom Hammond indicates that although Warner reserved the right to collect his $75,000 by deducting the amount from Bette's paychecks for *Dead Ringer,* the studio was already fully confident that *Baby Jane* was going to make enough money for the actress to repay her loan out of the 10 percent share of the film's net profits that Aldrich had agreed to in her contract (at a time when *Baby Jane* appeared unlikely to make much money at all).

With everything suddenly seeming to be going her way again, Bette felt confident of winning her third Oscar that April of 1963, when the other nominees for Best Actress included Katharine Hepburn for *Long Day's Journey into Night*, Geraldine Page for *Sweet Bird of Youth*, Lee Remick for *Days of Wine and Roses*, and Anne Bancroft for *The Miracle Worker*. Many years before this, Bette had been known to cast a jealous glance at Hepburn's career; but now she seemed not to realize the strongly contrasting levels of ambition signified by Hepburn's appearing in the screen version of the Eugene O'Neill play at a moment when Davis was thrilled to be doing *Baby Jane* and publicly trading barbs with Joan Crawford. Had Bette made the contrast with Hepburn for herself, perhaps she would have realized the wrongheadedness of her current strategy for retrieving her position in the film industry. Repeatedly Davis would insist on doing essentially trivial roles that—as in the old days at Warners—had been expressly tailored for her. As long as she recoiled from the kinds of demanding dramatic material in which actresses like Hepburn and Page delighted (roles that required the actress to stretch to their requirements rather than the other way around), there was really no place for Davis's career to go. By and large, the leading roles in commercial features that Bette coveted were routinely assigned to younger actresses: a fact she seemed as little prepared to accept as she was Anne Bancroft's being awarded the Oscar at the Santa Monica Civic Auditorium on April 8.

♈

With *What Ever Happened to Baby Jane?* came the opportunity to launch B.D. in an acting career. Aldrich cast Bette's tall, buxom fifteen-year-old-daughter in a small role, as the girl who lives next door to the depraved Hudson sisters. Since the move to Los Angeles, B.D.'s exceptionally mature manner and physical appearance allowed her frequently to operate on her mother's behalf. With no adult to accompany her, Bette's daughter had rented a temporary house for them to live in, enrolled her brother at Black Foxe Military Academy, and selected Honeysuckle Hill for their permanent residence. Bette, who encouraged B.D. to date at the age of twelve, appears to have viewed the idea of a film career for B.D. as a means to bind her daughter to her, as the pair gave interviews, traveled, and talked of making more films together in the near future.

"I'm always surprised when people ask how we get along—as if she'd swallow me, or something," said B.D. in *Look* magazine in December 1962. "I always say we're great friends."

In private, however, finding herself swallowed up by her mother was precisely what the teenager had begun to fear when Bette purchased a pink marble mausoleum in Forest Lawn Memorial Park. The actress grandly announced her intention to be buried there with B.D., Bobby, and Ruthie (whose silver casket she had ordered dug up from Fairhaven Memorial Park and moved here). Outside the mausoleum hovered a statue of "a goddess," sculpted to resemble Bette's daughter.

At Honeysuckle Hill, Bobby's melancholic presence in a room above the garage—"the crow's nest," as they called it—served as yet another omen to B.D. of the grim future that seemed to face her if she allowed her mother to control her life (including, perhaps, Bette's grandiose plans for her daughter's acting career). "Bobby was convinced by Mother that she was nothing without Mother," says her niece B.D. "She couldn't survive, she needed Mother, and so she was going to have to get on the ground and kiss Mother's feet every day that Mother would deign to care about her."

More and more, the teenager began to sense that Bette was planning a similar fate for her: "Mother's view of what she wanted from me was to be at her feet, have a few failed marriages, a whole bunch of affairs that ended in disaster, a few children along the way that I would bring home." It seemed to B.D. that, as she had done with Bobby, Bette wanted her to feel "emotionally incapable of existing without her." And says Bette's friend Charles Pollock, a Los Angeles antiques dealer: "Bette's ideal situation would have been to have B.D. at her beck and call for the rest of her life. Remember *Now, Voyager*? Bette wanted to make B.D. into an 'Aunt Charlotte' to keep her company and do her bidding in her old age."

It can only have confused the fifteen-year-old B.D. that, having repeatedly denied Gary Merrill's brutalities toward her daughter, Bette now pressed her to testify against the actor in Santa Monica Superior Court on January 16, 1963, as Davis renewed her efforts to keep him from seeing Michael and Margot.

Bette's attorney Murray Chotiner had already reported to Superior Court Judge Edward R. Brand that, in interviews with the children on November 26, he had learned from B.D. that Merrill had "been intoxicated on many occasions and committed acts of physical violence on those occasions"; and from Michael (who had spent intervals with his father since the divorce) that, preferring to be at home with his mother and sister, the ten-year-old "did not wish to spend any of the Christmas vacation with the defendant, nor alternate weekends with him."

When, in due course, Gary accused Bette of using the children as pawns, Bette responded by citing specific occasions when Merrill had been dangerously intoxicated in the presence of his son. Private detective Michael Parlow gave testimony that chronicled Merrill's carousing and womanizing at the Newporter Inn in Newport Beach, California, while the boy was in his custody. According to the detective, Gary would leave the ten-year-old alone in his room all night while he indulged in drunken revels in and around the hotel until seven the following morning.

Merrill had done himself no favors some months before by engaging in a violent quarrel with Rita Hayworth that caused them to be ejected from Au Petit Jean restaurant, where, by chance, Judge Brand happened to be dining. "I have seen this distinguished person behave in a nauseating manner in public," the judge declared in court on November 29, as Gary turned various shades of crimson. "He and his female escort [Hayworth] used language that would be disturbing in a brothel."

Nor did it help Merrill to be publicly accused of having "sadistically" burned a young model's ankles with a lighted cigar at 3:00 A.M. on February 11, in Mike's Pool Hall in the North Beach section of San Francisco.

Still, the judge found himself ruling in favor of Gary's being allowed to see and spend time with a son he clearly loved. Whereupon, according to Merrill, Bette suddenly called his lawyer with instructions that the boy would be delivered to them in two hours. "I couldn't figure out why," Merrill would recall. "When Mike got there, I learned he wasn't just coming for the afternoon, he was coming to live with me. Bette hadn't gotten her way in the trial, so she threw Mike at me like a loaf of bread. The limo drove up, and there was little Mike with his bags. Instead of leaving for New York as I had planned at that time, I stayed in Malibu for four months until Mike finished school. I drove him to school every morning and picked him up in the afternoon. About the time school ended, Bette had pulled herself together and took Mike back to live with her."

"I'm not an actress," B.D. told reporters in London, scarcely seven months after Bette had announced the teenager's plans to pursue a film career. "I did have a very small part in *What Ever Happened to Baby Jane?* and I enjoyed that greatly. But although I thought of acting as a possibility, I finally didn't like it as a career. I decided to get married."

This was no idle teenage fantasy. Bette Davis had mysteriously consented to allow her sixteen-year-old daughter to marry twenty-nine-year-old Jeremy Hyman, a vice-president of Seven Arts, the production company that had backed *What Ever Happened to Baby Jane?* (as well as having invested in the stage production of *The Night of the Iguana,* whose film rights the company had acquired). Asked why she was rushing into marriage at so young an age, when all four of her mother's had failed, B.D. replied, "Mummy's marriages don't reflect on mine for a large reason: She was a career woman, dedicated, even married to a career. I don't have that. I'm me. I've chosen the career of homemaker."

With this, although it is doubtful that either mother or daughter sensed quite what was happening, the history of the four women Eugenia, Ruthie, Bette, and B.D. approached full circle. Where once the vague idea of a theatrical career had symbolized little Ruthie Favor's longing to escape her mother's plans for her to have a husband and family of her own, now it was precisely in marriage that B.D. sought to escape Bette's no less constricting agenda.

"Having a mother who was so consuming a presence—would there ever be any room for anybody else?" asks Dori Brenner. "I mean, with Bette there was no more oxygen left in the room. So the healthiest thing that B.D. did was to say, 'Here's an exit. I'm taking it!'"

B.D. had discovered her husband-to-be at the Cannes Film Festival, where Bette was in attendance in spring 1963 to promote *What Ever Happened to Baby Jane?* On the day of the screening, Seven Arts (run by Jeremy's uncle Elliott Hyman) was to send an escort to look out for B.D. while her mother was occupied with publicity duties. When Jeremy appeared at their seventh-floor suite as the Carlton at the appointed hour, Bette assumed that the tall, slender Englishman was there for her—or so she later admitted to Charles Pollock.

Although Hyman had been assigned to squire the sixteen-year-old about for a single evening, in the ten days that followed they spent as much time together as decorum—and Bette—would allow. Back in Los Angeles, Davis had encouraged her daughter to date young men who B.D. often feared were really more interested in her famous mother than in her. Not so with Jeremy, who, aside from being crisply polite to Bette, showed none of the usual obsequiousness.

According to Davis's longtime assistant Vik Greenfield, Bette perceived herself as somehow in "competition" with B.D. for young men. It was as if the mother were intent on proving that she could take her daughter's boyfriends from her if she wished. "I think the reason that B.D. was really mad for Jeremy was that he never looked at her mother in any way at all," says Greenfield of B.D.'s instant attachment. "In fact, he barely tolerated her."

"What am I going to do about this?" Bette asked Robin Brown upon their return to the United States. Mother and daughter had stopped to visit with the Browns in Connecticut, where B.D. hastened to present herself to Jeremy's Westport relatives. Bette told Robin that after having known Hyman for less than two weeks, B.D. had stunned her mother by flatly declaring, "This is the man I'm going to marry!" Much as Bette lamented that age sixteen was far too young to marry, it was already clear to her that B.D. was "absolutely determined" to have her way.

At this point, Bette's sole consolation was that as far as she knew, Jeremy had yet to propose, but soon after they returned to Honeysuckle Hill, Hyman called from London to ask for the teenager's hand in marriage.

"It's about time! B.D.'s miserable without you," Bette told her future son-in-law when he asked to speak to her after B.D. had accepted his proposal. But to Robin, Bette quietly confessed her frustration over finding herself unable to do anything to stop the marriage; and later, to her hairdresser and traveling companion, Peggy Shannon, she confided her distaste for Jeremy on the grounds that he was an Englishman and a Jew.

The question remains: Why did Bette allow B.D. to marry Jeremy Hyman? She had only to decline to give her written permission, and Hyman would have been short-circuited in his attempts to marry Bette's underaged daughter. Here it is B.D. herself who best comprehends her mother's curious motives in approving the admittedly unconventional marriage: "That was easy because she knew I'd be back!" says the daughter. "That was just to show me. As she said, she always believed in letting her children make their own mistakes." B.D. believed that her mother gave the marriage no more than six months, after which Bette was certain that the teenager would come "crawling home." Thus, from the first, B.D. appears to have viewed her marriage at least partially in terms of a lifelong struggle with her mother. To allow that marriage to falter at any point would be to prove that Bette had been right all along.

With B.D. and Jeremy set to be married at All Saints Episcopal Church on January 4, 1964, Bette signed on to appear in the film *Where Love Has Gone*, based on a novel by Harold Robbins, to finance the cost of the wedding and the reception, at the Beverly Wilshire Hotel. Thus began a long-term pattern (observed by Peggy Shannon and Robin Brown, among others) of Bette doing certain films expressly to pay for this or that extravagant gift for B.D. and her husband.

Before leaving for their honeymoon in the Florida Keys and then going on to New York, where Jeremy was to begin work in Seven Arts' New York office, the newlyweds had a suite reserved for the night at the Beverly Hills Hotel. Camera in hand, several hours before the ceremony Bette stole into their rooms, where she lovingly made up the bed in black silk sheets, upon which she laid out the thigh-length white satin robe, trimmed in marabou, that she had selected for her daughter's wedding night.

TWENTY-FIVE

After *What Ever Happened to Baby Jane?* Bette had been certain that she was about to revive her Hollywood career. Contrary to her expectations, however, offers of major film roles simply never materialized. Of the films she did do in the immediate aftermath of the Aldrich picture—*Dead Ringer*, *The Empty Canvas* (made in Italy), *Where Love Has Gone*, and *Hush . . . Hush, Sweet Charlotte*—only the last, also directed by Aldrich, came close to *Baby Jane*'s box office success. And there, to Davis's utter bewilderment and consternation, her career stopped dead. She was left to make only a banal horror film, *The Nanny*, in England in 1965 and an episode of the popular television series *Gunsmoke* the year after that. By now she had sadly abandoned the house in Bel Air that was to have symbolized her successful return to film stardom and moved to an apartment, considerably more modest, in Beverly Hills.

Particularly because she failed to comprehend why *Baby Jane* had not led to the major movie roles she coveted, Bette found it increasingly unbearable to live in Los Angeles, where, for all her past glory, she was simply one of many former screen stars for whom the industry seemed to have little use. As long as she was going to have to go abroad to make films like *The Nanny*, Bette decided that she might as well follow her daughter to Connecticut, where B.D. and Jeremy had bought a new house, Wildwoods, in the town of Weston. Once before when Bette's career was at a low point she had enjoyed playing the screen legend with friends and neighbors in Maine; and so it would be again, in Westport, Connecticut, where many people were only too eager to listen to a famous actress's stories and take her drunken abuse.

When Bette turned up in Connecticut in October of 1966, she was in a state of personal and professional crisis. For ten months, she lived in Robin's romantic guest cottage. Finally, she bought a home of her own, Twin Bridges, on Crooked Mile in Westport, two miles from B.D. in Weston. Bette insisted to friends that she had come to Connecticut to be near Michael's boarding school, Loomis, Gary's alma matter in West Hartford; but to anyone who knew her well, it was obvious that B.D. was the principal attraction.

"Bette worshiped the ground that B.D. walked on, because, as she never wearied of reminding you, B.D. was her 'only natural child,' " says Charles Pollock. "Half the time, all she would talk about was her B.D. and how proud she was of her. Once Bette got on that subject she just wouldn't stop: 'B.D. did this and B.D. did that.' The only thing Bette didn't like about B.D. was her husband—him she hated." According to Bette's friend Stephanie Landsman (Vik Greenfield's sister), the actress hated Jeremy because he had taken her daughter from her: "Bette was always rather snide with Jeremy. She'd tolerate him for a bit, and then in the course of the evening she'd find something, some little incident, to jump on him for and rile him. Jeremy at that stage was pretty laid back. He'd just smile and not pay much attention to it."

"Have you quite finished, Bette?" the son-in-law would ask, to her evident disappointment and chagrin, it having been her intent to pick a fight with him.

After he abandoned the film business, B.D.'s husband worked as a commodity futures broker and the owner of a home services agency. But to friends like Charles Pollock, Bette complained that Jeremy was "a leech and a ne'er-do-well" who seemed somehow to have cast a spell over her daughter. According to Bette, Jeremy seemed scarcely to appreciate B.D.'s tireless efforts on his behalf. One of Bette's favorite stories about Jeremy told how B.D. had labored for hours to make him a special dessert of napoleon pastries. When B.D. served the pastries, Bette said, the demanding Englishman's only reaction was to take a bite and pronounce, "Not quite up to snuff, dearie."

Bette never seemed to give up trying to create problems between B.D. and Jeremy, much as Ruthie had worked to undermine Bette's marriages. But it seems equally true that on some level B.D. relished doing battle with her mother, whose years of violent collisions with Ruthie these two appeared to recapitulate. "They were all right as long as Bette was not dictatorial and telling B.D. what to do," says Stephanie Landsman. "The minute she tried to dictate to B.D., B.D. jumped at her. Or if she made a comment that B.D. thought was stupid, B.D. would tell her, 'Don't talk such rot; it's nonsense.' She'd stay pretty quiet afterward. It was as though she was rather in awe of B.D. B.D. was the only person I knew that could really manage her and keep her in tow."

For all Bette's incessant taunting of Jeremy (whom she called "Jer," while he called her "Mudder in Law"), a glance at her diary suggests that she was anxious to please him with gifts precisely calculated to suit his taste (a piece of silver from Asprey's in London; a sweater whose wool must be of a certain weight to meet Jeremy's standards); and when the question arises of giving her daughter an allowance, Bette reminds herself to seek Jeremy's permission first. "Bette gave B.D. everything, anything she wanted," says Robin Brown. For her part, however, B.D. regarded her mother's cornucopia of gifts less as evidence of Davis's generosity than as an unabashed attempt to "buy" her and her husband, much as Bette had bought Bobby's devotion through the years. Like Ruthie, Bette was willing to make sacrifices for her beloved daughter but expected to be paid back. "Ruthie never let Bette forget that what she had done for her in the early years had been at great cost," says Dori Brenner. "And in turn, Bette never let anybody around her forget what it had cost her to help them. Bette's generosity always had strings attached. Always."

"What did she say?" Bette would ask whenever Vik Greenfield returned from an errand at B.D.'s house. "Did she say anything about me?"

"No," her assistant regularly assured her. "We didn't talk about you at all."

"She's a better friend to you than she is to me," Bette would sigh, with great bitterness.

In truth, Greenfield recalls, "Of course we always talked about her! Anybody that knew her, you'd talk about her because Bette was so impossible."

Constantly at loggerheads with her daughter and her son-in-law, Bette, as recorded in her diary, filled long lonely days with increasingly detailed cleaning and cooking rituals that often baffled and amused casual observers, who could scarcely comprehend the degree of unbearable agitation they represented. People often wondered how the legendary movie star spent a typical day when she was not working; but close friends noted the symptoms of obsessive-compulsive behavior—the endless overly intense cleaning, checking, preparing, and rearranging—that devoured so much of Davis's time. "When Bette was depressed she didn't see people," says Dori Brenner. "She hid and literally polished the brass." Hour upon hour was devoted to compiling long, detailed lists of canned and frozen foods and cleaning materials: lists that Davis repeatedly reviewed and checked off. Something as simple as a tuna fish lunch for Vik Greenfield involved hours of elaborate, pointless preparation beginning as early as the night before, when Bette would carefully arrange the ingredients on the kitchen counter; again and again, she would be drawn back to the kitchen to confirm that everything was in its place. "Every time she would pass the food on the counter, she would have to touch each item—the obligatory laying on of the hands," recalls Charles Pollock. "Checking them for some reason or other." And she would endlessly rearrange the items on the counter, moving a soup can here, a tuna can there, in quest of some strange ideal order that only Bette seemed to comprehend.

As is often the case with obsessive-compulsive personalities, Bette's overemphatic neatness and organization in some areas stood in marked contrast to a lack of personal hygiene. "Bette never looked after herself properly," recalls Vik Greenfield. "In her house she would hardly take a bath a week, let alone wash her hair." When Bette was Charles Pollock's houseguest in Los Angeles, Pollock was initially baffled by her mysterious failure to spend much time in the bathroom, where, the maid reported, the tub and towels were clearly not being used. Finally, Davis seemed to notice Pollock's curiosity about her peculiar disinclination to take a bath or shower. "I don't bathe very often, but I'm not dirty," she made a great point of telling him. "I don't smell, do I?"

The personal and professional crisis that had caused Bette to move to Connecticut made her home there a less than optimal environment for Margot Merrill. "They should never have allowed Margot to stay with her on holidays," says Vik Greenfield, whom Bette regularly assigned to watch her retarded daughter when she came to Twin Bridges at Christmas and for a few weeks each summer. "She was very cruel to that child." And according to Dori Brenner: "Bette didn't give Margot any loving or kindness, at least not that I saw. Bette had no patience. We're not talking about a woman with little patience. We're talking about a woman with no patience. When I was there one weekend when Margot was there, I was horrified. Bette was more exasperated than usual and just yelled at her and pushed her around." Asked why Bette brought Margot to Twin Bridges, only to mistreat her, Brenner explains: "Bette in many ways went by the book. 'Okay, I've got to do it, I'll do it.' It certainly wasn't out of any compassion."

"The school would call and say, 'When is Margot going to visit again?'" recalls Margot's sister, B.D. "Mother would suddenly become aware that this was supposed to happen. She'd hem and haw and fuss and finally come up with a time." Whatever abuse she suffered at Bette's hands, the teenager always seemed anxious to spend time with Bette and Vik at Twin Bridges. "Even though it was very unpleasant, Margot never remembered it was unpleasant," says B.D., to whom Margot often turned in confusion when Bette insisted on reminding her that she was adopted—a concept she seemed to have considerable difficulty comprehending.

Scattered throughout Bette's diary for this period are the dates when Margot is due to arrive for a visit—almost always followed by the date when her daughter is scheduled to return to her school. And repeatedly around those dates one discovers Bette's frantic reminders to herself to replenish her supply of Miltown tranquilizers.

By far the most disturbing entry in Bette's diary comes on February 14, 1968, shortly after seventeen-year-old Margot has completed her first Christmas visit to Twin Bridges. To read Bette's private diatribe on what she describes as her retarded daughter's perverseness and deviousness is to make the blood run cold, especially when one reaches the horrifying pronouncement that rough physical discipline is the only thing the lying black Irish girl understands. Tragically refusing to grasp Margot's mental limitations for what they were, Bette all too clearly viewed her adopted daughter's misbehavior as a deliberate assault on her.

At Twin Bridges, Bobby no longer occupied the place in Bette's life that she once had. With B.D. married and Michael away at school, Bette had decided that her sister's services were no longer needed. Bobby moved to Arizona with her daughter. There, Bobby developed breast cancer and underwent a mastectomy. After the operation, Bette traveled to Phoenix with Vik Greenfield, who noted with horror Bette's rough treatment of Bobby, despite her recent medical ordeal. No sooner did Bette arrive than she launched into one of her usual tirades against her ailing sister, who seemed resigned to the fact that Bette was probably incapable of behaving any other way. From then on, while Bette continued to send her money and to see her on occasion, Bobby's poor health ruled out all thought of her resuming her former role in Bette's household.

"When you think of all those years when Bette was sitting there alone in Connecticut," says Dori Brenner, "you have to wonder— what did she wake up thinking at four o'clock in the morning?"

Although Vik Greenfield's presence in the apartment above the garage at Twin Bridges assuaged her barely concealed terror of being alone at night, Bette flung herself into a series of ill-conceived, often unconsummated love affairs with younger men whom her assistant describes as being mostly "of dubious qualities and talents—and obviously looking for a meal ticket." Her seduction routine hardly varied. When the man arrived at Twin Bridges, Bette would be waiting for him, drunkenly posed on a chaise longue in a manner that allowed her gradually to disclose the absence of any underwear. Time and again, friends like Robin Brown and Dori Brenner would discreetly inform Bette that one or another of these men was almost certainly homosexual. "Oh, no!" she would cry; or, "I'm going to be the one to change him!" In her raging loneliness, Davis actually proposed marriage to a number of these unattainable young men. Hungry for the attention and adulation they provided, Bette forced herself to overlook what, on some level, she knew perfectly well: that her "suitors," as she called them, incessantly gossiped about her with each other, often making merciless fun of the woman they purported to worship.

Scarcely more fulfilling was the actress's sparse professional life in this period, limited usually to a single more or less dismal film a year. By her own account, had she not desperately needed the money, Davis almost always would have turned down such unrewarding assignments as *The Anniversary* (another horror film, made in England in 1967), *Connecting Rooms*, *Bunny O'Hare* (1971), *Scientific Card Player* (shot in Italy in 1972), and *Burnt Offerings* (1976). To shore up her finances, several times in the Connecticut years Bette tried and failed to launch a new television series: the pilots *Madame Sin* in 1971, *The Judge and Jake Wyler* in 1972, and *Hello Mother Goodbye* in 1973.

"The fun has gone out of my work," she told Vik Greenfield, while shooting *Connecting Rooms* in England with Michael Redgrave in January 1969. "I do it now only because I have to." Similar sentiments appear in a January 1969 letter to Robin Brown, in which Bette declares herself uninterested in acting anymore but sorely in need of funds after a two-year hiatus from film work. "I'm a basket case!" she would nervously scream at her assistant before appearing on the set— and she seemed hardly more confident of her powers at day's end, when, as Greenfield recalls, "The minute she got to the dressing room, out came the bottle."

Davis welcomed her role as an impoverished cellist in *Connecting Rooms* because it came soon after she learned that B.D. was pregnant. Her diary and her correspondence with Robin are filled with lists of projected gifts for B.D. and Jeremy (although in a letter to Robin she wonders whether her daughter isn't pleased to be rid of her for the time being) and for the baby—Bette is confident it will be a girl—at whose birth that spring she eagerly anticipates being present.

But Ashley Hyman, born on June 19, 1969, was not the granddaughter Bette had expected; nor, to her chagrin, was she present at his birth, Jeremy having failed to call from the hospital until afterward.

Eighteen-year-old Margot was visiting Twin Bridges when B.D. gave birth. She kept asking B.D. if Ashley—whom Bette called "love pot"—was her "real" baby: had somebody else had him, who couldn't keep him? According to B.D., her sister "went wild" over the new baby, wanting to sit and hold him as long as B.D. would allow. But Margot's wonderment soon turned to agitation; she inquired if she was ready to get married yet and have children of her own.

On June 20, Bette arrived at the hospital with her camera, to begin taking the usual quantities of photographs. According to Bette's diary, even Sherry and his wife, Marion, were sent copies. And it was in this period that Bette unearthed photographs she had once taken of young Margot at Witch Way to reassure herself that, contrary to her worst fears, the child was normal—photographs that she now quietly placed in the trash.

But this was only a prelude to Bette's astonishing decision to wash her hands finally of Margot. After years of disputes about the girl, Bette signed over custody to Gary Merrill, despite the fact that she had often accused him of failing to monitor their adopted daughter properly while she was in his care. "That was the unpredictability of Bette!" says Vik Greenfield. "One minute she was upset that Merrill had been irresponsible toward Margot when the girl was staying with him, and the next minute she didn't want custody and turned it all over to him."

When Gary assumed custody of Margot, Bette struck B.D. as, quite simply, "relieved to unburden herself." "Mother had abrogated her responsibility, and that was it," says B.D. of Bette's decision. "She didn't have to bother anymore."

"Miss Davis, have you ever had a face-lift?" a young man called out during the lengthy question-and-answer period of Bette's one-woman show: a mélange of film clips and predictable banter with the audience in which the actress opened at New York's Town Hall in February 1973. Bette exhaled a great dragon plume of smoke, then descended into the auditorium, where, hovering above the questioner, she looked hard into his eyes and shouted, "Brother! Does this look like a face that's been lifted?"

By now it seemed to a good many of Bette's associates that she had despaired of even attempting to function as a serious actress. She appeared to prefer to incarnate the travesty figure whom one commentator wistfully described as "an amalgam of all her screen roles plus all her impersonators." Onstage in the one-woman show and at home in Connecticut, Bette sought to retreat from the painful reality of her current circumstances by endlessly, mechanically repeating the stories of her Hollywood glory days.

TWENTY-SIX

"Glad to see you!" said Bette, slurring her words as she guided her guests through the lushly planted walled garden and into the living room of Charles Pollock's West Hollywood home in 1973. "Oh, I'm so proud! Miss West, your host, Mr. Pollock."

Before turning to the eighty-one-year-old Mae West, Pollock nervously inspected his wobbly houseguest, Bette, for signs of damage.

"You have no idea of how drunk Bette was by that point," Pollock recalls. "She was so nervous and terrified at the idea of meeting Mae West that she couldn't stop drinking all day. When Mae and her two escorts finally arrived, Bette, who insisted on greeting them herself, was so snockered, I was sure she was going to break her neck as she stumbled to the front door—which of course she almost did!"

A few days before this, apprised that Bette Davis and Vik Greenfield were in town from Connecticut, Mae West had called to arrange a dinner at Perino's restaurant.

"Who the hell wants to sit in Perino's, with everybody gawking at the two old broads!" said the sixty-five-year-old Davis after accepting West's invitation.

"Bette, my house is your house," said Pollock, with whom Bette and her assistant invariably stayed whenever she came to Hollywood to "take the money and run" (as Davis called film work these days). "Why don't we just have Mae here for dinner?"

"Oh, that's wonderful! Wonderful!" said Bette, who—with her usual obsessiveness—began to plan every tiny detail of the evening. The only request that Pollock declined to indulge was that there be a roaring New England–style fire in the fireplace as Mae entered; he thought it inappropriate for the ninety-degree weather.

"How do you do?" said the arriving Mae West, who—like Davis—had no idea that the bartender was tape-recording their every word, the microphone concealed behind the ice bucket.

"Nice to know you," Pollock replied staring in disbelief at West's heavy white wool trousers, sweater, and jacket, as Bette eyed the tantalizing pile of logs in the fireplace, which Pollock had forbidden her to ignite.

"I can't believe it!" Bette screeched, a new surge of enthusiasm overcoming her as Pollock seated Mae in one of a pair of eighteenth-century French Régence chairs, facing a nineteenth-century Belgian painting of a dog dressed as a hotel concierge. "That you're here! I really mean it! There are few people in my life—in our industry—that I have felt are this great, and you are one!"

Suddenly a show tune could be heard in the background, Vik Greenfield having turned on the stereo.

"Listen, Mae! They're playing your record!" said Bette, collapsing into the other eighteenth-century chair.

"No, no," said one of Mae's escorts, discreetly trying to point out Davis's error. "That's not . . ."

"You know," Bette went on, ignoring him, "Mr. Pollock said, 'Would Miss West be insulted if she heard her record being played when she came in?' And I said, 'Records? I'd be thrilled to death if you played my records when I walked into a house!'"

"This is nice," said Mae, changing the subject, her voice barely a whisper beside Bette's trumpet tongue.

"Oh! This house!" Bette interjected, lifting a fresh drink from the tray Vik Greenfield was passing around to Mae's escorts. "It was a horrible little Spanish house! The front door was here. A staircase went up there. And the fireplace . . . Everything! Mae, have you been in Chuck's antique shop?" No answer. "Ever been to it?" No answer. "Know about Chuck's antique shop?" Still no answer. "Welllllllll! It is verrrrrry sophisticated!"

"I love this picture," said Mae, softly. "The dog. What's he got in his hand—a letter?"

"It's a dog as the concierge of a hotel delivering a letter to a guest," Pollock explained.

"That's terrific," said Mae.

"Can we get you anything?" Bette cut in, a note of hysteria in her voice, everyone but Mae West having taken a drink from Vik's tray.

"Orange juice," said Mae, whose escorts had notified Pollock in advance that Miss West neither drank nor smoked.

" 'Orange juice'—to Bette that was a code word for vodka," Pollock recalls. "She started drinking her 'orange juice,' as she called it, every morning around ten or ten-thirty. Orange juice laced with vodka. All morning. Then in the afternoon she switched to vodka with water, so people thought it was a glass of ice water. That she considered her 'light' drinking. Then, after nipping all day, at about five or five-thirty she hit the hard stuff—Scotch on the rocks. By the time we sat down to dinner, usually Bette was pretty well slushed, which meant it was fasten-your-seat-belts time."

This accounts for Pollock's standing policy, whenever Bette was his houseguest, of serving dinner at precisely seven. "Set routine: dinner on the table at seven o'clock and no later," says Pollock. "The minute the food hit Bette's stomach, it was like someone threw a switch and she sobered up! No matter how overdone she was, she suddenly gained control. Amazing thing to see. So I was always frantic to get dinner on the table and into her mouth by seven, especially when there were guests—otherwise, believe me, it could turn into a very hairy situation."

"We have orange juice—I'll get it!" said Vik Greenfield, dashing off to the kitchen before his pickled employer could fill Mae's glass with her version of the beverage.

"I don't believe I'm meeting you!" Bette took it from the top, very mellow now. "I have to tell you that. You and Garbo. I've met everybody else in this town. I have never met you—whom I have admired. And I have never met Miss Garbo—whom I have admired."

"I met her once," said Mae with scant enthusiasm.

"We never ever meet each other," Bette continued.

"Unless you're in the same studio," said Mae.

"This is right! Unless you're at the same studio!"

"If you're in the same studio, you sort of walk into people."

"Unless you're in the same studio, you never meet," Bette concurred.

"That's right."

"But my admiration for your work!" said Bette.

There followed a tense, embarrassing silence as Bette and the others waited for West to return the compliment; but Mae was preoccupied with her newly arrived glass of orange juice—taking a long, luxurious drink and then daintily placing it on the black marble top of the round Directoire table that separated the two actresses.

"Mae was just telling us on the way over," one of West's escorts kindly called to Bette from a sofa beneath the dog painting. "She said, 'I've just been crazy about everything Bette's ever done.' "

"Well, that's why we're meeting tonight!" declared Bette, expansive again—and anxious to raise a toast. "She wanted to meet me! I always wanted to meet her! And this is going to be a great evening!"

In an effort to get some food into Bette before things spun entirely out of control, Pollock placed an hors d'oeuvres tray on the table beside her. But as the host watched in horror, Bette, ignoring the crackers on the tray, thrust a slab of his caviar mousse pâté on a napkin and handed it to Mae, who accepted with evident confusion as to how she was going to eat it.

"Can I take that and put it on a plate for you and do it properly?" the embarrassed host asked Mae.

"No, no, no, honey," she replied, struggling to lick the pâté off the napkin. "I don't wanna make any waves."

Pollock figured it was time to get the dinner ready, as Davis seemed to have reached what he recognized as "the point of no return." He was on his way out to the kitchen when, to his alarm, he heard Bette cry: "But, Chuck, you didn't light the fire yet!"

"Something I discovered about Mae," said one of the escorts from the sofa. "Mae wrote her own scripts, as you know."

"Did you?" asked Bette.

"Yeah, on my pictures," said Mae.

"So did I!" said Davis, not to be outdone. "You know something? We wouldn't have our careers if we hadn't written our own scripts! You know that. There's not one soul in the world would ever have written a script that was good for us. When I did *Now, Voyager*, for instance—which is a great book by a woman named Mrs. Prouty—I used to go home every night, write out every word of dialogue from the book, and bring it back to the director and say, 'This we shoot today!' "

"Miss Davis!" exclaimed Vik Greenfield, appalled as Bette's face disappeared in a cloud of smoke. "We are not permitting smoking—we hear it bothers Miss West!"

For the rest of the evening, unless she slipped into the kitchen to grab a quick smoke with Chuck and Vik, Bette was compelled to do without the cigarettes that accounted for the many mysterious burn marks on various antique tables and chairs throughout Pollock's house which he referred to as Bette's "calling cards."

"I used to think, every night Bette was with me, we were just going to go up in flames," Pollock recalls. "She had those twitchy, nervous hands that always had to be doing or touching something—either clutching a cigarette, or checking the food on the kitchen counter, squeezing and patting and poking the food over and over again with those hysterical fingers of hers, or picking away at a bouquet of flowers on the table, until the thing was bald! It was as if something inside made her hands do those things; she couldn't stop them if she tried."

In the kitchen, where Pollock was hurriedly preparing chicken with sour cream and garlic (the sour cream expressly intended to coat Bette's stomach), the pie-eyed actress could be heard loudly reassuring Mae, in case she hadn't believed it the first time, "You always fascinated me! Always!"

Then, with what Pollock fondly describes as "the total innocence of a child," Bette added, "But, Mae. You don't talk anything the way you talk in the movies."

"Oh," replied Mae West, momentarily disconcerted. "You mean, 'in characterization.' When I was doing the character. Oh, no. Not in here. Oh, never."

Newly charmed by his friend's artless simplicity, Pollock returned to the living room, to discover that in his brief absence Bette had ignited the logs in the fireplace, which she was poking and prodding as flames shot in every direction.

Soaking wet and seemingly about to pass out, Mae took off her heavy wool jacket. Pollock rushed up behind her to open a window.

"Is that all right, Mae?" he asked.

"Oh, yeah, honey," she panted. "Much better. Much better. Thanks."

By this time, Bette was engaged in a fairly unpleasant exchange with one of the escorts, who happened to have mentioned someone he knew who worked at the Hollywood Roosevelt Hotel. Bette interjected that her first husband had worked as a musician in the hotel grill.

"Who?" the escort made the mistake of inquiring.

"Ham!" said Bette, as if the poor fellow were a dunce—how could anyone not know Bette Davis's first husband's name?

Silence.

"Ham Nelson sang at that grill every night!" she went on.

"Oh my God, yes," said the escort, catching on.

"That was his job—he used to play there."

"He was killed, wasn't he?" asked the other escort.

"Not Ham!" said Bette, indignant again. "Farney! Farney died at thirty of a brain hemorrhage. Oh, I tell you—the one good husband I ever had. You know, I look back on my life—the way I was brought up as a Yankee girl—and there's no way I can believe I've been married four times!" Here Bette's voice dropped, as she turned to address Mae. "And out of this one idiot, Sherry, I got the most beautiful daughter. I was just the luckiest woman in the whole world. You know, there isn't any way he could . . . It was like the immaculate conception. And I kept looking at her and watching her grow. Oh, he was a monster, this man—and she's the most beautiful girl. . . ."

"B.D. is heaven!" Vik chimed in.

"Well"—Bette continued her tipsy oration—"B.D. is out of this monster marriage, you see. And I think, in this world, we have many terrible experiences. I believe in this, like I can't tell you. And I never look back! I look forward."

"You went ahead," said Mae, with sympathy.

"How Sherry and I have this daughter . . . This horrible man! He was a horrible man!"

"In what way was he horrible?" asked one of the escorts.

"Well, he beat all of us up!"

"He beat you up?" said the escort.

"Oh my God!" Bette shouted. "Every man in the world beats me up! There's no man who doesn't beat me up!" Her voice subsided again, as she said, "Oh, men always beat me up."

"Why?" asked Mae, gently. "Do you make them angry?"

"No," said Bette. "It's not my fault. They just can't stand me. All the men who've been married to me say, 'I'm so exhausted being married to you.'"

"Well, you're a strong lady," said one of the escorts.

"My enthusiasm is exhausting, I think," said Bette.

"No, what I mean," said the escort, "the thing about you and Mae, you're enormously strong, but there's not one touch of lesbianism—"

"Lesbianism!" Bette cried. "*Me?*"

"No, no," said the nervous escort. "What I'm talking about—"

"I tried to turn for years!" said Bette, suddenly cackling with delight. "I thought it would be so simple. I have a great friend who's younger than me—she loves men and I love men—and I said to her, 'Now come on, we must get together!' "

At which the boys rocked with laughter, as Bette turned to Mae and asked, "Would you ever want to marry anyone at your age now?"

"Would I want to?" said Mae.

"Would you?"

Mae thought a moment, then started to say, "I'd—"

"I'd kill a man!" Bette interrupted.

"I'd wanna see him first," Mae came back, deadpan.

"If I had a man in my house, "said Bette, "I would murder him!"

"Oh, well," said Mae. "I always have a man."

"What?!"

"I always have a man."

"Well," said Bette, "you are very smart. I have never done that. I haven't had a man in so many years it's a riot! I'm a virgin. A complete old virgin! If a man ever got into bed with me at this age"—here a menacing glance at the sofa full of escorts—"I'd kill him!"

"Oh, but age has nothin' to do with it," said Mae, in her sweetest, most soothing tone.

"It has with me!" Bette shot back, her fury undiminished.

"Oh, it shouldn't."

"I had three children, and now they're all gone from my life," said Bette. "They're both married, and I live my own little separate life."

"Yes," said Mae, solicitous. "But you've got to meet a man now that inspires you."

"I haven't see one in twenty years that inspires me!" Bette cried. "And that's sad. Now I agree that's sad. But I really don't care. I can't stand men as husbands anymore!"

"Really?" asked one of the escorts. "Do you think it's because you're too strong?"

"Strong!" said Bette, enraged. "I was the best wife! I was never a strong woman as a wife! I was the biggest sucker you ever met!"

"You didn't cut their balls off?" asked the escort.

"Ohhhh, come off it!" Bette screamed. "Come off it! All you guys think of strong women this way! I wish men had enough balls not to be cut off! The stronger the woman is, the more she needs a strong man. You want to find strong men today? Go search the earth! I can't find them!"

"But if you did," asked the escort, "you'd marry one?"

"I'd never marry!" declared Bette.

"You don't have to just marry them," said Mae, an island of serenity in the tense room.

"Oh, I'd never marry again," said Bette, softly now. "A love affair would be good. But I'd never marry again. Oh my God, are you kidding? And end up supporting them? Jesus Christ! No, never. Women like Mae West and I, we have a rough go with husbands because we made lots of money and we had to be verrrrry smart about who we married. And I wasn't smart! I married men who were supported by me. Oh my God! I'd be so rich today without three husbands!"

At which the boys exploded with laughter again, as Mae tried to stop them by saying, "It's very possible."

"But I got one great daughter," Bette continued.

"You wanted children," said one of the escorts.

"No!" shouted Bette at the top of her lungs. "I did not want children! I am not the mother of the earth!"

"Apparently it's not what she felt," said Mae, trying to prevent the escort from saying more.

"I happened to have the luck with a lousy marriage to have a great daughter. Just luck! Just luck!"

"How lovely that is for you," said the escort. "Yes."

"My dear," said Bette, "I have three children. I am the luckiest woman in the world."

"Well," said the escort, "Michael's a great joy too, I'm sure."

"Michael is not a joy to me!" Bette exploded again. "He is the lousiest Aquarian bastard that ever walked the earth!"

"You have three children?" said Mae, deftly trying to calm things down.

"I have three children," Bette replied.

"Oh, that's wonderful," said Mae. "Do you have pictures of them?"

"Yes," said Bette, a changed person. "I have. Would you?"

"Yes, I'd love it," said Mae, shooing the others away as Bette searched for the photographs in her purse.

"Okay, I'll show you my grandson." Bette kept talking, lest Mae lose interest before the pictures had been produced. "I have one grandson. I have them, Mae. Somewhere . . . How dear of you!"

Charles Pollock and Vik Greenfield having repaired to the kitchen to finish the dinner preparations, the escorts talked to each other on the sofa—until Bette could suddenly be heard to cry for joy, "There's nobody like us!"

"That's for sure," one of the escorts chimed in.

"This is the crazy thing!" said Bette. "There's nobody else like us! Half the kids you could meet in the television area today, you might say, 'Now Miss West is coming on the set,' and they couldn't give a shit. Couldn't give a shit! These horrible little kids, they couldn't care less!"

"Who are they?" asked Mae.

"Horrible little kids!" Bette replied. "The kids who are doing all this television crap! Horrrrrrrrible television!"

It having been mentioned that the film *I'm No Angel*, in which West portrays a lion tamer, had been on TV recently, Mae took the floor.

"I always wanted to be a lion tamer, from a child up," she addressed the room. "I had an obsession to get in that cage with the lions. And then for my second picture they said, 'What do you wanna do next, Mae? Anything you wanna do!' 'Cause they knew I'd write it, they said, 'We wanna spend a lot of money on your next picture.' So I said, 'What about a circus story? You can spend a lot of money on that.' I thought: Well, here it goes now: I'll just get in that cage with the lions! That was my one ambition. It had been in my mind for so long—like an obsession: you wanna do it, you have to do it."

Here Pollock emerged from the kitchen, to discover Bette and the escorts listening in rapt silence as Mae recounted her big day at Madison Square Garden.

"I think they had about six or eight lions," said Mae, "and they had me sittin' there waitin' for about twenty minutes. I said, 'Well, here I am! I'm ready!' And the director comes over and he says, 'We're thinkin' of gettin' a double for you.' I said, 'What do you mean, a double! I'm gonna go in there!' So he said, 'One of these lions almost took the trainer's arm off. We just took him to the hospital.' I said,

'Well, get the lion that did it, and get it out of the cage, 'cause I'm goin' in!' So the director said, 'We don't know which one did it. There's a couple of lions in there, and they all look alike!' So I said, 'Go over and look for the one that has blood on him.' I just sat there and insisted on goin' in, 'cause this was built up in me since my father took me to Coney Island to see the lions. In my mind, I used to dream about bein' in a cage with the lions and with that whip—get them to jump over here and do that!—oh, it fascinated me so! Even when the director told me that they almost chewed the trainer's arm off, I said, 'Well, get that one out!' So they finally got that one out, and I said, 'Okay, wash off that blood!' And they cleaned it all up. And they were still tryin' to talk me out of it—but they couldn't, 'cause this was what I wanted to do for so many years! I had to do it! Finally, I got in there, and I had them snarlin' and jumpin' this way and that!—and I'm crackin' that whip!"

"Bartender!" called Bette, requesting a refill, then returning to Mae. "It is such fun! I have admired you. It's incredible, the movie business! Let's face it, I can't say I haven't made it!"

"You certainly have," said Mae.

"And I'm not going to say you haven't made it," Bette went on. "You see, there were reasons we made it. We're just special people!"

"It's called originality," came a small voice from the sofa.

"It's called originality," Bette echoed. "It's called originality. We have made it! And to meet you is an absolute ball!"

"Bette, what's your reaction to people doing imitations of you?" asked one of the escorts. "Professionals."

"Oh, that's the greatest compliment you can have!" Bette replied. "Eventually they become asinine, how they imitate you. But if you're not imitated—boy, you've not made it!"

"Because you're not an original," said the escort.

"That's right!" said Bette. "I do an imitation of Mae West, you know. Oh, yes, if you're not imitated, you've had it."

"I think we have a difference of opinion here," said the escort, casting a glance in Mae's direction. "I think Mae doesn't like imitations, right?"

"I like them," said Mae, trying to be diplomatic, "but not too much."

"You threatened to sue one of your imitators," said the escort, egging her on.

"Well, this one guy," said Mae, "he was a fan of mine. I let him live in my beach house. My three-hundred-thousand-dollar home. Fine boy, you know. I gave him a wig. I gave him a gown. He used to try them on. I wasn't living at the beach at that time, I was living in my apartment—so I'd go down there, and he'd have my wig and my gown on, and finally he had worked up this imitation of me. Terrible! I think he also does you, Bette. Who else does he do, boys?"

"He does Carol Channing!" said the escorts.

"That's' right," said Mae. "Carol Channing and Tallulah."

"Who is dead now!" Bette declared of her old nemesis. "So they should stop doing her!"

"He does Bette Davis," said one of the escorts. "He does Tallulah Bankhead. And he does you."

"Well, we're naturals to do!" said Bette. "We have a definite style."

"I stopped him!" said Mae.

"You can legally do that?" asked the escort.

"Sure," said Mae. "You see, he isn't doing me, 'Mae West.' He's doing 'Diamond Lil'—the characterization that I created and own. It's copyrighted! You can imitate anyone, you can imitate the President, anybody. But when he takes the characterization that I copyrighted, then he's infringing on my property, see? He's imitating the character that I created. That's the characterization. I don't do that in real life."

"Obviously, sitting here tonight, you don't," said Bette. "Sitting here tonight, you don't."

"No, I don't. So I stopped him. I had the lawyers write a letter and stop him."

"Have you seen some imitations of you, Bette, that you like and some that offend you?" asked one of the escorts.

"Miss West will tell you," Bette replied, "if you can't be imitated, you have not made it. I will never fault any imitation."

"Thirty minutes of 'Mae West'!" Mae continued. "And he was using all my material!"

"I don't see it like that," said Bette. "If they imitate you, you're lucky!"

"It was an act that I did in Las Vegas," said Mae, a note of exasperation creeping into her voice. "They filmed it, and he played me—all this great material I had!"

"And if they don't imitate you in this world—boy, you ain't got no status!" said Bette.

"See, this boy that I'm talking about," said Mae, "he did thirty minutes of 'Mae West.' Thirty minutes! He took a book that I have out, *The Wit and Wisdom of Mae West,* with all my wisecracks, all the clever lines that I put in my pictures. That book, I don't know if you ever read it. He took all of that material—and you want him to imitate you for thirty minutes? Do you know what that means? All of my material! All the stuff out of my brains! I used to maybe take a day to think of some great line, and here he was out there repeating it and getting good money for it!"

"Bette," called one of the escorts, "can you do an imitation of Mae?"

"Ohhh, not really," said Bette.

"Can you do the Mae West character, Bette?"

"Anything she wants to say." Mae laughed.

"Come on, do it," said the escort. "Can you do it well? Mae would be—"

Whereupon the other escort turned to Mae and asked, "Mae, have you ever thought about doing Bette Davis?"

"No!" said Bette. "There's no way she did!"

"Well," said Mae, taking Bette's measure, "I'd have to watch what she's doin', and then maybe after—"

At that moment, their host having announced that dinner was ready at long last, the two escorts rushed to lift Mae from her eighteenth-century chair; and Vik Greenfield, to help Bette from hers.

"Chuck is one of the great cooks!" Bette called across the Directoire table to Mae. "You're going to have a great dinner tonight. We're so thrilled you came here! I can't tell you!"

"This picture," Mae told Pollock, as she paused to admire the Belgian painting of the dog dressed as a hotel concierge. "I think I've seen it before. So impressive! So interesting!"

"And now," Bette declared to no one in particular, as they all made their way to the dinner table, "we must divide Miss West and me among the men!"

TWENTY-SEVEN

 n her February 1973 application for social se-
curity benefits, Bette listed her previous
year's earnings as approximately $26,000, in-
cluding residuals from prior work, and projected the same income for the following year.
Finding herself increasingly short of funds, in 1974 she was forced to
sell Twin Bridges and rent a more modest house in Weston, Connecticut, which she dubbed My Bailiwick. To save face in Westport,
she claimed not to need so large a house now that Michael was gone.
After graduation from the University of North Carolina at Chapel
Hill, Michael Merrill married his longtime girlfriend, Chou Chou
Raum, with whom he soon headed to Massachusetts to attend Boston
University Law School.

At Twin Bridges, Bette had often clashed angrily with Vik Greenfield. Greenfield called himself "the most fired man in America," for
all the times Davis had drunkenly dismissed her assistant, only to
plead with him to come back soon afterward. At one point, Greenfield
recalls, "She even offered marriage to me. Well, she offered marriage
to everybody, didn't she? It was one of her lines."

By the time she sold Twin Bridges, Greenfield had finally left her employ, Bette having tongue-lashed her assistant perhaps one time too many. But he returned from California to supervise the sad move to Weston, where he remained with Davis for two weeks. "After that," Greenfield recalls, "B.D. essentially took over for me, coming by every day or so to check on how her mother was doing." Not very well, according to B.D., who noted that Bette began drinking herself under the table as never before—the new house seeming to grow more squalid by the day.

After several unsuccessful stabs at launching a television series, Bette stunned her friends by accepting the lead role in *Miss Moffat,* the musical version of *The Corn Is Green.* Director Joshua Logan planned to take the show on a nine-month tour before landing on Broadway in the fall of 1975. Her decision to accept the role was a curious gesture on Bette's part, in light of her miserable experiences in *Two's Company* and *The Night of the Iguana,* after which she had vowed never to appear in a stage play again.

The role had been intended for Mary Martin, who dropped out after the death of her husband; offered to Katharine Hepburn, who politely declined; and then to Bette, who proclaimed that *Miss Moffat* would be her "swan song." "Thank God for this play," Davis told Joshua Logan. "It's going to save me from those flea-bitten films. The last one I read, they had me hanging in a closet. *Miss Moffat* has saved me—saved me."

Summoned from California to travel with her on tour, Vik Greenfield—who on the basis of sustained close daily contact knew Bette's habits and disposition better than most—sniffed trouble from the outset. "Bette tried never to show her fear," he says. "Remember, she was a ram—headfirst and thought about it later. But very early I said to myself, 'Bette's never going to make this—she doesn't have the stamina for it anymore.' " As early as the rehearsal period in New York, that August of 1974, the actress recorded in her diary her private fears about how much exertion would be required of her at their first stop, in Baltimore.

"Bette looked as if she hadn't been oiled properly," Greenfield recalls. "The jerky movements, the suddenness of her attack, made her seem rather like the Tin Man."

Exactly a week before the company was scheduled to proceed to Baltimore, Bette claimed to have injured her back during rehearsal. True to form, the following day, August 29, she checked into Harkness Pavilion, Columbia Presbyterian Medical Center—whereupon her physician called Joshua Logan to announce the possibility of a herniated disk. The Baltimore engagement's having been canceled on Bette's account, the management moved up the out-of-town opening to Philadelphia in October.

On September 20, Bette checked herself out of the hospital and drove to Connecticut, where she was soon sending word to her by now exasperated director that she had mysteriously injured herself yet again. To her daughter B.D., however, it seemed that, as Bette had often been known to do, she had quite simply willed herself to get sick—an estimate with which Vik Greenfield agrees: "That was just Bette's usual sick act; take my word for it, it was all mental and all an act."

"Don't you tell me my line!" Bette shouted, on opening night in Philadelphia, when one of the children in the cast whispered her dialogue to her as the confused actress seemed to fumble for words. "I know it! You're a naughty little boy!" Elsewhere, to her director's dismay, Bette left out bits of dialogue; repeated lines she had spoken only a moment before; and, worse, protested at another actor's ineptitude directly to the audience, only to realize her mistake and apologize immediately thereafter. Still, it seemed to Logan that Bette's performance improved as the days passed, the star's occasionally forgetting or misplacing lyrics amply compensated by her ability to attract audiences to the show.

This accounts for Logan's fit of agitation when Davis summoned the director to her hotel suite to announce that she was quitting the show. "Bette, I know this sounds silly to you," Logan reasoned, "but for your own sake you can't commit this kind of professional suicide. You've become sick and made two important productions suffer before. There were hundreds of thousands of dollars of other people's money lost because of it and dozens of actors put out of work. You mustn't be blamed for that again, Bette. This might be the end of your stage career."

"I can't help it. I'm in pain," said Davis. Logan kissed her on the forehead, only to realize afterward that the actress seemed to have "flinched a little" at his touch.

Embittered and alone, Bette returned to Connecticut, where My Bailiwick seemed smaller and more unsatisfying than ever. Vik Greenfield's departure in the aftermath of Miss Moffat had opened an immense chasm in her day-to-day life. Once again they had quarreled, and once again Bette had been too proud to attempt to patch things up with him—but this time the exasperated secretary would not be coming back.

With only the bottle and the occasional fan for daily companionship, more and more Bette set her sights on B.D., who feared that her mother had returned to Weston with renewed hopes of breaking up her marriage and forcing B.D. to move in with her. As her mother tended to do, B.D. responded to the pressure by becoming ill. Among other ailments, the daughter developed a serious case of colitis, which she blamed on stress from the daily tussle with Bette. B.D.'s feelings of panic are understandable when one considers that on several occasions when Bette failed to get her way with her daughter, she pretended to attempt suicide. If the daughter would not give herself over to Bette out of love and devotion, perhaps she would do it for reasons of guilt and fear. Finally, Bette's tactics backfired. Instead of luring B.D. back to her, Bette drove her daughter and son-in-law to sell their house in Weston and flee to rural Laceyville, Pennsylvania. They purchased a secluded property called Ashdown Farm. It was either leave Connecticut or allow Bette to destroy their marriage and force B.D. to become what Bobby had been; for B.D., as for her mother, there was no middle ground.

Bette had further occasion to reflect on the shambles of her life when the American Film Institute invited her to speak in honor of William Wyler, who was to be the fourth recipient of its Life Achievement Award in March 1976 (previous honorees were John Ford, James Cagney, and Orson Welles). Living in solitude now, for hours on end she would stare at her face in the mirror, thinking of what could be done to make herself presentable enough to see Willy again. The actress's diary records in detail her plans to hire a makeup man in Los Angeles, who would devote an entire day to painting her face and rigging up the painful straps concealed beneath her wig to give the effect of a face-lift. To Bette, Wyler symbolized both the professional and the personal dreams that, for all her years of violent struggle, had never come to fruition. The speech she prepared for his award ceremony came dangerously close to publicly declaring her feelings for him. "A director has to be your father," Bette wrote, "your analyst, possibly the man at that moment you fall in love with. Willy was all these people to me." At the last minute, a final hysterical look in the mirror seems to have convinced her that the "Bette Davis" mask of her one-woman show was not an image she wished

Willy Wyler to see. Pleading illness, Bette sent her speech and her regrets—she would not be able to attend Willy's celebratory dinner after all.

After the Wyler tribute, Bette was in despair over the wreckage of both her career and her personal life, when she heard early rumors that the American Film Institute was considering her to follow Wyler as the fifth—and first female—recipient of the Life Achievement Award. If Bette was not as enthusiastic at the prospect as her friends had expected her to be, it was because she had also heard that Katharine Hepburn had been the AFI's first choice. From a number of industry sources Davis gleaned that only when Hepburn had discouraged the AFI's overtures had attention turned to her. To make matters worse, there was no concealing that, on account of the self-inflicted devastation of Davis's acting career, she was an extremely controversial selection for the award. Important dissenting voices questioned whether such an honor ought to be bestowed on an actress whose recent film work had been so abysmally undistinguished. Despite these objections, and despite the vast quantities of trash that cluttered Davis's filmography, there remained the core of great films she had made with Wyler and others to testify that, whatever blunders she may have made in the course of her career, Bette Davis was indeed one of Hollywood's finest actresses and richly deserving of the award. Debates over her acting aside, the Bette Davis image as a model of female power, efficacy, and independence continued to exert a strong hold over the imagination of American women— making her a particularly apt choice as first female recipient of the AFI award. Long after the war years, such exhilarating Davis characters as Judith Traherne and Charlotte Vale still provided clear, compelling, upbeat images of a woman's capacity for far-reaching growth and transformation.

Defensive as always, Bette protested to Charles Pollock and other friends that she didn't really want the AFI to honor her. But as anyone who knew her well could easily see, Bette was terrified that, in the end, the AFI would designate another recipient. Rumors that she had been second choice after Hepburn seemed particularly nettlesome to Bette, who, much as she had long struggled to deny it to herself, had to have recognized by now the vastly different roads the two actresses' careers had taken.

In March 1977, escorted by Charles Pollock, Bette attended the AFI award dinner, where she was beside herself with excitement when Willy Wyler delivered a testimonial to her. Wyler was obviously joking when, referring to their dispute over the end of *The Letter* (should Leslie look away or not?), the director said that Bette would doubtless return to Warners immediately if given the opportunity to reshoot the scene her way. Where Wyler had meant to allude, affectionately but poignantly, to what he perceived as perhaps the beginning of the end of her career—the moment where she started to resist merely for the sake of resisting—Davis failed to grasp the irony of his remarks. Nodding vigorously, Bette seemed to be saying that yes, she would do it all over again exactly as she had in the past. The intervening decades had taught her nothing.

With the Life Achievement Award came a welcome new status in Hollywood, where Davis began to receive offers to appear in "quality" television dramas, whose focus on social and family problems provided excellent opportunities for an actress of Bette's years. In an Emmy Award–winning performance in director Milton Katselas's *Strangers* (1979), Davis portrayed a lonely old woman attempting to come to terms with the dying daughter from whom she had been estranged for more than two decades. In George Schaefer's *A Piano for Mrs. Cimino* (1982), Davis appeared in a story about the rights of the elderly to manage their own affairs; while in Schaefer's *Right of Way* (1983), she co-starred with James Stewart in a drama about rational suicide. Roles in these and other successful television productions marked a major turnaround in Bette's fortunes, providing substantially more income and prestige than the shoddy films to which, by and large, she had devoted herself in recent years.

Whether these television roles allowed Davis to resuscitate her gifts as an actress is another matter. In them, all too often she reminds us of a wax-museum figure—the physical likeness is there, but also a disconcerting bloodlessness. Looking at these films in the context of Davis's career, one can scarcely ignore the irony of an actress noted for expressive gesture and movement metamorphosing into one of the "talking heads" of issue-oriented television drama. In a way, Davis's television work in this period may even have encouraged some of her worst tendencies as an actress: the desire to "bloat" her performance with pompous, unnecessary dialogue that Julius Epstein had decried in the forties.

But there were significant exceptions: most notably Katselas's efforts to render her performance in *Strangers* more visual by cutting out pages of dialogue to compel Davis to act with her face and body. This tactic met with mixed results; while Davis's absence of speech in the opening sequence, where she encounters her estranged daughter for the first time in more than twenty years, focuses our attention on her face, one misses the silent soliloquy, the mute dialogue with her daughter, that would provide some clue to what the embittered old woman may be thinking or feeling. Watching this sequence, one senses that the director has attempted to give Davis the space to show what she can do but that the actress has resisted in fear. Vastly more satisfying is the scene where, following an altercation with her daughter, the mother flees to her room, slams the door behind her, and allows all the violent, painful long-buried emotions to pulse through her entire body in a cinematic moment of rare expressivity and power.

Bette's growing visibility and status in the industry convinced her once again to forsake New England for Hollywood, where, accompanied by Charles Pollock, she inspected and purchased a condominium on the fourth floor of the charming old Colonial House apartments off Sunset Boulevard. With B.D. gone from Connecticut, Bette had no reason to remain there. On August 7, 1977, B.D. had given birth to her second son, Justin Hyman, which seemed to make Bette feel her daughter's absence all the more strongly. Far from Connecticut, perhaps Bette would be able to block out of her thoughts the painful fact that B.D. had decamped for Pennsylvania to escape her mother's unbearable presence.

Bette's loneliness and fear of living by herself traveled with her to Los Angeles, where her crony Peggy Shannon, a film industry hair stylist, stayed with her for three months to help her unpack and set up the apartment. Bette, obviously frightened, wondered to Shannon whether she would be safe in the building. In the beginning, she set up only part of the apartment, to test herself. Although Shannon's busy schedule precluded her staying on with her friend, she spent many nights at Colonial House, decorating the walls of the new apartment (as Ruthie used to do) with Bette's vast collection of personal photographs—a large painted portrait of her beloved if increasingly elusive daughter B.D. serving as centerpiece.

In contrast with the no-nonsense professional persona Davis constructed for her television work in this period, she showed considerably less self-control at home. Neighbors were treated to exhibitions of loud, drunken, violent behavior. According to screenwriter Ginny Cerilla, a member of the condominium's board of directors, Bette's tirades could regularly be heard through the bathroom vents; and there were complaints about the actress's stomping back and forth all through the night, interfering with her neighbors' sleep. Before day-break one Monday morning, Cerilla had just returned from her Mal-ibu beach house to her third-floor apartment when she heard a loud crash on the floor above. Going upstairs to investigate, she discovered Bette Davis, dressed in pajamas and a robe, lying facedown, out cold in the fourth-floor hallway. Scattered beside her were the empty whiskey, gin, and vodka bottles she had been on her way to discard; their remaining contents had leaked out and were permeating the carpet. On its side, about two inches from her hand, lay the remains of a Scotch on the rocks; it, too, had seeped into the hallway rug.

"Miss Davis," Cerilla called as she scurried to clean up the mess. The screenwriter had just picked up the bottles and put them in the trash, when suddenly, without warning, Bette leapt at her "like a cat on a binge," screeching loudly as she dug her nails into her neighbor's flesh.

"Listen, you old biddy, you're getting into bed," said Cerilla as she nudged the incoherent Davis into her apartment. "You stay in here until Peggy gets here, and I don't want to hear another word."

"Who the fuck . . . ? I'm Bette Davis!" the actress screamed as Cerilla closed the door behind her.

In June 1979, it seemed as if Bette's loneliness was about to be mitigated. She hired twenty-two-year-old Kathryn Sermak as a sec-retary and traveling companion and, shortly thereafter, live-in assis-tant: the first person to agree to reside with her on a permanent basis since Vik Greenfield's defection. The shy, quiet young woman had professed ignorance of Bette Davis and her career when she arrived for an interview with the actress, who was about to leave for England to film *Watcher in the Woods*. Peggy Shannon, originally scheduled to accompany Davis abroad, was forced to stay behind to undergo back surgery, whereupon Bette had summoned an employment agency to provide a last-minute replacement.

Although Bette was heard to make cruel remarks about Kath-ryn's lack of knowledge and experience, it seemed to Marion Rosenberg, Bette's West Coast agent at the Robert Lantz Agency, that Davis was very much pleased with the young woman's "total subservience." Several of Bette's friends noticed Sermak's apparent willingness to endure Davis's abusive behavior. "It was extremely unusual to find somebody who would put up with any of that," says Rosenberg.

One day when Bette and Dori Brenner were dining with Charles Pollock in Los Angeles, Davis invited her friends to meet the new assistant, who was waiting in Bette's recently acquired black Thunderbird. When the actress's friends came outside, Brenner recalls their surprise at the sight of the young assistant. "Here is this girl," says Pollock, "and she's done up in a little black velvet suit—pants and little jacket and a chauffeur's cap." Brenner silently wondered why, in 1979, any young woman would allow herself to be dressed up that way.

"How do you stand it?" Stephanie Landsman recalls asking Kathryn when "Miss D."—as Sermak faithfully called Davis—was safely out of earshot. Before long, according to B.D. Hyman, Sermak did indeed weary of working and living with Davis. "She used to call me in the middle of the night and say, 'How do I get out of here?' " Although B.D. says that she advised Kathryn simply to pack her bags and walk out, no matter how Bette might rant and rave, Sermak remained in place, becoming increasingly indispensable to the actress, whom she came to call her "role model."

The young woman's malleable nature, her willingness to accept and follow Bette's always precise way of doing things, endeared her to the actress, who throve on having somebody around who seemed never to disagree with her. As Dori Brenner and other intimates could see, Bette assuaged her fears of things going wildly wrong in her life by constructing rigid, often irrational if harmless rules for everything. This was Bette's way of controlling her world.

♈

Not all of Bette's attempts to impose her own order on reality were harmless. Unlike the obsessive rules and rituals with which she sought to comfort herself by eliminating chance and spontaneity from her life, Bette's revisions of the past, the lies and fantasies she constructed about herself and the people she had known, frequently hurt others. Having long ago convinced herself that she was William Wyler's first choice for marriage, that he had married Talli only when he thought Bette had rejected him, in 1981 Bette sought to make a more public and lasting claim on the director, whose death on July 27 allowed her to proceed without fear of his correcting her fantasy with the truth. "He was the love of my life," she told one of her biographers, Whitney Stine, to whom she falsely claimed that when Wyler died, Talli Wyler had called to spare Bette the shock of learning the news on television or in the press.

"I must tell you, I barely knew this woman," says Talli Wyler. "For whatever sad reasons, she seems to have imagined that we were good friends over the years, but that simply is not true. And what she did after my husband's memorial service—we can laugh about it now, but when it was happening, only a few days after my husband died, I could not believe what I was hearing from her!"

On Friday afternoon, July 31, 1981, wearing a trim checked dress and jacket, dark broad-brimmed straw hat, and white gloves, the seventy-three-year-old Davis appeared at the Directors Guild Theater on Hollywood's Sunset Boulevard for the Wyler memorial service. Her eyes concealed behind tinted glasses, Bette struck others at the service as peculiarly hostile and unapproachable, as if daring anyone to intrude on her private grief. But the actress gave no clue to what was really on her mind until afterward, when close friends and family repaired to the late director's home on Summit Drive in Beverly Hills to pay their respects to his widow.

Despite its grand size and imposing aura, the Wyler residence was very obviously a family house, a place where children had been raised and love had prevailed. In all the years that Willy and Talli had lived there, Bette Davis had approached the heavy front door and stepped into the entry hall only twice. On the day of the memorial service, as Mrs. Wyler observed the actress make her entrance, she was reminded of how little Bette had had to do with the Hollywood milieu the Wylers had inhabited together for more than four decades. Davis had always seemed somehow to live at a great distance from the creative people, the leading directors, writers, and actors, who made up the Wylers' social set.

As Willy and Talli's daughter Catherine watched the grim-faced Davis move urgently across the crowded room toward her mother, she could not recall a single occasion on which she had seen Bette in this house, among her parents and their friends. From a distance, the sight of Davis leaning over to whisper something to Talli, who quickly ushered her into the dining room, made Catherine Wyler wonder intently—as she recalls—"what could possibly be going on in there between them."

In the silence of the dining room, Bette, who had pointedly requested a private interview, wasted no time in getting to the point. Fixing her gaze on the widow, she began to speak in a slow, deliberate, portentous manner that convinced Mrs. Wyler that Bette had carefully written and rehearsed what she had to say. "Talli," the actress declared, "I want you to know that during the forty-three years of your marriage, Willy and I did not have an affair."

Although it did not occur to Talli Wyler at the time, this strange meeting with Bette Davis eerily, unmistakably recapitulated the scene toward the end of *Jezebel* where, persuading Amy to allow her to accompany Pres to the leper island and thereby to claim him in death, the duplicitous Julie Marsden tells Amy what she wants to hear: that it is his wife, not Julie, whom Pres loves. That Davis would replay this scene with the grieving Mrs. Wyler suggests the extent to which, by now, the story of *Jezebel* and her short-lived personal relationship with its director had become inextricably tangled in her thoughts.

"How did Bette expect me to react to a line like that?" Talli Wyler would wonder years afterward. "I honestly don't remember how I answered her, or whether I answered her at all. But I can tell you what I was thinking: 'I never for one moment thought you were having an affair with my husband, Bette Davis. Last thing on my mind!' Isn't it wild that she would say something like that to me a few days after he died? To this day I have no idea whether she was telling me that out of some insane idea of kindness, or whether she was actually trying to put a doubt in my mind. Could any woman be that twisted and cruel?"

At the time of the memorial service, Mrs. Wyler had yet to hear the spurious story about the unopened marriage proposal that Bette had quietly been telling for so many years that even she had come to believe it. Thus the pang Talli Wyler experienced when, the year after her husband's death, the marriage proposal story started to appear in print. With Wyler gone, only Bette could declare the story untrue; and she certainly had no intention of doing that, as it was she who had disseminated it in the first place. No matter that the story gave great pain to Wyler's widow, who only much later discovered that Davis had been its source. This false version of events had obliterated Bette's feelings of rejection when Wyler long ago terminated their affair, and as always with Bette, her own feelings were all that counted.

So it was when, that same year, Ham Nelson's widow, Ann, read for the first time the equally untrue account of Ham's having black-mailed Howard Hughes after discovering the tycoon's liaison with Bette. Like Mrs. Wyler, Mrs. Nelson had no idea that Bette was herself the source of the painful story about her late husband, who had suffered permanent brain damage after falling off a roof in 1971 and died four and a half years later. In 1982, when Ann Nelson contacted Bette about the blackmail story, the actress made a great show of commiserating with her. But for all the indignation she expressed privately to Ham's widow, Davis declined to denounce the story in public. It was with this spurious version of events that Bette had long ago allayed her own guilt about deceiving her husband, by portraying him as having wronged her.

A year later, having listened on numerous occasions through the years as Bette endlessly, indignantly repeated her melodramatic account of Ham's blackmail of Howard Hughes, Charles Pollock could scarcely conceal his surprise when, in the course of drawing up a guest list for the seventy-fifth-birthday party he was planning for her, Bette matter-of-factly added the name of Ham Nelson's widow.

"Joan and I really don't know one another well," said Bette when asked about Christina Crawford's portrait of her mother, *Mommie Dearest*. "The book makes her a monster, I suppose, but one gets the feeling Christina couldn't have made it up, could she? No one could. I've often said to my daughter, 'What are you going to write about me?' and she said, 'Nothing,' and I say, 'Thank God!' "

Living at a great distance from each other, Bette and B.D. seemed to have established a tense truce, which was violated whenever the actress appeared at Ashdown Farm—sometimes in the company of Robin Brown, who noted B.D.'s strict "rules" for her mother's behavior during these visits, including repeated attempts to proscribe Bette's chain-smoking. Charles Pollock points out that no matter what B.D. might do or say to her, Bette persisted in blaming everything on Jeremy, whom she continued to regard as "the fly in the ointment, the hated villain who was creating all these awful problems between her and her daughter."

Precisely as B.D. appeared to have hoped, her durable marriage served as a strong statement to Bette. "There is no doubt that she was wildly jealous of the fact that B.D. had managed to establish a solid and permanent marriage," says Marion Rosenberg. "She never made any bones about it. She was just always furious at the fact that B.D. had accomplished something that she could never do."

B.D., however, continued to feel powerfully threatened by the specter of Bette's domination. Hence the Valium with which she soothed herself during her mother's visits, and the chronic colitis and other stress-related ailments she persisted in attributing to Davis's attempts to meddle in every aspect of her domestic life. Bette's interference included violent criticism of B.D.'s methods of dealing with her sons, Ashley (who had recently been diagnosed as suffering from "depressed child syndrome," which, if left untreated, could escalate into full-scale manic depression) and Justin.

When one of the boys fell down and scraped his knee, B.D. needed only to cuddle him and wipe the tears away for Bette to pace back and forth and shout, "You're making your sons into sissies! They've got to be men! They've got to learn to be tough!"

While Davis complained to Peggy Shannon and others that Jeremy Hyman had made a "slave" of her daughter, B.D. quietly wondered about what she perceived as her "emotional bondage" to her mother, who, even now, continued to dream of their being buried together with Ruthie and Bobby in the pink marble mausoleum at Forest Lawn. In 1980, Bette had been visiting Ashdown Farm when word came from Phoenix that her sister had died of a cancer-induced coronary. Bette's initial outpouring of grief quickly changed to anger when she learned that Bobby had made a deathbed request to be cremated. Bette insisted that they bury her as planned in the mausoleum; but she declined to attend the funeral, as she was about to start work on a new film.

TWENTY-EIGHT

n April 1983, as Bette celebrated her seventy-fifth birthday with a black-tie dinner at the home of Charles Pollock, attended by friends and film industry colleagues, her life finally seemed to have come together as it had not in many years. Starring roles in the successful television films *Strangers, A Piano for Mrs. Cimino,* and *Right of Way* had obliterated the sense of failure that had plagued her career in recent decades. Although these were by no means the important dramatic roles that Davis's prodigious talents might once have allowed her to aspire to, they provided the trappings of dignity and status that had eluded Bette for far too long. And now, to her great satisfaction, one other thing that had persistently eluded her was about to be attained at long last. After Davis's several botched attempts to launch a television series, a lucrative leading role in Aaron Spelling's new series, *Hotel,* for which Bette had already successfully completed a pilot, finally offered the financial security that she had nearly despaired of achieving. The generous terms Spelling offered to secure the screen leg-

end's services were guaranteed to make Bette a very wealthy woman. In keeping with her recently retrieved stature in the film industry, Bette seemed to have fashioned a more restrained and dignified public persona. The quietly elegant long gray satin dress she wore to her birthday party suggested that the frantic straining to seem younger than her years had been replaced by a new outward confidence and air of equanimity more befitting the woman of achievement she had once again become.

She seemed to have reached a new equanimity in her personal life as well. Although she continued to lament the loss of her beloved daughter to marriage, Bette believed herself finally to have come to terms with B.D., for whose most recent wedding anniversary, three months previously, she had given a black-tie dinner at La Scala restaurant in Los Angeles, where the Hymans had happily mingled with Rock Hudson, Robert Wagner, and other film personalities. And it certainly seemed to Bette that she had managed to cement her relations with her daughter and son-in-law when, upon their return to Pennsylvania shortly after the anniversary party, an eleven-day nationwide strike by the Independent Truckers Association in February imperiled Jeremy's business. Flush with her earnings from *Right of Way* and from the pilot for *Hotel*, Bette had been quick to offer financial assistance, for which B.D. had written to thank her mother: "I will never not be indebted to you for helping us through this frightening time and saving our home."

According to Peggy Shannon, mother and daughter talked on the telephone every Sunday. Although B.D. unquestionably remained Bette's emotional focus, her physical absence left Davis to become increasingly attached to Kathryn Sermak, who basically functioned as Bette had always hoped her daughter would one day agree to do.

But if Davis entered her seventy-sixth year with what seemed like well-justified optimism, all was hardly as she thought. Much as she believed herself to have struck a delicate balance with B.D., the daughter, unbeknownst to Davis, persisted in feeling overwhelmed and was even now quietly seeking a way to expunge her mother from her life. And although Bette was widely thought by the friends and professional associates who attended her birthday celebration to look the fittest she had in years, scarcely a month after the party, she was diagnosed as being gravely ill. That May, after a typically calamitous visit to Ashdown Farm, Bette had turned up in Westport, where Robin Brown (a widow since 1974) was about to leave for Maine to open her summer cottage. They agreed that Bette would remain in Brown's Westport home while Robin was briefly in Maine; but by the time Robin returned, her friend had departed. Bette had discovered a lump in her left breast while showering one morning, whereupon, without a word of explanation, she rushed back to Los Angeles to see her physician.

On June 9, 1983, Bette underwent a radical mastectomy at New York Hospital. Kathryn remained in her room day and night, tending to her needs and fighting with the hospital staff on the star's behalf, as she had learned to do by watching Bette fend for herself in better circumstances. Davis's illness appears to have been a transforming experience for her young assistant. "I was a mild, almost docile person when I came to her," Sermak would recall. "Had her illness occurred earlier in our relationship, I doubt that I would have been strong enough or tough enough to fight for her, when necessary, against the wishes of her nurses and sometimes her doctors."

Following surgery, Bette's chances of survival seemed poor. The tumor had been malignant; and more than half a century of heavy drinking and smoking seemed to have diminished her body's resources to repair itself. Overnight her steady supply of alcohol and cigarettes was cut off (although Stephanie Landsman suspected her of sneaking a cigarette now and then), leaving Bette even more overwrought than usual.

And then, nine days after the mastectomy, Bette suffered a minor stroke, which caused a permanent left facial drag and a temporary speech impairment and loss of strength in the left arm and leg.

Doctors declared that Davis would almost certainly never be able to work again, yet the actress was still in possession of her old driving force, as became clear when, again and again, she went to war with her nurses. She felt that some of these women enjoyed giving orders to the famous Bette Davis—a pleasure she was keen to deny them, especially when one nurse instructed her that she must say "please" when she wanted something.

At Bette's urging, Kathryn went to Paris for a brief, much-needed vacation with her boyfriend, and Stephanie Landsman filled in as companion to Davis. She found her "desperately frightened" that the facial distortion and speech impairment would be permanent; and, worse, that her assistant might not return, leaving Bette with no one to take care of her. Having failed to tell Robin and other close friends even of her impending mastectomy, Bette was resistant to visitors in the weeks following her stroke. She clearly feared what people would think when they saw her facial drag for the first time.

Although she had round-the-clock nurses, Bette wanted Landsman to remain day and night, as Sermak had; but her friend agreed to stay only sixteen hours daily. Sleeping on a sofa in Bette's room, Landsman was frequently awakened by Davis's frenzied "jumping up and down all night." Neither her slurred speech nor her limp kept Bette from dragging herself out of bed to rage against the night nurse, whom she repeatedly fired, only to be persuaded by the weary Landsman to get back into bed and allow the nurse to do her job.

"God, you're a cold bitch!" Bette told B.D., who visited her mother once during her nine-week stay at New York Hospital and, once again, at Manhattan's Hotel Lombardy that September. Davis, with Kathryn Sermak, had taken up temporary residence at the hotel until she was well enough to go home. By this point Bette could scarcely continue to delude herself that she had come to terms with her daughter. When Bette asked B.D. to visit her at the hotel before she returned to Los Angeles, mother and daughter bickered with equal obstinacy about what days and times would be mutually convenient. B.D. ruled out one date on account of a dentist's appointment and stipulated that no matter what day they might agree upon, she must leave New York early enough to be home before her younger son went to bed—although that would allow her only four hours with her mother.

When B.D. did finally come to New York, Bette hinted that she might like to recuperate at Ashdown Farm, but no invitation materialized. The extent to which even the ailing Bette continued to pose a monumental threat to her daughter is suggested by the strange decision B.D. made on the way back to Pennsylvania, in the chauffeur-driven limousine Bette had provided. She would write a book about her relationship with her mother. "B.D. thought I was going to die," Davis told her old friend Ellen Batchelder after the 1985 publication of *My Mother's Keeper*. "That's why she wrote that book—but I fooled her!"

To anyone who knows or has talked at length to B.D. Hyman, this can be only a partial explanation for her actions that fall of 1983 as she set to work on the memoir of life with mother that Robin Brown angrily describes as having proved far more devastating to Bette than her cancer and the stroke. To listen to B.D. Hyman talk at full spate for hours on end—humorous, intelligent, ardent, imagistic, and, above all, strong-willed—one realizes that she is very much her mother's daughter, in full possession of the remarkable driving force that Bette had inherited from Ruthie, and Ruthie from Eugenia. But where Ruthie finally had channeled everything she had into Bette, who in turn put her own ferocious, often self-consuming energies into her career, into her ceaseless rage against one and all, and—for better or worse—into her daughter, B.D. may have lacked an outlet for the boldness that coursed in these women's veins. It found expression now in B.D.'s public, unrepentent castigation of her mother.

"She was competing with her mother," says Robin Brown. "She wanted to be somebody."

If, as B.D. says, she wrote *My Mother's Keeper* to free herself from Bette at long last, the book's publication would have quite the opposite effect: invisibly, ineluctably binding her to her mother; forever after identifying B.D. Hyman as Bette Davis's faithless daughter, the one who wrote "that book."

◆

Prior to the mastectomy and stroke, Bette had appeared healthier and more robust than she had in years. Friends agreed that her recent professional successes had given her a new air of physical confidence and vigor. But when she returned to Los Angeles now, she seemed to have undergone a shocking metamorphosis. The perpetual grimace that she was so anxious to conceal from others was the least of it. Frail and painfully emaciated, Bette seemed to have shrunken to a fraction of her former size. To make matters worse, not long after she was installed at Colonial House she called Peggy Shannon to announce that she had broken her hip. The accident had occurred while she was trying to remove her bra. She had called for help, and when no one came immediately she decided to do it herself: a difficult undertaking in her feeble condition. "I struggled and I got so mad that when I finally was able to take off the bra, I threw it toward my television," Bette told Shannon. Spinning around, she fell on the floor and broke her hip.

There followed an intensive program of physical therapy to help her walk again, as well as to regain her capacity for normal speech in the aftermath of the stroke. Unwilling to allow people to see her ravaged state, Bette recoiled from the prospect of returning to the television series *Hotel*. Whatever joy she had once experienced in anticipation of having her own series, and however desperately she needed the income now, Bette refused Aaron Spelling's repeated invitations to resume work. Spelling was anxious to get Davis back on the series and made every effort to accommodate her needs. He went so far as to suggest that she appear on-camera in a wheelchair. Shooting schedules and scripts could all be revised to suit her, so long as she would come back to work. Bette repaid Spelling's generosity by publicly lambasting his series, which she snidely suggested they rename "Brothel." She claimed to have withdrawn from *Hotel* on account of what she derided as its racy plot lines, but her real motive for leaving was what friends recognized as her terror of going on-camera in her current condition. Bette's role on the series went to Anne Baxter, who had once played Eve Harrington to Davis's Margo Channing in *All About Eve*.

Following Bette's surgery, friends noted a substantial change in her attitude toward her young assistant, Kathryn Sermak. Dori Brenner perceived that the reins started to change hands "as Bette grew weaker and weaker physically—and also emotionally." And according to Stephanie Landsman, who had spent time with Davis at New York Hospital, Bette became desperate when Kathryn was gone—palpably terrified that the assistant would fail to return despite daily notes from Kathryn reassuring "Miss D." of how much she loved, adored, needed, and understood her; and referring to herself as the ailing actress's stepdaughter.

Kathryn's brief absence in Paris seemed only to have endeared her to Bette all the more (especially as B.D. hardly danced attendance on her mother during her illness). "She needed her in the worst way," says Robin Brown of Bette's deep attachment to the assistant who had shown such devotion in the hospital. "I think that she developed a relationship with Kathryn that was highly emotional."

At Colonial House, Peggy Shannon was saddened and astonished to see her once imperious friend repeatedly defer to the young assistant. "Miss Davis used to order her around and everything," says Shannon, "but then when Miss Davis was sick, she took over with such power. I saw it." Charles Pollock, too, was perplexed by the strange new dynamics: "When I used to go over to visit Bette or have dinner with Bette, Kathryn would either sit in her room, sit in the kitchen, or sit someplace else. She was not part of the party." But now all that seemed to have changed. "Bette was like nothing, and Kathryn was Bette," says Pollock. "Kathryn made ninety percent of the conversation. She sat there drinking and having the hors d'oeuvres. . . . As B.D. said, 'She became Mother.' "

At length, much as Bette seemed to have feared, the young assistant who had showered her with attention in the months since her operation decided to live on her own for a while. Once again Kathryn's absence made Bette feel the need for her all the more desperately. Assorted maids, cooks, nurses, and secretaries followed in swift succession at Colonial House, but no one seemed to do.

Robin Brown had declined Bette's suggestion that they live together again, as in the twenties. Peggy Shannon, too, turned down Bette's repeated invitations to move in with her, but that did not keep Davis from making what was for her perhaps the ultimate appeal for companionship. "Now, Peggy Shannon, have you ever thought about your burial?" Bette would say after a few drinks. "Well, I have that beautiful crypt, and it holds eight. B.D. and the kids aren't going to be buried there. Their life is on the East Coast."

Finally, in the summer of 1984, Kathryn agreed to join Bette in Malibu as her secretary during the writing of the slender memoir *This 'N That* with Michael Herskowitz. Davis lived in a rented beach house, the assistant in a nearby apartment. Planned as a tell-all about the men in her life, the book had evolved into an account of the actress's recent illness and recovery. Davis would dedicate the volume to her secretary and even pose with her for the back cover photo; Kathryn appeared with her employer on the book tour.

At Ashdown Farm, B.D. was in considerable turmoil as she worked on the manuscript that would become *My Mother's Keeper*. No matter how powerful the anger and rage she had long felt against her mother, B.D. was well aware of the harrowing ordeal Bette had just undergone in New York. She had seen for herself her mother's ravaged body. And through regular telephone contact, B.D. knew of Bette's further ordeal in Los Angeles after she broke her hip. It would be one thing for the daughter to write a venomous attack were Bette strong and healthy, quite another to do this to a sickly, petrified, seventy-six-year-old woman fighting to put her life back together.

While B.D. was secretly transferring to paper all her pent-up fury at Bette, she was constrained in her telephone conversations with her invalid parent to avoid mention of what she was doing, even as she listened to Bette's slightly slurred accounts of her arduous recovery. All this cannot have been easy for B.D., who had long sustained a powerful, passionate love/hate relationship with her overbearing mother.

This was not just any child taking up the cudgel against any parent. This was Bette Davis's B.D.—the daughter this powerful, possessive woman cherished above everyone and everything else on earth.

"People say Miss Davis's career came first," observes Peggy Shannon. "No! B.D. came first! She idolized this girl. This girl was her life."

B.D. shared her gnawing doubts with her husband Jeremy, who encouraged her to keep writing. Having sold his interest in the trucking firm that fall, after a period of sustained discord with his business partner, the man whom B.D. describes as "the leader" in their family would take an active role in the production of *My Mother's Keeper*. According to B.D., Jeremy worked with her to help relive the agonizing scenes of domestic violence experienced at Gary Merrill's hands, which she had hitherto preferred to banish from her thoughts.

Besides her ambivalence about what she was about to do to her mother, other pressures drove B.D. to the crisis point. Her own poor health caused her to fear that she would become a semi-invalid before long. Torn ligaments in her back, bone spurs, colitis, varicose veins, and obesity were among the problems that plagued B.D. in this period, driving her to seek relief in muscle relaxers and painkillers. So severe was her back pain that she dared not raise her arms or bend over; and yet, fueled by the driving force that appears, in one form or another, to have possessed all the Favor women, she often crawled about on all fours to toil in her vegetable garden. Despite these severe physical limitations, B.D. regularly moved hay bales, cared for her horses, and undertook other heavy farm work.

Her elder son's mood disorder was the source of further anxiety and heartache. Ruthie had spent time in a sanitarium many years before, Bobby had had a long history of mental problems, and now Ashley was experiencing regular bouts of depression. Although (like his aunt Bobby) Ashley had suffered from depression from early childhood, it had seemed to his mother that his spirits were improving when, in 1981, B.D. allowed the boy to appear as an actor in the television film *Family Reunion*, starring Bette Davis. After this, B.D. blamed Ashley's worsening condition on his collisions with his grandmother (who complained to friends that the boy reminded her of

B.D.'s husband, Jeremy, hence her persistent ill treatment of him). By the time Ashley was fourteen, his highs and lows were a fact of life in the Hyman family, whose physician warned that he could, without proper help, become a full-scale manic-depressive before he turned twenty.

Such were the problems weighing upon B.D.—ambivalence about the book she was writing, dread of her impending semi-invalidism, anxieties about her son—when, on January 19, 1984, in the midst of a snowstorm, a man arrived at Ashdown Farm to make a routine delivery. Falling into animated conversation with the couple, the visitor happened to mention that he was a born-again Christian. As B.D. told the visitor, she had often watched the Reverend Ernest Angley engage in miraculous acts of faith healing on TV. Perhaps it was the uninhibited histrionics of the televangelists—then at their peak of national popularity—that lured Bette Davis's daughter; or perhaps it was a throwback to the religious fervor of her great-grandmother Eugenia, whose long-ago rejection by Ruthie had made Bette's career possible. Four days after the stranger's visit, B.D. Hyman declared herself a born-again Christian; and a little more than a month after that, on March 9, 1984, while watching evangelist Pat Robertson on the Christian Broadcasting Network's *700 Club*, B.D. claimed to have been cured of her excruciating back pain.

Three weeks later, when the Hymans made a pilgrimage to one of the Reverend Ernest Angley's Pentecostal healing services in Akron, Ohio, B.D. was hoping for a cure for her myriad other ailments; but also for Ashley's depression and the partial deafness he suffered. At Grace Cathedral, the Hymans watched in wonder as Reverend Angley applied his famous healing touch to people who had arrived in wheelchairs and on stretchers, some of them cancer patients, to a little girl with five personalities and a man with a withered hand and, finally, a woman who was said to have been in a coma for six weeks until the minister caused her to rise from her stretcher and take a short walk accompanied by her nurse, while the congregation swayed and spoke in tongues all around them.

"What can God do for you, son?" the Reverend Angley asked Ashley Hyman.

When the fourteen-year-old disclosed that he was partially deaf and suffered from depression, the minister began by cupping the afflicted ear with his palm and shouting, "In the name of the Lord, come out!"

"He stared straight into my eyes," Ashley would recall the moments leading up to his sudden faint onstage. "First I could see red lines running from his eyes into mine, and there was a burning sensation in my head. He stood there, with his arms folded, and stared at me. Then the red lines turned blue, and my head suddenly felt cool. Rev. Angley stepped toward me, tapped my forehead gently with the palm of his hand and shouted 'Yayah.' "

"That's my son!" called B.D., as members of the ministry caught the boy in their arms and placed him on the floor, where he lay unconscious, experiencing what he would recall as a glorious vision of a white-robed Jesus who walked on a lake before ascending to Heaven.

"Hallelujah!" the Reverend Angley greeted Bette Davis's weeping, laughing daughter. "Now what can God do for you, Momma?"

Back at Ashdown Farm, B.D. was confident that the healing service had indeed cured her son's depression. When B.D. talked to her mother on the telephone, she reported the miraculous relief from colitis, calcium deposits in the ankles, and varicose veins she claimed to have undergone at Grace Cathedral—but not something else that had happened there: the Reverend Angley's declaration in the midst of his service that it was essential for families to cast out relatives who brought discord and unhappiness to the family unit, which B.D. gratefully interpreted as a sign from the heavens that, for all her doubts about writing her tell-all book, she must press on with the enterprise.

Hence, it would seem, B.D.'s curious claim, in a January 4, 1985, letter to Vik Greenfield, that God had helped her to write *My Mother's Keeper*.

♛

"Mother was a destroyer," says B.D. Hyman, some five years after the publication of her book, "and the thing that amazes me is that I wasn't destroyed. It is a miracle. Since having in the last several years developed a really amazing relationship with the Lord—and I'm not discussing religion; I'm just talking about a one-on-one relationship with God—I do truly believe that the only reason is that God protected me. Whatever his reasons are I have no idea—I don't have any great destiny. But the Lord graciously protected me."

In September 1984 (a year after she decided to write her book), B.D. signed a contract that provided for a $100,000 advance and spring '85 publication. By contrast with Bette's self-promulgated image as devoted mother—an image that she no doubt believed to be entirely correct—*My Mother's Keeper* depicted her as drunken, cruel, abusive, and manipulative. Particularly scathing was the largely accurate portrait of Davis's violent marriage to Gary Merrill. The Hymans having decided to sell Ashdown Farm and take off for the Bahamas before the book was published and the fireworks started, Jeremy headed south on October 2, in search of a new home.

On October 22, purportedly in hopes of influencing her mother to become a born-again Christian, so that a happy ending might be appended to *My Mother's Keeper*—of whose existence Bette remained ignorant—B.D. came to New York. Davis was en route to England to make the television film *Murder with Mirrors,* her first acting assignment since leaving New York Hospital. She had undergone months of intensive physical therapy, but Bette was nonetheless fearful of what the cameras would reveal. Qualms similar to those that caused her to turn down *Hotel*—fans seeing the facial drag and other aftereffects of the stroke—tortured her now.

Would she have the necessary stamina for film work? Were her speech and gait sufficiently repaired? And more important—for she had experienced some alarming memory lapses of late—would she be able to remember her lines?

Almost certainly the very last thing on Bette's mind just now would have been the blow that awaited from B.D., who—telling herself that her mother seemed substantially recovered from the worst effects of the stroke, if still a bit wobbly from her broken hip—highlighted her final meeting with her mother by declaiming the Sermon on the Mount from a green leather-bound Bible on whose cover she had had "Ruth Elizabeth Davis" engraved in gold leaf.

In England, Bette's anxieties, as always, got the better of her, causing her to lash out at cast and crew lest they perceive her as weak. "She shunned me and everyone else who tried to help," co-star Helen Hayes would recall. "She couldn't stand anyone she considered a rival, though no one was trying to compete with her. Her physical condition made her hypersensitive to any potential charges that she was no longer capable of playing the role or any other role. She refused to take a nap between scenes, because that might confirm what she feared people suspected: that she was too much the invalid to be the great star and consummate actress she had once been. Bette drove herself mercilessly; she was her own worst enemy, at least during this production."

But she could keep up her front no longer when, in November, word about B.D.'s book reached her from New York, where rumors of what Bette Davis's daughter had done to her were rife. Already weak, fearful, defensive, and insecure, entirely unprepared for anything like this, Bette reacted as if she had been bludgeoned. On the telephone, she pleaded unsuccessfully with her daughter not to publish the book. Filming was still in progress when she crawled into bed and remained there, ruminating endlessly about B.D.'s betrayal. Perhaps even worse than the humiliation she would experience when the memoir was published was the thought that B.D. had been secretly, insidiously planning and working on the book through their many conversations in the past year: conversations that now seemed horribly tainted. How could her daughter have sat there with her in New York, while preparing that terrible violation? After this—her friend Robin Brown recalls—Bette would feel that there was no one left whom she could trust.

With both sides gearing up for a possible legal struggle, Vik Greenfield suddenly emerged as an important player, his experience as Bette's longtime assistant (the man who had indeed seen and heard "all") rendering him an invaluable potential witness for either camp. Having agreed to corroborate B.D.'s account (which, like most of Bette's friends, he thought harsh but, sadly, all too accurate), Greenfield soon found himself summoned back to work for Bette.

Politely, he declined to abandon his current, considerably more tranquil situation as companion to an elderly invalid gentleman. On January 5, 1985, B.D. wrote Greenfield from her new home in the Bahamas, in an apparent effort to keep him in her camp. Reminding him of all the terrible things her mother had said about him behind his back, B.D. warned him to be careful, as Bette was prepared to do whatever was necessary to halt publication of the book. B.D.'s letter is sprinkled with references to her mother's satanic character and powers; and to B.D.'s hope that God—who had helped her to write the book and was already showing an interest in its sequel—would also help Bette to profit from reading *My Mother's Keeper* by agreeing to admit her sins.

Although the public was stunned by the reports of brutality and domestic violence in *My Mother's Keeper*, many of Bette's friends and associates sadly recognized a good deal of truth in the daughter's account. Still, not one of Davis's friends, even those who continued to profess great fondness for B.D., believed she was right to pummel her aged, ailing mother in print.

"It was really an obscene book, in my opinion," says Robin Brown. "I cannot believe that she would write that book. Bette adored this girl—she was her life! I thought it was an absolutely brutal thing to do."

"You read B.D.'s book and you keep saying to yourself, 'Yep! Right! On the nose!' " says Dori Brenner. "It is a correct portrait—yet it's so profoundly disturbing to me that B.D. did it. I can understand why she had to write it. But then you think: Stick it in a drawer; don't publish it!"

"B.D. had to write that book," says Charles Pollock. "It was a catharsis for her. She had to get out all that poison in her system. But I think her timing was terribly wrong. Much as I like B.D., I have to say she exercised poor taste and poor judgment. She should have had a little more sense and waited until after her mother was dead. Well, Bette had only herself to blame for what B.D. did to her. Bette created the woman who wrote that book, exactly as Ruthie had created her."

"People said Mother was a very emotional person who felt things very deeply—but she didn't," says B.D. Hyman. "Mother just played roles. She spent her whole life saying I was the only thing she ever loved—not 'person' but 'thing'—and then when I did something that made her furious, when I wrote the book, she just decided I didn't exist anymore. And from that moment until she died, I didn't exist." After *My Mother's Keeper*, much as B.D. may have expected her mother "to call, to scream, to yell, to insist on at least getting together in the same place at the same time so that she could scream at me," to the daughter's astonishment that isn't what happened at all. "She just turned it off," says B.D. " 'Okay, B.D. is now the enemy. That's it. Don't bother me anymore.' And she never wanted to go past that. Now, if you really love someone and they do something that hurts you deeply, you want to at least try and understand. Even if you can never see the reason, even if you can never forgive them, you want to understand what on earth happened. . . . If you cared that much, then your rage would be absolute, but you'd have to deal with it. You couldn't just throw a temper tantrum and then shut it off. That's what she did. Very strange."

▲

"Well, anyway, now we can go on picnics and have a baby sister!" Bette had exclaimed in 1918 when Ruthie told her and Bobby that their father had abandoned them. And now again, sixty-seven years later, in swiftly, resolutely cutting her beloved B.D. out of her life, Bette mimicked Harlow Morrell Davis's Yankee mask of indifference, a public role she had learned to play early on in the face of unspeakable rejection.

In private testimony to her feelings, however, her personal papers contained a thick file of B.D.'s interviews and reviews. "Look, I know it's upsetting that B.D. published that book, but it's not that bad," Peggy Shannon said, trying unsuccessfully to soothe her. "It's all stories I've heard you tell. It's nothing people don't already know."

By the fall, Bette was able briefly to lose herself in work on a new television film, *As Summers Die*, shot on location in Georgia. As she admitted to screenwriter Michael DeGuzman, committing a part to memory posed formidable new difficulties in the aftermath of her stroke. She apologized in advance, anticipating difficulties in case of any changes in the script. Davis's benign manner with the screenwriter was in marked contrast to her harsh treatment of the local maid she had hired—"just someone else to beat on," as producer Rick Rosenberg describes the good-natured Georgia woman. Yet when the film wrapped on the day before Thanksgiving, to allow people to fly home to be with their families, Bette seemed in no hurry to leave the motel—or the maid at whom she had quivered with rage from first to last. "This was so sad," the producer recalls. "Bette literally didn't have anywhere to go for Thanksgiving and ended up having it alone in her room with the maid."

As indicated in a June 10, 1985, letter to Vik Greenfield, as early as her nationwide tour to promote *My Mother's Keeper*, B.D. was anxious to learn whether her mother had read it yet. Although the book was supposed to have freed B.D. from Bette, it was evident that she was as inextricably tied to her mother as ever. Again that summer she wrote from Grand Bahama Island to express her surprise that Bette had not called her. Had Greenfield heard anything about what Mother was up to? And yet again, at Christmas, B.D. was writing to declare her sadness at how lonely Bette must be by now, Davis having steadfastly (foolishly, in B.D's view) refused to be in touch with her daughter.

These letters suggest that, having long been told by an adoring mother that she could do anything, B.D. hardly grasped the import of what she had just done to Bette.

On Grand Bahama Island, the Hymans had settled into a Federal

house on Sea Breeze Lane, where B.D. had launched a career painting horse portraits, while (according to B.D.'s letter) Jeremy was
doing the greater part of the writing on *Narrow Is the Way*, the
sequel to *My Mother's Keeper* that B.D. had announced during her
book tour. For all that, B.D. appears not to have discovered the
tranquillity she may have hoped for. The old conflicts with her mother
seem to have been revived in discord with Ashley, whom B.D. believed to be Satan's latest means of access into her marriage. The
young man's capacity to infuriate her caused B.D. to compare him to
Bette, who, ironically, had been known to lash out at poor Ashley
because he supposedly reminded her of Jeremy.

Bette fared little better than her daughter in the troubled wake
of *My Mother's Keeper*. Kathryn's 1985 departure to pursue an independent life in Paris came as a new source of unhappiness. In search
of companionship, Bette flew east for a visit with Robin, in whose
Connecticut home she wandered about with Kathryn's photograph
clutched to her chest.

TWENTY-NINE

framed photograph of B. D. astride a horse was on display near Bette's bed in her room on Cliff Island, Maine, where the actress was filming *The Whales of August* in the fall of 1986. Across Casco Bay, Bette could see Cape Elizabeth, which, she said, triggered a flood of memories of life with Gary and the children at Witch Way: a life whose fundamental decency B. D. had publicly called into question in her book but which Bette continued to regard with unalloyed nostalgia.

Aware of Bette's precarious health and the public humiliation of *My Mother's Keeper*, producer Mike Kaplan and others in the company made every effort to accommodate the seventy-eight-year-old actress—but she was not mollified. From the outset, to the horror of all, Bette's ninety-year-old co-star, Lillian Gish (cast as the sweet-spirited, blithesome younger sister Sarah to Bette's sharp-tongued, waspish Libby), became the particular object of her rancor. Known as "The First Lady of the Silent Screen," Lillian Gish had made film history with director D. W. Griffith in such classics as *Broken Blos-*

soms, Way Down East, and *Orphans of the Storm.* Quite simply, Bette had never appeared in a feature film with an actress of Gish's caliber before. But instead of treating her with courtesy and respect, "Bette was just terrible to Lillian," says actress Ann Sothern, who portrayed Tisha, the sisters' eccentric friend on the Maine island where they have summered for many decades. "I think that she felt intimidated by Lillian because Lillian *is* motion pictures. Who could ever criticize Lillian Gish? It's like criticizing the Statue of Liberty!"

"Hello, Bette," said Gish when they met for the first time on the tiny set, where there was only a single chair at the moment.

"Hello, Miss Gish." Bette made a great point of refusing to function on a first-name basis.

"Do you want to sit down?" Gish softly asked the younger actress, who responded with scarcely concealed rage.

"Bette was immediately offended that Lillian had asked her to sit down," Kaplan recalls. From then on, Davis was persistently rude to her co-star, as if Gish had committed some grave offense against her. "No one had ever been that way to Lillian," says the producer. "It was unbelievable!"

Part of what Marion Rosenberg describes as Davis's "appalling behavior" to Gish was her endlessly complaining about Lillian's hearing problem. When actor Harry Carey, Jr., greeted Gish on the set, Davis barked, "You'll have to yell. She can't hear a damn thing!"— although, as Carey points out, Gish, standing a few feet away, could clearly hear that cruel comment. Still, says the actor, "Lillian just closed her mind to Bette and went her own merry way; Bette had no effect on her."

On repeated occasions, as actor Vincent Price recalls, "Lillian did come back at Bette," whom she impishly pretended not to hear when she did, so that director Lindsay Anderson was constantly obliged to repeat Davis's lines. "I think this rather surprised Bette," says Price, to whom it seemed that Davis had vastly underestimated Gish's strength.

"She must be a very unhappy woman," Gish sighed to Ann Sothern as they watched Bette lash her tail and paw the ground with rage. And another time, Gish was heard to remark: "That face! Have you ever seen such a tragic face? Poor woman! How she must be suffering! I don't think it's right to judge a person like that. We must bear and forbear." Lindsay Anderson—noted for the films *This Sporting Life, If . . . ,* and *O Lucky Man!*—had correctly assessed David

Berry's charming, if rather slight, screenplay as requiring a certain "mythic casting," lest the enterprise dissipate into a mere "film for TV." The exceptionally fine cast Mike Kaplan assembled made this by far the best assignment Bette had had in years: a prospect that left her secretly "petrified," her agent Marion Rosenberg recalls. As always, however, Bette worked hard to conceal her fear (from others and perhaps from herself) with the usual off-screen histrionics.

"Bette was so ridiculous in so many ways," says Mike Kaplan. He repeatedly deferred to such pointless demands as having her Winnebago turned so that it would face away from the other actors' trailers lined up beside hers—Davis's sole reason being that "she just wanted to be different."

"All this kind of behavior went out twenty-five years ago!" Ann Sothern laughs. "There aren't movie stars like that anymore. Actors just get on with it."

Cast and crew quickly learned that to offer Bette one's arm to lean on was like showing a red rag to a bull. When, in order to shoot beside the water, cast members had to descend a particularly steep hill, Gish and Sothern were carried down on a sedan chair. Davis would not hear of it. "I'll get down myself!" she snapped, unwilling to show what she perceived as weakness. With the producer beside her, Bette was slowly, precariously making her way down to the shore when she stumbled and wrenched her already fragile hip. "She was in pain all that night," Kaplan recalls, "and all because she didn't want to be like the others."

Unlike other cast members, Bette insisted on attending the rushes every evening. More often than not, she arrived in a state of intoxication that caused her tongue to wag all the more uninhibitedly. "She'd talk all the way through them," recalls Harry Carey, Jr., "raising Cain and yelling, 'That should have been different! Why did you allow that?' "

Lindsay Anderson had spoken to Mike Kaplan of the sense of dread he experienced every time he saw Davis coming up the road toward him; but in his dealings with her on the set, he displayed what Carey describes as a John Ford–like "toughness." In one scene, where Bette insisted on getting up and walking over to look out the window while saying her lines, Anderson objected, "But, Bette, your character is supposed to be blind."

It was an exchange not unlike the violent quarrels she had had in 1941 during the filming of *The Little Foxes*, as William Wyler struggled to explain that an actor's movements on-screen must be motivated by character, while Davis stubbornly persisted in her fondness for eye-catching movement and gesture for their own sake. More than four decades had passed since *The Little Foxes*, but to judge by Bette's argument with Lindsay Anderson, she had learned nothing in the interim.

"This scene needs some movement!" cried Davis. "I will not sit here in this chair!"

"I want you to," said the director.

"Well, I won't!"

"Bette, let's get one thing straight," said Anderson. "There's one director on this picture, and that's me."

A torrent of expletives poured from Bette's lips as she limped off the set—only to return quietly some ninety minutes later, after which, without further discussion or ado, Davis followed the director's orders.

And she was wise to do so. Thanks to Anderson's impeccable direction, *The Whales of August* was Davis's finest performance in decades, a reminder of the subtle effects and restrained expressive style that had distinguished her acting at its best and had been woefully absent from her film work for far too long. No sooner had they finished filming, however, than Bette learned that she and Lillian were to be billed on a single card. Swelling with fury, Davis insisted that she deserved her own card, before Gish's. "It was all nonsense," says Kaplan. "She wanted first position and wasn't embarrassed about asking for it. With Bette, all that stuff meant a lot."

Publicity for the film posed similar difficulties. First, Bette refused to attend the film's world premiere at the Cannes Film Festival in May, where Gish and Lindsay Anderson were scheduled to appear. At Cannes, *The Whales of August* was hailed as a historic occasion: a meeting of two great actresses, representing the silent and the sound eras. While critics extolled both performances, slightly more attention and acclaim went to Gish. "There was a bit more interest in Lillian than there was in Bette," says Kaplan, "and she thought we were planning it that way." Angrily declining to attend the film's American premiere in New York on account of its having been scheduled to fall on Lillian Gish's birthday, Davis publicly blasted both Anderson and Gish (and took a few gratuitous potshots at the film), even as she was announcing plans for her own premiere of *The Whales of August*, at the Deauville Festival in September.

All of which had the effect of shifting press attention from the film's artistic merits to the mad, one-sided feud between Davis (who insisted to reporters that her refusal to attend the New York premiere had been "simply a matter of self-preservation") and Gish. It was a disaster for a small, serious film of this type, which needed exactly the right media attention to discover its natural audience. After many years of churning out great numbers of inferior films, Bette had finally found herself with a director and a company of actors capable of operating at a level of artistic enterprise appropriate to her abundant gifts as an actress. Whatever discord may have existed on the set, after the reviews she and the film received at Cannes there could be no doubt of what they had all achieved together and—more important—what *The Whales of August* was about to do for Davis's critical reputation. Bette's talk of "self-preservation" aside, that she proceeded to run her own presumably long-awaited triumph into the ground by willfully subverting the film's publicity suggests a fundamental negativity, a need to attack and demolish so intense that she was willing to destroy herself in the process.

After filming *The Whales of August*, Bette went to Paris to spend the holiday with Kathryn, who was working there for the young American fashion designer Patrick Kelly. Much as she had lamented to Ann Sothern and others what B.D. had done to her, the actress's other favorite subject appeared to be the loss of her devoted assistant. "She was always saying, 'I should have introduced her to more people. I should have done this for her and I should have done that for her,'" Sothern recalls.

In the spring, Kathryn returned to accompany Davis on the rather curious publicity tour for the memoir *This 'N That*. From first to last, Bette accorded Kathryn a bewildering prominence in the publicity. There was something exceedingly odd about the spectacle of the decrepit movie star appearing on television accompanied by the obscure, mostly silent young woman dressed in a starlet's skin-tight black satin dress with one bare shoulder and a single red satin opera length glove. Who was she? Why was she on a talk show when it was Bette doing all the talking?

On one program where the assistant did not appear, Bette insisted on showing her picture to the camera and singing her praises in absentia. Bette seemed somehow to be promoting her assistant's career—but as what? "If Kathryn had been an aspiring actress or someone that Bette was grooming to be something, it would have been different," says Marion Rosenberg. "But she wasn't. She was exactly what she was. What Bette was extolling her for being basically was a servant."

There was a strange subtext to Bette's often embarrassing public appearances with the young woman, whose devotion to her during her illness and afterward the actress seemed never to tire of recalling. Although Davis promoted *This 'N That* as an account of her illness, it was no secret that if people were rushing to read the book, it was for Bette's response to *My Mother's Keeper*. Except for a few evasive, unsatisfying pages, Bette hardly addressed her daughter's book in *This 'N That;* not so on the publicity tour, which sometimes seemed to be addressed to no one on earth but B.D., whose younger, more devoted, glamorous, and slender replacement Bette endlessly pushed forward as proof that, yes, she had a new daughter now.

There was considerable upset among Bette's friends about the garish outfits by Patrick Kelly that she wore on talk show interviews with Joan Rivers, David Letterman, and others. Announcing that Kathryn worked for Kelly—who happened to be in New York now in search of backers—Bette appeared on the Letterman show in a dress Kathryn was said to have brought from Paris: a short, form-fitting black knit with tiny buttons in many colors over the left breast to give the effect of a large heart. Her hat was a black felt beanie with an upturned brim cut into crownlike points, on which were sewn more buttons, red, yellow, blue, and white. An outfit that might have appeared whimsical on a twenty-year-old model seemed merely gaudy and ridiculous on the sickly seventy-nine year-old actress. One friend compared Bette's costumes of this period to the silly little suit worn by the monkey who accompanies an organ grinder.

Following the *This 'N That* tour, Kathryn went back to France, where Bette joined her in September to attend the Deauville Film Festival. On September 2, 1987, Davis had changed her will: Kathryn Sermak was designated to split Bette's estate with adopted son Michael Merrill, now an attorney in Boston. Sermak returned to the United States to live and work with Bette, whom she faithfully accompanied until her death.

▲

"What's the worst thing that can happen to you? You come home and find that Bette Davis has married into the family," says director Larry Cohen, describing the premise of Bette's final film, *Wicked Step-*

mother, whose script Cohen wrote with Davis in mind. "This family leaves their old widowed father behind and goes to Hawaii for two weeks. And when they come back, the first thing the father says is, 'I got married!' 'Oh my God, to whom?' Then Bette Davis comes out and says, 'Call me Mom!' "

Following her luminous performance in *The Whales of August*, Davis's agreeing to appear in Cohen's low comedy was a mistake from the outset. There was probably a certain perverse element in her decision to do *Wicked Stepmother*, comparable to the way she had sought to subvert and cancel out *The Night of the Iguana* with *What Ever Happened to Baby Jane?* But it was also the case that Cohen seemed to be the only person in Hollywood willing to hire her at the moment. According to Marion Rosenberg, Robert Lantz, weary of the actress's abuse, had dropped Bette from his agency's client roster, leaving her without her longtime agent to bring in offers. To make matters worse, Davis's ugly and irrational public display regarding *The Whales of August* left a good many producers afraid to work with her lest she stage a similar self-immolation during the publicity for their film. Although Davis sought futilely to attach herself to movie versions of *Steel Magnolias* and *Driving Miss Daisy*, her sole concrete offer was *Wicked Stepmother*, which came with the incentive of providing a credit as associate producer for Kathryn. After Bette had made a commitment to appear in the film, her new agent, Michael Black at ICM, advised her against the ill-conceived project; but she pressed on anyway, hoping that Cohen would start shooting on April 5, 1988. Bette told the director that when the press asked how she was going to spend her eightieth birthday, she wanted to shoot back: "Working."

As it happened, filming was postponed, and Bette celebrated in seclusion with Kathryn at a hotel in San Ysidro. The assistant hand-lettered a birthday dinner menu with a border of tiny red hearts, the word "Darling" scrawled in large letters on the bottom. To judge by Kathryn's copious photographs of the wizened actress, one can only wonder who ate the *foie gras et caviar, saumon fumé*, roast squab with bacon, spinach flan, *pomme de terre*, and *gateau speciale* listed on the menu. Five years earlier, surrounded by friends and professional associates, Bette had seemed robust, optimistic, and on top of the world at her seventy-fifth-birthday party. Not so at her eightieth, which she passed with her paid companion, and a magician and a flute player hired to entertain them in their hotel suite.

Looking at the small, shriveled figure seated forlornly on an immense bed as her large, incredibly sad eyes gaze into Kathryn's camera, it is not too much to suppose that Bette may already have been wondering whether she was in any condition to make yet another film. Indeed, when she and Kathryn appeared on the set of *Wicked Stepmother,* it became painfully obvious that her physical and mental capacities had diminished to a point that would make it difficult for her to complete the film satisfactorily.

"Don't you dare give me my line!" Bette shrieked when Larry Cohen's script girl gently tried to help her. "I'm famous for never forgetting my lines! How dare you!"

"That was tough," the director recalls, with evident sympathy for Davis's plight. "She didn't know her lines. She was great when she was talking, but when she was doing the lines that were written, she'd slow down quite a bit. You could see that she was having trouble and that she was angry at herself because she was having trouble."

To Cohen's further dismay, the bridgework in Davis's mouth had broken and kept slipping as she struggled to speak her lines. Repeatedly she tried to conceal her tongue's efforts to readjust the false teeth. "She had to pause in the middle of a line to shift her teeth," the director explains. "This distracted her to such a degree that she couldn't concentrate on what she was doing." But still, Davis pretended that nothing was wrong, blithely smoking five packs of Vantage cigarettes a day and making flirtatious remarks to the director and other men on the set—until one incident made it impossible to keep up the pretense that all was as it should be.

"I saw her lying there on the ground," says Cohen, who had stepped indoors for a moment, then glanced out the window, to observe Davis (who had often seemed to lose her balance on the set) stumble and fall in the courtyard of the house where they were filming, as her assistant and others rushed to help her. "I didn't know if I should go over there or not. I felt maybe I should stay away from her so as not to embarrass her."

Davis angrily declined offers of help as she struggled in vain to return to her feet. That even Kathryn was turned away suggested how important it was to Bette to be able to get up by herself. To admit the need for assistance would be to accept how sick she was—and that Bette was most unwilling to do. For some twenty minutes she lay on the ground, repeatedly trying to rise by her own strength, then falling again. Finally, the grips stacked up empty apple crates, which Bette grabbed onto, slowly, painfully clawing her way back onto her feet.

On examination, it was discovered that Bette had a large welt on her side. "She came in, and I told her that she could go home," Cohen recalls. "But she said she wanted to continue." When Davis had to go upstairs, where Cohen was shooting, she insisted on walking up without help.

Afterward, when the director went to talk to Bette alone, he was amazed to see her suddenly burst into tears. "I couldn't believe it," says Cohen. "That was the most vulnerable I ever saw her."

"I don't know what to do!" Davis wept. "I don't know if I'm any good in this part. I must see the dailies. I must see how I look."

There was one important problem. Time and again in the unedited dailies, she was seen to lose her balance, to forget her lines, or to fumble with her broken dentures. Cohen had already informed his producer that before the dailies were sent to the distributor, MGM, he wanted to remove any moments that might prove embarrassing to Davis. "I wanted them to see her as smooth as possible," says the director, "so I wanted to get in there and edit the dailies." But now, with Davis desperately insisting on seeing all the footage at once, there was—as Cohen explains—no time to take out the things she would not want to see. Cohen arranged a private screening on Saturday.

There was no denying the brutal evidence of what Bette saw. As the unedited footage made all too clear, she was simply in no condition to do film work anymore: a horrifying prospect to a woman who had thriven on work, and, at this point, had little else in life to sustain her. It was hardly the poor quality of the film that vexed her now, as Bette later liked to suggest, she had made plenty of bad pictures before. It was the sobering, terrifying knowledge of what she looked like in the unedited dailies that drove her to do something that even Bette Davis had never done in the course of her long and tempestuous film career.

"I'm sorry," said Bette when she called the director on Sunday, the day after she had examined the footage. "I made a terrible mistake and am leaving the picture." Before Cohen could say a word to stop her, she hung up—leaving him to salvage his film by rewriting the script to allow the Bette Davis character miraculously to metamorphose into the young actress Barbara Carrera.

🦋

Though Bette persistently implied that she had withdrawn from *Wicked Stepmother* because of the film's ineptitude, it was really the sight of her own tottering, fleshless figure on-screen that had caused her to flee. In the months that followed, that flight took Bette around the world as she poured her remaining strength into collecting a succession of international honors and awards. To hold in one's hand some of the private, strangely funereal photographs that Kathryn took of the infirm actress—"a tiny broken sparrow," as one friend described her—is to wonder why, in this ruinous condition, Bette continued to haul herself from one award ceremony to another. Throughout her life, work had been her refuge. Now, much as she struggled to suggest that the public appearances were a strategy to keep herself visible, to show that she was still vigorous and ready to go on-camera again, all this was really a substitute for the film work of which she was scarcely any longer capable. The essentially pointless peregrinations helped banish from her thoughts the lonely void her life had become.

Where once she and Wyler had meticulously timed and choreographed her every second on screen, now it was the obsessive details, the empty rituals, of her public appearances that soothed and absorbed her. Kathryn was drafted to play the directorial role: precisely noting each move Bette was to make, leaving nothing to chance. Typically, in anticipation of the Film Society of Lincoln Center's tribute to Davis on April 24, 1989, Bette studied Polaroid photographs of each corridor she would be expected to traverse, along with handwritten descriptions of the turns, steps, and platforms to be encountered en route. As in Ruthie's 1928 letter to her daughter on the eve of Bette's departure for Rochester, here were meticulous, reassuring instructions for everything she was to say and do, down to so seemingly spontaneous a gesture as the blowing of a kiss or the turning of her left side, her face still slightly askew, to the camera.

Only naturally, the omnipresent assistant and the extent of her control over the wraithlike star elicited a good deal of comment and speculation. Press reports noted the curious "role reversal" in which Davis and her secretary intermittently engaged. "Kathryn appears to be a masterful minder who enjoys the role," wrote English journalist Maureen Cozens. "It made a strange contrast to see the forceful star switch from holding court on her own account very ably, wittily, at times cuttingly, then turn hesitantly to the very up-front assistant to ask 'what should we do?' from time to time." And repeatedly, in describing Bette's enigmatic relationship with Kathryn—who, in the end, seemed even to emulate the actress's speech and gestures—

friends evoke Margo Channing's relationship with Eve Harrington in *All About Eve*. "It's interesting how life imitates art," says Dori Brenner, "and how Eve Harrington came back to haunt Bette Davis." And declares Peggy Shannon (the skeptical, protective Birdie to Kathryn's Eve?): "This girl took her whole personality, everything, from her." But as Brenner and others close to Davis seem to recognize, there is also a strong sense in which Bette herself was pulling the strings from first to last. Perhaps in seeming to lose control to her increasingly powerful assistant, Bette was attempting, as she so often had in the past, to lend drama, to give a more satisfying shape and substance, to her own life by recasting it in terms of an old movie plot. "I think it's a two-way street," says Brenner. "Bette never did anything she didn't want to do."

And says B.D. Hyman, as always uncannily in touch with a good many of her mother's most obscure motives: "Kathryn became what I was supposed to be. Mother found a willing victim. . . . She became an extension of Mother. She dressed like Mother. She talked like Mother. She had the same phraseology. . . . She just became totally drawn in, totally as if she were possessed by the presence of my mother, and became what I was supposed to be. And Mother indeed did call Kathryn her daughter at the end."

On several occasions in this last period, B.D. attempted unsuccessfully to contact Bette. "I had called Mother a couple of times just because I thought I ought to when I was in California," she recalls. "Mother knew I was on the phone, because I could hear her voice in the background, but I never even got past Kathryn."

The daughter's mistake, according to several of Davis's friends, was her failure to present herself at Bette's door. "B.D. could have cut Bette's throat, but if she went to her door and Bette opened it, Bette would have fallen into her arms, sobbing," insists Vik Greenfield. "You've got to realize they were two strong women. Neither was going to bend. But Bette would have bent if she had seen B.D. face-to-face. Eye-to-eye. She adored B.D.!"

There had been no reconciliation between mother and daughter when, in the summer of 1989, Bette was diagnosed as suffering from cancer again and secretly underwent radiation treatments in Los Angeles: an experience that seemed to drain the last sap from her. Her starveling appearance having given rise to tabloid reports that she was dying of self-inflicted malnutrition, Bette asked Rick Rosenberg whether she should publicly disclose her latest bout with cancer.

"They say I'm starving myself, but it's not the truth!" Bette told Rosenberg, producer of *Strangers* and *As Summers Die*, when they met to discuss a small film role he wanted to offer her. "Should I hold a press conference and tell them about the cancer?"

"No, don't worry about it," the producer counseled Davis.

On the way to dinner with Rosenberg, Bette and her assistant asked to stop off first for a drink at the Saint James's Club in Hollywood, where the producer watched as, with enormous effort, Davis slowly dragged herself up the stairs to the lobby.

"See, we won! We won!" crowed Bette, clawlike fingers excitedly indicating a large photograph of her, displayed among star portraits in the lobby.

"What did you win?" asked Rosenberg, as all heads turned to watch Bette Davis on her way to the bar.

"I'll tell you," said Bette, clearly savoring all the attention, although much of it was doubtless morbid fascination with her death-like appearance. "I was here a couple of weeks ago, and they had my photograph way in the back. I talked to the manager, and they moved it up for me. I wanted to return unannounced to see if they had moved it back after I left, or if it was still in front, where it belongs."

Having promised to call Rick Rosenberg about the new film role after she returned from Europe, Bette left for Spain on September 13. Whether she sensed that she was dying is impossible to say, but there can be no question that she was horribly ill and failing badly as she allowed herself to be painted and bewigged for her public appearances at the San Sebastián film festival. Bette and her assistant lingered for several days at their hotel, where Bette developed what was initially thought to be flu.

Far too weak to return to the United States, Bette heeded her doctors' advice that she fly to Paris on Tuesday, October 3, to check into the American Hospital in Neuilly. A private jet was hired, but Bette would not even consider the proposal that she be carried aboard on a stretcher. She demanded that she be dressed and made up to give the impression that nothing was wrong. In Neuilly, the hospital staff initially expressed the hope that Bette would be strong enough to fly home in a few days, but scarcely a day had passed before her rapidly deteriorating condition made that most unlikely. And so it was that on Friday, October 6, 1989, with only her hired companion at her side, Bette Davis died at the American Hospital at the age of eighty-one. Although Kathryn would later make a great point of insisting that in her final days Davis never once uttered B.D.'s name, anyone who knew Bette well would find it hard to believe that on her deathbed she failed to think of her beloved daughter and the tragic events that had separated them.

Six days later, according to Bette's long-standing plan, she was buried in Forest Lawn Memorial Park with Ruthie and Bobby. The marble statue modeled on B.D. served as a poignant reminder that Bette Davis's daughter was not there to mark her passing.

"*I* always said Bette would come out on top no matter what she did, but it didn't work out that way at the end," says Robin Brown of her lifelong friend.

And of Bette's last years, her daughter B.D. declares: "She had her fame and her public; that's what she wanted, and that's what she had. And that's all she had."

In the months prior to Gary Merrill's death from cancer on March 5, 1990, a Merrill family member wrote to B.D. at her home in Charlottesville, Virginia, to suggest that she might want to go to Falmouth, Maine, to visit him in his last days. B.D. replied that although God had permitted her to forgive Gary, she had no interest in seeing or speaking to him again. Merrill's will pointedly excluded B.D. by name, "for reasons which I am sure she will understand." Gary appointed Michael Merrill as trustee of the Margot Merrill Irrevocable Trust, to which Bette had contributed when she signed over custody of their adopted daughter, who continued to reside at a special facility for the retarded.

On December 30, 1990, a little over a year after her mother's death, B.D. wrote to Vik Greenfield that shortly after Thanksgiving, doctors had discovered cancerous tumors on her ovary and informed her that she had a limited time to live. Although her condition degenerated rapidly, Bette Davis's daughter refused to enter a hospital. She preferred to remain at home and pray to God to heal her.

According to B.D., on December 7, 1990, her prayers were answered—the cancerous tumors disappeared, and her health was miraculously restored.

B.D.'s news about her long-troubled son, Ashley, was considerably darker. Early on, the boy had expressed a serious interest in following in his grandmother's footsteps by becoming an actor. His unhappy experience working with Bette in the television film *Family Reunion* notwithstanding, Ashley persisted in his desire for an acting career. Even after the irrevocable split with Bette occasioned by the publication of *My Mother's Keeper*, Ashley had retained his interest in dramatics and participated in the amateur productions of a little-theater group in the Bahamas. In time, however, immersed as he was in the world of evangelism and uninhibited religious fervor to which his parents had attached themselves, the young man exchanged his theatrical ambitions for a desire to become a minister. According to B.D., Ashley had been studying to be a minister when a bout with manic depression landed him in a Virginia mental hospital, where lithium treatments gradually improved his condition. Two years later, although Ashley was still hospitalized, he was able to spend weekends and holidays with his family. Thwarted for the time being in his career plans, Ashley, according to his mother, was bringing the message of born-again Christianity to his fellow patients, many of whom were said by B.D. to have found God through the young man's evangelism.

Less than a year had passed before B.D. was declaring, much as she had in 1984, that God had healed Ashley. At Christmas of 1991, to the astonishment of her mother's friends, B.D. contacted Vik Greenfield to announce that once again a miracle had occurred to restore Ashley's health. She also reported her twenty-two-year-old son's marriage to a young woman called Mary, who had recently devoted her life to Jesus after witnessing Ashley's latest miraculous cure.

Following her mother's death, B.D. had told Charles Pollock that she was relieved to be free of Bette at long last. The fierce

lifelong struggle with her mother seemed to be over. But it is hard
not to see the powerful aftershock of that struggle in the troubles that
beset B.D. and her family even now that her mother was gone. In
B.D.'s embrace of her great-grandmother Eugenia's evangelical zeal,
in the impassioned Pentecostal pronouncements in which she cloaked
herself before Bette's friends, one hears a daughter still raging against
her mother, one observes a woman desperately struggling to resolve
a conflict that, even now, seems to cast its shadow over her.

B.D. is correct when she characterizes Bette as a "destructive
force"—for that is what the Favor women's famous driving force
largely became. In Ruthie, Eugenia's evangelical zeal became a vague
but no less ardent aspiration to assert and express herself, to become
something in the world of men. Precisely what that something might
be remained frustratingly unclear to Ruthie until at length she transferred her dreams to Bette, whose fulfillment the mother claimed in
place of her own.

In the thirties and forties, Bette Davis inspired America with
dynamic portraits of strong-willed women who scorned the passive
roles traditionally accorded to their sex. Long after World War II,
when Davis's indomitable characters had provided an important
model of female strength, the enduring power of the Davis screen
image continued to stir filmgoers with its eloquent message of a woman's capacity for transforming herself and the world around her.

Confusing the actress with her image, the woman with some of
the characters she played on-screen, Bette Davis's biographers have
tended to view her as a woman who struggled, who fought for her art
against the mighty studio system and won. In most tellings, if Bette
Davis was almost always at war in the course of a turbulent career of
more than half a century, it was for better parts, better directors,
better films; and above all, it was to enhance her options as an actress
and a woman. On examination, however, the facts tell a less inspiring
story. Anxious as we may be to discover in Bette Davis's life the
example of a woman's courageous struggle to expand the boundaries
of her art and to demand the opportunities that have been unjustly
denied her, all we really find is an endless series of irrational, mis-
guided, all too often self-destructive battles, to which the woman
ultimately sacrificed her prodigious gifts as an actress.

There can be little question that Davis's performances in *Jezebel*
and *The Letter* are among the finest acting ever recorded on film.
Viewed in the context of the rest of Davis's career, however, there is
also something terribly sad about them: suggesting as they do all that

Bette was capable of as an actress and failed to achieve in the years that followed the perverse and self-consuming conflict with Wyler during the making of their third film together. By the time of *The Little Foxes*, Bette had fearfully dug in her heels. Unlike Fontanne, Cornell, and the other stage actresses she had once admired, Bette, upon attaining the stardom she and Ruthie had hungered for, saw no reason to take risks in order to perfect her craft as Wyler urged her to do. Thenceforth, for Bette Davis it would be strictly a question of staying on top, of remaining a star, of making certain that her portrait was up front where it belonged; the hollow struggle to accomplish that preoccupied her virtually until the day she died. Anyone tempted to believe that Davis left Warner Bros. in search of more challenging acting opportunities need only consult the long list of mostly inferior films on which she repeatedly squandered her talents in the years that followed. Even the magnetic personality and matchless screen presence Davis brought to the most execrable of productions did not camouflage the sorry spectacle of a great talent pigheadedly wasted.

More and more, in the absence of anything even approaching artistic aspiration, Davis's ferocious energies were absorbed by the offstage histrionics with which she gleefully subverted films and plays good, bad, and indifferent. *The Night of the Iguana* and *Two's Company; The Whales of August* and *Wicked Stepmother*—it was all somehow the same to Bette, whose ceaseless war footing the public continued fondly to regard as betokening the same irrepressible spirit Davis had shown in her legendary court battle with Warners.

Davis had waged that battle mainly over money and power, not over better films, as history has tended to record. Although, like Cagney's fight with Warners, Bette's struggle against her contract did have the effect of chipping away at the studios' all-embracing control over the individual actor; and although, in 1936, her contentious persona did project a socially useful image of a woman boldly and unabashedly speaking up for herself, before very long Davis's pugnacity had calcified into a mannerism as self-indulgent and gratuitous as any of the nervous, unnecessary, ticlike gestures Wyler lamented in her acting.

While Bette Davis liked to think of herself as a Hollywood rebel, she differed in important ways from a quarrelsome, recalcitrant figure like Orson Welles, who, like Davis, spent much of his working life in a perpetual state of siege. But where Welles was always fighting *for* something, Davis only knew how to fight *against*—and therein lay all the difference.

BETTE DAVIS: STAGE, FILM, AND TELEVISION CREDITS

STAGE

BROADWAY (Cukor-Kondolf Company, Rochester, N.Y., 1928; dir. George Cukor)

Summer theater productions (Junior Players and Cape Playhouse, Dennis, Mass., 1928)

Repertory (Cukor-Kondolf Company, Rochester, N.Y., 1928)

THE EARTH BETWEEN (Provincetown Playhouse, New York, 1929; dir. James Light)

Blanche Yurka Ibsen Tour, 1929

Summer theater productions (Cape Playhouse, Dennis, Mass., 1929)

BROKEN DISHES (Broadway, 1929; dir. Marion Gering)

Summer theater productions (Cape Playhouse, Dennis, Mass., 1930)

BROKEN DISHES (tour, 1930)

SOLID SOUTH (Broadway, 1930; dir. Rouben Mamoulian)

TWO'S COMPANY (tour, Broadway, 1952–53; dir. Jules Dassin)

THE WORLD OF CARL SANDBURG (tour, Broadway, 1959–60; dir. Norman Corwin)

THE NIGHT OF THE IGUANA (tour, Broadway, 1961–62; dir. Frank Corsaro)

MISS MOFFAT (tour, closed in Philadelphia, 1974; dir. Joshua Logan)
BETTE DAVIS IN PERSON AND ON FILM (tour, first performance 1973)

FILMS

(Note: Years cited indicate release dates)
BAD SISTER (Universal, 1931; dir. Hobart Henley)
SEED (Universal, 1931; dir. John M. Stahl)
WATERLOO BRIDGE (Universal, 1931; dir. James Whale)
WAY BACK HOME (Radio Pictures, 1932; dir. William A. Seiter)
THE MENACE (Columbia, 1932; dir. Roy William Neil)
HELL'S HOUSE (Capital Films Exchange, 1932; dir. Howard Higgins)
THE MAN WHO PLAYED GOD (Warner Bros., 1932; dir. John Adolphi)
SO BIG (Warner Bros., 1932; dir. William A. Wellman)
THE RICH ARE ALWAYS WITH US (First National/Warner Bros., 1932;
    dir. Alfred E. Green)
THE DARK HORSE (First National/Warner Bros., 1932; dir. Alfred E.
    Green)
CABIN IN THE COTTON (First National/Warner Bros., 1932; dir. Michael
    Curtiz)
THREE ON A MATCH (First National/Warner Bros., 1932; dir. Mervyn
    LeRoy)
20,000 YEARS IN SING SING (First National/Warner Bros., 1933; dir.
    Michael Curtiz)
PARACHUTE JUMPER (Warner Bros., 1933; dir. Alfred E. Green)
THE WORKING MAN (Warner Bros., 1933; dir. John Adolphi)
EX-LADY (Warner Bros., 1933; dir. Robert Florey)
BUREAU OF MISSING PERSONS (First National/Warner Bros., 1933;
    dir. Roy Del Ruth)
FASHIONS OF 1934 (First National/Warner Bros., 1934; dir. William
    Dieterle)
THE BIG SHAKEDOWN (First National/Warner Bros., 1934; dir. John
    Francis Dillon)
JIMMY THE GENT (Warner Bros., 1934; dir. Michael Curtiz)
FOG OVER FRISCO (First National/Warner Bros., 1934; dir. William
    Dieterle)
OF HUMAN BONDAGE (RKO, 1934; dir. John Cromwell)
HOUSEWIFE (Warner Bros., 1934; dir. Alfred E. Green)
BORDERTOWN (Warner Bros., 1935; dir. Archie Mayo)
THE GIRL FROM TENTH AVENUE (First National/Warner Bros., 1935;
    dir. Alfred E. Green)
FRONT PAGE WOMAN (Warner Bros., 1935; dir. Michael Curtiz)
SPECIAL AGENT (Cosmopolitan/Warner Bros., 1935; dir. William Keigh-
    ley)

DANGEROUS (Warner Bros., 1935; dir. Alfred E. Green)
THE PETRIFIED FOREST (Warner Bros., 1936; dir. Archie Mayo)
THE GOLDEN ARROW (First National/Warner Bros., 1936; dir. Alfred E. Green)
SATAN MET A LADY (Warner Bros., 1936; dir. William Dieterle)
MARKED WOMAN (Warner Bros., 1937; dir. Lloyd Bacon)
KID GALAHAD (Warner Bros., 1937; dir. Michael Curtiz)
THAT CERTAIN WOMAN (Warner Bros., 1937; dir. Edmund Goulding)
IT'S LOVE I'M AFTER (Warner Bros., 1937; dir. Archie Mayo)
JEZEBEL (Warner Bros., 1938; dir. William Wyler)
THE SISTERS (Warner Bros., 1938; dir. Anatole Litvak)
DARK VICTORY (Warner Bros., 1939; dir. Edmund Goulding)
JUAREZ (Warner Bros., 1939; dir. William Dieterle)
THE OLD MAID (Warner Bros., 1939; dir. Edmund Goulding)
THE PRIVATE LIVES OF ELIZABETH AND ESSEX (Warner Bros., 1939; dir. Michael Curtiz)
ALL THIS AND HEAVEN TOO (Warner Bros., 1940; dir. Anatole Litvak)
THE LETTER (Warner Bros., 1940; dir. William Wyler)
THE GREAT LIE (Warner Bros., 1941; dir. Edmund Goulding)
THE BRIDE CAME C.O.D. (Warner Bros., 1941, dir. William Keighley)
THE LITTLE FOXES (RKO, 1941; dir. William Wyler)
THE MAN WHO CAME TO DINNER (Warner Bros., 1941; dir. William Keighley)
IN THIS OUR LIFE (Warner Bros., 1942; dir. John Huston)
NOW, VOYAGER (Warner Bros., 1942; dir. Irving Rapper)
WATCH ON THE RHINE (Warner Bros., 1943; dir. Herman Shumlin)
THANK YOUR LUCKY STARS (Warner Bros., 1943; dir. David Butler)
OLD ACQUAINTANCE (Warner Bros., 1943; dir. Vincent Sherman)
MR. SKEFFINGTON (Warner Bros., 1944; dir. Vincent Sherman)
HOLLYWOOD CANTEEN (Warner Bros., 1944; dir. Delmar Daves)
THE CORN IS GREEN (Warner Bros., 1945; dir. Irving Rapper)
A STOLEN LIFE (Warner Bros., 1946; dir. Curtis Bernhardt)
DECEPTION (Warner Bros., 1946; dir. Irving Rapper)
WINTER MEETING (Warner Bros., 1948; dir. Bretaigne Windust)
JUNE BRIDE (Warner Bros., 1948; dir. Bretaigne Windust)
BEYOND THE FOREST (Warner Bros., 1949; dir. King Vidor)
ALL ABOUT EVE (Twentieth Century–Fox, 1950; dir. Joseph L. Mankiewicz)
PAYMENT ON DEMAND (RKO, 1951; dir. Curtis Bernhardt)
ANOTHER MAN'S POISON (Eros/United Artists, 1952; dir. Irving Rapper)
PHONE CALL FROM A STRANGER (Twentieth Century–Fox, 1952; dir. Jean Negulesco)

THE STAR (Twentieth Century–Fox, 1952; dir. Stuart Heisler)

THE VIRGIN QUEEN (Twentieth Century-Fox, 1955; dir. Henry Koster)

STORM CENTER (Phoenix Productions/Columbia Pictures, 1956; dir. Daniel Taradash)

THE CATERED AFFAIR (Metro-Goldwyn-Mayer, 1956; dir. Richard Brooks)

JOHN PAUL JONES (Samuel Bronston Productions/Warner Bros., 1959; dir. John Farrow)

THE SCAPEGOAT (Du Maurier-Guinness/Metro-Goldwyn-Mayer, 1959; dir. Robert Hamer)

POCKETFUL OF MIRACLES (Franton/United Artists, 1961; dir. Frank Capra)

WHAT EVER HAPPENED TO BABY JANE? (Seven Arts–Aldrich Associates/Warner Bros., 1961; dir. Robert Aldrich)

DEAD RINGER (Warner Bros., 1964; dir. Paul Henreid)

THE EMPTY CANVAS (Joseph E. Levine/Embassy, 1964; dir. Damiano Damiani)

WHERE LOVE HAS GONE (Joseph E. Levine/Paramount, 1964; dir. Edward Dmytryk)

HUSH . . . HUSH, SWEET CHARLOTTE (Aldrich Associates/Twentieth Century–Fox, 1964; dir. Robert Aldrich)

THE NANNY (Seven Arts–Hammer/Twentieth Century–Fox, 1965; dir. Seth Holt)

THE ANNIVERSARY (Seven Arts–Hammer/Twentieth Century–Fox, 1968; dir. Roy Ward Baker)

CONNECTING ROOMS (London Screen/Hemdale, 1971; dir. Franklin Gollings)

BUNNY O'HARE (American-International, 1971; dir. Gerd Oswald)

THE SCIENTIFIC CARDPLAYER (LO SCOPONE SCIENTIFICO) (Dino De Laurentiis/CIC, 1972; dir. Luigi Comencini)

BURNT OFFERINGS (PEA/United Artists, 1976; dir. Dan Curtis)

RETURN FROM WITCH MOUNTAIN (Walt Disney/Buena Vista, 1978; dir. John Hough)

DEATH ON THE NILE (Paramount, 1978; dir. John Guillermin)

WATCHER IN THE WOODS (Walt Disney/Buena Vista, 1980; dir. John Hough)

THE WHALES OF AUGUST (Alive/Circle Associates, 1987; dir. Lindsay Anderson)

WICKED STEPMOTHER (MGM Videotape, 1988; dir. Larry Cohen)

SELECTED TELEVISION

MADAME SIN (ITC Productions, 1971; dir. David Greene)

THE JUDGE AND JAKE WYLER (Universal, 1972; dir. David Lowell Rich)

SCREAM, PRETTY PEGGY (Universal, 1973; dir. Gordon Hessler)

THE DISAPPEARANCE OF AIMEE (Tomorrow Entertainment, 1976; dir. Anthony Harvey)

THE DARK SECRET OF HARVEST HOME (Universal, 1978; dir. Leo Penn)

STRANGERS: THE STORY OF A MOTHER AND DAUGHTER (Chris-Rose Productions, 1979; dir. Milton Katselas)

WHITE MAMA (1980; dir. Jackie Cooper)

SKYWARD (GE Theater/Major H-Anson Productions, 1980; dir. Ron Howard)

FAMILY REUNION (NBC, 1981; dir. Fielder Cook)

A PIANO FOR MRS. CIMINO (CBS, 1982; dir. George Schaefer)

LITTLE GLORIA . . . HAPPY AT LAST (NBC, 1982; dir. Waris Husscin)

HOTEL (ABC/Aaron Spelling Productions, 1983; dir. Jerry London)

RIGHT OF WAY (HBO/Post-Newsweek Video, 1983; dir. George Schaefer)

MURDER WITH MIRRORS (Hanjeno/Warner Bros. TV, 1985; dir. Dick Lowry)

AS SUMMERS DIE (1986; dir. Jean-Claude Tramont)

ACKNOWLEDGMENTS

Allegra Huston, my editor at Weidenfeld & Nicolson in London, first suggested that I write a biography of Bette Davis. This book would not have been possible without Allegra's intelligence, counsel, and support. She was there for me every step of the way. I am deeply grateful for all she has done.

Also at Weidenfeld, I would like to thank George Weidenfeld for his continued support of my work; and Natalina Bertoli for her help and good cheer.

At Summit Books in New York, I want to thank Jim Silberman, who was confident that it would be possible to write a serious biography of a movie star and who shared my belief that Bette Davis merited such a book. Also at Summit, I would like to thank Dominick Anfuso, who took over the editing after Jim's departure and made many helpful suggestions; and Cassie Jones, who assisted with important details.

Lois Wallace has been the best agent anyone could want. I will always be grateful for her support and cool head in moments of crisis. Also at the Wallace Literary Agency in New York, Tom Wallace was a source of much help and excellent advice, particularly at the inception of this book.

In Los Angeles, Leith Adams, curator of the Warner Bros. Archive at

USC, made an immense contribution to this biography. Without his astonishing mastery of the complex network of Warner Bros. papers, I would never have been able to unearth the story of Davis's Warner years. Also at USC, Ned Comstock was, as always, an unfailingly intelligent and generous guide through the other special collections in the Doheny Library.

In Boston, Dr. Howard B. Gotlieb persuaded Davis to deposit her personal papers in Boston University's Department of Special Collections. In the intervening years, he has meticulously assembled the finest collection of Davis materials for which any biographer could dare to hope; and he has made those papers available under the most efficient and effective conditions possible. Also at Boston University, I would like to thank Karen Mix, whose encyclopedic grasp of the Davis papers I benefited from throughout my research. Karen is a model archivist: knowledgeable, imaginative, and superbly organized.

Michael Merrill, Davis's son, graciously facilitated my work in his mother's papers at Boston University.

A number of Davis's oldest and closest friends have gone out of their way to enable me to write this book, even when it meant breaking a consistent habit of not giving interviews about their friend. Above all, I am grateful to Bette's dear friends Robin Brown and Ellen Batchelder, who shared their invaluable memories and perceptions with me. Besides talking to me at length on numerous occasions, Robin was always a telephone call away whenever I had a question that needed to be answered immediately. She also allowed me to examine her lifelong correspondence with Bette. Ellen Batchelder was not only unfailingly generous in providing me with details about every aspect of Bette's life; Ellen gave me the greatest gift any biographer could dream of, when she invited me to meet Bette Davis's girlhood friends at the first Newton High School reunion held after her death. Meeting these strong, vivid, remarkable women—Yankees all—enabled me to see Bette's life in a whole new light. My afternoon with the "Newton girls," and my individual interviews with them afterward, provided a lesson in the value of female friendship.

B.D. Hyman, Bette Davis's daughter, talked to me at length about her mother. I am tremendously grateful for her willingness to share her memories and insights with me, as well as to provide important leads for further research—including the names of several people whom she must have known would view her own actions toward her mother in a less than favorable light.

Dori Brenner, Vik Greenfield, Charles Pollock, and Peggy Shannon—Davis's close personal friends of later years—must also be singled out for their great warmth and generosity in tirelessly answering my questions and otherwise assisting my research. It is impossible adequately to acknowledge their unfailing kindness.

I am indebted to so many people who have given generously of their time to help me put this story together. They interrupted their busy schedules more times that I can count to answer my questions, share their memories and perceptions, or provide me with vast quantities of documentation. Bette Davis's life was long and complex, and I could never have told her story without the help of the following: Benny Baker, Ron Bernstein, Gay Bersteeg, Julian Blaustein, Paula Laurence Bowden, Harry Carey, Jr., Ginny Cerilla, Connie Cezon, Larry Cohen, Peter Constandy, Fielder Cook, Frank Corsaro, Margaret Fitts Currier, George Davis, Michael DeGuzman, Melinda Dillon, Dr. Robert Dores, Liz Dribben, Rosalie Dunne, Julius Epstein, Leslie Epstein, Rudi Fehr, Elsa Feminella, Geraldine Fitzgerald, Helen Elwell Fox, Sam Gill, Carlos Goez, David Greene, Skip Guard, Faith Wing Hawkins, Gordon Hessler, Richard Hoyt, Waris Hussein, Jill Jackson, Mike Kaplan, Milton Katselas, Brigitte Kueppers, Adrienne Lambert, Richard Lamparski, Stephanie Landsman, Jerry London, Virginia Koops McGill, Jerry Merrill, Robert Ellis Miller, Janet Munch, Ann Nelson, Barry Oliver, Patrick O'Neal, Michael Parness, Vincent Price, Irving Rapper, Marion Rosenberg, Rick Rosenberg, George Schaefer, Connie Sellecca, Vincent Sherman, Virginia Hodder Sherrill, Mr. and Mrs. William Grant Sherry, Ann Sothern, Dr. John Sussman, Daniel Taradash, Eleanor Harding Thomas, Renato Tonelli, Elizabeth Valkenier, Robert Valkenier, Betty White, Arthur Wilde, Meta Carpenter Wilde, Bob William, Catherine Wyler, Margaret "Talli" Wyler.

Finally, I must thank my husband, David, who somehow always manages to keep me alive through these other "lives."

NOTES ON SOURCES

The major primary sources for this biography included personal interviews conducted by the author; privately held, unpublished letters given to the author by Davis's friends; Davis's personal papers on deposit at the Mugar Memorial Library at Boston University; the Warner Bros. archive at the University of Southern California; and a wide variety of documents drawn from other archives and government agencies. Where there are disparities between my account of Davis's life and earlier published versions, including Davis's ghostwritten autobiographies, *The Lonely Life* and *This 'N That*, I have followed the information provided in the primary sources.

The people I interviewed included a number of Davis's closest friends who have not spoken publicly before. I was especially fortunate to have the cooperation of Bette's two lifelong friends Ellen Batchelder and Robin Brown, who provided a wealth of information. Other Davis friends, family members, and associates who graciously gave me their time for this biography are listed in the Acknowledgments.

Several of Davis's friends allowed me to read unpublished letters from her and her daughter B.D. Hyman. The most important letters were those Bette wrote to Robin Brown over the course of several decades. Robin

Brown also permitted me to examine William Grant Sherry's letters to her and her late husband, Albert Brown. Davis's friend Charles Pollock gave me access to his private correspondence with Bette and B.D. I was also able to consult letters from Bette and B.D. to Davis's longtime assistant Vik Greenfield. B.D. Hyman's correspondence with Vik Greenfield provided essential information on *My Mother's Keeper* and its aftermath.

Davis's extensive personal papers were deposited at Boston University in several installments. The first arrived in 1968, and the last came after her death in 1989. The vast treasure trove of Davis materials includes personal and professional correspondence, personal diaries, scrapbooks, photographs, annotated scripts, and assorted personal memorabilia.

The dozens of scrapbooks, composed and copiously annotated by Ruthie, Bette, B.D., and various assistants, are an extremely rich resource for the biographer. Documenting Davis's life from first to last, the scrapbooks constitute an astonishing archive of the most intimate memories and emotions. For Bette, the scrapbook form often functioned in place of a diary, allowing her to juxtapose word and image to record the details of her daily emotional and professional life as she was experiencing them. Bette's extensive handwritten annotations frequently disclose a private side of her very different from the carefully calculated public persona she constructed for interviews and her two published memoirs. With regard to the scrapbooks Bette assembled in youth, my conversations with a number of her girlhood friends enabled me to decipher some of the more cryptic private references and allusions. In addition to Davis's ongoing commentary, the scrapbooks are invaluable for the wide range of documents Bette preserved in them: marriage licenses, divorce papers, contracts, and other legal records. There are revealing letters from her father and mother, as well as from other family members, friends, lovers, husbands, and professional associates. In a number of the scrapbooks, the annotations of Bette's mother, Ruthie Davis, and daughter B.D. Hyman reveal much about these two most important characters in Bette's story.

Given the sustaining role that photography played in Ruthie Davis's life, it should come as no surprise that the Davis archive contains thousands of photographs, from all periods of Bette's life and career. In the course of more than half a century, a camera seems to have been an omnipresent feature of every household Bette occupied, providing the biographer with an extraordinary visual record of the tiniest details of Davis's daily existence from childhood to old age. Best of all, perhaps, Ruthie and Bette's shared obsession with photography often resulted in images that disclose every bit as much about the person taking the picture as about the thing being photographed.

Finally, the annotated scripts in the Davis papers are an indispensable source of information about the art of the actress. Bette's handwritten notes and marginalia provide a rare glimpse into how she approached a part, how she shaped a character, how she envisioned a scene in terms of the whole, and how she worked with her various directors on stage and screen.

For Davis's film career, the other major repository of documents is the labyrinthine Warner Bros. archive at USC. Fortunately for the biographer, it was the rule at Warner Bros. in Bette's day that everything must be carefully written down and preserved. Every phone conversation and contract negotiation, every script idea and altercation on the set, was committed to writing for possible future reference. Letters, legal papers, interoffice memos: everything was meticulously preserved, making it possible for the biographer to trace Davis's every second on and off the set, her every move at the studio in the course of eighteen stormy years there. The Warner files contain all of Davis's many letters to Jack Warner, Hal Wallis, and others. There are letters from her directors, including William Wyler, Edmund Goulding, and Irving Rapper, detailing their work and conflicts with her. And there are vast quantities of notes by Warner lawyers and by Jack Warner himself, assessing Davis's motives, strengths, and weaknesses during her various violent collisions with studio authority, both in and out of court. Each of Davis's films possesses detailed production and legal files, as well as voluminous daily production reports that allow the biographer to pinpoint creative problems, decisions, and conflicts. The Warners collection contains legal, personal, story, research, publicity, and contract files on Davis and all the actors, directors, and production people whom she encountered at the studio. Providing as they do a multiplicity of perspectives on the making of each of Davis's films, the thousands of documents in these files afford an up-close look at film history as it was actually unfolding.

Other archives and offices consulted for this biography included: Lincoln Center Library for the Performing Arts (Theatre and Dance Collections); Academy of Motion Picture Arts and Sciences; U.S. Department of Justice, Federal Bureau of Investigation, Washington, D.C.; U.S. Social Security Administration, Washington, D.C.; University of California at Los Angeles, Theatre Arts Library; U.S. Central Intelligence Agency, Washington, D.C.; Records Office, Northfield Academy; Records Office, Mount Pleasant Cemetery; Records Office, Mount Auburn Cemetery; Suffolk County Probate Court, Boston, Mass.; Superior Court, Yuma, Ariz.; Los Angeles Superior Court, Civil Division, Los Angeles, Cal.; Superior Court, Santa Ana, Cal.; Los Angeles County Coroner, Los Angeles, Cal.; Clark County Recorder, Las Vegas, Nev.; Vital Statistics Branch, Sacramento, Cal.; County Records Center, Los Angeles, Cal.; Vital Records Office, Hartford, Conn.; Office of Vital Records, Vermont; Registry of Vital Records, Boston, Mass.; Santa Monica Superior Court, Santa Monica, Cal.; Cumberland County Superior Court, Portland, Me.

NOTES FOR CHAPTERS 1–4

At Boston University, vital information on Bette's youth and family background came from scrapbooks #1; #6; #32; #55; and #57. Also consulted were Bette's "Baby Book"; "Ruthie's Book"; Ruthie's 1934 gift scrapbook to Bette, "The Tales of a Simple (?) Life! Lived and Sojourned in sixty three places!"; uncatalogued scrapbook "G"; Rev. Paul Favor's unpublished memoir of the Favor family; and Ruthie Davis's two unpublished memoirs of life with Bette and Bobby.

Other essential background came from my conversations with Bette's Newton High School classmates at their 1990 reunion, the first since her death. Additional data came from the Newton High School yearbooks for 1923 and 1924.

For an understanding of Ruthie's Delsarte training and all it meant to her, I examined her 1892 chautauqua Delsarte manual: Emily Bishop, "Americanized Delsarte Culture." Of many books on dance consulted, four proved particularly useful: Edwin Denby, *Dance Writings;* Elizabeth Kendall, *Where She Danced;* Ted Shawn, *Every Little Movement;* and Suzanne Shelton, *Ruth St. Denis.* The Kendall book was especially important for its discussion of the points of contact between interpretive dance and pictorialist photography.

Background on the Yankee view of divorce came from Judson Hale, *The Education of a Yankee.*

Other facts came from the following documents: death certificate, William A. Favor, December 4, 1911; death certificate, Eliza M. Davis, May 31, 1906; death certificate, Harlow Morrell Davis, January 3, 1938; birth certificate, Ruth Favor, September 16, 1885; birth certificate, Ruth Elizabeth Davis, April 5, 1908; birth certificate, Barbara Harriet Davis, November 5, 1909; marriage certificate, Harlow Davis and Ruth Favor, July 1, 1907; announcement of Harlow Davis and Ruth Favor marriage; program of Lowell High School Annual Exhibition in Calisthenics, May 21, 1901; Betty Davis's report card, Grade 4, Winchester Public School; Minnie Stewart Davis's tombstone, Mount Pleasant Cemetery, Augusta, Maine; program of Cushing Academy Graduation, June 28, 1925; program for Repertory Theatre, Boston, 1925, *The Wild Duck;* Bette's script for Booth Tarkington's *Seventeen;* letter from Harlow Davis to Bette, n.d.; letter from H. M. Grant to Ruthie Davis, June 2, 1924; letter from Warren Blake to Bette, summer 1925; letter from "Dr." Steve to Bette, January 24, 1926; Harlow Morrell Davis's Last Will and Testament, July 27, 1926.

NOTES FOR CHAPTERS 5–6

At Boston University, vital information on Bette's early stage career came from scrapbooks #1; #2; #3; #4; #12; #32; #55; and Ruthie's 1934 gift scrapbook to Bette.

Other material came from the following documents: letter from M. Olga Rogers (John Murray Anderson School) to Ruth Davis, May 21, 1928; letter from Ruthie Davis to Bette, April 27, 1928; letter from James Light to Bette, November 17, 1928; telegram from James Light to Bette, November 27, 1928; telegram from James Light to Bette, January 3, 1929; telegram from James Light to Bette, February 4, 1929; telegram from Marie (Robin Brown) to Bette, November 5, 1929; telegram from Charlie (Ansley) to Bette, November 1, 1929; telegram from Ruthie Davis to Bette, April 30, 1928; postcard from Marion to Harlow Davis, 1930; letter from Bette to Harlow Davis, May 6, 1929; telegram from Bobby Davis to Bette, October 15, 1930; letter from Rev. Paul Favor to his wife, Gail, March 6, 1929; card from Bette to Harlow Davis, 1929; note from Harlow Davis to Bette, 1929; letter from Bette to Harlow Davis, April 5, 1929; letter from Harlow Davis to Bette, March 25, 1929; letter from Harlow Davis to Bette, April 8, 1929; Bette's response to Harlow's April 8, 1929, letter, n.d.; telegram from Harlow Davis to Bette, March 5, 1929; note from Blanche Yurka to Bette, 1929; note from Charles Ansley to Bette, 1929; card from Charles Ansley to Bette, October 15, 1928; telegram from Marie Simpson (Robin Brown) to Bette, October 15, 1928, letter from Harlow Davis to Bette, March 25, 1929; note from Ruthie Davis to Bette, July 21, 1929; telegram from Ham Nelson to Bette, October 1930; telegram from Arthur Hopkins to Bette, May 16, 1930; Bette's annotated script of *The Wild Duck*; typescript of Bette's first interview, April 1929; Bette's first radio speech, handwritten on United Shoe Machinery Corporation stationery, 1929; Bette's contracts with the John Murray Anderson–Robert Milton School of Theatre and Dance, October 19, 1927, and February 6, 1928; program of Examination Plays of the Junior Dramatic Class, January 27–28, 1928; Memorandum of Agreement, Provincetown Playhouse, March 2, 1929; Bette's contract with the Actors' Theatre Inc. (Blanche Yurka), April 4, 1929.

NOTES FOR CHAPTERS 9–17

At Boston University, vital information on Davis's film work at Universal and Warner Bros. came from scrapbooks #4, #6; #7; #8; #9; #10; #11; #12; #13; #14; #15; #16; #17; #18; #19; #20; #21; #22; #23; #24; #25; #26; #27; #28; #29; #30; #31; #32; #33; #34; #35; #36; #37; #38; #39; #40; #41; #42; #43; #44; #45; #45a; #46; #47; #48; #49; #50; #55; #56; uncatalogued scrapbooks C, P, and G; Ruthie's 1934 gift scrapbook to Bette; uncatalogued Brown Album, Pink Album, and Black Album ("Houses, inside and out"). Also Rev. Paul Favor's unpublished family history and Ruthie Davis's unpublished memoirs.

At the University of Southern California, Los Angeles, the Universal Collection—Shooting Record of Pictures 1930–1931–1932 and the John Stahl Collection provided information about Davis's Universal period.

Also at USC, I consulted the wealth of documentation on Davis's career at Warners on deposit in the Warner Bros. Collection. In addition to studio files on Davis and her films, I examined the collection's files on Hal Wallis, Jack Warner, Henry Blanke, Casey Robinson, William Wyler, Lenore Coffee, Edmund Goulding, Vincent Sherman, Julius and Philip Epstein, Michael Curtiz, Robert Lord, Darryl Zanuck, Irving Rapper, John Huston, Steve Trilling, Al Alleborn, R. J. Obringer, Archie Mayo, Al Green, William Keighley, George S. Kaufman.

Other essential Warner material was located in the Jack Warner Collection and the Bill Schaefer Collection (Warner Bros. Films—Casts/Grosses '22–'67) at USC.

At the University of California, Los Angeles, William Wyler's personal papers were an invaluable resource for this biography. Few people in Hollywood understood Davis's work as an actress as well as Wyler did. Read in conjunction with Bette's annotations on her scripts for the films she and Wyler made together, Wyler's notes, rewrites, and annotated scripts provided much fascinating information about their creative collaboration.

At the Academy of Motion Picture Arts and Sciences, I examined the Hal Wallis Collection, the Perc Westmore Collection, the John Huston Collection, the Edith Head Collection, the Hedda Hopper Collection, and the Irving Rapper Collection.

Of many books on the Hollywood studio system consulted, four proved particularly useful: Rudy Behlmer, *Inside Warner Bros.;* Neal Gabler, *An Empire of Their Own;* Ethan Mordden, *The Hollywood Studios;* and Thomas Schatz, *The Genius of the System.*

Other material came from the following sources: Bette Davis's FBI file #100-352574; Bette's letters to Robin Brown, various dates; William Grant Sherry's letters to Robin and Albert Brown, various dates; letter from A. L. Roper, Toeplitz Productions, to Bette, August 27, 1936; letter from Helen Hayes to Bette, n.d.; letter from Ham Nelson to Bette, n.d.; letter from Bette to Teddy Newton, n.d.; marriage license and marriage certificate, Harmon Oscar Nelson, Jr. and Ruth Elizabeth Davis, August 18, 1932, Yuma, Arizona, Superior Court; divorce papers, Harmon Oscar Nelson, Jr. vs. Ruth Elizabeth Davis, Case #D174595, Los Angeles Superior Court; death certificate, Harlow Morrell Davis, January 3, 1938, Middlesex County, Mass.; Mount Auburn Cemetery records, Cambridge, Mass.; Mount Pleasant Cemetery Records, Augusta, Me.; marriage certificate, Robert Woodbury Palmer and Ruth Favor Davis, November 27, 1945; marriage certificate, Otho W. Budd and Ruth Favor Davis, April 27, 1950; divorce papers, Barbara F. Pelgram vs. Robert Cole Pelgram, Case #23491, February 28, 1945, Judicial District Court, Clark County, Nev.; marriage certificate, David Roscoe Berry and Barbara Davis Pelgram, June 25, 1947, Clark County, Nev.; birth certificate, Arthur Austin Farnsworth, January 2,

1909; death certificate, Arthur Austin Farnsworth, August 31, 1943; marriage certificate, William Grant Sherry and Marion Dolores Richards, August 11, 1950.

NOTES FOR CHAPTER 17–EPILOGUE

At Boston University, vital information on Davis's post-Warners years came from scrapbooks #50; #51; #52; #53; #54; #55; #56; #59. Also uncatalogued scrapbooks: 1951 Life at Beach with Gary Merrill; Big Black Book; 1959–1960, annotated by B.D.; Keep as is—Gary and me; White Leather Scrapbook 1961–1963, annotated by B.D.; White Leather Scrapbook (1969); Lots of B.D.—houses, Charlotte; B.D.; Scrapbook of trip to Cannes and B.D. romance with Jeremy Hyman; Scrapbook of Italian trip, annotated by attorney Tom Hammond; Houses, inside and out; Big Brown Book 1976–1978; Miss D. and relatives; Very Special Photos 1980s; Awards—*Family Reunion* Party 1982; 1988–89 A Lot with Kath; AFI Award; Festival de Deauville; *Whales*; Plus de Deauville and Kennedy Center Awards; Caesars-Paris; Assorted Family and professional.

I also read Davis's personal diaries for 1958, 1967, 1968, 1970, 1971, 1972, 1973, 1974, 1975, and 1976.

Other material came from the following documents: Bette's letters to Robin Brown, various dates; Bette's letters to Charles Pollock, various dates; Bette's letters to Vik Greenfield, various dates; B.D. Hyman's letters to Vik Greenfield, various dates; B.D. Hyman's letters to Charles Pollock, various dates; B.D. Hyman's letters to Bette, various dates; Michael Merrill's letters to Bette, various dates; Gary Merrill's letters to Bette, various dates; letter from Gary Merrill to Robin Brown, n.d.; death certificate, Ruth Favor Davis, July 5, 1961; Tennessee Williams's unpublished letters to Bette, various dates; Tennessee Williams's unpublished letter to Bette, Maggie, Allen, and Pat, n.d.; Tennessee Williams's unpublished Author's Notes on Last Scene: For Maggie and Pat, n.d.; card from Bobby Davis to Bette, n.d.; divorce papers, Barbara Merrill vs. Gary Franklin Merrill, Case No. D 399, 466, Los Angeles Superior Court; birth certificate, Barbara Davis Merrill (altered when Gary Merrill adopted B.D.); letter from Michael Merrill to Gary Merrill, July 1962; affidavit of Michael Parlow, investigator, February 18, 1964; divorce papers, Bette Davis Merrill vs. Gary F. Merrill, Case No. WED 2895, Los Angeles Superior Court; Last Will and Testament, Gary F. Merrill, July 14, 1989; Consent of Parent or Guardian to Issuance of Marriage License for marriage of Barbara Davis Sherry to Jeremy Aubrey Hyman, December 23, 1963; Davis's handwritten notes on her actions regarding *Miss Moffat;* Kathryn Sermak's notes to Bette at the time of Davis's 1983 hospitalization; letter from Pierre Kalfon to Kathryn Sermak, August 22, 1987; Kathryn Sermak's annotated publicity schedule for Bette Davis; handwritten speech for Bette Davis's Lincoln Center Film Society tribute; Kathryn Sermak's notebook and yellow pad; Bette Davis's Social Security Administration file, U.S. Department of Health and Human Services.

Important background on Davis's film and stage work in this period came from her annotated scripts for *The Night of the Iguana*, *All About Eve*, and other projects, deposited at Boston University. The Warners archive at USC provided information about her participation in *What Ever Happened to Baby Jane?* and *Dead Ringer*; with additional material coming from the Jack Warner Collection, also at USC. Other career data came from the MGM Collection and the 20th Century–Fox Collection at USC.

SELECTED BIBLIOGRAPHY

Allen, Frederick Lewis. *Only Yesterday*. New York: Harper, 1931.
Astor, Mary, *A Life in Film*. New York: Delacorte, 1971.
Atkinson, Brooks. *Broadway*. New York: Macmillan, 1970.
Au, Susan. *Ballet and Modern Dance*. London: Thames and Hudson, 1988.
Bainbridge, John. *Garbo*. New York: Doubleday, 1955.
Balazs, Bela. *Theory of the Film*. New York: Dover, 1955.
Bankhead, Tallulah. *Tallulah*. New York: Harper, 1952.
Behlmer, Rudy. *America's Favorite Movies*. New York: Ungar, 1982.
———. *Inside Warner Bros*. New York: Fireside, 1987.
———. *Memo from David O. Selznick*. New York: Grove Press, 1972.
Berg, A. Scott. *Goldwyn*. New York: Ballantine, 1989.
Billquist, Fritiof. *Garbo*. New York: Putnam, 1960.
Bishop, Emily. *Americanized Delsarte Culture*. Meadville: Chautauqua Century Press, 1892.
Blum, Daniel. *A Pictorial History of the American Theatre*. New York: Greenberg, 1950.
Brown, Jared. *The Fabulous Lunts*. New York: Atheneum, 1986.
Calder, Robert. *Willie*. New York: St. Martin, 1990.

Carey, Gary. *More About* All About Eve. New York: Random House, 1972.

Cheney, Gay. *Basic Concepts in Modern Dance*. Princeton: Dance Horizons, 1989.

Cole, Toby, and Helen Krich Chinoy. *Actors on Acting*. New York: Crown, 1970.

Considine, Shaun. *Bette and Joan*. New York: Dutton, 1989.

Cornell, Katharine. *I Wanted to Be an Actress*. New York: Random House, 1939.

Courtney, Marguerite. *Laurette*. New York: Rinehart, 1955.

Craig, Edward Gordon. *Index to the Story of My Days*. New York: Viking, 1957.

Croce, Arlene. *Afterimages*. New York: Knopf, 1977.

Davis, Bette, with Sandford Dody. *The Lonely Life*. New York: Berkley, 1990.

Davis, Bette, with Michael Herskowitz. *This 'N That*. New York: Berkley, 1988.

Denby, Edwin. *Dance Writings*. New York: Knopf, 1986.

Dody, Sandford. *Giving Up the Ghost*. New York: Evans, 1960.

Dyer, Richard. *Stars*. London: BFI, 1979.

Edwards, Anne. *A Remarkable Woman*. New York: Pocket Books, 1985.

Feibelman, Peter. *Lilly*, New York: Avon, 1990.

Federal Writers' Project. *Massachusetts*. Cambridge: Riverside Press, 1937.

Fitzgerald, F. Scott. *The Last Tycoon*. New York, Scribner, 1941.

———. *This Side of Paradise*. New York: Macmillan, 1988.

Flanner, Janet. *Janet Flanner's World*. New York: Harcourt Brace, 1979.

Flynn, Errol. *My Wicked, Wicked Ways*. New York: Putnam, 1959.

Fonda, Henry. *My Life*. New York: Signet, 1982.

Foster, Susan Leigh. *Reading Dancing*. Berkeley: University of California Press, 1986.

Fraser, Antonia. *The Warrior Queens*. New York: Vintage, 1990.

Freedland, Michael. *The Warner Brothers*. London: Harrap, 1983.

Frewin, Leslie. *Dietrich*. New York: Stein and Day, 1967.

Friedrich, Otto. *City of Nets*. New York: Perennial, 1987.

Funke, Lewis. *Actors Talk About Acting*. New York: Avon, 1961.

Gabler, Neal. *An Empire of Their Own*. New York: Crown, 1988.

Gill, Brendan. *Tallulah*. New York: Holt, 1972.

Grobel, Lawrence. *The Hustons*. New York: Scribner, 1989.

Hale, Judson. *The Education of a Yankee*. New York: Harper & Row, 1987.

Harris, Radie. *Radie's World*. New York: Putnam, 1975.

Haskell, Molly. *From Reverence to Rape*. New York: Holt, 1974.

Hayes, Helen. *My Life in Three Acts*. New York: Touchstone, 1990.

Henreid, Paul. *Ladies Man*. New York: St. Martin, 1985.

Higham, Charles. *Bette*. New York: Macmillan, 1981.

Huston, John. *An Open Book.* New York: Knopf, 1980.

Hyman, B.D. *My Mother's Keeper.* New York: Morrow, 1985.

Hyman, B.D., and Jeremy Hyman. *Narrow Is the Way.* New York: Morrow, 1987.

Ibsen, Henrik. *Four Great Plays.* New York: Bantam, 1981.

Kanin, Garson. *Tracy and Hepburn.* New York: Primus, 1988.

Kendall, Elizabeth. *Where She Danced.* Berkeley: University of California Press, 1979.

Kofler, Leo. *The Art of Breathing.* New York: Werner, 1897.

Leatherman, Leroy. *Martha Graham.* New York: Knopf, 1966.

Le Favre, Carrica. *Physical Culture Founded on Delsartean Principles.* New York: Fowler and Wells, 1892.

Levenkron, Steven. *Obsessive-Compulsive Disorders,* New York: Warner, 1991.

Lichm, Mira. *Passion and Defiance.* Berkeley: University of California Press, 1984.

Logan, Joshua. *Movie Stars, Real People, and Me.* New York: Delacorte, 1978.

Madsen, Axel. *William Wyler.* New York: Crowell, 1973.

Magriel, Paul. *Isadora Duncan.* New York: Holt, 1947.

Mantle, Burns. *The Best Plays of 1927–1928.* New York: Dodd, Mead, 1928.

Marx, Samuel. *Mayer and Thalberg.* Hollywood: Samuel French, 1988.

Maugham, W. Somerset. *The Letter.* London: Pan, 1980.

———. *Of Human Bondage.* New York: Penguin, 1989.

Mazzo, Joseph. *Prime Movers.* New York: Morrow, 1977.

McClintic, Guthrie. *Me and Kit.* Boston: Little, Brown, 1955.

McGilligan, Pat. *Backstory.* Berkeley: University of California Press, 1986.

Merrill, Gary. *Bette, Rita, and the Rest of My Life.* Augusta: Tapley, 1988.

Mordden, Ethan. *The American Theatre.* New York: Oxford University Press, 1981.

———. *The Hollywood Studios.* New York: Knopf, 1988.

———. *Movie Star.* New York: St. Martin, 1983.

Morgan, Anna. *An Hour with Delsarte.* Boston: Lee and Shepard, 1889.

Morgan, Ted. *Maugham.* New York: Simon & Schuster, 1980.

Morin, Edgar. *The Stars.* New York: Evergreen, 1960.

Morley, Sheridan. *Tales from the Hollywood Raj.* New York: Viking, 1983.

Mosley, Roy. *Bette Davis.* New York: Donald Fine, 1990.

Negulesco, Jean. *Things I Did and Things I Think I Did.* New York: Linden, 1984.

Newall, Beaumont. *The History of Photography,* New York: Museum of Modern Art, 1964.

Nickens, Christopher. *Bette Davis.* New York: Doubleday, 1985.

Norman, Dorothy. *Alfred Stieglitz.* New York: Aperture, 1990.

Paopolos, Demitri, and Janice Paopolos. *Overcoming Depression*. New York: Perennial, 1987.

Quirk, Lawrence J. *Fasten Your Seat Belts*. New York: Morrow, 1990.

Rapoport, Judith. *The Boy Who Couldn't Stop Washing*. New York: New American Library, 1990.

Reade, Charles. *Peg Woffington*. London: George Allen, 1899.

Ringgold, Gene. *The Films of Bette Davis*. Secaucus: Citadel, 1985.

Robinson, Jeffrey. *Bette Davis*. New York: Proteus, 1982.

Roddick, Nick. *A New Deal in Entertainment*. London: BFI, 1983.

Rollyson, Carl. *Lillian Hellman*. New York: St. Martin, 1988.

Rosenblum, Naomi. *A World History of Photography*. New York: Abbeville, 1984.

Rourke, Constance. *American Humor*. New York: Doubleday, 1931.

Schatz, Thomas. *The Genius of the System*. New York: Pantheon, 1988.

Shaw, George Bernard. *Major Critical Essays*. New York: Penguin, 1986.

Shawn, Ted. *Every Little Movement*. Princeton: Dance Horizons, 1963.

Shelton, Suzanne. *Ruth St. Denis*. Austin: University of Texas Press, 1981.

Sontag, Susan. *On Photography*, New York: Farrar, Straus & Giroux, 1977.

Spoto, Donald. *The Kindness of Strangers*. New York: Ballantine, 1985.

Stebbins, Genevieve. *Delsarte System of Expression*. New York: Werner, 1902.

Stevenson, Elizabeth. *Babbits and Bohemians*. New York: Macmillan, 1967.

Stine, Whitney. *I'd Love to Kiss You*. New York: Pocket Books, 1990.

———. *Mother Goddam*. New York: Hawthorn, 1974.

Tarkington, Booth. *The Flirt*. New York: Doubleday, 1913.

———. *Seventeen*. New York: Harper, 1932.

Terry, Walter. *Ted Shawn*. New York: Dial, 1976.

Thomas, Bob. *Clown Prince of Hollywood*. New York: McGraw-Hill, 1990.

Vermilye, Jerry. *Bette Davis*. New York: Pyramid, 1973.

Wallis, Hal, and Charles Higham. *Starmaker*. New York: Macmillan, 1980.

Warner, Jack. *My First Hundred Years in Hollywood*. New York: Random House, 1965.

Williams, Dakin, and Shepherd Mead. *Tennessee Williams*. New York: Arbor House, 1983.

Williams, Tennessee. *Collected Stories*. New York: Ballantine, 1986.

———. *Five O'Clock Angel*. New York: Knopf, 1990.

———. *Memoirs*. New York: Bantam, 1976.

———. *Three by Tennessee*. New York: Signet, 1976.

Wood, Audrey, with Max Wilk. *Represented by Audrey Wood*. New York: Doubleday, 1981.

Yurka, Blanche. *Bohemian Girl*. Athens: Ohio University Press, 1970.

Zolotow, Maurice. *Stagestruck*. New York: Harcourt, Brace, 1964.

INDEX

Abbott, George, 64
Academy Awards, 85, 112, 113–15,
    119, 155, 167, 168, 210, 218, 232,
    258, 288–89
Actors Studio, 271, 272, 273, 274
Actors' Theatre Inc., 70, 72
Adams, Maude, 78
Agate, James, 151
Aherne, Brian, 166
Akin, Zoë, 167
Aldrich, Robert, 285, 286, 287, 288,
    289, 295
Alice Adams, 112, 114
All About Eve, 240–46, 248, 252, 254,
    275, 286, 333, 353
Alleborn, Al, 163, 166, 167, 206, 223,
    230
Allen, Jim, 41, 44, 48
All Quiet on the Western Front, 85, 90,
    93
All This and Heaven Too, 178
American Academy of Motion Picture
    Arts and Sciences, 204, 241
    see also Academy Awards
American Film Institute (AFI), 318–20

Anderson, John Murray, 60, 61
Anderson, Judith, 198
Anderson, Lindsay, 344–46
Anderson, Maxwell, 80, 112, 171, 172
Andover Theological Seminary, 15
Angley, Ernest, 336–37
Anna Christie, 85
Anna Karenina, 158
Anniversary, The, 301
Another Man's Poison, 254
Ansley, Charles H., 66, 67, 76, 101,
    110
Arliss, George, 85, 95, 96, 99, 115,
    128, 133
art photography, 22–23
Ashdown Farm, 318, 326, 338
As Summers Die, 341, 354
Astaire, Adele, 58
Astaire, Fred, 58
Atkinson, Brooks, 255
Atlantic Monthly, 26
Aydelotte, Betty Jane, 176

Bacon, Lloyd, 135
Bad Sister, 91, 92–93

Bainter, Fay, 81
Baker, Benny, 66, 67
Ball, Franklyn, 145
Balzac, Honoré de, 32
Banca Comerciale Italiana, 123
Bancroft, Anne, 289
Bankhead, Tallulah, 153, 158, 169, 193, 194, 195, 197, 198–99, 200, 243, 313
Banks, Monty, 124
Barrie, James, 64
Barry, Philip, 158
Barrymore, Ethel, 66, 220
Barrymore, John, 112
Barrymore family, 79
Barthelmess, Katherine Wilson, 61, 254
Barthelmess, Richard, 61, 102, 253–54
Batchelder, Ellen, 25, 35, 40, 93, 97, 98, 99, 100, 121, 268, 269, 331
Bates College, 14
Baxter, Anne, 242, 252, 333
B.D. Inc., 211, 219, 222, 223, 224, 229, 232
Before Breakfast (O'Neill), 68–69
Behrman, Stanley, 255
Beloved Vagabond, The, 122
Bennett, Richard, 79
Benrimo, J. Harry, 65
Bergman, Ingrid, 241
Bergner, Elisabeth, 222, 223, 241
Berkeley, Busby, 151, 152, 153
Bernhardt, Curtis, 223
Berry, Barbara, *see* Davis, Barbara Harriet
Berry, David, 344–45
Berry, David Roscoe, 238
Bersteeg, Gay, 267, 268
Beyond the Forest, 234
Bill of Divorcement, A, 112, 158
Black, Michael, 349
Black Foxe Military Academy, 289
Blair, Mary, 68
Blake, J. Warren, 44, 45, 48, 49, 52, 53, 79
Blanke, Henry, 163, 167
Bloch, Bertram, 62
Bogart, Humphrey, 140
Bordertown, 111–12
Boston Post, 91
Bourke-White, Margaret, 31
Bowden, Charles, 276

Brand, Edward R., 290, 291
Branson, Justice, 127, 129, 130, 131, 132, 133, 138
Breen, Joseph I., 180, 181
Brenner, Dori, 142, 197, 259, 263, 292, 297, 298, 299, 300, 323, 333, 340, 353
Brent, George, 99, 100, 109, 118, 146, 150, 163, 175, 176–77
Bride Came C.O.D., The, 197
Broadway (Dunning and Abbott), 64–65
Broadway theater, 58, 286
Broken Blossoms, 343–44
Broken Dishes (Flavin), 77–78, 79, 97
Brontë, Charlotte, 151
Brontë, Emily, 150, 184
Brook, Clive, 122
Brooks, Richard, 265
Brooks, Van Wyck, 39
Brown, Albert, 228
Brown, Robin (Marie Simpson), 60, 122, 159, 176, 211, 267–68, 333
  background of, 55, 65, 101
  on B.D. Hyman, 297, 326, 331, 332, 339, 340
  Bette's career and, 62, 68, 69, 301
  Bette's friendship with, 55, 56, 80, 117, 147, 174, 175, 177, 178, 185, 225, 247, 253, 265, 266, 269, 274, 293, 300, 330, 334, 342
  career of, 55, 65, 67, 72, 78–79
  marriages of, 78–79, 80, 174, 228, 329
Browne, Lennox, 28
Browning, Elizabeth Barrett, 28
Bruehl, Anton, 31
Budd, Otho W., 247–48, 268
Budd, Ruthie, *see* Davis, Ruthie Favor
Bunny O'Hare, 301
Burlesque, 58
Burnt Offerings, 301
Butternut, 212, 231
Byron, Arthur, Jr. (Bunny), 78–79, 80

Cabin in the Cotton, 101–3, 106, 107, 109, 253
Cagney, James, 87, 117, 120, 126, 318, 359
Campbell, Kathleen, 27
Campbell, Lawton, 79
Camp Mudjekewis, 32–33, 38, 39

Cannes Film Festival, 292, 346, 347
Canning, Alice, 22, 23
Cantor, Eddie, 58
Cape Playhouse, 65, 79
Carey, Harry, Jr., 344, 345
Carpenter, Meta, 197, 205, 207, 209–210, 286
Carrera, Barbara, 351
Carroll, Lewis, 42
Carroll, Madeleine, 122
Casablanca, 216
Case of the Howling Dog, The, 110–11
Cassidy, Claudia, 278
Casuarina Tree, The (Maugham), 180
Catered Affair, The, 265
Cat on a Hot Tin Roof (Williams), 271
Cerilla, Ginny, 322
Chandler, Helen, 95
Channing, Carol, 313
Chatterton, Ruth, 99, 117, 140
Chertok, Jack, 220
Chevalier, Maurice, 122
Children's Hour, The (Hellman), 82
Chotiner, Murray, 290
Christian Broadcasting Network, 336
Cinecittà, 122
Civic Repertory Theatre, 58–59
Claire, Ina, 198
Clarence White School of Photography, 31
Clarke, Thurmond, 165
Clovelly, Cecil, 70, 73
Clymer, John, 94
Coburn, Charles, 65, 67
Cohen, Larry, 348–49, 350, 351
Cohen, Mark, 161
Colbert, Claudette, 58, 241, 245
Colman, Ronald, 78
Colonial House, 321
Colt, Samuel Blythe, 66
Comet over Broadway, 151, 152
Comoro, Hedda, 217
Conn, Carl, 113
Connecting Rooms, 301
Conroy, Frank, 47, 64
Cooper, Gary, 85, 194
Cooper, Gladys, 62, 206
Coquette, 58
Cornell, Katharine, 62, 67, 78, 149, 174, 186, 187, 188, 190, 194, 359
Corn Is Green, The, 220–22, 227, 232, 316

Corsaro, Frank, 8, 270, 279–80
  on Bette's instability, 276–78, 279
  Bette's resentment of, 9, 271, 272, 273, 274, 280, 283, 284
Cousin Bette (Balzac), 32
Covered Wagon, The, 97
Cozens, Maureen, 352
Craddock, Jane (Mlle. Roshanara), 46–47, 48, 70
Crawford, Christina, 326
Crawford, Joan, 98, 285–86, 287, 290, 326
Crestalban, 28–29, 30, 31, 32, 60
Crews, Laura Hope, 65
Crisp, Donald, 148
Cromwell, John, 107, 109
Crosland, Alan, 110–11
Cruze, James, 97
Cukor, George, 64, 65, 66–67, 158, 169
Cummins, Oscar, 158, 171
Currier, Guy, 46
Currier, Marie, 46
Curtiz, Michael, 101, 102, 103, 106, 109, 137, 171
Cushing Academy, 43, 48, 52

Damita, Lili, 154
dance, interpretive, 22, 45–48, 85, 144, 148
Dane, Essex, 62
Dangerous, 112, 113, 114, 147, 167
D'Annunzio, Gabriele, 122
Dark Horse, The, 101, 103
Dark Victory, 157–64, 165, 173, 175, 286
  Judith Traherne character in, 8, 158, 159, 162–64
  stage version of, 153, 158
Davis, Barbara Harriet (Bobby):
  Bette accompanied by, 152, 156, 222, 231, 236, 238, 239, 252, 265, 266
  Bette's career and, 95, 99, 103, 107, 112, 135
  Bette's relationship with, 98, 109, 212, 238–39, 260–61, 268, 290, 300, 318, 327
  birth of, 19, 253
  charity ball organized by, 154
  childhood of, 19–20, 23, 24, 25, 27–28, 29, 31, 32–33, 36, 37–38, 41–42, 47, 55, 57, 59, 63–64, 340

Davis, Barbara Harriet (Bobby) (*cont.*)
  daughter of, 177, 231, 249, 260
  death of, 327, 355
  health of, 38, 92, 93, 300
  marriages of, 121–22, 139, 177, 238
  mental illness of, 25, 55, 92, 99, 100,
    103, 104, 110, 112, 139, 171, 177,
    178, 207, 260–61, 290, 335
  as pianist, 32–33, 38, 47
Davis, Bette:
  Academy Awards and, 112, 113–15,
    119, 155, 167, 168, 218, 232, 258,
    288–89
  acting style of, 61, 69, 75–76, 80,
    102, 109, 186, 196–97, 203, 205,
    217–18, 224–25, 243–45, 272, 316,
    317, 320–21, 346, 358–59
  agents of, 233, 323, 345, 349
  alcohol problems of, 93, 212, 248, 273,
    301, 303, 305, 316, 322, 330, 345
  ambitions of, 51, 52–53, 54–55, 67,
    80, 101, 105, 179
  at auditions, 70, 93–95
  bequests made by, 348
  birth of, 16
  as chain-smoker, 173, 270–71, 307,
    326, 330, 350
  childhood of, 16–54, 340–41
  dance training of, 46–48, 60–61, 102,
    144
  death of, 327, 354–55
  direction resisted by, 196–97, 198–
    199, 202, 205, 206, 215–18, 223,
    233, 234, 320, 345–46
  at drama school, 56, 57, 59–60, 62
  fans of, 8, 217–18, 219, 245, 282
  film persona developed by, 9, 85,
    90–91, 164, 205–6, 231, 232, 245,
    302, 319, 358
  film roles vs. life of, 49–51, 73, 74–
    75, 107, 109, 162, 175, 176, 214,
    243, 251, 325, 333, 353
  finances of, 48, 70, 80, 96, 99, 107,
    112–13, 117, 118–19, 120–21, 123,
    125, 129, 134, 136–37, 138, 156,
    201, 219, 230, 267, 288, 294, 300–
    301, 310, 315, 328–29, 333
  first film of, 90–91
  in foreign films, 122–32, 134, 266–
    267, 295
  friendships of, 35, 40, 93, 97, 207,
    321

  as grandmother, 301, 311, 335–36,
    342
  health problems of, 23, 27, 29–30,
    71–73, 106, 113, 137–39, 146, 152,
    163–64, 170–71, 173–75, 200, 206,
    220, 248, 255–56, 284, 316, 317,
    329–31, 332, 333, 334–35, 338,
    348, 350, 353–54
  Hollywood contracts of, 70, 80, 96,
    99, 102, 112–13, 117–21, 123–25,
    129, 156, 219, 232, 233–34, 288
  imitations of, 312, 313
  loneliness of, 300, 317–18, 321, 322,
    334, 341, 342, 349, 352
  love affairs of, 142, 146–47, 150, 152,
    154–57, 160–62, 163, 176, 178,
    184, 185, 200, 209–10, 217, 220–
    221, 222, 225, 242, 243, 247–49,
    250, 273, 275, 300, 308–10,
    323–26
  marriages of, *see* Farnsworth, Arthur
    Austin; Merrill, Gary; Nelson,
    Harmon Oscar, Jr.; Sherry,
    William Grant
  memoirs of, 33, 49, 59, 255, 334,
    347, 348
  as mother, 231, 236, 246–47, 252–53,
    254, 258, 259–64, 267–68, 269,
    289–94, 296–98, 299–300, 301–2,
    308, 309, 310–11, 316, 317, 318,
    321, 326–27, 335, 338, 339–42,
    353, 355, 356, 357–58
  as mother-in-law, 296, 326, 327,
    336
  name of, 16, 32
  obsessiveness of, 21–22, 30–31, 64,
    98, 140, 141, 258, 266, 277–78,
    298, 304, 323, 352
  physical appearance of, 35, 46, 55,
    63, 69, 80, 88–89, 93, 94–95, 96,
    97–98, 135, 145–46, 152, 155, 172,
    273, 282, 302, 318–19, 329, 330–
    331, 332, 338, 348, 349–50, 351–
    52, 353–54
  pregnancies of, 108, 150, 151, 184,
    185–86, 187, 188, 229, 230–31
  as producer, 211, 219, 222–24, 229,
    232, 233
  professional rivalries and, 112, 113–
    114, 168–69, 174, 194–95, 198–
    200, 243, 273, 289, 343–44, 346–47
  publicity on, 96, 116, 117, 122, 124–

126, 134–35, 139, 152, 192–93, 278, 286, 346–48
reviews of, 69, 76–77, 91, 111, 278, 283, 346
in school plays, 28–29, 52, 62, 63
screen tests of, 78, 79, 93–95
stage work of, 7–9, 62–80, 255, 256, 270–84, 302, 316–17
strong characters preferred by, 62, 80, 232, 245, 358
studio conflicts of, 9, 109, 110–11, 113–14, 116–37, 138, 151–53, 173–178, 192, 207–9, 229–30, 233, 234, 287–88, 359
television roles of, 301, 320–21, 328–329, 332–33, 335, 338–39, 341
temperament of, 66, 73, 89, 93, 96–07, 98, 100, 109–10, 140, 206, 209, 220–21, 223–24, 230, 234, 235–40, 252, 274, 283–84, 285, 322, 331, 344, 345, 349, 359
unreliability of, 229–30, 276–77, 316–17, 319
voice of, 60
youthful romances of, 30–31, 38–41, 42, 43–45, 48–49, 52, 53–54, 56–57, 60, 61, 66, 67, 76, 78, 79, 98, 100–101
Davis, Edward, 14
Davis, Eliza, 14, 16, 18
Davis, Harlow Morrell:
Bette's career and, 52–53, 54–55, 56, 69, 70–71, 74–76
death of, 147, 269
education of, 14, 15, 16, 17, 18, 20
as father, 16, 17, 18–21, 23, 36, 37, 39, 49, 51–53, 54–55, 56, 71, 74, 251, 253
first marriage of, 15–17, 21, 24, 25–27, 37, 50, 52, 100, 104, 117, 147, 155, 251, 341
second marriage of, 25, 34, 55, 117, 147, 160
Davis, Mildred Favor, 13, 18, 24, 25, 33, 34, 59, 104, 109
Davis, Minnie Stewart, 25, 34, 55, 117, 147, 251
Davis, Myron, 24, 25, 34
Davis, Owen, 142
Davis, Ruthie Favor, 11–14, 33–34, 79, 109, 175, 211, 292
Bette's career and, 9, 30, 32, 46, 47–
48, 54–60, 62, 63, 64–66, 68, 69, 72–74, 76, 77–78, 80, 88–90, 93, 95–96, 97, 101, 103, 108, 114, 115, 121, 122, 127, 132, 133, 134, 139, 152, 171, 201, 332, 336, 352, 358, 359
Bette's romantic relationships and, 40–41, 42, 56–57, 60, 76, 98, 103–4, 110, 127, 155, 156, 227, 229, 297
Bobby Davis's emotional problems and, 25, 55, 92, 93, 99, 100, 103, 104, 178, 268
death of, 9, 268–69, 290, 327, 355
Delsarte studied by, 11–12, 22, 23, 77–78
divorce of, 25–27, 36, 37, 340–41
emotional problems of, 21, 22, 23, 24, 71, 335
financial issues and, 27, 31, 43, 46, 49, 53, 54, 59, 60, 107
first marriage of, 15–17, 21, 24, 25–27, 34, 50, 51, 52, 100, 104, 117, 147, 155, 251, 253, 340–41
grandchildren of, 177, 262, 268
health of, 28, 33
homes chosen by, 71–73, 98–99, 107, 191–92, 231, 265, 268, 321
later marriages of, 100, 225–26, 231, 247–48, 268
as photographer, 22–23, 31–32, 35, 36, 37, 38, 42, 43, 45, 46, 49, 50, 53–54, 89, 101, 141, 191–92, 226, 231, 254
physical appearance of, 53–54
religious beliefs of, 13, 139
as seamstress, 37, 39, 54, 97
as working mother, 28, 29, 31, 33, 36, 43, 45, 49, 50, 53–54, 59, 60
as young mother, 16–27
Days of Wine and Roses, 289
Dead Pigeon, The, 288
Dead Ringer, 288, 295
Deauville Film Festival, 346, 348
Deception, 229, 230, 232
DeGuzman, Michael, 341
Delsarte, François, 12, 83, 148, 149, 151
Delsarte system, 11–12, 22, 23, 28, 32, 45, 46, 47, 77–78, 85, 144, 148, 149
Denby, Edwin, 61

Denton, Hall and Burgin, 126, 132, 133, 134, 136–37
Design for Living, 169
Desire Under the Elms (O'Neill), 94
Dewey, Thomas E., 135
Dickinson, Dorrel, 201–2
Dictator, The, 122
Dieterle, William, 108, 113, 148, 150, 163, 166, 167
Dietrich, Marlene, 85
Disraeli, 85, 96, 115
Divorcee, The, 85
Donovan, Maggie, 195
Driving Miss Daisy, 349
Dunham, George J. (Gige), 39, 40, 41, 43, 44, 48, 80
Dunning, Philip, 64

Eagels, Jeanne, 113, 181
Ealing Studios, 124
Earth Between, The, 63, 64, 65, 67–69, 70, 76, 94, 101
Ebenstein, Morris, 126
Eddy, Mary Baker, 139
Edelman, Lou, 135
Einfeld, S. Charles, 182, 192
Elizabeth the Queen (Anderson), 80, 169, 170, 171, 172–73, 195
Elliott, Maxine, 78
Ellis, Francis C., 226
Elwell, Helen, 36
Emmy Awards, 320
Empty Canvas, The, 295
Entwistle, Peg, 49, 50, 51, 105–6
Epstein, Julius, 216, 218, 320
Epstein, Philip, 216
Ervine, St. John, 69
Espy, Reeves, 195, 201
Excess Baggage, 65, 67

Fairbanks, Douglas, Jr., 98
Family Reunion, 335, 357
Famous Mrs. Fair, The, 63
Farnsworth, Arthur Austin, 266
  Bette's career and, 177, 185, 192–93, 201
  Bette's relationship with, 176, 177, 178, 192–93, 210, 211–12, 213, 214
  death of, 210–14, 308
Farrell, Charles, 99, 104
Favor, (Harriet) Eugenia, 26, 33, 77–78

domineering personality of, 13, 18, 27, 292, 332
evangelical commitment of, 13, 336, 358
as grandmother, 17, 19, 22–23, 24, 27, 30
Ruthie Davis's marriage and, 14, 15, 24, 226
Favor, Gail, 69
Favor, Mildred, *see* Davis, Mildred Favor
Favor, Paul, 13, 14, 15, 28, 59, 68, 69, 226
Favor, Richard, 13, 15, 18, 24
Favor, Ruthie, *see* Davis, Ruthie Favor
Favor, William Aaron, 13, 18, 24
Feathered Serpent, The (Wallace), 95
Félix, Elizabeth (Rachel), 151, 152
Fellows, Bob, 143, 145, 148
Film Society of Lincoln Center, 352
Finkel, Abem, 142
Fisher, James, 241
Fiske, Minnie Maddern, 78
Fitts, Margaret (Miggie), 36, 38–39, 40, 42, 49
Fitzgerald, F. Scott, 41, 86, 122, 175
Fitzgerald, Geraldine, 149, 157–58, 162, 175
Flannagan, James A., 165
Flavin, Martin, 77, 78
Flesh and the Devil, 87
Flirt, The (Tarkington), 90
Flynn, Errol, 171, 172, 173
Fog Over Frisco, 108
Fonda, Frances, 143
Fonda, Henry, 143, 146
Fontanne, Lynn, 62, 63, 67, 80, 169, 171, 172–73, 174, 194–95, 359
Ford, John, 112, 114, 318, 345
Fox, Sidney, 88, 90, 91
Francis, Kay, 117, 158, 165–66
Freedman, Dave, 210
Free Will Baptists, 11, 12, 14, 15
Freund, Karl, 92–93
Front Page Woman, 112
Fuller, Loie, 47
Funny Face, 58
Furse, Dudley, 119, 120, 137, 152, 199, 201, 202, 210, 211, 213, 237

Gang, Martin, 112, 113, 116, 117, 118, 119

Garbo, Greta, 85, 86–87, 107, 158, 174, 305
Garden District (Williams), 271
Garden of the Moon, 153
Gardner, Robert, 237
Garland, Robert, 158
Garson, Greer, 210
Gas, Air and Earl (Bloch), 62
Gaudio, Tony, 182, 185, 186, 187
Gaumont-British, 126
Gaynor, Janet, 88, 99
Geddes, Virgil, 63, 67–68, 69, 72
Genthner, Myrtis, 32
Gielgud, Sir John, 218
Gilpin, Laura, 31
Girl from Tenth Avenue, The, 112
Gish, Lillian, 86, 87, 343–44, 345, 346–47
Glass Menagerie, The (Williams), 271, 272
Globe, 23
God's Country and the Woman, 118, 119
Golden Arrow, The, 114, 116, 117, 118
Goldwyn, Samuel, 78, 142, 182
   Little Foxes produced by, 193, 194, 195, 199, 201, 202
   Wuthering Heights produced by, 150, 181, 184
Gone With the Wind, 142, 177
Good Hope, The (Heijermans), 58
Goodman, J. L., 104
Gordon, Ruth, 62, 79, 169
Goulding, Edmund, 137, 142, 180, 209, 240–41
   Dark Victory directed by, 157, 158, 159, 161, 162–63, 164
   Old Maid directed by, 167, 168–69, 170
Graham, George Greenfield, 61
Graham, Martha, 60–61, 63, 67, 102, 187
Grant, H. M., 41
Great Lie, The, 192, 193
Greed, 86
Green, Alfred E., 99, 101, 109, 113, 114
Green, Paul, 102
Greenfield, Vik, 252, 296, 300, 302
   on B.D. Hyman, 293, 297–98, 308, 316, 337, 339, 341, 353, 357
   as Bette's companion, 299, 300, 301,

303, 314, 315–16, 317–18, 322, 339
   at Mae West dinner, 303, 304, 305, 307, 308, 311, 314
Greenwich Village Follies, 61
Griffith, D. W., 112, 114, 343–44
Guardsman, The, 172–73
Guinness, Alec, 266
Gunsmoke, 295

Hacker, Frederick, 238, 240
Hall, Alice, 78
Hall, Francis Lewis (Fritz), 56–57, 60, 61, 66, 76, 78, 79, 253–54
Hall, Gladys, 252
Haller, Ernest, 143, 144
Hammett, Dashiell, 113
Hammond, Percy, 158
Hammond, Tom, 288
Happy Returns (Dane), 62
Hart, Moss, 204
Hastings, Sir Patrick, 128, 129–31, 132
Hayes, Helen, 58, 338
Hayward, Leland, 180
Hayward, Susan, 241
Hayworth, Rita, 269, 291
Hazelton, George C., 65
Heaven (Moody), 42
Hecht, Ben, 150, 184
Hedda Gabler (Ibsen), 72, 75
Heijermans, Herman, 58
Heisler, Stuart, 254
Hell House, 93
Hellman, Lillian, 82, 193, 195, 196, 197, 198, 199, 200, 202, 209
Hello Mother Goodbye, 301
Henley, Hobart, 91
Hepburn, Katharine, 112, 155, 174, 289, 319
   Academy Awards and, 112, 113–14, 289
   stage roles declined by, 272, 316
Herskowitz, Michael, 334
Hiller, Wendy, 167
Hodiak, John, 252
Hoeber, Arthur, 23
Hollywood Canteen, 208
Hollywood Hotel, 138
Honeysuckle Hill, 288, 289, 290
Hopkins, Arthur, 79
Hopkins, Elizabeth, 27

Hopkins, Miriam, 140, 142, 167, 168, 169
Hopper, Hedda, 286, 288
Hornblow, Arthur, 59, 62
Hornblow, Arthur, Jr., 78
Hotel, 328–29, 332–33, 338
House Divided, A (Clymer-Van Every), 94–95
Housewife, 109, 110, 129
Howard, Leslie, 108
Hudson, Rock, 329
Hughes, Howard, 154, 155, 156, 157, 160–61, 162, 326
Hush . . . Hush, Sweet Charlotte, 295
Huston, John, 94, 142, 161, 166, 204
Huston, Lesley, 161
Huston, Walter, 94, 161
Hyman, Ashley, 301, 327, 335–37, 342, 357
Hyman, Barbara Davis Sherry (B.D.):
  Bette's relationship with, 264, 268, 289–90, 292–94, 296, 297–98, 308, 316, 317, 318, 321, 326–27, 329, 331–43, 353, 355, 356, 357–58
  birth of, 231
  as born-again Christian, 336, 337, 338, 357, 358
  childhood of, 235, 236, 242, 246–47, 248, 249, 251, 252, 253, 254, 258, 259–60, 262, 263–64, 265, 267, 269, 335
  in films, 289, 290–91
  on Gary Merrill, 259, 263–64, 265, 266, 267, 269, 356
  health problems of, 318, 327, 335, 336, 337, 357
  homes of, 296, 318, 338, 341–42
  on Kathryn Sermak, 323, 334, 353
  on Margot Merrill, 299, 302
  marriage of, 292–94, 296–97, 318, 326–27, 329
  memoirs of, 331–32, 334–35, 337–43, 348, 357
  as mother, 301, 321, 327, 335–37, 342, 357
Hyman, Elliott, 287, 292
Hyman, Jeremy, 292, 293–94, 296–97, 318, 326, 329, 338, 341–42
  B.D. Hyman's memoirs and, 335, 342
  Bette's resentment of, 296–97, 301, 326, 327, 337

Hyman, Justin, 321, 327
Hyman, Mary, 357

I Am a Fugitive from a Chain Gang, 111
Ibsen, Henrik, 49–50, 69–70, 72, 73, 74, 107
ICM, 349
If . . . , 344
I'll Take the Low Road, 123, 124, 126, 127, 129–30, 134
I'm No Angel, 311
In This Our Life, 204
Italy, film industry in, 122–23
It Never Rains, 88
It's Love I'm After, 137

Jacobson, Max, 255, 273, 274, 281
Jazz Singer, The, 88
Jezebel, 8, 140–50, 159, 222, 286, 358
  Academy Award for, 155, 167
  Bette's gestural expressiveness in, 47, 81–85, 143–45, 148–49, 164, 168, 186
  Bette's life vs. role in, 162, 325
  casting of, 142, 169
  fitting room sequence in, 81–82, 83–85
  shooting schedule for, 143, 145, 146, 147–48, 150, 151
  Wyler's direction of, 47, 81–85, 139, 140–50, 168, 169, 173, 182, 184, 196
John Murray Anderson—Robert Milton School of Theatre and Dance, 60, 61, 62, 71, 78
John Paul Jones, 267
Jolson, Al, 88
Jowitt, Sir William, 128, 130, 131, 132, 134
Juarez, 163, 165, 166–67, 168, 173
Judge and Jake Wyler, The, 301
June Bride, 232

Kaplan, Mike, 343, 344, 345, 346
Katselas, Milton, 320–21
Kaufman, George S., 204
Keighley, William, 118, 204
Kelly, Patrick, 347, 348
Keyes, Homer, 212–13
Kid Galahad, 137
Kinnell, Murray, 95

Knight and the Lady, The, 171
Koch, Howard, 182, 183, 190
Kohner, Lupita, 161
Kohner, Paul, 161
Kondolf, George B., Jr., 65, 66, 67
Koops, Doris, 49
Koops, Virginia (Sister), 36, 37, 39, 40, 42, 49, 50, 51–52
Korda, Alexander, 126, 130
Koster, Henry, 265

Lady from the Sea, The (Ibsen), 72, 73, 75
Laemmle, Carl, 82, 88
Laemmle, Carl, Jr., 88, 90, 92, 93, 95, 101
Laff That Off, 67
Landsman, Stephanie, 296, 297, 323, 330, 331, 333
Lang, Fritz, 92
Lange, Dorothea, 31
Last Laugh, The, 92
Last Tycoon, The (Fitzgerald), 86
Laughton, Marie Ware, 46
Laurence, Paula, 276, 285
Lawrence, Gertrude, 241
Leeds, Barbara, 248, 251–52
Le Gallienne, Eva, 58–59, 76
Leigh, Vivien, 177
Leighton, Margaret, 270, 271, 277
   audience response to, 276, 282
   Bette's resentment of, 273, 274, 275–276, 278, 280, 284, 286
LeMaire, Rufus, 95
LeRoy, Mervyn, 106
Letter, The (film), 8, 179–91, 286, 320, 358
   Bette's life vs. role in, 214
   casting of, 178, 179–80
   shooting of, 185–89, 193, 196, 320
   Wyler's direction of, 178, 179–90, 196, 320
Letter, The (Maugham) (play), 62, 179, 180, 181, 184, 186–90, 194
"Letter, The" (Maugham) (short story), 179, 180–81, 187
Letterman, David, 348
Levee, Mike, 110, 117, 118, 121
Lewis, Ralph, 119
Light, James, 62–63, 65, 67, 68, 69
Lindbergh, Charles, 56
Little Caesar, 87

Little Foxes, The (film), 193–203, 220
   Bankhead's stage performance and, 194–95, 197, 198–99, 200
   Bette's life vs. role in, 214
   loan-out deal for, 193–94, 201
   shooting of, 199–203, 205, 281, 286, 345–46
   Wyler's direction of, 193, 195–203, 205, 281, 345–46, 359
Little Foxes, The (Hellman) (play), 193, 194–95, 197, 198–99, 200
Litvak, Anatole, 153, 178, 185, 192
Lloyd's of London, 201
Lochland School, 262
Logan, Joshua, 316, 317
Lombard, Carole, 111
London Film Productions, 130
Lonely Life, The (Davis), 33, 49, 59, 255
Long Day's Journey into Night, 289
Look Homeward, Angel (Wolfe), 25
Lord, Pauline, 62, 79
Lord, Robert, 111, 112, 170–71, 182, 188, 189
Lost Sheep, 88
Lubitsch, Ernst, 169
Luciano, Charles (Lucky), 135, 136
Lunt, Alfred, 63, 171, 172, 173
Lynch, George, 147

MacArthur, Charles, 150, 184
MacDowell Colony, 46
MacEwen, Walter, 142, 158, 181, 182
MacKenzie, Aeneas, 166
Madame Sin, 301
Magic Slipper, The, 48
Maltese Falcon, The (Hammett), 113
Mankiewicz, Joseph, 240–41, 243, 244, 245, 254
Man Who Came to Dinner, The, 204
Man Who Played God, The, 95–96, 128
Mariarden arts colony, 45–48, 64, 70, 79, 148
Marie Antoinette, 167
Marked Woman, 135–36, 137
Martin, Mary, 316
Mary of Scotland, 112, 113, 114
Mattison, Frank, 216, 217, 218
Maugham, W. Somerset, 62, 107, 108, 109, 178, 179, 180–81, 184, 187, 188, 189–90
Mayer, Louis B., 87

Mayo, Archie, 111, 112, 113, 137
MCA, 208, 233
Menace, The, 93, 95
Merlo, Frank, 281
Merrill, Barbara Leeds, 248, 251–52
Merrill, Chou Chou Raum, 315
Merrill, Gary:
  alcohol problems of, 248, 258, 261,
    263, 266, 269, 273, 284, 290, 291
  Bette's affair with, 242, 243, 247–49,
    250
  Bette's marriage to, 248, 251–52,
    254, 255, 258–59, 262, 263, 264,
    265, 266, 267–68, 269, 273, 288,
    343
  career of, 239, 241, 257, 264
  death of, 356
  as father, 253, 254, 258, 259, 261,
    262–64, 266, 290–91, 296, 302,
    356
  violent behavior of, 257–58, 259,
    263–65, 266, 267–68, 269, 273,
    281, 290, 335, 338
Merrill, Jerry, 254, 259, 265, 267
Merrill, Margot:
  adoption of, 253, 254
  Bette's rejection of, 263, 268, 299–
    300, 302
  custody of, 269, 290, 356
  mental illness of, 258, 261–63, 301–2
Merrill, Michael Woodman, 310, 315,
    356
  adoption of, 258
  career of, 348
  childhood of, 25, 259–60, 261, 262,
    264, 266, 269, 290–91
  education of, 289, 296, 300, 315
Metro-Goldwyn-Mayer (MGM), 85,
    86–87, 351
Metropolis, 92
Mexico, Red Cross in, 208–9, 210
Midsummer Night's Dream, A (Shake-
    speare), 47–48, 58, 70
Milliken, Carl, 90
Milne, A. A., 65
Miracle Worker, The, 289
Miss Bennett's, 29, 30, 31
Miss Moffat, 316–17
Molnár, Ferenc, 172
Mommie Dearest (Crawford), 326
Moody, Dwight Lyman, 42
Moore, Paul, 201, 202, 211, 213

Morning Glory, 112
Morocco, 85
Morris, Gouverneur, 96
Mountain Justice, 118
Mr. Pim Passes By (Milne), 65
Mrs. Johnson's Tea Room, 56
Mr. Skeffington, 211, 215–18, 219, 232
Mrs. Miniver, 210
Mulberry Bush, The, 58
Muni, Paul, 111, 117, 163, 166–67, 168
Murder with Mirrors, 338–39
Murnau, F. W., 92
Mussolini, Benito, 122, 132
My Bailiwick, 315
My Mother's Keeper (Hyman), 331–32,
    334–35, 337–43, 348, 357

Nanny, The, 295, 296
Narrow Is the Way (Hyman), 342
Nazimova, Alla, 79
Negulesco, Jean, 152, 254
Nelson, Ann, 325–26
Nelson, Harmon Oscar, Jr. (Ham):
  Bette's career and, 110, 113, 114,
    122, 125, 127, 133, 137, 139, 165
  Bette's marriage to, 103–4, 107, 108,
    109–10, 147, 152, 153–54, 155–56,
    159–61, 162, 163, 165, 192, 207,
    229, 325–26
  death of, 326
  employment of, 79, 106–7, 122, 127,
    153, 165, 308
  family of, 53, 54
  as singer, 52, 53
Nelson, Lois, 53
Newton, Teddy, 159, 160, 174
New York Herald Tribune, 158
New York Times, 91, 111
New York World Telegram, 158, 198,
    205
Night of the Iguana, The (Williams),
    270–285, 292, 316
  Bette's departure from, 283–84, 349
  on Broadway, 7, 8–9, 275, 282–85
  in out-of-town tryouts, 275–82
  publicity on, 275, 276, 278, 280, 286
  rehearsals for, 270–71, 274
Ninotchka, 174
Northfield Seminary for Young Ladies,
    42, 43
Now, Voyager, 8, 204–7, 209, 210,
    224–25, 290, 306–7

Oberon, Merle, 150, 180, 184
O'Brien, Pat, 126
Obringer, Roy, 158, 167–68
    Bette's absences and, 175, 177, 201
    in contract negotiations, 114, 117,
        118, 119, 120–21, 156, 157, 180,
        194, 207, 208, 234
    English litigation and, 129, 137, 138
    loan-out refused by, 112, 113, 126
Of Human Bondage, 8, 107–11, 112,
    117, 190, 286
    Academy Awards and, 113, 114, 167
    Bette's abortion and, 108, 229
Old Acquaintance, 208, 209–10
Old Maid, The, 167–70, 171, 173
Olivier, Laurence, 156
O Lucky Man!, 344
O'Neal, Patrick, 8, 9, 282–83
    Bette's resentment of, 273, 274, 275,
        276, 278–79, 283–84, 286
    in rehearsal, 270, 271, 274
    on women's roles, 272, 280, 282
O'Neill, Eugene, 63, 69, 94, 289
Orphans of the Storm, 344
Orpheus Descending (Williams), 271
Orr, Mary, 241
Orry-Kelly, 195
Out-Door Players, 46
Outerbridge, Paul, 31

Page, Geraldine, 289
Palmer, Robert Woodbury, 100, 225–
    226, 231
Palmer, Ruthie, *see* Davis, Ruthie
    Favor
Paramount Studio, 78, 85, 181
Parker, Jean, 155
Parlow, Michael, 291
Parsons, Louella, 192
Payment on Demand, 237, 239, 241,
    242, 254
Peckett's Inn, 175, 176
Pelgram, Barbara, *see* Davis, Barbara
    Harriet
Pelgram, Charlie, 121
Pelgram, "Little" Bobby, 121–22, 177,
    238
Pelgram, Ruth Favor (Fay), 177, 231,
    249, 260
Period of Adjustment (Williams), 271
Perkins, R. W., 129, 136, 137
Petrified Forest, The, 113

Phone Call from a Stranger, 254
photography, art, 22–23
Photo-Secession, 22
Piano for Mrs. Cimino, A, 320, 328
Picasso, Pablo, 23
Pickford, Mary, 154
Play with Music, A, 67
Plottel, Joseph, 125
Pollock, Charles, 292, 319, 323, 326,
    328, 333–34
    on B.D. Hyman, 290, 296, 326, 340,
        357
    on Bette's compulsive behavior, 298
    as Bette's escort, 320, 321
    at Mae West dinner, 303, 304, 305,
        306, 307, 311, 314
Pollock, Gordon, 89
Pomeroy, Charles A., 267, 268
Porter, Ethnan, 11–12
Porter, Sadie, 11, 12, 13, 14, 28
Price, Vincent, 344
Prince of India (Wallace), 11, 13
*Private Lives of Elizabeth and Essex,
    The*, 171–73, 174
Production Code Administration, 180,
    181, 186
Proudlock, Ethel Mabel, 180–81
Prouty, Olive Higgins, 306
Provincetown Playhouse, 63, 67, 70–71
Public Enemy, 87
Pygmalion, 167

Quality Street (Barrie), 64

Rachel (Elizabeth Félix), 151, 152
Raffles, 78
Rains, Claude, 207, 210
Rapper, Irving, 204–5, 206, 209, 220,
    221, 229, 254
Raum, Chou Chou, 315
Red Cross, 208–9, 210
Redgrave, Michael, 301
Reinhardt, Max, 58
Reinhardt, Wolfgang, 166
Remarque, Erich Maria, 90
Remick, Lee, 289
Repertory Theatre of Boston, 49
Richards, Marion, 235, 237–39, 242,
    246, 249–52, 301
Rich Are Always with Us, The, 99
Right of Way, 320, 328, 329
Riley, Alice C. D., 62

Riley, Lewis A., 221, 222, 223, 225
Ripley, Clements, 142
Riverbottom, 191–92, 212
Rivers, Joan, 348
RKO, 107–8, 111, 112, 113, 114, 237, 241, 242
Robbins, Harold, 294
Robert Lantz Agency, 323, 349
Robertson, Pat, 336
Robinson, Casey, 153, 158, 159, 167, 168, 169, 170
Robinson, Edward G., 87, 117
Rockwell-O'Keefe, 153, 156
Rogers, Anna A., 26
Roosevelt, Franklin, 208
Roosevelt, Theodore, 20
Rosenberg, Marion, 322–23, 326–27, 344, 345, 348, 349
Rosenberg, Rick, 341, 354
Roshanara, Mlle. (Jane Craddock), 46–47, 48, 70
Ross, Bob, 164
Rubber, Violla, 272

St. Denis, Ruth, 22, 46, 61, 144
St. Just, Maria, 283
St. Mary's School, 60, 64
Sanders, George, 242
Satan Met a Lady, 113
Scapegoat, The, 266
Scarface, 111
Schaefer, George, 320
Science and Health with Key to the Scriptures (Eddy), 139
Scientific Card Player, 301
Screen Actors Guild, 153
script approval, 87, 109
Seager, Duck, 43
Seastrom, Victor, 86
Seed, 93, 97
Selznick, David, 142, 158, 177
Sergeant York, 194
Sermak, Kathryn:
  bequest made to, 348
  as Bette's companion, 322–23, 329, 330, 331, 333–34, 347–48, 349–50, 352–55
  in Paris, 330, 342, 347
Seven Arts, 287, 292, 293
700 Club, 336
Seventeen (Tarkington), 38, 39, 40, 52
Seventh Heaven, 99

Shannon, Peggy, 293, 294, 327, 332, 333, 353
  on B.D. Hyman, 327, 329, 335, 341
  as Bette's companion, 321, 322, 334
Shaw, George Bernard, 49–50
Shawn, Ted, 46, 61, 102, 148
Shearer, Norma, 85, 154, 167
Sherman, Hedda Comoro, 217
Sherman, Vincent, 141
  Bette's affair with, 209–10, 212, 217, 221
  Mr. Skeffington directed by, 215–18
Sherry, Barbara Davis, *see* Hyman, Barbara Davis Sherry
Sherry, Marion Richards, 235, 237–39, 242, 246, 249–52, 301
Sherry, Skippy, 230
Sherry, William Grant, 230
  Bette's marriage to, 225, 226–29, 235–40, 241, 242, 246–49, 252, 259
  as father, 231, 246–47, 249, 251, 301, 308
  second marriage of, 249–52
  violent temper of, 227, 235–40
Sherwood, Robert, 113
Shumlin, Herman, 198, 209
Silhouette Shop, 46
Simpson, Marie, *see* Brown, Robin
Sisters, The, 153, 173
Skirball, Jack, 237
So Big, 99
Solid South (Campbell), 79
Sothern, Ann, 344, 345, 347
Special Agent, 112
Spelling, Aaron, 328–29, 333
Stacey, Eric, 220, 221
Stahl, John, 93, 97
Standard Steel Motor Car Company, 39, 40
Stanwyck, Barbara, 58, 99
Star, The, 254
Steel Magnolias, 349
Stein, Jules, 208, 233
Stephenson, James, 187, 188
Stevenson, Robert, 181, 182–83, 190
Steward, William Crozier, 180–81
Stewart, James, 320
Stewart, Minnie, *see* Davis, Minnie Stewart
Stieglitz, Alfred, 22, 23
Stine, Whitney, 324
Stolen Life, A, 222–25, 229, 232

Storm Center, 233, 265
Strange Interlude (O'Neill), 63
Strangers, 320–21, 328, 354
Streetcar Named Desire, A (Williams), 271, 272
Strictly Dishonorable (Sturges), 79, 80, 88, 94
Sturges, Preston, 79
Sullavan, Margaret, 140, 150, 167
Sullivan, Barry, 239–40
Summerville, Slim, 93
Sweet Bird of Youth (film), 289
Sweet Bird of Youth (Williams), 271

Tailwagger's Club, 154–55
Taplinger, Bob, 178, 185, 192
Taradash, Daniel, 265
Tarkington, Booth, 38, 40, 41, 52, 90, 112
Taylor, Laurette, 62, 79
Temple Players, 65–67
Terry, Ellen, 63
Thalberg, Irving, 86, 174
That Certain Woman, 137
Theatre, 59
Their Anniversary (Riley), 62
These Three, 82, 169
This 'N That (Davis and Herskowitz), 334, 347, 348
This Side of Paradise (Fitzgerald), 41
This Sporting Life, 344
Thompson, Harriet Keyes, 13
Three Comrades, 167
Three on a Match, 106
Toeplitz, Ludovico, 122–28, 130, 132, 133
Toeplitz Productions, 122, 126, 130
Toland, Gregg, 82, 202
Tracy, Spencer, 106
Trenholme, Helen, 111
Trouble in Paradise, 169
Turney, Catherine, 224
Twelve O'Clock High, 239
Twentieth Century-Fox, 241
20,000 Years in Sing Sing, 106
Twin Bridges, 296, 315
Two-Faced Woman, 174
"291," 23
Two's Company, 255, 256, 316

Ulmann, Doris, 31
United Shoe Machinery, 20, 21

Universal City, 88
Universal Pictures, 82
Universal Studios, 79–80, 89, 90, 92–93, 94, 95, 96, 97, 177

Van Every, Dale, 94
Velez, Lupe, 155
Vidor, King, 234
Virgin Queen, The, 265
von Sternberg, Josef, 85
von Stroheim, Erich, 86

Wagner, Robert, 329
Wallace, Edgar, 95
Wallace, Lew, 11
Wallis, Hal, 137, 158
  Bette's health problems noted by, 135, 152, 201
  Bordertown produced by, 112
  in contract disputes, 118, 120, 121, 177, 201
  Jezebel produced by, 142, 143–44, 146, 147–48, 150
  Letter filming and, 180, 181, 182, 188
  Now, Voyager produced by, 206, 207
  roles assigned by, 135, 151, 153, 162–63, 167, 172
Walsh, Raoul, 233
War Bond Drive, 207–8
Warner, Ann, 152, 161
Warner, Jack, 87, 101, 103, 110, 161, 203
  agents' negotiations with, 232–33
  Bette placated by, 203, 209, 210, 215, 216–17, 218–19, 221, 222, 223, 224, 229, 230
  Bette's conflicts with, 110, 116–21, 122, 123–35, 136–37, 138, 173–78, 192, 207–9, 233, 234, 287–88
  on Bette's husbands, 192–93, 210, 212, 229
  loan-outs and, 108, 112, 113–14, 124, 181, 193–94, 200–201
  roles assigned by, 111, 114, 151–52
  star billing controlled by, 171, 194, 195
Warner Bros.:
  Academy Awards and, 85, 115, 119
  Baby Jane distributed by, 288
  Bette's conflicts with, 109, 110–11, 113, 123–37, 151–53, 229–30, 359

Warner Bros. (*cont.*)
  Bette's departure from, 234, 254,
    359
  contracts negotiated by, 87, 95–96,
    102, 103, 109, 112–13, 116–21,
    123–25, 138, 156, 157, 173–76,
    219–20, 233–34
  films produced by, 101, 106, 166,
    181–82
  independent productions for, 206,
    211, 218–19, 232
  Jezebel produced by, 81, 140, 141,
    142, 143, 146, 148
  loan-outs made by, 108, 111, 193–94,
    201
  male stars at, 87, 96, 106, 166
  plot sources used by, 135
  production style of, 99, 143, 173–74
  publicity efforts of, 96, 192–93
Warner Bros. v. *Nelson*, 127–32
Warrior's Husband, The, 112
Wasserman, Lew, 233
Watcher in the Woods, 322
Watch on the Rhine (Hellman), 209
Waterloo Bridge, 93
Watkins, Linda, 70
Way Back Home, 93
Way Down East, 344
Welles, Orson, 157, 318, 359
Wellman, William, 99
Werner, David, 79–80, 88, 90
West, Mae, 58, 303–14
West, Nathanael, 175
Westmore, Perc, 172, 195, 207
Whale, James, 93
Whales of August, The, 343–47, 348
Wharton, Edith, 167, 232
What Ever Happened to Baby Jane?,
    285–90, 292, 349
Where Love Has Gone, 294, 295
White, Clarence, 22, 23, 31
Whiting, Margery, 29, 60
"Why Marriages Fail" (Rogers), 26
Wicked Age, The, 58
Wicked Stepmother, 348–52
Wild Duck, The (Ibsen):
  Bette's performance in, 70, 72, 73,
    74–77, 95, 101
  Peg Entwistle in, 49–51, 105
William, Bob, 193
Williams, Emlyn, 220
Williams, Tennessee, 7, 276, 285

casting decisions and, 9, 271–72,
    283–84
  direction taken over by, 281
  rewrites promised by, 272, 273, 274,
    275, 277, 278, 279–80
  writing style of, 270, 271, 281, 282
William, Warren, 103
Wilson, Katherine, 61, 254
Wilson, Lois, 97, 98
Wind, The, 86
Windust, Bretaigne, 232
Wing, Faith, 35, 40
Winter Meeting, 232
Winters, Shelley, 283
"Wisdom of Eve, The" (Orr), 241
Wit and Wisdom of Mae West, The
    (West), 314
Witch Way, 257, 258, 263
Wolfe, Thomas, 265
Women Love Diamonds, 87
Wood, Audrey, 276, 277
Wood, Vernon, 119–20, 121, 173
Woollcott, Alexander, 63
World of Carl Sandburg, The, 267
World War II, Hollywood in, 207–9
Wright, Gilbert, 210–11
Wright, Tenny, 143, 152, 166, 216, 223
Wright, Teresa, 200
Wuthering Heights, 150, 156, 180, 181,
    184
Wyler, Catherine, 184, 324
Wyler, Leopold, 161
Wyler, Margaret Tallichet (Talli), 184,
    185
  on Bette's acting, 141–42, 195,
    198–99
  on *Little Foxes*, 196, 198–99
  marriage of, 156–57, 161–62, 180,
    323–26
Wyler, Melanie, 161
Wyler, Robert, 161
Wyler, William, 82, 208
  Academy Awards and, 210
  on acting technique, 196, 203, 220,
    281, 346, 359
  AFI tributes and, 318–19, 320
  auditions conducted by, 94–95,
    97–98
  Bette's affair with, 142, 146–47, 150,
    152, 154, 155, 160, 161–62, 178,
    184, 185, 200, 323–25
  death of, 324

House Divided directed by, 94–95
Jezebel directed by, 47, 81–85, 139, 140–50, 168, 169, 173, 182, 184, 196
Letter directed by, 178, 179–90, 196, 320
Little Foxes directed by, 193, 195–203, 205, 281, 345–46, 359
marriages of, 150, 156–57, 161–62, 167, 180, 184–85, 323–25
perfectionist tendencies of, 140, 141, 143, 148, 352
screen tests conducted by, 94–95, 140–41

studio interference and, 181, 206
Wuthering Heights directed by, 150, 156, 180, 181, 184

Yellow Jacket, The (Benrimo and Hazelton), 65, 72
Young, Francis, 30
Yurka, Blanche, 49, 50, 70, 72–77, 95

Zanuck, Darryl, 241, 242
Ziegfeld Follies, 58

8/98